Translated from the 4th Brazilian edition of *Os Religiosos, vocação e missão.*
Um enfoque exigente e actual (Rio de Janeiro: CRB, 1986).

BRAZILIAN EDITIONS:

First edition: July 1977
Second Edition: September 1979
Third Revised and Enlarged Edition: February 1982
Fourth Revised and Enlarged Edition: January 1986

TRANSLATIONS:

Italian (Ed. Ancora: Milan)
    First Edition: December 1984
    Second Edition: December 1988
Spanish (Soc. Ed. Atenas: Madrid)
    First Edition: January 1985
    Second Edition: October 1987
French (Éditions du Centurion: Paris)
    First Edition: April 1985
    Second Edition: September 1987
    Third Edition: September 1988
German (in preparation)
Polish (in preparation)

CONTENTS

Preface to the English Edition   *xi*
Acknowledgments   *xvi*
Introduction   *1*

Chapter One   *An Apostolic Vocation*   *3*

The Problem of Identity   3
Religious Vocation and the Clerical Dimension   4
Openness to Others   6
Identification of Religious Life within the Context of
    Apostolic Vocations in the Church   8
The Life of the Gospel: Determining Element in
    Decision Making   11

Chapter Two   *The Vow of Poverty*   *13*

The Poverty of Being and of the Person   15
The Dialectic of the Poverty of Being and of Having   17
The Poverty of Having   21
Poverty and Gratuity   25
Poverty and Administration   26
Poverty and Mission   27
Conclusion   31

Chapter Three   *Religious Life and the Preferential
                     Option for the Poor*   *33*

The Starting Point for a New Sensitivity   34
Religious Life: The Dynamic of a History   38

Religious Life: Presence and Leaven in the Process of
  Transformation   40

Chapter Four *The Vow of Chastity*   **46**

Inversion of Perspectives   47
Chastity and Interior Poverty   48
Chastity and the Totality of the Person   50
Chastity and Maturity   52
Chastity and Communion with God   54
Chastity and Gratuity   57
Operative and Functional Chastity   59
The Core of Consecrated Chastity in Religious Life   60

Chapter Five *The Vow of Obedience*   **62**

Obedience in Religious Life   63
The Presence of the Spirit and Co-Responsibility   65
Obedience and Discernment   66
The Community and the Superior: Ecclesiological
  Perspectives   68
The Community and the Superior: Psychosocial
  Perspectives   69
Obedience, the Person, and Mission   71
Conclusion   75

Chapter Six *A New Vision of Religious Obedience*   **77**

The Proper Character of Religious Obedience   78
Present-Day Focus and Perspectives of Religious
  Obedience   79
  From the Imitation of Christ to the Sharing
    in His Mission   79
  From Autocracy to Subsidiarity   81
  From the Level of Virtue to the Fullness of Life   85
Conclusion   87

Chapter Seven *Human Decisions and the Will of God*   **90**

Two Conceptions of Obedience   91
  Previous Conception of Obedience   91

Present Conception of Obedience   92
Human Decision and the Will of God   95
    First Hypothesis   95
    Second Hypothesis   96
Conclusion   101

Chapter Eight   *Obedience, the Preferential Option for
                                the Poor, and Conscientious Objection*   **104**

A New Ecclesial Context   104
Conscientious Objection   106
Conscientious Objection and the Exercise of Obedience   107
Preferential Option for the Poor and Conscientious
    Objection   109
The Option for the Poor and Its Mediations   111
Conclusion   116

Chapter Nine   *Fundamental Dimensions of a Religious
                                Community*   **120**

Outlining the Topic   120
Solidarity   121
The Individual Person   121
The Religious Community   124
God's Rhythm   128
Conclusion   129

Chapter Ten   *The Mission of Evangelization*   **131**

Some Major Problems of the Church   131
The Image of the Church   132
Priority Tasks and Missions   134
Evangelization and Religious Life   135
    Evangelization   135
    Religious Life   136
Jesus Christ the Evangelizer and Religious Life   138
    Jesus Christ the Human Being   138
    Jesus Christ the Man for Others   140
    Jesus Christ the Prophet   141
    Jesus Christ the Son of God   143

Chapter Eleven *Women Religious in the Church*   *148*

Religious Life in the Church   148
Women in the Church   152
Women's Religious Life in the Church   155
Women Religious as Women in the Church   160
   The Communitary Dimension   162
   The Vocational Dimension   163
Perspectives   165

Epilogue   *171*

Appendices   *173*

Preface to the First Brazilian Edition   173
Preface to the Second Brazilian Edition   176
Author's Preface to the Third Brazilian Edition   178
Author's Preface to the Fourth Brazilian Edition   184

About the Author   *187*

For James E. Sullivan, O.M.I., in great gratitude for his dedication to the ongoing formation of religious men and women in Brazil. For Edmund N. Leising, O.M.I., praising his creative service to the poor in Brazil.

For Sister Mary Milligan, R.S.H.M. in gratitude for her Preface to this English edition of the book.

For Sister Marcilia, in Campanha, MG, Brazil, and Sisters Donna and Mechthild, in Jerusalem, and all the Sisters of Zion throughout the world, in deep gratitutde.

For the Professors, officials and students of the Washington Theological Union for their support in the Fall Semester 1987.

For the Franciscan Community of the Holy Name College, in Silver Spring, MD, which received me more as a brother than as a guest in the Fall Semester of 1987.

For the English-speaking men and women religious who came to Brazil as witnesses to Jesus Christ for the service of our people and our Church.

PREFACE TO THE ENGLISH EDITION

ONE OF THE needs of our times is to build bridges, to create spaces of dialogue, to ensure the interfacing of diverse realities. Summit meetings which bring opposing powers into negotiation, international conferences which situate national concerns in a broader context are the order of the day. Dialogue between South and North, between West and East, between woman and man, between young and old is meant not to enable one of the protagonists to triumph over the other but rather to create a "space" where respect and collaboration can grow for the good of all.

This present book by Fr. Marcello de Carvalho Azevedo responds to the need to build bridges. Again and again in this book, he creates new "space" where various elements of religious life are presented so that they interact with one another in freedom and creativity. Never are diverse aspects or necessary distinctions allowed to stand in opposition to one another. Rather, relationships and interdependent connections are made explicit. The poverty of being is related to the poverty of having; obedience to conscience and obedience to those in authority are put into dialogue with one another; relationships are drawn between the priestly and lay vocations, between the person and the community, between traditional values and life-giving insights of our own times.

If the interfacing of diverse aspects of reality is a characteristic of *Vocation for Mission*, it is no doubt because Father Azevedo has lived such interfacing in his own person. A Brazilian by birth, he lives and works on three continents—South America, North America and Europe. He brings the richness and values of those three continents into dialogue with one another. The blending of geographical diversity is paralleled by the variety of his intellectual formation and his pastoral experience. Degrees in philosophy, cultural anthropology and theology bring Marcello as close as one can become today to being a "universal scholar." To the writing of this present work, Father Azevedo has brought his own personal experience which includes that of provincial superior, of president and executive director of the Brazilian National Conference of Religious (CRB) as well as that of teacher and scholar. These various ministries have enabled him to draw on the experiences of many other persons as well. The various chapters of *Vocation for Mission*, written over an extended period of time, are the fruit of his listening to his own and others' experience. They have been revised, added to and updated for the English edition.

This book appears in English at a crucial and graced moment for religious life. The twenty years since Vatican II have been a time of great joy and acute pain—both signs of life. A renewed ecclesiology and emphasis on the solid and authentic sources of religious life have purified religious' way of living of many non-essential elements. Apostolic religious institutes of women especially have come to understand that their form of life is relatively new in the Church. Looked at from the long perspective of history, one might say that it is still coming to birth. Only in this present century were non-enclosed women professing poverty, chastity and obedience recognized canonically as religious.

In the wake of Vatican II, religious institutes focused on the Gospel and on the original intuition which led to the founding of each institute. This contact with the authentic sources of the ecclesial life which we call *religious* renewed both apostolic energy and a sense of theological identity in those institutes. Among the insights gleaned in these post-conciliar years, two in particular enable religious life to create a future in fidelity with its past.

The first of these insights is that apostolic religious exist in the Church for mission; service/ministry is their *raison d'être*. For them, activity is not an accessory; it is not one among many elements of equal importance. *Perfectae Caritatis* described such institutes as communities where "the very nature of the religious life requires apostolic action and services, since a sacred ministry and a special work of charity have been consigned to them by the Church and must be discharged in its name" (*PC* 8). For religious in these institutes, ministry is the axis of their life, coloring all its other elements. Community life, prayer, the living of the vows—all of these are *for mission.* The way in which each of these realities is lived reflects "being-for-others." Though the phrase "consecration for mission" has been with us for a while, its implications are as yet far from fully realized.

Founders and foundresses of apostolic communities were moved by the needs of the people of their time and responded to those needs in a variety of ways. This response was understood not only as an expression of union with God but also as a means to that union. In the vast majority of cases, apostolic religious institutes were born because a concrete need was recognized. Most founding persons did not create a religious community and then look for some useful apostolic activity. Rather the movement was the contrary. A particular need in society was obvious. In an extraordinarily unified view, the founding person(s) understood that a full Christian response to that need required the total, visible dedication of a community. The radicality of a life of obedience, chastity and poverty was both a sign and a means of such a response.

Holiness for apostolic religious lies in oneness with Jesus who was sent, whose life was poured out for the world. Apostolic religious are surely not unique in the Church in this regard, but they are publicly committed to living a dedication to others in a total way. For them, vows of chastity, poverty and obedience are the modality of their apostolic commitment. These vows form the heart of the apostle. They provide a constant pedagogy teaching the religious disciple to be free enough to lay down his or her life for others (cf. Jn 10:17–18).

Traditionally, chastity has been considered the keystone of the vows, the highest expression of love from which poverty and obedience flow. But one might make a strong case that for apostolic religious it is obedience which is the lynchpin of the vows. In the Johannine Gospel which portrays Jesus as the one sent by God, obedience is the deepest expression of Jesus' love for the One he experienced as Father. That love finds concrete expression in doing the will of the One who sent him (cf. Jn 4:34; 5:30; 6:38; 8:24), in doing at all times what God has told him to do (Jn 14:31). Obedience, willingness to be sent is the very identity of Jesus as well as the deepest manifestation of his love of God and of other people.

The second insight which will profoundly affect apostolic religious in the years to come is that the poor and the disinherited are a privileged place of God's self-revelation. A variety of factors in today's international society have increased Christian awareness of the scandal of economic inequalities which cause some to live in inhuman conditions of misery while others live in an excessive abundance which might also be termed inhuman. Response to situations of injustice has been recognized as an integral element in the life of Christian discipleship. And the Gospel preached to the poor is today, as it was in Jesus' time, a clear sign of the coming of God's reign.

Certainly for apostolic religious, the return to the "sources of all Christian life and to the original inspiration behind a given community" (PC 2) has developed a sensitivity which allows them to perceive the call of God in this situation. Like all other Christians who take the gospel seriously, they are moved to respond in some way, to act in favor of victims of poverty and injustice. Once again, they do this in creative fidelity to the inspiration of their origins.

But what religious, along with many others in the Church, are coming to understand is that there is a particular face of God revealed among the poor. Throughout the history of Israel and of the Christian Church, inadequacy, weakness and poverty have been privileged places for the divine presence and action. Saint Paul, for example, could remind the very diverse Christian community at Corinth that because there were among them so few who were powerful or wise, so few who came from "good families," God had chosen them, called them together to be saints. "God chose what is foolish and weak in the world to shame the wise and the strong." The poor, the weak, the disinherited are in a privileged way God's people, those among whom God resides, those who reveal God's presence.

Today, the Latin American church in particular reminds us of this truth. It is a Christian insight, not a geographically localized one. Humbly and with conviction, those who have "handed over their lives to God's service" and the service of others "in a special act of consecration" (*PC* 5) are challenged to seek the face of the Lord among the poor.

In this present book, Father Azevedo has addressed in a variety of ways *consecration for mission* and the *revelation of God among the poor*. It is not by chance that he has devoted four chapters to obedience and two to the option for the poor. His vision, formed by his own experience, furthers theological reflection on these realities and motivates to action. With great balance, he addresses a multiplicity of aspects, never watering down the challenge of the gospel which comes to question our lives. The various aspects treated are always judged in the brilliant light of the absolute priority of God and the relativization of all else. With practical good sense, with theological exigency, with exquisite balance, Father Azevedo never leaves this priority of God in the abstract. Indeed, one might say that the whole of *Vocation for Mission* draws the implications of that absolute priority in the flesh of everyday life. May that "incarnation" be a source of help for all who read this book, yes; but may it be especially a source of hope and an encouragement to act.

Los Angeles   Mary Milligan, RSHM
December 8, 1985

ACKNOWLEDGMENTS

I GRATEFULLY acknowledge my debt to the following persons who are somehow related to the present English edition: Sister Mary Milligan, who kindly accepted to write the Preface; my Jesuit fellows Luis Garcia de Souza, Allan Deck, Robert Faricy, Michael Garanzini, David Kay, Edouard Bourassa, and Harold Rodriguez; all the English-speaking religious, both men and women, who read this book in other languages and who agreed to help me prepare the English edition of it; the Franciscan Friars of Holy Name College in Silver Spring, Maryland, who extended their hospitality during the time I did the final correction of the present translation; Mr. John W. Diercksmeier, the translator, and Mr. Robert Hamma, the editor at Paulist Press, for their endurance in coping with that difficult task for about three years.

INTRODUCTION

DURING NINE YEARS as president of the National Brazilian Conference of Religious Men and Women (CRB), I have seen and heard many things; I have thought and prayed; I have lived intensely. The CRB has been for me a cross-section of observations, knowledge, and information about people and situations, about things and institutions. I have lived with the vicissitudes and experiences of many congregations; I have known of their experiences, both positive and negative. I have shared the hopes of many people and the disappointments of many others. No other position has given me the opportunity for such a wide and exhaustive view, for such a realistic and diversified perception of the daily life of the religious of Brazil. At the same time, the very character of the CRB, with its intense national and international relationships on different occasions, also made it possible for me to become profoundly conversant with the evolution of religious life in several countries.

I have participated in meetings, congresses, encounters, and assemblies on the intercongregational level. I have attended the provincial and general chapters of various congregations. I have worked directly with men and women religious in many countries. I have had the opportunity to be in continual contact with officials of the Church, from the Congregation of Religious in Rome to the National Conference of Brazilian Bishops (CNBB) and the episcopal conferences of other countries, the Brazilian dioceses and their bishops, and in the various regions of Brazil, I have been, to a greater or lesser extent, involved in many areas of religious work.

On many occasions, I had the opportunity to listen; and on others, I was invited to speak; later, I was asked to write. I resisted this because what I said was always deeply related to the people to whom I spoke. Apart from this context, I believed that it would lose its meaning. But people insisted, and I ended up writing and publishing. At the request of many religious and encouraged by Father Marcos de Lima, who worked with me for seven years in the CRB, as director of its journal *Convergência* and its publications, I accepted the idea of bringing together in one book the articles that seemed to be the best. And here they are.

Yet, what is one to do? Should I retouch them, rewrite them and enrich them with footnotes and bibliographies? I have preferred not to do that because these articles would cease to be what they are: an expression of life and the manifestation of my fundamental convictions about religious life as I lived them and as I presented them in more specific circumstances. This is the most important characteristic of these works. They are not erudite, nor do they pretend to be so, because they were directed at a specific audience and the important thing was that they could be understood by those people. Therefore, I refused the sophistication of using technical terminology. These articles are the result of lived experience. They are not primarily theological or philosophical, just as they are not only sociological or psychological. They do not aspire to a specific place in these categories considered in isolation. They contain a little bit of everything, like life, which organically integrates distinct elements. They are published together solely because that is how the people who benefited from them asked them to be published. May they continue to cause people to think and pray that the mission of religious in the Church and in the world may respond to the present demands of the service to God and to our brothers and sisters.

Chapter One

An Apostolic Vocation

The Problem of Identity

FEW ISSUES have affected religious men and women in recent times as much as that of their *identity*. A great deal has been said about it. In its name, norms have been set and people have been judged by them. But every attempt to specify and define religious life more clearly has resulted in a dead-end street. Many documents from general chapters clearly testify to this difficulty. A closer study of these documents reveals the fragile ambiguity of the results and, above all, their inadequacy in the light of the reality in which religious life is actually lived.

Traditionally, religious life was presented in the Church as the vocation to holiness by means of the fulfillment of the evangelical counsels. Later, it came to be considered as a "state of perfection." In the novitiate and in later formation, the attempt was made to ground it in specific Scripture texts, such as those of the rich young man and others. Added to this was the fixation on practices and habits, norms, rules, and customs—an entire choreography that endured for centuries and was eventually incorporated into the definition of religious life, making it impossible to be recognized apart from this "scenario."

Little by little, biblical studies came to restrict and relativize a specific and textual basis for religious life, although without denying its evangelical inspiration. Historical study documented the much later appearance of religious life in the Church. These studies showed, as well, the diverisity of inspirations and experiences manifested in the lives of people around whom what we call *religious life* was born and grew.

3

Furthermore, the Second Vatican Council, which avoided the
207 §2 expression "state of perfection," underscored the vocation of all
Christians to holiness, preventing holiness from constituting an
exclusive or privileged characteristic of any specific apostolic vocation within the Church.

The diversity of situations, schedules, and activities, as well as
the secularization of the world itself, with new demands for presence and participation that often were incompatible with the age-
old style assigned to "religious life" was breaking down and questioning what seemed to be untouchable and unchangeable in the
external image and the ambience of religious life.

Religious Vocation and the Clerical Dimension

Suddenly, religious were faced with the worrisome question: Who
are we and what are we doing in the Church?

The uncertainty of the answer was sharpened due to the
postconciliar phenomenon that deeply affected everyone, especially women religious. Religious priests used to receive a formation that was primarily oriented toward the ministerial priesthood
and less toward the conscious growth of their religious vocation.
After ordination, their pastoral activities absorbed so much of their
time and their strength that they almost forgot the "religious"
dimension of their lives. This, however, was not the case with
women religious. Contemplative cloistered sisters lived within
their convent walls and active sisters were likewise restricted to
very specific activities (health, social work, education . . .). These
activities had to be compatible with countless remnants from the
cloister (such as the daily schedule, strict cloister, and lack of communication with the outside world). Women religious were thus
considered to be a separate caste in the Church. Advised by
priests, their chapters or assemblies presided over by bishops,
they were always directed by men who decided for them, especially in the areas of formation, the apostolate, and administration.

---

*The numbers in the margin refer to the new Code of Canon Law (1983). See the
preface to the fourth Brazilian edition, p. 184.

They were both protected and scorned, although things were never called by their proper names. The facts speak for themselves. Studying these facts reveals a language of which we are truly ashamed, even though it has yet to disappear entirely.

Suddenly, as the number of priests diminished because of departures and the lack of vocations, women religious were urgently called to fill in for priests in almost all areas. This started in Brazil, in Nizia Floresta, RN, as early as 1954. Our ability to rationalize positions that the march of events is undoing and to change to opposite positions rapidly and with some good reason is a phenomenon worth studying in a more objective future. It is certainly amazing that, in less than ten years, women religious were released for wider pastoral activity, setting aside a large part of what they did before. A guilt complex was created for them in terms of their own regular occupations. There was an agressive way to put pressure on them in such a fashion that, after an entire week of eight- to ten-hour days of work, their difficulty or impossibility of attending to catechism classes or to the parish Masses on Saturdays and Sundays was considered to be a transgression, repeatedly interpreted as a lack of "church awareness" and of sensitivity to the needs of the local church.

Nevertheless, for centuries, in view of its original inspiration, religious life was not strictly linked to clerical pastoral activity— that is, word and sacraments, parish and catechesis. Religious did everything, and this did not pose a problem for their identity in the Church. 588 §1,2,3

The Second Vatican Council made it clear that religious life does not belong to the hierarchical structure of the Church. In this sense, religious are, as such, structurally farther from the position of the hierarchy and the clergy in the Church. Consequently, they are closer to the laity and the faithful, who constitute the "base" of the people of God. In fact, there are a great number of religious— brothers and women religious—who, by their very nature and vocation, are not linked to the presbyterate or the episcopacy. Moreover, truly clerical orders and congregations, such as the Franciscans, had origins that were characterized by a nonclerical calling. It can be said with assurance that the religious vocation or religious life does not necessarily imply, from historical or struc- 207 §1
573 §1
574 §1
654 607 §3
588 §1,2,3

tural perspectives, an orientation toward clerical pastoral activity as it embodies the *munus pastorale* inherent to the vocation of bish-
1001   ops and priests.

Openness to Others

The critical relativization of the textual, biblical foundation, in which religious life was once supposed to be rooted, makes it possible to understand that religious life is actually grounded in the Christian vocation itself, in the baptismal vocation. In this sense, the religious vocation, which is clearly different from the episcopal and presbyteral vocations, is not very different from the Christian vocation of the faithful. Neither the faithful nor religious are called to holiness by means of living the ordained ministry of the priest-
207 §1   hood, or the fullness of the priesthood as lived by the bishops.

Due to their baptismal vocation, the faithful and religious are
96   called to realize the Gospel plan in its totality. There is nothing,
204 §1   then, in the Gospel that may be specific to the faithful, nor is there anything that may be seen in the evangelical counsels that must be realized by religious only. Therefore, it would be difficult for us to use this path to discover the identity of religious. Bishops, priests,
588 §1,2,3   religious, and the faithful have all been called to the realization of the Gospel plan, which is the following of Jesus Christ and the continual embodiment of his mission in the world for humanity.
208   Bishops and priests have, in the New Testament itself, a well
204 §1   defined and unique model that religious do not have.

Religious appeared much later in the life and consciousness of the Church, when bishops, priests, and the faithful strayed from their generous and total fidelity to the Gospel plan. That is when men and women were raised up by the Holy Spirit. By their lives, much more than by their words, they acted as the Church's "memory," calling it to a return to its original vocation of following Jesus Christ. Religious want to live the very core of the evangelical intuition: on the one hand, the absolute priority of God, of the God who is revealed in Jesus Christ; on the other hand, the consequent relativization of everything else—especially what humanity normally tends to absolutize, thus rejecting the primacy of God and straying far from God.

This desire to live and to be the radical incarnation of the Gospel has historically led religious, first, to a total surrender to God, and only later to neighbor because of the love of God. There was no concern to be part of this or that sector of the pastoral activity of the Church, as officially represented by the clergy. There was, however, a constant search for actualizing the Gospel life, wherever religious were.

For a long time, the great concern of religious did not go beyond their own sphere; rather, they were self-centered and primarily sought personal salvation. All of this came to be particularly emphasized in the modern individualistic phase that so much characterized recent centuries of the Church's spiritual tradition, even to our day. However, little by little, a path was opened toward a gradual overcoming of this dominant, individualistic dimension and toward a greater openness to one's neighbors and their most urgent needs.

The official Church, represented by the bishops and the presbyterate, knew and accepted the religious lifestyle. Gradually, it encouraged individuals, recognized them, and relied on them implicitly and discreetly. Later, it expressly legitimized their way of life.

This ecclesial legitimation was of capital importance in the history of religious life. The saints (founders) as well as the heretics are people who normally perceive with similar acuity the deficiencies of the Church, its limitations in the following of Christ, its treason and hypocrisies, and its capitulations as well. The heretic, however, absolutizes the struggle to correct or overcome the limits, thus becoming isolated from the ecclesial context. The saint (founder), on the contrary, remains in communion with the Church, working from within it, and renouncing immediate results. The founder is sanctified in the endurance of an effort and a hope that may go beyond the limits of a lifetime. The growth of the Church is the only important thing. The saint questions, disturbs, reforms, and converts with his or her life more than with verbal denunciation, although this too has its place.

588 §1,2,3

573

This total dedication to the realization of the Gospel in the heart of the Church completely encompasses the life of the individual who, in reality, is exclusively consecrated to this and to live life in service to it. Self-centered concern for one's possessions, family, or future takes second place or simply disappears, relativized by the power of God's absoluteness. The formal and juridical transformation of this surrender to a form of life that was already legitimized by the Church was historically embodied in the so-called *vow of consecration*, recognized by the Church before 1202. This vow was accepted by the Church itself and was converted as such into the proper and significant expression of that lifestyle.

Identification of Religous Life within the Context of Apostolic Vocations in the Church

Public profession before the people of God, as recognized and legitimized by the official Church, is what began to characterize religious life.

The individual, through the power of the Spirit, intends to realize the Gospel fully and radically in his or her life. This is a concrete way of being present in the world and in the Church. This means a renunciation of many aspects of life that are legitimately and validly accepted by the majority of people. It is true that God does not call everyone to incarnate the Gospel plan in this way. However, the fact of calling certain individuals throughout the centuries to this lifestyle and of sensitizing the Church to it caused the maturation, little by little, of what we today call the vocation to religious life. Once recognized and legitimized by the Church, this way of life officially became one of the great apostolic vocations. Its distinctive character is not the vocation to holiness (common to all Christians), but *the public profession—recognized, legitimized, and appreciated by the Church—of the will to live fully and radically the Gospel plan, coherently and as the primary objective of one's life*. This is the only thing that justifies religious life in the Church. This *identifies* the religious among the many vocations in the Church. This identification will depend on the legitimation and recognition

573 §1
207 §2

574 §2
576
578

573 §1
574 §1
654
607 §3

by the Church, because religious life as such always appears as an ecclesial phenomenon, and not as the informal initiative of a Christian or of a group of believers.

Consequently, it is clear that neither activity nor the style of activity nor the characteristics of that activity constitute the identity of religious life; rather, its identity is given by the qualitative character of its presence, publicly expressed to God through the Church. Therefore, to a certain degree, every form of activity within the Church and the world has always been, and should always be, open to religious as long as they maintain the basic objective of wanting to express the totality of the Gospel plan by means of the full and radical realization of the following of Christ in one's own life. That is how one explains the multiple and varied activities of the different religious orders and congregations within the Church throughout the centuries, as distinct branches of the same tree.

To the degree to which the religious vocation does not belong to the hierarchical structure of the Church, and is distinguished more by an internal consistency of life than by an external organization in terms of its dynamic of action or presence, religious life incarnates a *charismatic* presence in the Church. The tension and the balance between the *prophetic* and *charismatic* dimensions in the ecclesial context is an indispensable condition for preserving religious life in the Church. To attempt to enclose it within certain structures, so as to make it lose the charismatic breath that constantly liberates it, would deprive the Church of an important instrument of renewal and conversion. But the exacerbation of its prophetic dimension can lead it to rupture, above all through its possible alienation and actual differentiation from the entire people of God.

The saints, the founders, and those who intensely lived the call to evangelical radicality attracted many to their way of life. After the eremitical phase (which is not properly a form of religious life, although it was its precursor) the gathering of a group, of a *community*, led by the same spirit and gravitating around a central figure, became a constant in the appearance of distinct forms of religious life. Yet, as differentiated and plural as the concept of *community*

587 §2
207 §2
576
577
607 §3
619
652 §2
663 §2
719
599
601

107 §2

207 §2
574

578
598 §1
631 §1

607 §2
608, 665
686, 687
602, 603

696 §1
578

573 §1,2
574 §2
654 may be in various orders and congregations, the awareness of belonging to an apostolic body and to a specific community, together with the public profession of consecration, distinguishes and characterizes religious life within the Church.

Nevertheless, these same saints and founders, or their immediate successors, were aware of the human impossibility of a life based exclusively on the intense thrust of the Spirit without a minimum of organization. Therefore, they tried to give it a structural base, within the parameters of their time and their own personal history. The danger of many of their successors lay in the absolutization of that structure and in trying to perpetuate it, unaltered, for all time, especially in times of rapid change such as the five centuries of the modern age and, particularly, our own century. They forgot that, having relativized much more fundamental elements, they could not absolutize what was actually meant as a tool and assistance.

It is understandable that the clinging to the structural and normative models would be stressed by the consciousness of the weakening of the original spirit. The rule thus ceased to be a means for a constant return to the liberating creativity of the Spirit and instead became the guarantee for an external mimicry of a spirit that felt itself to be empty and sterile.

From the year 1202, the single vow of consecration began to be expressed as the three vows of poverty, chastity, and obedience, which are still observed in our day. The institutional growth of religious life in countless orders and congregations, as well as the 577
603, 675
676, 604 social interaction of individuals and groups within and outside of the religious institution, led to the demand for greater rigor in the codification of these vows. The result is a feature common to every spiritual process: on the one hand, there is the unavoidable need to specify and define; on the other hand, this same process sets up barriers and boundaries that, given human frailty, lead to accommodation and mediocrity. Large religious corporations that came to possess a sophisticated normative legislation in the area of poverty and obedience, for example, have been snared and blocked for many years by this same juridical apparatus that had lost its liberating power, and had paralyzed individuals as well as the group as a whole.

The Life of the Gospel: Determining Element in Decision Making

During the special chapters called for by the "motu proprio" *Ecclesiae Sanctae,* and afterward, many congregations and orders found in their own legislation a powerful obstacle to renewal, which was desired after centuries of a stagnant model that was incompatible with the demands of people and the world in our day. The same thing happened to the institutional Church. The rapid aging of the 1917 Code of Canon Law led, in 1959, to the consciousness of a necessary reform of the juridical expression of the Church. Such a reform proved to be a difficult task: on the one hand, there was the unavoidable need for the Church, like any human grouping, to find the proper expression of its laws; on the other hand, the precariousness of every attempt to fix juridical formulas for long periods of time was apparent. The multiple and rapid expressions of life, in the world as in the Church, began to demand deeper roots and criteria that could be compatible though with a flexibility in their application. In the past, we knew static models and remedies, as well as rigid instructions and norms. Yet this belongs to the past. Now we feel the need for a spiritual process of personal and communal discernment that continually confronts us with the reading of the Gospel, as related to a complex reality that has become a determining and indispensable element in decision making.

It was a dominant or even exclusive juridical focus that led us to see the vows, in formation as well as throughout life, from a narrow perspective. The reaction to this was a multitude of theories. Some of them declared religious life in the Church and in the world today to be sociologically unwarranted. Other opinions questioned the vows as the valid expression of its meaning. During the past few years, there has been the proliferation of formulas of commitment to express the surrender of life to God and to humanity in a religious community, without recourse to the classical vows of poverty, chastity, and obedience. Moreover, the lack of a *textual* biblical foundation for the three vows has also been played against them.

I do not pretend to offer a scriptural justification for each of the vows. I want, rather, to help toward understanding that, through a new and rich focus of the vows, we can find in them for our time a significant expression of this personal and communal option for the full and radical living of the *Gospel plan,* around which the *identity of religious life* in the Church is defined. This living is not reduced to the vows, much less to a juridical-legal treatment of them. The identity of religious life is not exhausted by the vows, yet they can be one of its meaningful expressions and mediations.

This happens as long as the vows express the radicality and the scope of the comprehensive involvement of the individual for God and for one's brothers and sisters within the Church and in that specific vocation which we call *religious life.* This happens, as long as the vows are seen in the *total picture of the Gospel plan,* which encompasses:

— the reference of one's life to God in terms of the kingdom, that fundamental intuition and concretization of salvation history;

— the consciousness of the centrality of Jesus Christ, in whom and through whom the love of God is given and proclaimed to us, for the salvation and liberation of humanity, both individually and socially;

— the active participation in carrying forward, under the guidance of the Holy Spirit, the mission of Jesus, seeking the consistent integration of life and faith within us;

— the task of doing so not only within the limits of our individual horizon, but also and above all as a living part of an apostolic community of faith, which makes concrete the love of God and neighbor in the hearing and acceptance of the message, in the search for its full realization, and in the witness to all people of God's plan of salvation for them.

This book deals with all of this.
This is what this book is about.

Chapter Two

The Vow of Poverty

SALVATION HISTORY reveals the initiative of God, who calls Abraham as a person, giving him the hope of the promise. Abraham answers with *faith* and *hope*, the inexplicable but indisputable certainty that God has the power to fulfill what is proclaimed. God spontaneously chooses the people of Israel, Abraham's posterity, making them the chosen people, the object of divine love. Yahweh seals the covenant with them, the central axis of the entire history of salvation. Yet all of this is a pale reflection of God's great initiative made manifest in Jesus Christ.

God, who is love and communion, becomes human in Jesus Christ. In him, that love is made intelligible and accessible, the love that humanity could not see in countless figures and theophanies during so many centuries of divine pedagogy. Jesus, God made human, is sent to humanity for humanity. The mystery of the incarnation can only be explained in terms of mission, in the same way that any type of vocation in Scripture can only be understood in the light of mission. Moreover, there is no vocation, either before or after Jesus Christ, that can be understood without reference to the mission of Christ himself.

Every religious today is called by the Lord to realize in our day the history of salvation. Through us and with us, God seals the new covenant. God assumes the totality of our being and we respond with everything we are. We intend to publicly incarnate this covenant before the Church and the world, and it is this public profession and our coherence with it that practically identifies us with a specific vocation among so many people called to other paths.

A powerful spiritual current centered this vocation on the *imita-*

tion of Jesus Christ, a perspective that is historically grounded. Another ancient spiritual tradition focuses that vocation on the *following* of Jesus Christ. To follow Jesus Christ is not to repeat and imitate what he did, but rather it is to reincarnate his presence in the world, to follow today the steps he took in former and distinct times, in a constant and challenging epiphany that never ends. God, in Jesus Christ, must be made manifest through us so that humanity may understand that God *is* and that only God truly *is*, in an unfathomable capacity *to be* forever.

The incarnation of the Word, made human in Jesus Christ, is a radical option for the *poverty of being*. No one has expressed this more concisely and precisely than Saint Paul in the Letter to the Philippians (2:6–8). We continue to be impressed by Jesus' consistency throughout his life with this existential option, through which he manifests the gratuitous love of God for humanity.

Another mysterious and significant dimension is added to this radical poverty of being of a God who becomes human: Jesus sets up house among materially poor people, continually stressing the possibility they have to enter the kingdom of heaven due to the simple fact of their being poor.

This double outpouring, in which Jesus Christ manifests his preference for poverty, cannot be absent in the option and in the life of those who have been called to the following of Jesus Christ. *Poverty of being* is the emptying of power and prestige, a form of wealth to which all people instinctively tend. *Poverty of having* resides above all in the conscious and experienced affirmation of the precariousness of things and their inability to give the happiness every person desires. Both of these, which in Christ are the affirmation of his freedom, are meant to bring about in us a total *freedom* from everything that is not God, that is, from people and things, from spiritual and material goods. Poverty is not, properly speaking, not having, but rather it is being *free* to be without having. To follow Jesus Christ is to profess freedom, to intend to be free. This is a vision that goes beyond the juridical level of understanding the vows, the public profession of the radicality of religious in their realization of the Gospel plan. This freedom must not be reduced to something personal only. It must also have a communal and institutional character because, although it is a public profession of the act of an individual, this act is realized within the context of a community in which each and every one decides, before God, the Church, and people, to live the options of Jesus Christ in order to continue his mission to the world.

The Poverty of Being and of the Person

We have almost always been educated to an idea of poverty along the lines of not possessing or depending on the use, especially individual use, of things—particularly in their material dimension. But material poverty lacks consistency if it is not the result and expression of a poverty of being and of the person. We must patiently construct our interior and Gospel poverty, individual as well as communal and institutional, especially in terms of our spiritual, cultural, and moral values. Once more, the problem resides in our ability to maintain a great freedom regarding them, without allowing ourselves to manipulate them through any selfish ideologies of prestige or power.

There is a profound relationship between this and the apostolic meaning and scope of our personal values in the area of the spirit. It is only from the angle of mission that the qualification of religious as persons and as professionals is justified. The personal growth of the religious cannot be primarily undertaken as a response to the deeply human desire for personal fulfillment, considering it as a conditioning element and a teleological determinant of the entire process of the individual's improvement. The religious vocation does not seek personal fulfillment for itself, as if it were a definable and reachable goal. Moreover, the public profession of Gospel radicality carries with it the seed of constant personal advancement and the demand for transcendence that stems from the following of Christ written into the very reason of being as an apostolic vocation. Consequently, separated from this apostolic perspective, the personal growth of the religious becomes a type of richness that somehow breaks the internal coherence of his or her consecration. Therefore, to pursue a career, in terms of qualification only as well as a sign of status and power, is incompatible with authentic religious life, in the same way as that vocation is incompatible with any kind of ambition in terms of being, having, or doing. This understanding of our position in the world, in consonance with this facet of our vow of poverty (rarely understood in this way), carries with it, among many other practical consequences, an irrevocable purification of our decision-making processes. It necessarily implies the elimination of every non-evangelical dynamic of power, as well as of any imposition of power trends or ideologies within our communities and our chapters. Poverty and mission are the only perspectives from which religious can treat the subject of authority. And only from the perspective of poverty can authority be properly rather than demagogically understood as service. We can already perceive here the profound relationship that exists between poverty, one of the vows that expresses our consecration, and obedience, which manifests it from another angle.

The poverty of being and of the person, having a poor heart, the poverty of spirit, prepares us solidly for humiliation, misunderstanding, and injustice. These are accepted not as a violation or an affront, but rather as integral parts of the response to a fundamental option of life that continues to follow that of Jesus Christ, who became human "assuming the condition of a slave." It is poverty that makes us feel, at times, the emptiness of people around us, an experience of existential loneliness that leads us to seek and find in God our unique and authentic support in the difficult moments of our life or mission. This is, without a doubt, one of the basic experiences of Jesus Christ in the Gospel. In the individual or communal process of decision making, we frequently realize the contrast between God's criteria and our own principles and exigencies; we become aware of the inevitable confrontation between the options of Jesus Christ and the demands of our internal richness of the spirit.

Poverty of being and of the person sustains and causes interior freedom to grow in us, and its principal fruit is peace. It is a poverty that eliminates the spontaneous feeling of surprise or rebellion when we run up against our personal limitations and, especially, when we experience them incarnated in our own sinfulness. The highest form of poverty assumed by Christ was to become sin before God without ever having sinned. And yet, there are few things we resist as much as the acceptance of sin within us. Poverty is liberating because it leads us to accept, in peace, the awareness of our own limitations; it also helps us to engage in a peaceful and ongoing process of overcoming those limitations, an impossible dream indeed. But poverty also grants us a great interior freedom among people. The individual who is poor, in his or her being and in his or her person, is an independent and free person, without petulance or snobbishness. Nothing will be able to sway that individual to serve power or prestige, intimidation or flattery, or anything that is an expression of wealth from which the person has been freely liberated. Here, poverty is part of truth, while wealth, prestige, and power often emerge from the underworld of lies, doubletalk, and hypocrisy. It is crucial to remember that, in religious life, poverty of being and poverty of the person should not be limited to the strictly individual dimension, but must permeate the spirit of the entire community. Only in this way will we create the conditions for discernment in order to identify the imperatives of our mission. In this way also we will experience peace while we seek the Lord's will and do it effectively, with a poor heart in spite of the conflicts that are involved.

The Dialectic of the Poverty of Being and of Having

Moreover, this poverty of being and of the person gives us the capacity for a coherent material poverty that does not become a source for harassment or an escape disguised in prestige. Jesus Christ preferred the poor and opted for the lowly and the oppressed. He chose his apostles and disciples from among the weakest. But he always acted in terms of his mission. It is not that the rich cannot hear his message. It is difficult for them, however, to be open to God's priority, to be aware of their poverty as a creature before God, and, above all, to realize the need for Gospel openness to others, to one's neighbor, to those whom we should love with the gratuity with which God loves us. The coordinates of wealth and power, and the resultant pride and prestige, become a centrifugal force that normally tends away from God and that God openly resists. Nevertheless, the majority of people, including the poorest in terms of possession, desire material wealth and envy those who have come to possess valuable goods, either through the slow process of hard work or by the sudden stroke of good fortune. A large part of humanity converts the struggle for wealth, although they may never actually possess it, into the reason for their sweat and tears. This ongoing temptation to absolutize the possession of goods can only be transformed by a radical poverty of being and of the person, a true poverty of spirit. It is difficult indeed to create a climate for an effective poverty of being and of the person amid an abundance of goods. This is why, in religious life, our poverty only touches the mission of Christ when it includes the double arrow of his option: poverty of being made specific in the poverty of having. Then will we relativize what the natural inclination of humans tends to absolutize.

It is important that the explicit profession correspond to an authenticity of life. In this sense, the touchstone of poverty is the apostolic mission, in a free attitude of service. This mission demands adequacy and reference to the world in which we live and evangelize, and consequently a true and consistent involvement in that world. The basic difficulty with our own and the world's understanding of our "poverty" is in making the obvious meaning of the word compatible with the current personal and institutional reality of religious life. I believe we have lost much of the original meaning of poverty in terms of having, as well as in terms of being and of the person. I am sure that the Christological and evangelical cement has cracked, and this is the only reliable reference point for the public profession of poverty by religious.

Many congregations have recently opted for the materially poor. This decision was taken within a wider ecclesial intuition: the profound link between evangelization and the integral advancement of the human person. It has been an expression of a greater maturity of the Church in our day to capture the need for an implantation of justice as the unavoidable component of peace. This manifests the twofold path along which the Spirit leads the entire Church: to know, first, that in Jesus Christ the Word was made fully *human* (and not only spirit) and, second, that we must build up here, in time, the entire person that historically is on the path toward his or her eschatological destiny.

Therefore, the mission of the Church encompasses everything that is human. That is why the social dimension of the Church's concerns—the faith that does justice—will only be understood by those who are willing to accompany it on its journey of deep conversion led by the Spirit. This process did cause a true transformation of the Church. We now have a new Church facing the world, one that follows Jesus' incarnation by sincerely moving toward a poverty in itself and an effective presence among poor people. Yet, the discernment of criteria for its decisions has not been an easy task for the Church.

This synthesis—of a justice that is promoted as a service of faith to the whole human person—gives consistency to our option for the poor. Without it, we would be doing exactly the same thing as other people do out of different motivations, and we would have to ask ourselves why we should then act this way, claiming to profess something we no longer live. This leads to our discouragement and to the disenchantment of others. It is the beginning of the death of what, at one time, gave us life.

Only this synthesis can give meaning and credibility to our living witness among the poor, in such a way that the process of their own liberation does not become a source for them of bitterness or the promise of hatred.

The decision to opt for the poor or to be among them has not always been an expression of life and of public profession of religious and their congregations, an endeavor coherent with the evangelizing mission and the following of Jesus Christ. It often, and at times exclusively, runs along the line of a mere material liberation of the poor, adding its efforts to those of other movements for the overcoming of hunger and misery so as to promote social justice in the world. This is good and consistent with the mission of the Church. And we cannot hesitate or refuse to do it because of the many undesirable consequences that may occur such as misunderstandings especially among those who continue to see the Church as a worldly power only. The *political* scope, in the basic and etymological sense of the term, of human actions and therefore of the (human) options of religious cannot be under-estimated or eliminated.

However, from the point of view of the public profession of religious poverty, that decision is only effective through an existential attitude of relativizing aspects that are normally absolutized by us or even by the poor. Dialogue and true involvement demand a double process. On the one hand, there must be the relativization of ourselves, our values, and our ideas. This liberates us and opens us to others so as to understand in the materially poor the dimension of a poverty of spirit in which we can educate ourselves. This will not take place easily if we are rich in being and in having and thereby unable to understand the language of poverty. On the other hand, it is also possible, and even frequent, that the one who is poor in possessions may be rich in spirit. If we are poor in being and in having, perhaps we will become the means for others to discover the immense wealth of poverty of spirit, without which material poverty is nothing but privation, the simple lack of goods and possessions. This discovery will liberate the poor and prevent that person, who is oppressed on one level, from becoming an oppressor of those who are dispossessed on a lower level. This is the only way for the presence of religious among the poor, as they become poor with the poor, to encompass and rightly to transcend the limits and objectives of mere material or cultural improvement. Such an improvement can be achieved by the public sector or by private initiative, but this is radically distinct from the actual mission of Jesus Christ. This mission is to evangelize while promoting and to promote while evangelizing, thereby leading people to interior freedom and the ability to relativize what cannot be absolutized. This is an immense task for which the majority of religious are not prepared. Personally or institutionally, they have not integrated the two Christological poles of poverty—that of being and of the person, and that of material possessions—the only true and full meaning of the first Beatitude. Without translating the following of Christ into our own lives, we cannot carry out his mission through which the evangelization and, therefore, the complete liberation of the individual will bear the fruits of justice in the world as the consistent demand of a living faith.

The Poverty of Having

The devaluation of the relationship between poverty of being and the poverty of having, reducing poverty to the aspect of having, as stressed by the concepts of use and dependence, has been one of the factors that has most contributed to the falsification of an authentic understanding and living out of the full sense of poverty throughout the history of religious life. The relative individual poverty of the religious as a person became then compatible with the growing institutional wealth of the congregation on the local, provincial, or worldwide level. Every one of the religious communities consented to live on some or all of these levels, according to a model of small-scale, individualistic capitalism of its own kind.

Some religious people, normally well paid and often exempt from taxes, assume a lifestyle that is discreet but well insured. Their economic income allows them to feed, as a group, the innate human and upper-class tendency implicitly to absolutize goods and property. They soon find pretexts to avoid the need to collaborate and to help, and even to give up some of their things or share them with others. They find reasons for building up their security and provisions much more than is necessary. Therefore, they hold on for many years to unproductive land and property that has no benefit or social function. This attitude leads, in reality, to the elimination from religious life of an elementary and honest dimension of poverty. This is one of the personal forms of inconsistency with the public profession of Gospel radicality. Such an attitude makes this apostolic vocation, which can only be recognized in the total consistency with which it is publicly professed, unintelligible to others and to the Church.

When the matter is not goods and values, land and property, it can become personal titles, degrees and courses, interminable and insatiable qualifications. They are understood and sought not so much from the apostolic perspective of service to others, to the world, to one's own congregation, or to the Church but rather as a source of that self-complacency within each one of us toward the gratifying and documented statement of our own excellence.

The evangelical living of the vow of poverty demands a total replacing of the current ways of living religious life. The problem does not reside in forming a dependence on the undisturbed use of all that is possessed in fact, but in achieving responsibly, on a personal and institutional level, the dialectical confrontation of each one of our options with the christological foundation of poverty that we profess as one of the aspects of our consecration to God of all that we are. This demands of us a profound interior freedom and a true *kenosis* that conforms us to the incarnation of Christ and unmasks our pseudo-involvement in the world of the poor, in order to lead us to an authentic communion with them.

THERE REMAINS one more lost dimension in the living of poverty: our participation as religious in the *world of work*, with all of its consequences. And, nevertheless, this seems to be, in today's world characterized by work, one of the great inconsistencies of many religious with respect to their public profession of Gospel poverty. The vast majority of men and women who work and who live from their work do not understand the working life of a great number of religious.

The truth is that we have led many young religious to a genre of life that, working less than their peers, allows them to vegetate in our houses, often enjoying refined conditions of life. It seems unbelievable to admit how a large number of religious of working age are able to avoid the universal law of work. Even in developed countries and, what is worse, in the third world, many religious often live at the margin of the demands of work and the economic coordinates of today's world in terms of everything that means and carries with it austerity, discipline, sacrifice, difficulties, insecurity, and risks. Our livelihood is guaranteed; can we exempt ourselves from the day-to-day living of the inhabitants of our cities? Did not passivity, the lack of fighting spirit, the absence of creativity, and not having to struggle to survive diminish within us the heroic inspiration of our lives? We have been falling into mediocrity and alienating ourselves from a world where those who struggle enthusiastically survive and where jobs are attained through competition and kept if carried out sufficiently well. It is amazing to see just how many religious, who enjoyed unique educational opportunities and professional preparation, shy away from life and are considered incapable of tasks that lay people carry out with less formation and training or that those religious themselves carry out when they leave religious life. No less shocking is the frequency with which seemingly responsible religious play games with their communities, going this way and that, prompted by inspirations or impulses that disappear as rapidly as they arose. The stagnation of many and the lack of preparation of others convert quite a few congregations into a type of other-worldly caste, incomprehensible in the real world in which we must live. In almost every congregation, there are individuals who are closer to those who suffer and struggle with them and who tirelessly put up with the chronic fatigue of so many others, but who ask themselves anxiously if the apostolic body to which they belong is truly in the position to evangelize.

Furthermore, a revision would be very necessary to translate into economic terms the chronograms and internal disposition of time, schedules, methods and systems of work of our provincial and general chapters, our style of administration, our conferences and meetings, our vacations and entertainment, and—in general and above all—our dynamic of formation and action. Many religious are already tacitly conscious of the disproportion between the time dedicated to all of this—with the consequent costs involved—and the effective result that is obtained. We are not speaking of falling into one of the characteristic absolutizations of our time: the myth of efficiency and efficacy. However, relativizing them and enriching them with the human and gratuitous dimensions of life, we cannot live in today's world within the outlines of an ancient, agrarian civilization that does not value time. We cannot yield to a paternalistic and infantile conception of religious leadership. The problem seems to pose itself precisely in the realm of poverty. I am considering poverty here in its relationship to aspects such as the economic dimension of time, the participation on the part of people, the objectivity of goals and priorities, and therefore the sensitive reading of current demands of mission that were less felt in other ages. A greater sensitivity in this area would allow for the integration of economic and methodological coordinates with the perspective of a true poverty in the midst of a world of work. We cannot go on working, and even less in the name of the Gospel, with archaic methods in a world characterized by advanced technology. To admit that we might continue with a domestic and patriarchal style of life unveils a tremendous contrast and a rupture between what we are, backed by the goods we have been able to accumulate, and the way of life of the majority of people of our time. This is more a problem of mentality and attitudes than of actual facilities and furniture in our offices. It is not just a matter of providing machines and sophisticated instruments for simultaneous translation, electronic voting equipment, word processors, and computers. The actual problem lies in the area of the effective use and rentability and use of these things in economic terms, in the light of an updated perspective of poverty.

RELIGIOUS FREQUENTLY make the serious mistake of equating poverty with the rejection of all economic initiative. Many of us want to be only dedicated to the "spiritual" or the "pastoral," omitting from our concerns the economic dimension, its demands, and its rigorous rules. With house, food, studies, clean clothing, car, entertainment, vacations, and travel all assured, some of us speak of poverty in the abstract, but live completely at the margin of the ordinary people and of the concrete situation that surrounds us, including our own pastoral work. Economic problems are something serious and cutting for the people. While any family restricts its purchases or its vacations to its financial possibilities, a good number of religious lack sufficient judgment to apply these criteria to their own case. They are incapable of any objective rendering of accounts, and they interpret as distrust any demand along this line, although it is the daily reality of anyone who works. Religious have not been educated for the discipline of accountability—one of the great schools of poverty. They thus allow themselves basic errors and imprecisions, the consequences of which cause no suffering since their place is assured as it is a high quality of life, independent of the quality of their work. They live a pseudo-poverty, a theoretical and unincarnated poverty, one that is rather sheltered from any consequence that may affect the person. Such a poverty is completely detached and alienated from the concrete events of the life of humanity. It is a meaningless poverty that does not attract men and women who sincerely seek today to translate the Gospel into their own lives.

Poverty and Gratuity

A first consequence of that false poverty is the paternalistic attitude that, avoiding any economic consideration, distributes the goods and provisions of the house and the community in the name of a well-intentioned but, consciously or unconsciously, demagogic and inauthentic poverty. It is nothing more than the affluent generosity of one who has his or her life assured. Not one of the truly poor with whom the religious may work would be able to display such a generosity. Thus, despite appearances, the religious would be actually acting as a small lord of the past and not as a poor among the poor. Furthermore, this same assurance of their life leads many religious often to carry out their work for free, leading people to think that religious can always work for free or for a purely symbolic remuneration. No attention is paid to the sacrifice of a few upon whom the support of the entire community falls and who assume the odious task of looking out for the penny while the others freely share in hundreds.

This also tends, in well-situated communities, to perpetuate the paternalistic image of the one who lets fall the crumbs of overabundance and has a "clear" conscience because he or she "helps" the poor. A large number of individuals and religious communities find themselves in this situation. All commentary aside, we could equate their position with that of many wealthy people who appear in the newspapers because of some of the gestures of generosity. Within a true perspective of poverty, I conceive "gratuity" as the total personal and institutional freedom in relation to the equitable and actually received remuneration. Only this freedom leads the religious to give that retribution, wholly and unreservedly, to the service of the apostolic body which is the community and, through it, to the service of other poor people. It is interesting to note how many "generous" people who carry out gratuity in the first sense are incapable of it in the second sense. They are lavish with the remunerations that should officially go to the community, but they are late or do not give to the community the recompense they have received from their personal work. In the background of all this is often hidden the analogous attitude of those who resist paying taxes because they believe their money will not be rightly

used by the administration. In religious life, it is of utmost importance that individual poverty, the true freedom of the person in
terms of things and goods, find its correspondence with an identical attitude of the entire community. The individual and the community are mutually educated in the faithful and radical living of
Gospel poverty that demands this integration of criteria if it does
not want to frustrate the generosity of some people or to cause in
others irrecoverable cracks and evasions that are destructive of an
authentic religious life.

Poverty and Administration

One often hears religious speak, with a certain disdain, of the
work of the bursars, treasurers, and administrators while singing
the praises of pastoral and spiritual works. But this is again the
two-edged sword for the community living of poverty. A false or
authentic vision of religious life, a correct or ambiguous orientation of poverty in the provinces or congregations depends very
much on treasurers' mentalities. They are charged with the responsibility of concerning themselves with good administration and
the satisfaction of the needs of their communities. This is indispensable if we do not wish to live utopically in a world characterized by economics and if we do not desire to return to the system
of alms and the conditioning aid of the rich to cover some chronic
community and provincial deficits. A good administration, however, can limit itself to economic or commercial criteria only, without an awareness of or a reference to the religious dimension of
poverty. In this case, the bursars and financial commissions can,
in fact, become fatal and final arbiters to the apostolic orientation
of a work, of a province, and even of an entire congregation. As a
result of a decentralized division of labor in the province, provincials and their immediate advisors, without a sufficient knowledge
of the subject, may commend economic decisions to their respective sector. But the economic dimension is, and will continue to
be, a partial and limited component of the wider decisions of a
province. There may actually be important motives—of a religious, ecclesial, and/or apostolic and political nature—that may
urge specific decisions at a provincial level, in spite of the opposi-

tion of those responsible for the economic sector. The latter should be helped and encouraged to reconsider their decisions in this respect and to seek new elements for redirecting them otherwise. Without the perspective of an authentic evangelical freedom, many provinces or communities can be locked in a rigid apostolic immobility. They can go on simply doing business or avariciously accumulating common possessions. All of this is far from religious poverty and the real demands of mission.

However, the treasurer who carries out a good administration and who also cares for and regulates the religious postulates of poverty becomes at the same time a pedagogical factor of realistic involvement in a school of non-utopic poverty and freedom. That person becomes a liberating element in the province or in the house and a generative factor of the regular and generous exercise of a healthy apostolic gratuity which avoids the constant and limiting dependence on benefactors. The individual treasurer does this out of an alert and critical appraisal of the apostolic usefulness of goods, avoiding the unnecessary accumulation of wealth, reducing idle space, being conscious of the need for unproductive or long-term investments, such as libraries or formation, which are crucial factors in the improvement of apostolic activity. All of this presupposes a new conception of the treasurer's mission. He or she cannot be considered as someone who is turned to from time to time, but rather as someone with whom the wider and evangelical criteria of apostolic activity are honestly discussed. It is important that the treasurer be greatly sensitive to the reality of the people, and especially to the poorest. A treasurer must be aware of the wider policy of the province, as well as participate in designing and developing mission projects. This will create new conditions for revising one's own hierarchy of values. Little by little, the interior freedom will emerge which must preside over the administration of a religious community, as opposed to the direction of an enterprise that only pursues production or profits.

Poverty and Mission

Let us keep in mind this wide and realistic view of Gospel poverty. It certainly overcomes the narrow limits of a merely legal or spiritual understanding of our vow. It demands a great interior consistency with our public profession. A difficult but real question then arises existentially in the present situation of religious life: To what group do we belong, to the rich or to the poor? Or, perhaps, don't we form a third one, a specially privileged class? Are we those who have a great deal, but without the preoccupation and fear of the rich, without having to work as they do, without having to think of the threat of competition or of the problems inherent to unforeseeable economic factors, more or less favorable, without having to seek credit or financing, or worrying about the ups and downs of the marketplace? The examination of our unique situation leads us to admit, with surprise, the existence of a certain ambiguity in our lives. Our friendship with the wealthy, the appearance of our comfortable and privileged life due to the services we perform, does facilitate our being accepted by people. Our ability to move so many people to philanthropy, and everything that has been accumulated throughout the centuries which in some way has been incorporated by us, makes it very difficult for us realistically and seriously to live a radical and Gospel poverty. If this is so, where do we begin our conversion?

A complex world, full of contrasts, stands before us and challenges us. But this is the world we must evangelize, the one in which we must announce the Gospel message to all people, in which we must live and work with all people. Strikingly enough, our religious vocation, understood correctly, has an enormous actuality in this world. More than ever before, it should be recognized and legitimated by the Church, because people need, more than ever, someone to give intelligible witness to the absolute priority of God and to the consequent relativization of what people, especially people of our day, try to absolutize.

Many religious have opted, with generous sincerity, for dedicating themselves exclusively to those who are poor in material goods, to the needy *barrios* and shantytowns. Others, beyond this physical presence among the poor, saw the necessity of questioning the very structures of our world that have caused these situations. For the poor, for the marginalized, for so many in today's world who lack the basics of food, clothing, health care, and employment and who cannot satisfy the most elementary, educational, and living necessities—for these people the religious cannot be limited to being an instrument of aid and assistance. The religious must become a builder of justice and bring to those who hold the power and wealth the cry of those without a voice and without representation. The society of the hungry, of the emigrants, of the marginalized, of those who have been stopped, and of the oppressed needs our presence. Yet we must absolutely avoid making their situation a tourist attraction for us. We are not allowed to go to them in order to use them for our own spiritual and even ideological claims. Our mission is to help them liberate themselves, to unveil the meaning of their existence in the situation within which they live, struggling with them, to overcome it. We must not use them in order to gain personal or community goals.

Every superficial attempt to place communities or fraternities among the poor, communities that are ill-prepared or disengaged from their surroundings or insensitive to particular situations, is indeed irresponsible, religious tourism. We would be raising in the poor a new awareness, without offering them alternatives or without seeking those solutions with them. We would be pointing out concerns of which they are not conscious. We would be irresponsibly politicizing them to confront problems from which, as the situation becomes more severe, we distance ourselves more and more, until we show ourselves to be cowardly absent, or securely protected when push comes to shove. How many times has our position as people without family commitments, and particularly with the powerful backing of our communities, led us idealistically to provoke situations that are unbearable for entire families, for parents and youngsters alike. Because of our words, they throw themselves into heroic actions and, eventually, we leave them in the lurch! Fortunately, we can be proud of our brothers and sisters who have faced the consequences of their actions, even to the point of death. However, it is still very easy to speak and to write documents or manifestos. It is rather difficult for us to do serious analysis of complex realities and to bring about a consistent, critical, and far-reaching effort that seeks the liberation of the poor in the context of unjust structures. These will not be changed with words but with the prolonged effort of a life

sealed by the strength of the Spirit and with an effective sharing in
the building of a new society together with all people.

But the world is not made up only of the poor and the inhabitants of shantytowns. An equally great challenge is the society of
abundance and consumerism, the areas of sophisticated culture,
the universities, the artistic, scientific, and mass communication
media, the financial and commercial, the industrial and technological world, as well as urban and rural workers. All of this needs our
presence, and it would be tragically myopic for the Church to
overlook such challenging areas. The very historical evolution of
religious led them eventually to side more with affluence than
with poverty and suffering. Moreover, through a total osmosis,
religious seem bound to assimilate quickly not only life patterns
but even the very principles of this affluent life. The reaction that
is really needed can be neither simple nor naive. There is a radical
difference between merely being with the rich and being a stimulat-
ing and evangelizing presence among them. The real challenge,
however, is that this difference is rooted within us, and we must
demand it of ourselves without waiting for it to be demanded by
others. The same thing is true for non-wealthy sectors that are also
not poor or marginated and from which the Church and religious
clearly shy away because they are difficult, critical, and demanding. The Brazilian church has been placed on the path toward a
communitarian understanding of its evangelizing activities: the
appearance everywhere of *basic ecclesial communities* is a springtime
that fills everyone with hope.[1] But we must ask ourselves why
these communities arise primarily in rural areas and among
middle-aged people, while urban communities and the youth (two
characteristics of Brazil) continue to be a challenge. The evangelizing presence among university students and industrial workers
still is a small percentage of pastoral activity. We are either on the
sidelines of the means of communication, or we show a regretta-
ble, outdated presence. We certainly have no significant evangelizing impact among the majority of college students or their parents,
or among the doctors and medical workers of our hospitals. Many
of us would not even know how to begin a dialogue with scientific
or artistic areas, not to speak of the business world against which

we entrench ourselves without enough knowledge of its internal dynamic.

The mission of Jesus Christ, continued today by us, cannot be reduced to the borders of our limitations. The Gospel poverty we profess is precisely what is going to liberate us to offer a clear and challenging presence on all these fronts. We lack the interior freedom—that only the poverty of being and of the person can give us—that allows us to say that it is necessary to go to those poor in material goods, but it is also necessary to be converted in order to maintain a poor heart before those who are not poor in material things but who have need of God. It is as difficult to evangelize them as it is to convert ourselves. But the same power of the Spirit that allows us to understand today the cry of the oppressed should be enough power in us to allow others to see the face of Christ. He wants the salvation of all people and wants everyone to know in him, through and in spite of the limited instrument we are, the manifestation of the love of God, without which neither we ourselves nor anyone else will be able to transform structures. The Gospel is a universal project for everyone. That Jesus Christ would show preference for the poor does not mean that he excludes the rich, although he alerts them to the difficulty involved in wealth because it enslaves the individual and makes one forget God and neighbor. But between those very rich and very poor in material goods, there is a large group that we are disregarding, at least rationally in our theories. Perhaps we are in fact also excluding them because we are not what we should be. There is a loss of evangelizing thrust among us religious that is born from the realistic awareness of our limitations, though unaccepted existentially by us because we do not possess a poor heart.

Conclusion

The approach to Gospel poverty that we publicly profess before the Church and before all people, and especially before God, embraces the whole of our action and of our being. To try, with the power of

God within us, to offer all of this to the Lord and to people seems to me to reveal a striking meaning and scope of the vow of poverty. Yet, at the same time, it prepares us for the challenge of a conversion that involves the translation of all of this into life. If by God's grace we achieve this, the light that is in us will shine for the people and Jesus's mission will be continued by us. However, if we do not achieve it, our light will be extinguished and our salt will have lost its flavor. God will know how to raise others to continue through history the manifestation of divine love to all people in Jesus Christ, the Son of God, our Savior and Liberator.

Note

1. See Marcello Azevedo, *Basic Ecclesial Communities in Brazil. The Challenge of a New Way of Being Church* (Washington, D.C.: Georgetown University Press, 1987).

Chapter Three

Religious Life and the Preferential Option for the Poor

AMONG THE CHANGES experienced by religious life after the Second Vatican Council, there is one that touches the very depths of its being and action. It acts as a catalyst and inspiration for other changes. It serves as the criterion for evaluation and credibility of what mobilizes religious today, gives meaning to their lives, and challenges them. I am referring to a new sensitivity toward the poor, toward the poor people of the world, toward poverty in humanity.

The constancy and the insistence with which this problem is now present in the individual consciousness of religious men and women throughout the world is impressive. It looms as a paramount concern of their life and work in many local communities, a new dimension of their identity. It has become the central axis of the reflections and decisions of many general chapters in the last few years, opening other avenues for mission or communicating a fresh vigor to the ongoing mission.

The sensitivity toward poverty is certainly not new in the Church or in religious life. Beneath all of its forms of material or spiritual poverty, of illness or ignorance, of need or rejection, of loneliness or insecurity, of discrimination or oppression, this many-faced poverty, as it is perceived in the concrete lives of people, was on many occasions the starting point or first priority of various religious orders and congregations throughout history. From the beginning of the thirteenth century, religious life was expressed juridically, through the explicit vow of poverty, as one of the central dimensions of the full consecration to God in this

33

specific modality of apostolic vocation in the Church. Following the poor Christ led to a radical Gospel coherence in the lives of many saints. It was the touchstone of many spiritual trends or traditions that would translate for the Church the endless fertility of this Gospel seed. But the Church was conscious also of the limits of its fidelity and of the contradictions of its personal and institutional life. The Church, however, never discarded this primal idea of being poor with the poor Christ and of going out to meet those whom he clearly preferred, when dwelling among us, making himself poor—he who was God—and living as a poor man among the poor people of his time. Upon this foundation and in this spirit, he recruited his disciples; and in this way he also loves us, today's disciples.

It is nothing new, then, that religious life is concerned with poverty. What is surprising is the *new sensitivity* toward the poor and toward poverty in the world that today characterizes religious life. What is disconcerting and challenging is the internal dynamic of this perspective. Such a vision becomes the key element of a profound and inclusive transformation of both individual religions and their communities within the ecclesial context in which we live.

From where does this new vision come? What has caused religious to discover this dimension of their faith and of their own existence so powerfully in the last few years? Why, at the same time that so many are encouraged and full of hope, do others experience doubt, resistance, or skepticism? Why, in various communities or entire institutes, does this new sensitivity toward the poor become a sign of contradiction, a life stimulus, and/or a source of disunity or misunderstanding? From where do the problems come? How do we identify them and try to give a valid answer to them? How do we examine and gradually integrate so fertile an intuition that, nevertheless, runs the risk of becoming sterile or being the cause of dispersion?

The Starting Point for a New Sensitivity

We live in a paradoxical world. *On the one hand*, humanity can point to extraordinary conquests in science and in the technological translation of its knowledge about itself and about nature. It achieves highly sophisticated processes of information, organization, production, and consumption on all levels. On the theoretical level, humanity is capable of codifying, as never before, a charter of human rights that, at least in principle, purifies and rectifies centuries of discrimination and arbitrariness, the entire unacceptable gamut of archaic imperatives that various cultures consecrated as taboo or customary law. This world is conscious, on a global scale, of genuinely human values, such as the fundamental equality between persons, which makes fraternity possible among people of any level; liberty, which must be sought in all of its expressions, on the individual and social levels; solidarity as the palpable project of an efficacious love that approaches and unites people around common goals and leads them to cooperation in the widespread overcoming of limitations and needs. People today have an inclusive and simultaneous perception of the world as a whole. They have the conditions to be able to operate globally and efficaciously on the entire mass of humanity.

On the other hand, in spite of all this potential and capacity, the real world in which we find ourselves and in which we live is characterized by the hunger and malnutrition of almost two-thirds of its inhabitants, by illiteracy, illness, and unemployment, by the primary lack of the basic conditions of life for a vast number of peoples. This world smothers the freedom of hundreds of millions of people. Societies are shaped along the lines of institutional violence, patent or covert, which shows or enjoins itself destructively in the short or long run. There are systems of domination that impose, on very wide areas, an economic and political dependence that conditions or oppresses their people. The hands of a few hold the fate and destiny of many. There is no hope that the many may sometimes break through the state of things or emerge freely toward a dreamed autonomy.

There are countries whose administrations tolerate or, what is worse, install corruption as part of the very institution of the state. Bribery, illegal commissions, the corruption of individual consciences, and the bartering of public responsibilities destroy, like a terminal cancer, the social fabric, degrade society, and disintegrate the dignity and identity of the nation. Conscious of all this, ordinary people feel defenseless and suffer the demoralizing and unbearable weight of so much corruption.

These are all forms of poverty on a macrosocial scale, lived by individuals or supported by entire societies. What is *new* in the perception of this phenomenon is the evidence that our world, in contrast with the convictions and possibilities described previously, is organized in such a way that it produces and reproduces this poverty. What is *new* is the clear intuition that, based on the premises upon which states and societies operate, there is no hope of escape. There is, indeed, the certainty of a more and more serious and extensive worsening of this poverty. What is *new* is the understanding that such poverty is not episodic or by chance, but rather has become systematic and structural. What is *new* is the persuasion that poverty is the result of a long evolutionary process that, by the will of a few, is forced upon humanity, directly or indirectly, in an inexorable and uncontrollable way. What is *new* is the proof that, one after another, the calls and attempts to stop or redirect this process are frustrated. What is *new* is the evidence that this poverty is the product of an internalized lack of respect for people, for their admitted rights, and for their uncontestable aspirations. Poverty is the result of the oppression of many people, of orchestrated manipulation and exploitation, perhaps less on the level of a conscious, singular act of an individual than on the level of the economic and political systems that humanity has created. These systems operate primarily and irresistibly from the actual standpoint of structural injustice that is their presupposition and the very principle of their insatiable hunger. This is really what is *new*; this is a creation or a perversion of modern and postmodern times.

The prophets of Israel and the saints of the Church in other times could not have such a global insight into the poverty of their time. No matter how much they shared in the daily poverty of those around them, they could not perceive as we do the worldwide interaction of factors that produce the poverty of the many that "you will always have with you" to whom Jesus referred. The certainty of inevitable poverty is sad. The organization of the production of poverty on a global scale and the irreversible destruction of humankind is tragic.

The conscious openness to humanity as a whole and the deep communion with the true history of that humanity—two increasing tendencies in the recent position of the Church in several parts of the world and of many religious within the Church—convince us that this poverty cannot be considered as a natural fate. It is, rather, the result of selfishness, which is translated into active and efficient injustice. It is, therefore, not only an unbalance in the proper equity, but also the clear denial of love and truth. In the Christian perspective, such injustice perverts and subverts both the plan of God as well as the dignity and destiny of human beings. Thus, the final reality, *that poverty which is the fruit of injustice*, bears within it the sign of sin.   *Social sin*

We are conscious of the fact that while humanity today can create a more just society and world, in fact it does not want to do so. Omission or indifference, conformity or cowardice, can submit us to this situation or lead us tacitly to join in it. We then become co-responsible for such injustice. This posture is incompatible with the faith that we profess: a faith in a God who is Father and who wants the best for all people. He is present and accessible in Jesus Christ, through whom we all are children of God and brothers and sisters to one another, fully liberated by love in forgiveness and reconciliation. This faith teaches us and leads us to make of the human mediation the necessary pathway to God. It measures the quality of our relationship with God by way of our relationships with others (Mt 25). For this faith, therefore, the injustice inherent in those structural forms of poverty that our world generated or tries to perpetuate is intolerable. To work, then, to overcome this injustice is to live out faith in the full scope of its meaning; it is to give to God an answer that is transmitted through service to others, just as God wanted to pass through the Word made flesh to speak and interact with humanity. To live faith without this demand for justice is to separate oneself from the plan of God and to take on in some manner the aberration that humanity created.

The sharpness and density of those insights gave the Church and religious within it that *new sensitivity toward the reality of poverty in the world*. Such a perception challenges religious to a radical and consistent living of faith. This is what precisely gives meaning to our consecrated life in the Church and the world of today.

Religious Life: The Dynamic of a History

Religious life is a form of apostolic vocation that is characterized by complete consecration to God on the part of certain men and women. Their public expression is translated by the vows of poverty, chastity, and obedience, professed and lived in a specific community that the Church accepted and legitimated. The peculiar modalities of this form of living the Christian vocation cross history from the fourth century to the present day.

Like layers that are superimposed in a geological cross section, religious life is manifested on various levels that emerge from the eremetical experiences and are affirmed in the early cenobitic life. It gains force and is spread with Eastern and Western monasticism. From the twelfth or thirteenth century onward, new paths were opened by the mendicant orders who confronted the urban challenge generated by the profound transformation of medieval economics. The sixteenth century gave us original and unexpected models of religious life. Just like their predecessors, these beat with the total rhythm of the Church. They respond, from the most intimate part of the Church, often with prophetic intuition to its urgent need to proclaim the Word and to share in the sacrament and in the gracious gift of the Spirit, serving and saving people wherever and however they are found. The discovery of new lands leads the Church to an immense expansion, but also to a perception of the complexity and diversity of these newly known peoples. Among so many faces of the same humanity, the Church is discovering the profound and common traits of a suffering and needy humanity, hungry for God. From the seventeenth to the nineteenth century, many institutes arose that wanted to remedy the indigence of individuals, the impotence or perversion of societies, in the service of all people. They were congregations of men and women who teach in the schools, cure and comfort in hospitals, proclaim the word in catechesis and in devotional acts, but, above all, in the missions, near or far. The footsteps remain in the sands of the world of those who evangelize under so many different forms and by an infinite number of paths.

With lesser or greater variations, religious life feeds and lives a little bit of all these models and inspirations up until the 1970s. Just as it is true that the layers were formed gradually and superimposed over time, so it is true that they met and were fruitful, interacting throughout an ongoing and penetrating historical osmosis. Within the diversity of its multiple activities and in the endless variations of its expressions, there exists a thread of uninterrupted continuity: this is the desire to be, in the midst of people, a presence that translates evangelical radicality as well as teleological life orientation into what will become definitive for humanity.

Religious life is, then, in history, a living fabric of contrasts and tensions, of creativity and movement, of confirmation and improvement, from which emerges the same thread which is sensitivity for people. It is from here that religious life becomes, in the Church, a specific response by men and women to God, in service to their brothers and sisters. It is not the simple ratification nor the static and fixed repetition of the same paradigm. The inspiration for the *fuga mundi* gives it an initial impulse and, in fact, crosses it from beginning to end in the authentic meaning of a critical distance from the "world" in its Johannine sense—the world of darkness and sin, which rejects God and massacres humanity—thus lending an eminent service to people in their fidelity to God, but also, and often disgracefully, in the perspective of an effective distancing from people, from their aspirations and destiny. Religious life often lived an involution on itself that converted it into a refuge from the world and a potential for alienation.

The *new sensitivity to poverty in the world*—the fruit of the structural injustice that hurts humanity and denies God—introduces in religious life a different layer in the geological cross section of its history. This layer is characterized by the emphasis on *mission* and on its urgency. It is defined not by flight from the world, but by the sending of religious into it, to this very world which is people, the most needy among them, those whom Jesus preferred and to whom he said he was sent (Lk 4:16–21), to the point of defining and describing his own identity in terms of them (Lk 7:18–23). That is how religious life gives continuity today to the Gospel inspiration and connects itself with its past history. But, from the perception of *poverty as the fruit of injustice* on a large scale, men and women religious begin to translate their witness and service to faith into a perspective of mission that is indissociable from the building, with people and for people, of a just society where people may open themselves to God and to others.

The preferential option for the poor is the catalyst for this entire perspective of being and doing. Are the poor not the astounding majority of this suffering humanity in which once more we see the face of the crucified Christ? Are they not, in fact, the distressful presence that leads us to intuit deeply the cruel paradox of our world, notable for human conquests and marked by the oppression and destruction of so many people? Are they not the ones who pedagogically help us to perceive the emptiness of a faith that is not the transforming and constructive force of a just world where there is space for truth and love? Are they not, on the other hand, the ones who call into question the very authenticity of a love and a truth that tolerate the products of injustice or even make pacts with them?

What does this new sending out mean, this mission that religious life grasps today, as do other groups, beginning from an ever more sensitive ecclesial consciousness of people, in their total relationship to God and to other people? How do we understand, in the present context of the Church and the world, the *preferential option for the poor*, this dense and current expression that so well synthesizes the profound inspiration of so much we have just said?

Religious Life: Presence and Leaven in the Process of Transformation

From a purely sociological standpoint, religious life—above all in first world countries—presents a worrisome picture in this moment of the Church. It seems as if it were being diluted, vanishing in an irrecoverable way, afflicted by the aging of those who live it and by the lack of fertility, even sterility, that does not allow it to reproduce any longer. Few young people seek it and see in it an acceptable and inspiring form of life, one that is able to fulfill their generous desires to serve God and people.

However, perceived from other angles and on a deeper level, primarily in the countries of the third world and in some sectors of the first world, religious life is experiencing the breath and vigor of a new and promising perspective. A religious life that captures, in the frequency of today's world, the modulation that expresses the meaning of its apostolic vocation in the Church: to be in our day, through a radical consistency of life, the presence and witness of God's truth and love toward humanity, as manifested for us in Jesus Christ. The far-reaching horizon of a religious life, which religious want to embrace in its entirety, is findiing its more convincing and trustworthy expression precisely in *attention* to the poorest, in *docility* to the message of which they are the carriers, and in *presence and communion* among the poor. These three elements can help us in a serene reading and a fuller understanding of that ecclesial *preferential option for the poor*.

Although, in its widest usage, this formula may be linked to the Puebla Conference, it is becoming more and more a part of the consciousness and the patrimony of the present-day Church, as much in the documents of the universal Church as in the various episcopal conferences, including some of the first world. In making the preferential option for the poor at Puebla, the Church of Latin America took an extraordinary step. It made itself ready to enter into a process that is new with respect to centuries of its past history. The Puebla option is not meant to be an idealization of the poor and their poverty: it does not use them for the eventual ecclesiological hermeneutic that tries to redeem itself from its secular compromise with wealth. Such a focus would be assuming the inauthentic hypothesis that the poor are satisfied with their situation of being poor, a situation that they would maintain and even cultivate in the name of the Gospel preferences. This somewhat romantic perspective of a people resigned to their own poverty lacks realism and cannot be accepted either by the Church or by the poor themselves. The Gospel does not authorize us to canonize the disgrace or to resign ourselves to human misery. Neither was this option made in the unsustainable illusion of being able to reestablish, through and with the poor, the hegemony of premodern religious legitimation. This option does not intend to create with them a type of ghetto, a defensive entrenchment against both the conflictive reality and the pluralistic influences of the world in which we live. Such a position necessarily flows into sectarianism or fanaticism; it shares the weakness of every dualism that annihilates the capacity for criticism and discernment.

The *preferential option for the poor* implies the *"change of social perspective."* This has to do with accepting, in the reading or interpretation of reality, a new angle or starting point. To change "social perspective" means for the Church, and for religious within it, the serious effort to look at the world and society, at the Church itself, and at all of humanity from the perspective *of the poor,* from their urgencies and needs, their values and callings, from their possible and valid contribution in their own advancement and in the desired construction of a just society.

Only this new and distinct perspective of reality, from the point of view of the poor, will make possible the effective change in the criteria and decision-making processes, be it on the ecclesial, social, cultural, or economic level. This new reference point is what will allow the quality of our presence and the totality of our apostolate as religious to be put at the service of the poor and, as such, at the service of the effective transformation of the present-day world, directly or indirectly. In education or in research, in the means of communication or in publishing, in pastoral activity of every kind and, above all, in the work and collaboration with the laity, this perspective will make us evangelizers of today's world. And we will not primarily be such by stressing liturgical and sacramental practices, or because of spiritual or devotional orientation, or due to the transmission of mental knowledge of the contents of faith or even because of the solicitous announcement of the Word. We will be such, with this and in all of this, through the attempt to raise up the internal challenge that our faith be made consistently explicit in the conscious effort to make possible, through the persevering construction of a new society based on justice and the reorientation of people toward Gospel truth and love.

Only this looking at the world from the point of view of the poor, in the awareness of the infrahuman situation of such a majority of people, will be able to change the canons by which the organisms of decision making are currently structured on all levels and then make viable for humanity the so-desired new international order. It is certainly not the role of religious to act directly on the front line of many initiatives that necessarily are defined and are mediated by the contrasting political powers and economic alternatives. But, because of the new sensitivity toward the structural character of poverty in our world, it is incumbent upon us to give to people, by means of our life and the weight of our apostolic activity in the entire world, the tools for reflection and the operative contribution that may make viable and urge the building of a better world, a more human one.

On the inter-ecclesial level, the conception of reality from the point of view of the poor can also lead us to help the Church as a whole to understand complex ecclesial situations that are distant and distinct from those that are lived at its center. New perceptions can then lead to new evaluations and thereby to new pastoral paths.

Therefore, to give preference to the poor in the context of the world and the Church of today is not only to intensify generous, but perhaps paternalistic, aid from our abundance of human and material, intellectual and spiritual, resources. And it does not exclusively have to do with being involved in its midst and sharing directly with them in the daily and arduous evolution of their painful existence. It is, before all else, to situate the poor actively at the very root of our criteria of analysis, evaluation, and interpretation of reality, at the center of our discernment and decision making, at the focus of our being and our apostolic activity as religious in search of a more humane and, as such, more just ground in which the seed of the Gospel may fall with the hope of fertility.

The *preferential option for the poor*, however, is not only that priority attention toward the poor. It also includes our acceptance of the message which is carried by them. This message demands from the whole ecclesial body a disposition of not always considering ourselves as the only active pole of evangelization. It is basic that we allow ourselves to be evangelized by the Gospel inspiration that exists in those that Christ himself chose preferentially.

This pragmatic attitude places the institutional Church on the path back toward its origins. The Church of Jesus Christ, in its primitive model of evangelical inspiration, is far from the dominant religious paradigm of pre-existing cultures and even of the Judaic tradition from which it emerged. It is an original Church. The apostles and disciples of Jesus Christ were not a separate caste, nor were they chosen for their birth or titles. Chosen from among the people for service to people, they go out from the people and are for the people just as Christ himself was. Their rise to evangelical power within the community should not distance them from the people. Historical consequences often led the Church to be co-opted by the dominant religious paradigm in many cultures and to lose or eclipse much of its authentic new-ness. The preferential option for the poor could reintroduce the Church in its original perspective: to live without imposing human power and, therefore, to be fundamentally free to help people to embrace the power of God and to answer the calls of humanity.

It is here that the charismatic and prophetic dimensions of reli-gious life are emphasized. In changing their social perspective, religious are liberated from the traps of non-evangelical power. This creates spaces in the Church that are free of ambition, of anxiety about a career and about the search for prestige, and of the games of pressure groups. Because of the quality of their presence and because of the strength of their witness, religious can be freely open to listening to the Spirit and to an ever-necessary conversion. Only thus will they be leaven in the ecclesial mass of dough.

Finally, the *preferential option for the poor* is not, nor can it be, an instantaneous act. This change of social perspective that purifies and reformulates our criteria of analysis and decision making, this docility that consents to being evangelized by the poor and not only to evangelize them, is necessarily a *process*. Before and while transforming the world, this process transforms us, opening us to the direct or indirect presence of the poor and, above all, to the *communion* with them. To be with the poor—and this living and life experience always carries with it a profound redemptive power—is to live history from its reverse, that side that is not written. It is to feel existentially—not only to know it—the weight of need, injustice, impotence, insecurity, and uncertainty. All of this demands a new learning. Those who do not live close at hand this other side of humanity, those who ignore it or try to forget it, lack this pedagogy. It is a pedagogy that the Church knew through-out its history, given that it was always open to helping the poor. In the past, however, the Church rather perceived them in their singularity of individuals or in the modest horizon of local realities. And it was also often out of remission of individual sin that it tried to lessen their poverty. Today, on the contrary, without denying the reality and the impact of individual sin, the Church has also grasped the unbearable scope of social sin, a primary generator of that macrosociety which impoverishes people. From there springs the Church's decision not to align itself uncritically with all trends of society. From there arises in the Church the urgent call for being alongside those who suffer, the option for looking at reality from their point of view. This profound communion, which is one way of concretizing the option for the poor but not the only one, is taking in fact a particular form in the Church by the insertion of many men and women religious among the poor. The poor, who are simultaneously evangelized and evangelizers, make the Church present in their own reality, but they also discover at the same time how profoundly they already are and live as that faith community which is the Church.

Chapter Four

The Vow of Chastity

THE INNATE HUMAN tendency to absolutize material goods and
to lay a foundation with them for positions of power and prestige
in relationship to other people is apparent in our daily experience.
Perhaps for this same reason, we have not recognized the wide
ramifications and the influence that can come from this inclination. The Christological and anthropological focus on poverty in
the previous chapters helps us to realize how decisive is the radical
living of the Gospel plan in this area of the poverty of being and
having. It reaches both the individual and the institutional levels
of a religious community. We profess that poverty publicly before
God, before the Church, and before humanity.

Another powerful, instinctive human tendency is the absolutization of human love. We can experience that love as characterized by an affective egoism, which is affirmed in two directions:
the domination of the beloved person to the point of turning such
a possession into a kind of master key for one's own happiness,
and the inability to understand that a real love can be lived and
incarnated in the total giving of oneself, without a necessary
sexual-genital expression of that love.

The wave of pornography and the growing permissiveness that
have invaded Western nations are manifestations of this way of
seeing things. Often, the analysis of the discussions and proposi-
tions, in legislatures or in representative groups, as well as com-
mentaries on the media, reveal a significant presence of selfish or
hedonistic motives in the development of norms that involve human problems, such as the state's influence on the official control
of birth rates, abortion, homosexuality, divorce, and pre-marital
sex. We do not want to oversimplify the facts nor do we want to

ignore the extraordinary complexity of the situations that surround each one of these problems. But we cannot close our eyes before the widespread insistence upon a common denominator: the claim that sexual, especially genital, freedom liberates the person for love or, conversely, that the person will not be free or mature in the capacity to love if one does not tear down the walls that have been raised throughout the centuries in terms of his or her sexual expression. This assumption that sexual-genital freedom liberates the individual for love includes the iconoclastic demolition of many cultural and religious taboos. Many, in fact are taboos; but others are not. Nevertheless, everything is left behind as if they all were.

All of this has coincided with great and relatively recent discoveries in biology and in psychology related to the knowledge and value of human sexuality in the context of individual personality and social behavior. This is not the place to explore this aspect, which has been studied in countless books and articles, especially in the last twenty years. Among Catholics, the appearance of publications that have attempted a rereading of the phenomenon and its application for the Church to the entire moral and psychological focus of the sexual question is even more recent. The indisputable result of all these studies is the fact that love and sex are the absolutely central and all-embracing axis of the psychosomatic structure of every human person, from the beginning to the end of his or her life.

Inversion of Perspectives

Did not religious life also fall into an absolutization of affective egoism, although from the opposite side? Was it not fostering an egoism by conceiving of the vow of chastity as a flight from the world and as separation from people, as well as the passive, timid, and frightened elimination of all affective relationships between persons? Don't we meet religious who are concerned with and proud of a purity lived in fidelity, but lived for itself? Is this not a tacit but real denial of the love and gracious self-giving to others? Is it not shocking to find people who are consecrated to God but who are arrogantly distant from people, with a superiority complex that sets them apart from others? Who of us has not known religious capable of a subtle and constant cruelty, yet whose purity is without question? Some individuals are cold and harsh, capable of hurting and putting down others, of oppressing the weak, with their attitudes or their actions, with a word or a glance, in action or by omission; some people are experts in festering revenge and camouflaged aggression cloaked in hard and fast discrimination. However, basic psychological intuition would make it clear that they were frequently led to this extreme, especially toward other religious, prompted by an unconscious and singular jealousy with regard to masculine/feminine figures around them. Is it not that conception of love and purity that is at the root of so many problems of relationship within community?

Who has not known religious who are authoritarian and inaccessible, attentive to the smallest details of norms and the law, inflexible with themselves and whose purity is without question, but who, by being so rigid and lacking in true love, become curious aberrations? Many powerful and authoritarian male figures display feminine traces and manners; strongly dominant persons are impressively sensitive, however, to any type of courtesy and adulation, desiring praise and applause and being very vulnerable to the repercussion of their own image in feminine/ masculine surroundings.

The vow of chastity is often reduced to the observance of mere moral purity. It is not lived as a liberating force of our potential for love. It became, in this way, a protective overcoat for our comfort, our individualism, and our self-satisfaction, for an easy and uncommitted organization of our lives, a guarantee to not be bothered and to be able to deny others whenever we are asked for things that conflict with our more inconsistent and selfish desires and tendencies.

Chastity and Interior Poverty

When chastity is lived without a profound interior poverty, which is the fruit of the consciousness and experience of one's own frailty, it easily leads one to judge others. It might be helpful to point out a distinction between purity and chastity. Purity belongs more properly to the legal, ritual, or morally ethical realm. It may be faithfully observed without grasping the actual scope and meaning of chastity. Chastity always presupposes purity, but it transcends it and gives it the breath of life and spirit. Purity can be a problem that is not posed for an older or infirm individual, because one of the ways in which life is manifested has been extinguished in them. Chastity is a gift for everyone and a conquest of their entire life, until death, because it touches the whole person. Purity can be lived, as we have seen, with pride and hardness of heart; chastity, on the contrary, is always as humble as Saint Francis' Sister Water, "soft, precious, and chaste." Chastity belongs to the world of oblative and gratuitous love because it is conscious of being a gift that must also be given. What Saint Paul says about love cannot always be said about purity. Chastity, however, would be irreconcilable if it were not patient and kind. It cannot be arrogant or envious. It takes joy in truth. It understands; it believes; it hopes; it supports. Chastity is essentially on the order of charity and love. Like love, it is always affirmation and presence. In the midst of the poverty of our possibilities of love lives the full hope of the LOVE that transcends us. Loving God in charity, one is open to others. And in the love of others, one is sure of being open to God.

The resistance of many young people today to live the commitment of the vow of chastity resides less in chastity itself than in the ways we have conceived of and concretized it throughout the centuries. They often see in us religious a kind of cold and distant love, the inability for a real and unrequited giving, gratuitous and open to all. That is why they shake when they meet religious who are capable of this, of existentially incarnating in their lives one of their deepest and most undefinable desires. In this world so dominated by the demand for a self-interested and pervasive sexual-genital expression, one of the greatest contributions to be given by religious to people is to reveal to them, with their committed lives more than with their words, the possibility of a true giving and openness to others, being happy in people's happiness; being faithful and delicate in love, fleeing from every desire for domination or exclusivity; and being able to live in peace, without the demand for a sexual-genital expression that is commonly understood as a necessary way of expressing love.

Chastity and the Totality of the Person

Chastity is an anthropological situation that affects the whole human person in his or her spiritual and material dimensions. It is a result of the correct orientation of the affective and sexual psychosomatic totality of the person in a consistent and integrated concretization of his or her life as an individual and as a member of the human community. In this sense, chastity is not a privilege or a characteristic of a state or way of life; its distinctive character is given by its different forms of realization. All of them, however, affect human life, whether one's life is the fruit of a conscious and free choice or whether it is the result of an existential situation that does not always depend on one's decision. Indeed, chastity, more than a partial aspect of the person, touches upon the wholeness of the individual and is situated on the level of an all-embracing, personal, and existential attitude. It is not, therefore, only purity in the realm of the sensitive; much less can it coexist with the ambiguity of a formal purity that allows for compensations in the affective spiritual plane. And this, once more, can be applied to all forms of human life. That is why chastity, respectively corresponding to any form or state of life, to any apostolic vocation, is at the same time radically common and specifically distinct.

In the specific case of religious life, vowed chastity presupposes a necessarily conscious and free choice. This is the consequence of the acceptance, from within the depths of the person, of a gift of God that is offered in the vocation to this style of life. Consecrated and publicly professed chastity in religious life, as an apostolic vocation in the Church, concentrates in God the affective potential of the individual and, in light of and by the power of God, opens the individual to the personal but not exclusive love of one's neighbor.

The religious is called to be a living witness in the world to the exclusivity of the love of God as an absolute and definitive response to our human desire for love. In not considering human love as the only path and expression of the exclusivity of the love of God, consecrated chastity is somehow outside of the natural pattern of human evolution. It acquires a markedly transcendent and eschatological dimension. In this way, it anticipates our ultimate situation. Religious chastity cannot be considered as the goal of some human ideal nor can it be understood in light of human reason alone. Consecrated chastity, though, is part of the universal plan of God for humanity. Religious men and women are consecrated for *mission*, which is to manifest to all people, through the giving of their limited and poor love, the traces of the infinite riches of God's gratuitous love. This is where religious chastity is integrated in the Gospel inspiration of our entire life, making present again the very mission of Jesus Christ. By becoming *human*, he wanted to reveal to us what we could not by ourselves understand about God. In the consecrated religious' attitude of love, a personal and gratuitous love, people are able to perceive the reality of the great love that the Lord is revealing to them, a LOVE which is himself, that is, God. Therefore, for religious, chastity is not a defense and, strictly speaking, neither is it simply a virtue. It is the meaningful expression of the very character of their apostolic vocation, possibly the most profound and individualizing one, because it affects the totality of their being. One must be fully conscious of all of this when making the public profession of consecrated chastity. Indeed, that profession does not only suppose a clear call from God, whose response only comes from faith; it also demands the notable maturity of a well-integrated person.

A well-defined, firm, and clear option for this type of life is basic to the formation of young religious. It is more important than the isolated and partial, and consequently little existential, acquisition of simple habits of individual purity, which may lead him or her to a distancing from others and a self-sufficient pride in his or her presumed and proper virtue. As we have already said, daily life often puts us in contact with people who, from the pedestal of their purity, set up criteria for the evaluation and interpretation of the actions and intentions of others. Purity that is observed apart from the context of chastity tends to become something ritualistic and formal, rigid and intransigent, that easily condemns and almost never understands. Experience tells us, however, that profoundly chaste people possess at the same time the naturalness and the goodness of the Lord as manifested by his gratitude to Mary Magdalene for her love, by his patient teaching with the Samaritan woman, by his compassionate and discreet mercy with the woman caught in adultery, but, above all, by his evident ability to love well. Jesus loved Martha, Mary, and their brother Lazarus. John is known as the beloved disciple of Jesus. Yet, to all of them, Jesus revealed the Father. And in forgiving the adulteress and in not allowing the crowd to throw a single stone, as was the law, Jesus gave her the true meaning of life: "Go, and sin no more."

Chastity and Maturity

If the clarity of the option for chastity is important at the beginning, its growth and maturation throughout one's life is fundamental. Difficult and concrete situations, the spiritual discernment about them, the concern with the criteria of the spirit and not of the flesh (Rom 8), the enlightenment of the Lord as to the subconscious motives for our actions and as to the "disordered inclinations" of our hearts—all of this is the true school of the ongoing formation of our chastity, in which we will never reach the final goal. It causes the option of our younger years to mature, day after day, throughout our lives. This constant checking ourselves, at the same time vigilant in our frailty and aware of it, allows us to be open to all people, with a truly free heart. It makes the personal intensity of our love clearly shine forth our firm consciousness of the pervasive and transcendent presence of God's love in us, as the decisive option of our life.

What we are saying lessens our concern and perplexity about so many people who have recently abandoned religious life. There are two aspects that cannot be ignored in analyzing this phenomenon. On the one hand, it is true that until recently the entire religious formation used to unilaterally stress formation for purity. Religious life once was largely supported by its isolation from the world and from people (legislation regarding cloister,

for example, was based fundamentally on the defense of purity)
and by a solid structure. Countless defensive resources were
thereby given to safeguard purity, but without always arriving in
fact at sufficiently exploring the personal dimension of the option
for chastity lived in this way. The old structures—largely inadequate for contemporary life—were recently broken down. The
media, especially television, penetrated the cloister. Interpersonal
relationships were intensified. There were religious, well prepared for purity, who nevertheless realized that they had been
mistaken in the way of conceiving of a life that did not correspond in fact to their very option. One cannot generalize on that
matter or undervalue the influence of inauthentic simplifications
or justifications. But the experience of the leaders of religious
orders during the past twenty years does away with any doubt
that, at the root of many who left, purity was not the problem.
This, rather, was the much more basic and decisive fact of the
lack or ambiguity in the conscious personal option for this particular way of life in consecrated chastity. Once so vital a question
was posed, it became necessary to find a solution. In many cases,
there was no other way but to reorient one's own life, valuing
possibilities that had been kept unfolded because of the false
existential situation in which the individual found himself or herself. It is just as certain, furthermore, that until recently formation for religious life had given too much value to the spiritual
element alone in order to resolve deeper questions regarding the
totality of the person. This reductive approach favored the permanence in religious life of inept but generous people and/or of
conformist and mediocre individuals. The former used their spiritual and ascetic voluntarism to overcome intolerable life situations by means of an heroic effort of fidelity; the latter, in the
midst of a comfortable inertia, held onto their chronic incapacity
for an authentic commitment. Both groups are not qualified for
that mission and, certainly, they have not been called by God to
the religious life, although they continue in it spontaneously or
supported by others in a dramatic, existential mistake.

It will not be easy to find well-conceived channels for an initial
and ongoing formation that will shelter us from such formidable
mistakes. But it is absolutely necessary not to forget that professed

consecrated chastity in religious life today has meaning only if it is solidly anchored in a conscious option. It must be a liberating option that builds up an integrated person in the context of a community of people to live the love of God and to manifest it to one's brothers and sisters, without demeaning them or turning against them. Furthermore, this option will help the religious to realize that the fullness of love is a lifelong task, an endless path. Like all human choices, including those made from the perspective of faith or in virtue of God's grace, the option for consecrated chastity is also subject to ups and downs. It can only be lived from a profound attitude of the poverty of being and of a self-accepting person in love. That attitude helps one to advance patiently day after day in the building of one's fidelity; it continually allows people to be educated by others and to seek support in God's love, source of all love. We realize how much chastity and poverty are interwoven in the human design of religious life.

Chastity and Communion with God

We thus express a highly important double aspect for the proper positioning of the ongoing option for consecrated chastity. Jesus Christ brought and manifested to humanity the *love* of God, which is trinitarian communion. As a logical consequence, he carried out his mission in continual communion with the Father and the Holy Spirit. Our communion with God through Jesus Christ is the only source that allows our religious chastity to be an expression of love. We only can love a real and concrete *Someone.* God must be, for us, *someone* truly living through faith, in whom "we live, move, and have our being," with whom we speak and by whom we are spoken to. *Someone* for whom we set aside time and interior space. *Someone* whom we see in the darkness of our searches and whose design and will we try to discover in the midst of the frailty of our intuitions or in the precariousness of our reflections. This *someone* lives and exists, and we must communicate with that *someone* through faith. This intimate communion with the Lord will never be able to be replaced by constant communication with others, through whom God speaks to us intensely and in whom we find

God in surprising and often mysterious ways. Nor can it be replaced by the simple reading of reality and events, although they help us to discover the way of bringing together the little pieces of the mosaic of our lives. We will truly discover the love of God in the continually deepening immersion into prayer. Through it we contemplate God in the midst of life; we recognize God's presence in others. Only in prayer will we find the language to show God to others and the intelligence to discern and embrace God's love that is shown to us through others.

The community must be, in religious life, the special place for this manifestation. Public profession of one's consecration to God in a community is another element that grants identity to religious life among the apostolic vocations in the Church. It is true that the conception and the reality of community are very different in various congregations. But, whatever the kind of community, the communion of persons is fundamental: it is indeed the unavoidable condition for the manifestation of love. The conversion necessary for achieving communion in our communities may be much deeper than that required to live poverty in religious life. And yet, community is a decisive condition and climate for our consecrated chastity. Purely formal communities, based on the physical juxtaposition of people and on the coordination of schedules and communal activities, are the causes of the incurable sterility of many religious. These communities trigger a centrifugal process that leads religious to spin in various orbits and to create their own satellite communities. Such surrogate communities at times may fulfill an integrating function in defense against the scattering of the actual religious community. But they can also produce disintegration and gradually lead religious to miss the real meaning of their religious project.

When consecrated chastity is lived in communion with God and with others, it leads the individual to fullness as well as to a serene and profound freedom. The individual radiates with a joy and happiness that in itself is a real and unmistakable presence of the love of God. This is what the Gospel allows us to imagine, I would suggest, when it speaks with great discretion of the Virgin Mary.

The neatness of her option, the simplicity of her being, the unexpected richness of her consciousness of poverty, her openness to God, her availability to others, the calm depth of her intimate meditation on the language of God in her Son, the unfathomable mystery of her love for Joseph, the strength of her presence at the foot of the cross, and her living communion with the early apostolic Church are the expression of the extraordinary strength of a chaste and fulfilled personality who embraces the gift of God and is sure of her option because God has done marvelous things in her.

Consecrated chastity in religious life, as lived in the way we are trying to describe it here, can become a reference point for believing in the possibility of chastity in other situations or states of life, such as chastity in marriage, chastity in non-consecrated celibacy, pre-marital chastity, or chastity stemming from life circumstances such as illness, widowhood, war, absence, or the fact of not being married.

The personalized and exclusive intensity of the human love between a man and a woman finds its full human expression in the spiritual/material dimension of sexual union. But only the consciousness of the transcendence of God's love makes it possible to relativize even that very qualified love between spouses. This is a love that can indeed be stronger than death, a love that is capable of taking the risk of a lifetime, of accepting the other as that person is. This is a love that leads to a mutual, daily improvement, through the dynamics of love itself, in the peaceful acceptance of the limitations in each person. This is only possible in a true living of conjugal chastity, which emphasizes the primacy of love being able when necessary also to relativize the demand for its genital expression. This living is not simply reduced to the level of continence, which might not be chaste. It is rather the right orientation of the psychosomatic and sexual-affective totality of the spouse in the consistent and integrated concretization of their life in the world precisely as spouses and as parents. When it is lived evangelically, matrimony is the discovery of the love of God through the human mediation of mutual love between spouses. It is a sacrament of the gratuity of love, a gratuity that can grow to be heroic in the full and mutual acceptance of spouses and their children. Religious learn from them the capacity to accept in love the risk of life and to be able to place the happiness of the other before one's own happiness. Conversely, the religious known by the spouses in the profound dimension of his or her chastity will become a reliable stimulus for the relativization of the demand for genital expression when the many circumstances of life oblige them to curtail it, without threatening love.

Consecrated chastity can, in the same way, give great support and inspiration to those who have to live chastity as a specific and existential situation before marriage, or to those who have to live it as celibates whether because of personal choice or because of life circumstances. The religious can learn from these people, especially in times of crisis, not to absolutize naively or subjectively marriage as the unavoidable alternative of life. Many others, through their own decision or through life circumstances, have to live a similarly consistent non-conjugal chastity, even lacking the vocation to live the consecrated way of religious life. In their life and by their own experience, religious reassure these people that chastity is really possible, but only in light of and through the power of God's love as lived in a constant and intense openness to the good of one's neighbor. As a result, the young person before marriage as well as the adult celibate will find in the complete and open chastity of the realized and integrated religious a fertile inspiration to overcome personal selfishness and self-sufficient introversion. They will learn, above all, in the ethical impossibility whether momentary or definitive of sexually expressing love the little known reality in our world that sex is not love but rather only one of its possible manifestations and, therefore, not absolutely necessary to make true love real.

Chastity and Gratuity

The capacity to relativize sex can reveal the very core of love: its *gratuity*. To love is to be fulfilled with the good of another, to be happy in another's happiness. When our love carries with it this gratuity, it brings us closer to God's love in us, a gratuitous love that will never have a proper correspondence. This love is actualized precisely in communion: a continual giving and taking, a being what one is and an embracing—not only accepting—what the other is without trying to tailor that person in my image. The living of this reality, according to the character of one's personal vocation, is to love in chastity. And even spouses who do not realize thusly their own surrender, even in the sexual expression of their love, do not live love.

It is important, therefore, for every person to live in calm and committed fidelity to his or her own vocation, whatever it may be. This is the only way for one to be truly free, because true love is liberating. For that reason, consecrated chastity thus understood should help us to be persons who radiate a mature joy, forgetting ourselves and attentive to others, but, first, full of God; it should be indeed a true sign in the world of the goodness of God made human in Jesus Christ.

All of this raises the question of the intelligibility of consecrated chastity. It is not coincidental that one of the central themes of the theology of religious life in this century, especially since the Council, has been the subject of *sign*. Just as the issue of identity was of constant concern to religious as well as to their chapters, the question of sign also captured their attention for a long time. Experience and reflection over many years lead me to two considerations: if religious intensely live their consecrated life, they will have greater influence upon and a real meaning for others the less they are concerned about being a sign. Religious life, as it continues the mission of Jesus Christ and relativizes what humanity normally absolutizes, contrasts powerfully with people's innate tendency, especially in our day. The fact of religious having distinct criteria and coherently trying to translate them into life calls people's attention, makes them uncomfortable, and challenges them. But not actually because of this do religious become a "sign" for others. Only when those attitudes cease to be grasped as something imposed, and are perceived as spontaneous manifestations of love, only then will they be understood as the reflection of a deep joy and not simply as the result of obedience to a norm or law. People begin then to capture a "sign" that is not intelligible by normal categories. *However*, we cannot naively expect a world as pansexualized as our own to understand easily the meaning and scope of our chastity. There is a preliminary problem that cannot be undervalued, much less ignored: a great number of people do not easily believe that we live in chastity. To profess it and to live it faithfully today, in spite of everything, is one of the most concrete ways to realize the poverty of our being and of our person in the context of the world (see first chapter on poverty). There are also those who are incapable of believing this because their idea of love necessarily passes through the filter of selfishness. It is impossible for them to imagine a life that, especially in the manifestation of love, does without a dimension like the sexual-genital, which is an appropriate expression, although not a necessary one, of the gratifying recompense of love between people. Nevertheless, consecrated chastity does not lose its Gospel and redemptive meaning by the simple fact that it may not be understood or that it may not become a sign. I would rather say that this is a very way of really sharing in the mission of Jesus. He also was not always well understood by those who lived with him and has not been either by many other people throughout the centuries.

Operative and Functional Chastity

In defining the reasons for chastity in religious life, and in trying to explain it to young people, great emphasis is often placed on its functional and operational dimension. Religious chastity is presented more in terms of consecrated celibacy, which makes religious freer and more open to the frequent mobility that characterizes their life. They can be sent to any place, according to the demands of the mission, without the burden of a family and the education of their children. This certainly has its pragmatic value and makes mobility much easier. But it cannot be said that celibacy is necessary for mission. Protestant missionaries, the majority of whom are married, make a greater sacrifice in facing the needs of their mission. The diplomatic corps and especially the dynamic universe of present-day, multinational corporations constantly transfer executives. They work in various countries, learning other languages and other customs; they try to understand other cultures, giving up their own habits, and accommodating themselves to the lifestyles of other peoples, as a means of expanding the marketplace. From ancient times, business and economic necessities converted the individual into an untiring and suffering, indomitable and tenacious, vagabond. Internal migrations, emigrations from one country to another, the phenomenon of migrant workers who come from poor countries or regions to the industrial centers, have demanded of individuals and whole families a much greater sacrifice than that which would be required of us due to the functional character of our celibacy. We are moved from one house to another, but they are always our houses. We find ourselves with our own brothers and sisters. We are backed by a history and by the work that precedes us. And even when we strike out into the unknown to begin something new, we are backed by an institutional world of support that will not fail us. The same can be applied to the diocesan, priestly ministry, to which the public profession of celibacy is juridically, but not intrinsically, united.

However, the profession of consecrated chastity, one that also necessarily involves celibacy, is something inherent to the very nature of this apostolic vocation, which the Church itself has recognized and legitimated and which we call *religious life*. Consequently, even when the church would come to adopt another discipline for secular priests, this would not affect religious priests. Therefore, the operative and functional dimension cannot be the determining reason for our religious chastity, and even less the original source of its inspiration.

The Core of Consecrated Chastity in Religious Life

The core of chastity resides in the plan of God. Throughout history, the Lord has raised up men and women who have been called to the fullness of his love and who have been able to love him with such an intensity that they could do without an imperative need for human mediation. They were able to experience an intimate communion with God, and were granted the grace of spreading his gratuitous love to others, and to discover in others God's love for them. So great was the intensity of this experience that, again moved by the Holy Spirit, they believed themselves to be able to make it their own for life. Living in this way, they sanctified themselves and they sanctified the Church itself, which recognized and legitimated their way of life. At the root of consecrated chastity there is always a profound experience of communion with God, which is a gift from God and the explicit sign of his presence in that person. So great was the radiation of those men and women (founders) that they attracted others to their own lifestyle. Although the depth of the original experience is not always repeated, God's initiative remains, as the gift of the One who calls without completely revealing the ultimate meaning of that call. God assumes the person and places him or her within the fullness of his plan to reveal his love to others. This was done fully in Jesus Christ, but God continues to do it through thousands of people. They fragmentarily incarnate some aspects of the fundamental *mission* of manifesting to people, through their way of life, that all of the love of humanity stems from the love of God. Therefore, there is no human love that can be considered ultimate and absolute, no one without the possibility of being transcended. The public profession of the vow of consecrated chastity relativizes human love and, by the same token, unveils the greatness of that love; it opens human love to the perspective of its own improvement toward the eschatological communion with the fullness of God's love, of which it is already an anticipation.

Chapter Five

The Vow of Obedience

SAINT PAUL presents Jesus Christ as "obedient unto death, death on a cross." A strong spiritual tradition of the imitation of Christ grounded the meaning and the need for obedience in religious life and in the Church in the proof that Christ was obedient, but without asking the actual reason for that obedience of Christ. And yet, it is the answer to that question that can give ground and light, in the *following* of Jesus Christ, to our obedience as religious, as his disciples.

The obedience of Christ is not a virtue that he could more or less emphasize, in the same way that he could point up certain virtues while leaving others aside, even though he possessed all virtues. The obedience of Christ is intimately linked to his own being the Son of God made human, the Word made flesh as a man for all people. It arises from the very reason for his incarnation and his mission. Jesus obeys the Father because the Father has a plan for him. That is the reason for Jesus' repeated insistence that he has come to do the will of the Father, and in that he finds nourishment. During the crucial moments of his life, he realizes the Father's plan and asks that not his will but the Father's be done. His time was the Father's time. It was up to the Father to tell Jesus when his hour had come.

Everything that happened in his life was somehow linked to the gradual unfolding of the will of the Father throughout the centuries, in the context of salvation history. At times, the Father made his plan for LIFE appear more explicitly, signaling it with key figures that would allow people, in the future and at a distance, to perceive the traces of God amid the myriad of human events. The patriarchs and the prophets pre-figure and proclaim what will be

62

fulfilled later in Christ and what Jesus himself would do to fulfill the Scriptures. In this "fullness of time," God, after having spoken to humankind in many ways, speaks again through his Son. Jesus knows that in him are fulfilled millennia of human hope fed from the beginning by the Spirit of the Lord.

But he also knew that history continues. If people previously walked without knowing with certainty what their hopes were, now they know that the whole of history is full of Christ. God revealed in him his plan for humanity. With an enormous wing, the pendulum of salvation history oscillates between the peak of the manifestation of God's love revealing himself to humanity in the incarnation of his Son, and the end of history itself, the parousia of the final revelation of the glory of the Lord. Within this wide historical-eschatological arc is where we find ourselves today, we who live after the coming of the Savior.

God's plan, as outlined throughout all of Scripture, becomes much more specific in the words of Jesus himself, as the Gospel gives them to us. His mission consisted in the fulfillment/realization of the will of God. Therefore, the central goal of the *following of Christ* consists in continuing to fulfill the will of the Father in the world. This is the goal of our life, of all of us who are called to share in the riches of the love of God in Christ. This is the vocation to which we have been called. This is where we become disciples. This is where our holiness is achieved.

Obedience in Religious Life

Among the apostolic vocations in the Church, there is one that publicly professes an effort to be consistent with the Gospel project. That vocation is recognized and legitimated as such by the Church, which continues the mission of Jesus Christ in the world. Therefore, those who dedicate themselves fully to God for the service of others are called to recapitulate the presence of Christ in the world. For them, the search for the will of the Father and its reality in daily life is something unavoidable; it is the very reason for their life, a reason that makes explicit the Christological foundation and perspective of obedience.

In this way, obedience in religious life is not properly an ascetic means that may be used arbitrarily by people, nor is it a virtue for today to be forgotten tomorrow, nor even less is it a domination by some over others. Neither is obedience in religious life something similar to countless obediences necessary within human societies, which are normally regulated through laws and prescriptions.

Obedience in religious life is something much more profound. It concerns the direct relationship between God and the individual, between God and each person, between God and all people. Consecrated obedience involves a responsible answer to the call for radical living of the Gospel plan, thus prolonging in the world the presence and mission of Jesus. The individual obedience in religious life is related to and lived within a community. This is also expected to be a sign of the Lord's presence. As a result, the internal laws that rule it as a *religious community* and that consolidate its growth and movement affect the most intimate levels of every person, and in no way can be based exclusively on the socio-methodological improvements of the dynamic processes of relationship, behavior, and interaction, although these processes may serve them.

The search for the will of the Lord is not something incumbent upon some of the members of a community only, but rather it is the task of everyone. And if each one tries, day after day, to carry out a personal search for the will of God, how can one exempt oneself or be excluded from the communal search for the will of the Lord on the level of the local community or of the religious order or congregation? The purely vertical conception of obedience that was imposed for centuries upon religious, and which reduced the search for the will of God to the superior of the community, forgot two fundamental theological aspects.

The first one is the active and constant presence of the Holy Spirit in each and every one of us. The Spirit makes use of anyone, and not only of those in authority, to manifest to everyone God's designs. Therefore, the attention, of superiors as much as of the entire community, to the manifestation of the Lord through each one of the members of the apostolic body is a basic requirement of religious obedience. It can happen that the Lord may speak to us through the most humble among us, because the Spirit does not always speak according to human wisdom. Was that not the case in the synagogue in Nazareth? Was it not through the son of the carpenter that he revealed to the priests and the scribes the unusual plans of God for his people?

There is another aspect that has also been forgotten: the *sense of co-responsibility* for the right understanding of the mission of the apostolic body, incumbent upon everyone and not only on the superiors. This should put us in a position to understand the signs of God through everyone and also to liberate us and to be able to manifest the impulses of God in us. Was it not how Yahweh sent the prophets to speak to the kings and priests? Was this not the path of the great conversions within the Church itself? Was it not his love for the Church that caused the poor Francis to present himself to Innocent III, who vested the supreme temporal and spiritual power of the day?

The Presence of the Spirit and Co-Responsibility

Human society is organized for the attainment of the common good. Its basic assumptions, though, dispense with what is properly the will of God. But the religious community comes together with the explicit objective of continually discovering this will. Only God can tell us what he wants of us. God is the origin of all religious authority and, as such, of all obedience. God revealed himself in many different ways before the coming of Christ. He did it in a privileged way through the tradition and the written documents of the people of Israel. In Jesus Christ and through him, God was manifested fully. God speaks to us in the Scriptures and in tradition, through the Church and events. It is incumbent upon each community, therefore, to listen to and to receive this Word, under the influence of the Spirit, within the particular circumstances in which it is found, and to know here and now the will of the Father for the community. This, and only this, will effectively be its "common good."

This presence of the Spirit in everyone and the consequent co-responsibility of everyone in mission makes obedience at once more universal and much more demanding. From a purely vertical conception of obedience, the permission of the superior in a certain way was seen as legitimating the action of the subordinate, making room for known personal and institutional aberrations. From the new standpoint of obedience, however, I am expected to face my Lord in the most intimate depth of my heart before searching for the will of God with the superior or with the community. I have to focus on the very criteria of Christ's mission that I am supposed to continue within the context of my community and through my and our apostolic work. The result is twofold. First of all, I am the one to first assume the responsibility for what I intend to demand or ask of my superior or community. Second, starting from the narrow angle of my own perception, I will be open to widen my perspective with the help of others and to purify and correct it if necessary. Together we seek the will of the Lord.

Obedience and Discernment

We can thus realize the current reappraisal of *personal and communitarian spiritual discernment.* Discernment can be seen as the attitude underlying the prayerful process of identifying the will of God as much as the *method* and technical resource for making viable this search for what the Lord wants. This is not the place to do an in-depth analysis of discernment, which has been the subject of many excellent studies. It is important, however, to bear in mind that discernment presupposes *three elements.* Without them, the practice of obedience as we are presenting it here is impossible. First, discernment demands the *interior freedom* of each person. That freedom is the fruit of his or her conversion, of the intention not to be led by less pure motives and by sin, particularly in the area of love and truth. This interior freedom is the prior condition for attaining right decisions in terms of mission. We should not confuse our personal goals with the will of God. Second, discernment demands of us a deep attitude of a poverty of being and of the person, which leads us to *listen to one another* in the awareness that God can speak to us through others. Third, there is no discernment without a reference to *known reality*. A possible, complete information on the object of decision and a serious study of its context and situation are required for an honest discernment that tries to find the will of God in truth and in love.

Once these three conditions are achieved on a *personal* level, they must also be attained on the *communitarian* level. In the same spirit of faith, personal discernment, which leads to specific results in terms of the individual's life, will thus be continued with reference to the goals of the common mission of the whole apostolic group to which this person belongs. The community or the group confirms or widens the individual perspectives, especially in relationship to the third element, that of knowledge of and information on the object of discernment. The need for overcoming or modifying the results of personal discernment should not be excluded. In fact, religious obedience and communal discernment cannot be reduced to the individual level only. The relationship to the apostolic body is central to religious life. The individual religious is always a person committed to his or her community, which is the actual scenario of mission and obedience. In searching for the will of God, the superior can enhance participation by the mutual listening within the community. The manifestation and confrontation of points of views, in a climate of love and truth, improve the process of discernment. Decisions that are adopted by the means of a wider consensus are likely to commit the people involved more consciously and responsibly. A good superior will then confirm the decision that matured within the communal environment that he or she was able to create. But this is not the concern of the superior only. All of the members of a religious group should be equally committed to the honest process of the search for the common good in terms of the goals and the mission of the community. That mission can then emerge as the fruit of consensus and as an expression of a conscious and shared responsibility. However, there is another type of superior: the autocratic one who always eliminates or discards, even from the beginning, the process of communal discernment. This will eventually be replaced by the disastrous affirmation of his or her courage to make decisions alone, a fragile and often fearful courage, if we are aware that courage is not always a responsible act.

The Community and the Superior: Ecclesiological Perspectives

Some recent trends have attempted to minimize and even eliminate the need for a superior in religious congregations and communities.

The first reason for this would be the charismatic nature of religious congregations, which would be in contradiction to any hierarchical dimension in their organization. The second reason is the autonomy and primacy of the individual, who is supposed to be called in a very personal and unique way, according to the inspiration of the Spirit at the most intimate level. We will return shortly to this second aspect. As for the first, we must not lose sight of some important aspects. In the Church, there is neither hierarchical nor charismatic exclusivity. The people of God, as a whole, finds itself beneath the activity of the Holy Spirit: bishops, priests, deacons, religious, and lay people. The dimension of service that some assume in the Church through the sacrament of orders, being part of the hierarchical body of the Church, not only does not deprive them as persons of the Spirit's activity, but enriches them precisely in terms of the service they render. As a result, the charismatic dimension is also present in the hierarchical dimension of the Church.

Religious do not rise up in the Church as something essential to it. They spring from the conscience of the church and are hierarchically legitimated by it. When the hierarchical Church approves this or that order or congregation, it does so from the knowledge of its nature, of its original, spiritual experience (charism), and of its intended mission or apostolic service. Such a project for life is normally submitted to the Church, be the design contained in a Formula or Summary of the institute, be it more developed in a Rule of Life or in the Constitutions. The actual role of the hierarchical Church is the recognition of that new apostolic group and its public legitimation as a specific vocation within the ecclesial community. The same Church that approves and legitimates that project desires both its continuity and its fidelity to it. This also is a concern of all the members of the group, but it is a special mission of some of them, a responsibility that is given them through election or appointment by the group itself. This mission of service, which is authority, comes also from the hierarchical Church, which confers upon the group, through its representatives, the defense of the common good of the entire apostolic body. As such, the hierarchical Church maintains its interest and vigilance over the group on a universal level through the Pope and on the local level through the bishop. In this way, authority in religious life is, according to the relationship to the authority of the Church that approves and legitimates it, a form of hierarchical presence within a charismatic community. This presence is realized on various levels, the most common being the general, provincial, and local levels. Therefore, the superior has and will always have his or her own meaning and mission within the ecclesial context of religious life in its publicly recognized institutional expressions.

The Community and the Superior: Psychosocial Perspectives

Experience and social psychology have widely shown that no human group lives without a superior (coordinator, chief, leader, or any other name one wants to give that individual). Either the group gives itself its own superior or it has one given to it. When, sometimes, the group naively wants to do without a superior, someone naturally arises from within the group, either with or without the group's consent. The very fact that a human group states that it does not need a leader means, generally, that there is already one.

The appearance of a natural leader or superior has many advantages in the various groups of society. Experience has shown, however, that this is not the normal or the best way of entrusting to some people the service of authority in religious communities. The reason is that the superior in religious communities should not be primarily concerned with the external organization. This has its own laws that are often already verified from the standpoint of efficacy and method. The religious superior today moves rather along the line of a great attention to the mystery of persons, to the divine pedagogy with respect to each one, to the human evolution and history of each individual, in order to seek together the common will of the Father for the apostolic community. The religious superior is, therefore, the first one to be concerned with an ongoing process of discernment and also the first in not being able to dispense with it or take distance from the others. The superior thus consults, listens, intuits, and unifies the communitarian elaboration of major decisions, making use of his or her admittedly wider vision, based on the knowledge of everyone else. The superior, therefore, is the first in obeying, responsibly aware of his or her role in the process by helping people to make choices, to evaluate and to question their options, and to face the more serious and bitter decisions that the group may at times be too afraid to face. At times it may be up to the superior, after having heard the group, and faced with some hesitancy or lack of overall consensus, to have to make the decisions. This will be done in light of the fundamental criteria and the apostolic tradition of the community or congregation that is trying to find the will of the Lord.

All of the above makes the mission of the religious superior a rather delicate and difficult one in the non-vertical conception of obedience. More than anyone else in the group, the superior is supposed to be extremely attentive to the signs of God and of the times, wherever they may be manifested. Conscious of his or her mission in raising up the process of discernment and in creating conditions for freedom that allow a constructive sharing, the superior cannot impose his or her opinion or diplomatically lead the process toward his or her pre-determined intentions. The lack of transparence undermines the image of a superior in the eyes of a group. Limitations might be tolerated, but duplicity always is unacceptable. Furthermore, such a process of discerning the will of God creates within the community a profound union of hearts and minds and is nourished by it. That union is rooted in a poverty of being and of the person, the ability to know one's limits and to accept others as they are, the willingness to share our values and to act together in a loving service of people.

Obedience, the Person, and Mission

Such a perception of obedience brings about some dialectical situations. On the one hand, the presence of the Spirit, who speaks to each individual, as well as the common co-responsibility for mission, presupposes a mutual knowledge among the members of the group and the knowledge of them all by their superior. Every one of us has a kind of personal code by which we filter what we think God is telling us. This code is the result of our history and our complex reality of our values and limitations, of our education and our experiences. All of that has been forming within us the substratum of our opinions and attitudes, the soil that makes the seed within us either sterilized by the rocky ground or smothered by the weeds, or, rather, fertile and fruitful, bearing fruit in some other way. Without knowing that code, people will not understand the deep meaning of our language, the real scope of our projects and actions. This demands of us a great transparency and authenticity. Here again, the poverty of being and of the person is required to reveal to and share with others what we really are and to make possible to them also to be what they are. That transparency is an important element of truth, of our truth especially; it is also a key factor of religious obedience.

But there is another, almost antithetical, aspect. In every individual, there is an underlying historical continuity that must not be lost. It is difficult to completely modify that ongoing path, although it may be pedagogically reoriented. In the industrial chain of production there are tests and processes to check the objective quality of the product and to eliminate what is deficient. There is nothing like it where a human person is involved. We must start from the concrete reality of each individual in order to attempt, with and within that particular person, to give continuity to his or her history. This idea leaves less room for a conception of obedience that prevailed for so many centuries, always wanting to contradict the nature of persons and things. People would be prepared for one task and later ordered to do something else without any special preparation whatsoever, all in the name of obedience and supposedly on the level of faith. Superiors would arbitrarily contradict people so as to allow them to "grow in virtue," reprimanding them without a cause so as to make them grow in "humility." All of this is against truth and, therefore, is something ephemeral and meaningless. There must be an unbroken continuity between what a person brings to religious life as existential baggage in ontological and psychological terms and what we do in order to help the person to grow in light of his or her consecration to God and the apostolic ministry. The relatively high incidence of religious who are emotionally or affectively unbalanced or significantly reduced in their creative capacity and effective fulfillment quite frequently has its origin in that rupture. We often pay a fatal price for it.

This is one of the principal tasks of the superior, which cannot be shared with all of the members of the community, although there may be those who naively ask for it to be shared. Attention to people and, particularly, to this continual and progressive integration and unification in their lives and missions entails, in fact, an open and profound dialogue between the superior and each one of the members of the long-lasting process. It cannot be prescribed or instituted once and forever. It demands that religious truly want to manifest themselves. The criterion and the motive of self-revelation is the central concern with their growth for mission, which is the function of their progressive integration as persons and as members of this apostolic body. On the part of the superior, a great respect for the person is necessary. In fact, it is only the nature of that service in authority that allows him or her access to those intimate levels of the individual. They are shared with the superior in a perspective of faith and in the exclusive relationship to the common mission. Very probably, they would never be spontaneously manifested even in the context of a profound friendship.

Within that complex dialectical scenario as just outlined and that is so much involved in religious obedience, we can understand how difficult it is to attempt to replace the specific role and mission of the superior by the common acting of the whole community. This can hardly be done without deeply hurting the individual members of the group.

It may happen that the superior has to make a final decision on behalf of an individual or of the mission without having reached either a consensus or even a simply majority of the community in support of it. A superior certainly can do it and this must, in turn, be a service to the community. After going through an unsuccessful discernment with the group, the superior can act on the basis of an objectively better or more comprehensive information about the persons and/or situations that are involved.

I am speaking here of the ordinary instances of a religious administration on a local, provincial, or general level. I do not have in mind some collegial bodies, such as the chapters on the provincial or general level. In most of these assemblies, religious authority is constitutionaly, equally vested in all of their members. They all take common responsibility for the decisions before the Church and the whole order or congregation.

In the realm of ordinary government, communities without a superior or with only an ongoing and continual institution of collegial government have not proved to be experientially valid. The reasons for this have already been explained. Either the individual persons do not find a favorable climate for the manifestation of themselves, or authority ends by being diluted in the various members of the collegial administration. These are no longer seen as a reference point for the unique exercise, in faith, of the obedience of one person to another. The resulting adaptation and accommodation damage the mission. The community comes to be run according to the socio-psychological rules of any human group. In this way, obedience is emptied of its transcendent dimension, the only dimension that can legitimate its existence and save it from destructive factors, especially those of politics and power. Deprived of its fundamental relationship to faith, religious obedience does not distinguish itself from the obedience to traffic laws or to the rules of the strictly functional organization of the group and to the regulation of merely human institutions and societies.

However, when the function of the superior is preserved and well fulfilled, an extraordinary service can be rendered to individuals and to the group as a whole. The key element of this service is the growing adequacy *of the individual to mission* and *of the mission to the individual*. Sometimes the mission must be limited because of individual needs; sometimes urgent demands are addressed to the person because of the needs of mission. The first aspect would give us sufficient reason to close those areas or institutions for which we no longer have enough personnel. By keeping them open, we will be causing serious damage to those whom we impose on or ask to continue the task. They will do it alone or deprived of the minimal conditions for survival as human beings within the context of their religious vocation. The second aspect allows us, in the name of mission and aware of the sacrifice that is demanded, to ask that certain tasks and functions be undertaken by individuals who must almost go beyond themselves in order to accept and to perform those tasks. This seems to contradict what we previously said about the continuity of each person's history. In fact, we mentioned the need for the community as well as for the superior to search for a better knowledge of the person and for the correlation of person to mission and mission to person. There is indeed a contradiction. But we were then speaking of the ordinary, regular process of obedience in religious life. We may sometimes have to face extraordinary situations, and this is what we are now talking about. The very option to follow Christ and the radical realization in our lives of the Gospel project relativizes our personal autonomy to that very point. Here indeed is the heart of consecration in obedience.

People tend instinctively to absolutize their autonomy as an expression of their freedom. Religious consecration in poverty relativizes the need for material and spiritual goods and our innate tendency toward prestige and power. Religious consecration in chastity relativizes human love and the imperative need for its sexual expression. Religious consecration in obedience, paradoxically, is an affirmation of freedom. It does manifest the person's autonomy to accept freely the gift of God and to direct his or her freedom toward the continual and communal search for God's will. This searching process may lead us to tough consequences. It might unveil the contrast between our own concrete ideals or goals and God's will upon us. The latter must always prevail for us to give continuity to the mission of Jesus and to his presence among all people through us.

Conclusion

The Christological criteria in searching for the will of God as the driving force and teleological orientation of every personal or communal process of discernment, as well as the free and consistent option to relativize one's own autonomy, aiming at realizing and achieving what was recognized as the will of God for me or for the community, constitute the identifying elements of religious obedience. Here lies its own characteristic when compared to other types of obedience. The public profession before God and the Church and before all people of assuming that obedience for mission as one's life program distinguishes *religious* vocation from other apostolic vocations within the Church.

The difficult balance between the two previously mentioned poles—that is, attention to the *person* and attention to the *mission* in fulfilling God's will—is a major factor for a true living of the Gospel project of obedience in religious consecration. Often, there is much insistence on the first element: we emphasize the person to the point of missing the awareness of his or her responsible belonging to an apostolic body. Therefore, a fragmentation and proliferation of individual plans make of any common project an impossible dream. When everyone decides for oneself what is one's mission without further consideration, the corporate mission will be damaged with serious consequences for the service of people and for the kingdom. The institutionalization of such a process will reverse the meaning and the perspective of religious community. The commitment to community will then be seen much more along the lines of companionship than along the actual insight of a common inspiration (charism) for a mission that is collectively assumed. Of course, this tends to a gradual weakening of the group and of its visibility. Its members cannot minimize the risk of increasingly gravitating around other orbits until the group is spinning far from its original design. Yet, the exaggerated stress on the second element, mission, without enough attention to the person, leads to gradually destroying both the person and the mission, thus destroying or frustrating God's plan.

Religious obedience can only be fulfilled existentially through a profound communion with God and with one's brothers and sisters in that vocation. Such a process demands a self-education in love and in truth, a constant attention to the action of the Holy Spirit upon the community and upon each one of its members. When assumed and lived in this way, religious obedience is a deeply human and evangelical fulfillment of freedom, that highest human characteristic that has been given to us.

Chapter Six

A New Vision of Religious Obedience

"AUTHORITY-OBEDIENCE" COULD have been the title of this chapter. For centuries, these were key points in the study of the subject. We were almost always introduced to the understanding and living of the vow of obedience through them. This often led us into dualisms and dichotomies, especially in those situations in which we were really faced with the difficult, concrete, and mysterious experience of having to *obey* indeed.

However, I believe that a more complete vision of obedience lessens or overcomes that duality in terms of its potentially irreducible oppositions or contradictions. In religious life, *we all obey*, those who command as well as those who do not. Those who serve without authority in the various areas of mission obey. Those who serve in authority also obey. Consequently, to pose the problem of religious obedience today in terms of superior versus subordinate—to use these overloaded words from the past—is to lose sight of an entire theological and spiritual evolution that has taken place.

Yet, to limit oneself to sociological models of authority and obedience—such as totalitarianism and democracy, centralization and participation, majorities and minorities—in the search for the key to studying and interpreting the present context of religious obedience is to risk compromising and falsifying the insight of its identity and the perception of the internal strength of what is original in it.

The Proper Character of Religious Obedience

In religious life, obedience is situated on the level of faith and truth. It is made concrete and is realized in a dimension of love, justice, and freedom. This obedience can be understood only from the wider perspective of mission—the proclamation and realization of the kingdom—which justifies it and gives it meaning. Therefore, obedience affects the entire person, in one's relationship with God through Jesus Christ and with people, our brothers and sisters. Consequently, religious obedience cannot be reduced to a purely functional dimension in the organization and productivity of the group, institution, or community, as it frequently happens with the obedience that regulates relationships in view of the common good and of the efficacy of the entire group or of intermediate situations of society as a whole.

In religious life, obedience is an existential dimension of the individual who lives this specific vocation in the Church and in the world, a person consecrated for mission. In this sense, religious obedience grafts into our life, from the roots of our baptism and religious profession, the obedience of Jesus Christ, with which it is linked. We may seldom find specific instances of true obedience in our own personal or community history, as well as the occasion for quite explicit acts of obedience. However, this will not affect the need for and the continuity of a deep and consistent attitude of obedience. This is an integral part of our vocation and mission, just as it was for Jesus.

I will not continue to develop this theme because I have already done so in the previous chapter on the vow of obedience.[1]

The idea and practice of obedience in religious life has undergone profound change in the last twenty years. It has been enriched and deepened. A superficial glance and the collection of anecdotal case studies and strange situations could give the impression that obedience has suffered a certain decline and even a loss of meaning. But if we dig deeper, if we compare previous ideas with the current understanding of obedience, we can discover a greater demand for interior consistency, a more emphasized sense of mutual co-responsibility in mission, and a living awareness of the need to integrate the double relationship of the person with God and with one's brothers and sisters. And we insist that this is true for those who serve in positions of authority as much as for everyone else. All are radically affected. In this sense, there is no doubt that today we understand and live obedience in religious life in a new way.

Present-Day Focus and Perspectives of Religious Obedience

This chapter is meant to help us better understand certain aspects of that evolution. I am limiting myself to theological and intra-ecclesial elements, setting aside for now the socio-cultural aspect of contemporary extra-ecclesial life and its influences on religious obedience.

Without pretending to be exhaustive, I want to treat only some of the principal tendencies of this evolutionary change in the concept of religious obedience. They are not necessarily related to each other. Put together, however, they show us different aspects of a process that ends by modifying the previous concept and practice of obedience.

From the Imitation of Christ to the Sharing in His Mission

There is a step *from* obedience centered on the imitation of Jesus Christ *to* obedience understood as sharing in the mission of Jesus Christ, who is obedient. This *Christological* approach moves the emphasis from obedience conceived somewhat statically as a moral virtue to placing the accent on obedience conceived dynamically in terms of the continuity of the mission entrusted to us by the Father and by Jesus Christ. In the former, the principal concern is to do what Jesus did and to transfer to my life his fidelity to the historical context of his life. In the latter, however, what is sought is to do what Jesus would do in the very particular situations within the temporal, spatial, cultural, and social coordinates in which I find myself. As we have already stated,[2] obedience is not a virtue that Jesus could have or not have, but rather it was the very foundation of the meaning of his life: "I have come to do the will of the Father who sent me." That central inspiration of the life of the historical Jesus, and not the simple materiality of the actions in which his obedience was sought and concretized, becomes the driving force of our life in which the risen Christ lives and is made present. Therefore, religious obedience as such is not primarily concerned with the moral improvement of the consecrated person, as is the case of other virtues as we will discuss later.[3] As long as, by vocation, we are called to be the Lord's presence and witness and to continue his mission in the world today, obedience—this constant attention to the will of the Father, its identification, and its fulfillment—is a constitutive part of our life. In our obedience, he continues to obey, in the same way that he continues to act through our actions to proclaim and bring about the kingdom.

The characteristic and principal consequence of this change of focus is that it places obedience on the horizon of *mission.* Thus, we are faced with a task that is incumbent upon all of us. To discover the will of the Father and to translate it into reality is something from which we ourselves as well as no one else can exempt us, whatever may be our role and function. Consequently, whether or not I hold a position of authority in the group, I cannot command or obey without reference to mission. This is as true on an individual level as it is in the social circle of my group, community, province, congregation, or Church. Therefore, the reason for commanding or obeying must always relate to the mission plan. This is a central criterion for comprehending the very nature of religious obedience and for identifying, in context, the very process of what it means to obey.[4]

By linking our obedience in terms of continuity to the obedience of Jesus Christ, we are urging the need for a great interior freedom that leads us to purify the obediential motives of our service in the context of mission, whatever may be the actual institutional model of obedience in our religious order or congregation. This is a basic condition for being able to harmonize with Jesus' mission and to continue it. Therefore, everything that obscures the clarity of the search for the will of the Lord and looks for a diplomatic solution or for decisions that are based on power or prestige, opportunism or recourse, defensive immobility or aggressive vanguardism, betrays the fundamental inspiration of religious obedience, as much in someone who leads as in the one who obeys, whatever may be the character of the decision-making process in the institute.

Each and every one of us is involved in the responsibility for the specific character of our life and work, a responsibility that cannot be transferred to anybody else. To obey will always be to "own" what I do, to do in a very personal way what only I can and must do in terms of mission only. To command will always be to "own" the fact that whatever is asked or demanded of others is essentially defined within the perspective of mission. At times this will be very clear, while at other times it will not; and there will be times when it will become something paradoxical and conflicting. In all of these circumstances, religious obedience is meaningful. Yet, the more perceptible human limits may be in this identification of the Lord's will and, as such, in the definition or design of a concrete mission, the more the responsibility in the search grows, the more the darkness surrounding obedience appears, the more it is actually revealed in its identity as religious obedience: that which is only understood and lived in the *light of faith*. At the same time that this helps to distinguish it from other forms of human obedience, the fact of framing it in terms of mission reveals to us the evangelical content inherent to this dimension of our vocation and religious consecration that is demanded of each and every religious.

From Autocracy to Subsidiarity

In the present conception of religious obedience, the step is taken *from* the idea of authority as the expression, affirmation, maintenance, and/or reinforcement of a hierarchical structure *to* the understanding of authority seen as part of the apostolic body which it serves specifically in a function within the wide and organic context of the diversity of functions. In other words, one passes from placing an exclusive and dominant emphasis on *verticality*, inherent to an institutional, hierarchical model, to giving relevance to *subsidiarity*, which must also be present, without losing the hierarchical dimension.[5]

In the previous conception there is an undeniable hypertrophy of authority that easily becomes absorbing and centralizing. At the same time that it is involved in everything and orders even the smallest details, it drowns and neutralizes initiative and creativity in those who are not in authority. It reduces or underestimates the need for consultation and sharing. It empties or eliminates the meaning of participation and the practice of co-responsibility, stressing the dependence of everyone on a single source of decision. It brings with it the lack of perception of and sensitivity to the organic and subsidiary body, a perception that is crucial in the living out of mission. It is, above all, an impoverishment—if not a degradation—of people who are not motivated or who are suffocated in their apostolic motives. This purely vertical conception of obedience explains the interior paralysis of many religious, as well as the devaluation of true talents (sometimes demonstrated before entrance to religious life), the insecurity and infantilism. All of this often leads to an inferiority complex of people who lose confidence in themselves or who go on to live a domesticated and alienating servility.

On the part of those in authority, this conception of obedience tends to convert them into autocrats. They believe that everything depends on them. They feel responsible for the actions and attitudes, and the smallest details of those who obey them. They often grant to their decisions an almost messianic dimension, and they make God responsible for what is only their partial view of things and people. In this situation, authority tends to meddle in everything, to always have the last word, to take the place of subordinates. This type of conception of obedience reinforces to a great degree the insecurity of shy people who are in authority who, lacking leadership qualities, almost always take refuge in the jurisdiction they have. They substitute the exterior affirmation of their power and authority for the interior security they lack. Almost all of us have had the experience of this type of obedience, which has given rise to pre-potent and distant superiors and heroic or mediocre subordinates.

In another way, this exclusively vertical line of obedience can, at times, be a seemingly legal basis for the affirmation of people who, by their nature or formation, are dominant or ambitious and who understand authority not as service, but as a way of feeding their desire to climb to the highest peaks of power.

It would be naive to think that this model has disappeared. Not only do we find it here and there, but we see it subtly reinforced under the guise or pretext that it alone incarnates authentic religious obedience, without secular contamination, and it alone guarantees unity in uniformity, the salvation of the Church and of religious life in the challenging context of a pluralistic world.

Changing the emphasis toward subsidiarity in the process of obedience places authority in an organic context and corrects many of the described distortions, without affecting its hierarchical character. All of the members of the apostolic body, on any community level (local, provincial, or general), capture the meaning and importance of their own parcel of responsibility within the totality of mission. People feel worthwhile when they experience themselves free to be spontaneous in their creativity with regard to their own field of activity, without losing sight of the whole and the meaning of proportion. Government tends to decentralize. A majority of the decisions is made with the consultation and participation of the various people and with the interaction of facts and factors that are involved. Those in authority see themselves as participants in the whole process, and are seen as such by the others. Emphasis is placed on the service that is rendered, and not on the authority held. In other words, the *power* that is held is looked at from an evangelical perspective. It becomes the extension of the power given to Jesus by the Father to proclaim the kingdom, a power that Jesus exercised as a *service of love*. Instead of a form of unilateral dependence, it emerges as the awareness of interdependence: eventually everyone depends on everyone else and all need to count on one another. No one can take another's place. Without undermining obedience, one moves from autocratic centralization toward subsidiary decentralization. Thereby, the importance and necessity of various functions is perceived and, among them, with its own scope and connotation, the function of the one who carries out the service of authority in this perspective of the kingdom.

At the root of this change in the position of religious obedience there is a particular *anthropological* conception of people and soci-

ety. It is a conception that is far from the stable and static vision of
a stratified and pyramidal society. It stresses the fundamental
equality of people as persons and as children of God and, in the
specific case of obedience, as people called to the same mission. In
this way, it recovers the forgotten or lost newness brought by the
Christian message, when compared with other previous religious
conceptions. This newness anticipates by far the modern democratic awareness of the value of the individual based on the liberty
and equality of all. It also recognizes that this communion of people in mission demands distinct services and various assignments.
This does not mean that one person may be superior to another,
but rather that they have different responsibilities within their
reach, within their surroundings, and in the character of the relationships that consequently are established within the apostolic
community or that refer to situations outside of it, on the level of
decision making as well as on the level of representation.

In this conception of obedience, there is also an *ecclesiological*
vision that conceives of the Church as a body or as the people of
God. This perspective found expression in the ecclesiology of the
Second Vatican Council: in the appreciation of collegiality, in the
introduction to the Church of institutional instances of decentralization, such as the synod of bishops, conferences of priests and
bishops, and others. Within religious life, among many practical
initiatives that would be impossible to enumerate, what perhaps
best indicates the acceptance of this change is the process of revising the Constitutions. This process was carried out by a large
number of congregations according to the "motu proprio" *Ecclesiae
Sanctae,* and was achieved by many institutes with a striking quan-
titative and qualitative participation of their respective members.

Finally, at the heart of this change of position on obedience is
the extension to religious life of the rediscovery of the theology of
the Holy Spirit and of the meaning and scope of the Spirit's action
upon each and every Christian. This *theological* fact proved to be
extremely significant for the renewal of individual and shared
prayer, as well as for spiritual discernment. These two elements
have enriched and even redirected the entire process of decision
making.

In light of the Spirit's activity, there is also the manifestation of

the prophetic dimension in the Church and in religious life. Perceived and lived by people and communities on various levels,
this prophetic dimension became a catalyst for mission and, consequently, a new and distinct source of perspectives for obedience.
The prophetic dimension cannot be an end in itself nor can it be
absolutized in hegemonic terms of exclusivity. Starting from the
announcement or denunciation of particular and well defined elements, the prophetic dimension in biblical terms grasps and unveils the right meaning of the mission, the insight into God's initiative as a work of salvation. It comes as the bearer of new life,
which assumes what already exists, redirecting it and transforming it. In this prophetic key, I see the *preferential option for the poor*
and the change in the *social perspective* of the Church as it was
requested by the hierarchy of Latin America at Puebla. That option
has been a fertile element in the review, restructuring, and
reconfiguration of mission by many institutes, with profound and
wide-ranging consequences for the entire conception and living of
obedience. (See the second chapter on poverty).

From the Level of Virtue to the Fullness of Life

From the ascetical and moral conception of obedience, as situated within the context of temperance and/or mortification as ends
in themselves, obedience became the *full expression of the person*
through one's own integration and free commitment to vocation
and mission.

As long as we search, in the sincerity of truth, for the discovery
of God's will for us in each moment of our lives, we are already
obeying existentially, through the totality of life itself, or, in other
words, through what we are and what we do. In this process,
religious do not have the same autonomy as lay Christians, although the latter are limited by other paths. Through the vow of
obedience, religious determine, and to a certain extent delimit, the
sphere of this autonomy. They do so, above all, in terms of the
proper character of the institute in which they are professed, in
terms of the spiritual tradition that feeds it, in terms of the specific
characteristics of the mission that the institute is proposing, and in
terms of the means that it chooses or accepts as instruments of this

mission. Naturally, all of this necessitates and to a certain extent
conditions the path of the obedience of religious. But, in principle,
we are already being faced here with a concrete consequence of
the religious's *obediential option*. Thus, religious obedience is not
opposed to the development of the human person. In every human option or decision, in effect, freedom is both self-affirming
and self-limiting. Affirmation and limitation are parts of this same
free act of deciding. The option for the architectural plan of a
house, for a product that is bought, for a profession that is embraced, or for a lifelong stable marriage is, at the same time, a free
decision and a free renunciation of other alternatives. Within this
dialectic of affirmation and limitation, every person must find the
parameters of his or her own growth and fulfillment. And there is
no reason why religious life should be any different.

Therefore, once the initial option for this vocation is consciously
and freely made, *obedience,* as a means for manifesting or discovering what God wants for us, must be a *unifying and integrating
principle* of our person. It should lead us, without too many contradictions or slip-ups, to be what we should be and, as a result, to
discover the meaning of our lives. We have been called to this,
although we are bothered by the occasional turbulence and inevitable accidents found in every human life.

To think of obedience in this way is to refuse a non-integrated,
reductive view of an obedience that is centered on isolated and
unconnected acts, thus becoming arbitrary and displeasing because it loses sight of the central axis of the lives and mission that
are involved. Obedience is not an element of mortification or control. It is a factor for the inner construction of the person, on the
deepest level of his or her option and fundamental orientation in
life. Religious obedience is not a game of domination or submission. It is the conscious search for the meaning of mission and its
specific means by all who are involved in the process: companions
of vocation and mission in their respective areas of responsibilities
and functions, aware of their values and limitations, within the
apostolic body which is the religious institute operating within the
local and universal Church.

This necessitates that the *"obediential space"*—that is, the whole
set of aspirations and intentions, of plans and means, of actions and

tensions, in and through which the life of obedience unfolds—be characterized by mature personal relationships, impregnated by faith and love, hope and truth, and transparent freedom. Moreover, it presupposes that the actors in this obediential space, at the same time that they are open to God, be open to each other, listening, accepting, and showing mutual trust, knowing that they can count on one another. This is very difficult to do in daily life, given the reality of who we are as human beings. But that is the path by which we reincarnate the full meaning of the obedience of Jesus Christ, which unified his life and led him to what the Father wanted of him.[6]

Finally, in light of this openness to God and to our brothers and sisters, we are able to read and analyze reality, our own and that of the world in which we find ourselves, which constitutes our field of activity. Only thus will we come to sense the "signs of the times" and the new calls of the Lord. They make us see the faults and failings that we must change. They strengthen us for new commitments to the kingdom. They give us the power to continue history and not to repeat it only. It is incumbent upon us all, as individuals, whether or not we are in positions of authority, to accept as our own the path of our institutes, bringing to it this life meaning. In this way, we will realistically build the present, faithful to what we must preserve and value from the past and with forward looking insights that ground the future. Although freely conditioned and limited by our option, we live a life of obedience that does not immobilize us or belittle us, but rather frees and fulfills us; it does not suffocate us but rather completes us. Only in this way will we be able to make present to humanity today the *hour* of Jesus Christ in its intersection with our own *hour*, this time of God that walks within us.

Conclusion

We are not always sufficiently aware of the *processes* that have resulted in such sweeping changes. We did not always understand the internal workings of the decisive factors by which these processes took shape and were incorporated in life. Therefore, it was meaningful to reanalyze here the origins and evolution of some changes. Doing so helps us, on the one hand, to now capture the *evolutionary* character of these processes, the results of which are obvious. It allows us to be aware of the fact that, more than analytical or ideological changes, many of these transformations emanate from life itself, in the cross-complex of factors whose interaction, matured in time, are rooted in the solid and realistic ground of life. To perceive these things and to foresee their consequences is to live according to the Spirit, who allows us, in faith, to grow in the freedom of accepting what the Lord inspires and to live it faithfully in strength, discernment, and wisdom. In this way, the feelings of Jesus Christ, who through us continues God's work, live in us, through the gifts of the Holy Spirit. And Jesus does so by assimilating us to his obedience to the Father, the key to his own mission and the ultimate meaning of his life.

Notes

1. The reader will forgive me if I return at times to topics previously discussed, although in another way. This highlights the mutual complementarity of the themes.
2. See Chapter 5.
3. See Chapter 6.
4. This is applied directly to institutes of religious life, whose model of obedience is non-capitular: those in which, even when there is wide consultation with individuals and communities in the decision-making process, the decisions are made, in the final and deliberative stage, by those in positions of authority. But this reference to mission, as the criterion and fundamental reason for decision and obedience in religious life, is equally applied to capitular institutes of religious life. In the latter, decisions generally are made on the deliberative level of the community, through election, votation, or consensus. The superior is, so to say, commissioned by the community, through his or her specific function, to serve the community, in effective solicitude for the implementation of decisions made. In both institutional models of obedience, everyone must be directed toward mission and, so, decide. It is good to be aware that, on certain occasions, whether foreseen or not, whether or not they are stipu-

lated by Constitutions, there can be decision-making processes that give the non-capitular community deliberative power. This is the case, for example, of the general and provincial congregations of the Jesuits and of the general or provincial chapters of many non-capitular congregations that have, as an elective or legislative body, deliberative powers. It is also possible to have procedures of non-capitular decisions that fall upon capitular communities, at least on the same level of an authority, which can be intrinsic or extrinsic to the religious institute in question. This is the case, for example, of possible interventions by the provincial superior on the local level or by the general superior on the provincial level, or even a bishop's involvement in the pastoral concerns of the institute.

5. Note that I am not speaking of a step from the vertical to the horizontal, from the monarchical to the democratic. This is not the question here. The transposition of sociological categories to religious life that is ruled by a dimension of faith is always somewhat inadequate. Being a community of human beings, every institute has a sociological dimension and can be analyzed from that perspective. But the sociological, as such, does not exhaust the meaning of religious life and is not in a position to reach its depth and its inspiration. Therefore, the sheer sociological approach to religious obedience always misses a central aspect for the full understanding of the phenomenon it attempts to analyze.

6. There is much to explain and develop in this area. It is not possible for me to do so here without going beyond the proportions set by the various parts of this chapter. The reader may find some fundamental elements related to this *unifying perspective of obedience* in the preceding chapter.

Chapter Seven

Human Decisions and the Will of God

THIS CHAPTER continues the reflection, begun in the previous chapter, on the subject of obedience. We could also examine other factors or tendencies that helped to create this new conception of religious obedience. The reader will remember that I limited myself to considering only three aspects directly related to the theological dimension and to pointing out their influence on the perception and life of obedience.

There would be another line to explore: that of the *socio-cultural impact of present-day life* upon people and religious institutions and, consequently, upon the relationships established between them by obedience. But it is not possible for me to enter here into such an extensive topic. However, it is necessary to state that it exists and that it affects us deeply. The question of religious obedience cannot be reduced to it alone, nor can that question be interpreted exclusively or primarily in terms of it. In the study of the subject, certain theological aspects prevail, which we have already treated, because the ultimate meaning of religious obedience must be understood always from the horizon of faith and mission. Socio-cultural factors, when related to obedience, must also be read in this same light. Only from the perspective of faith and mission do we find criteria for a correct evaluation and for an adequate placement of religious obedience within the wider scenario of social relationships between people in the contemporary world as they are reflected in *obediential space*.[1]

What we have said in the two previous chapters is sufficient to pose a profound question with which we often find ourselves faced in the life of obedience: *the interrelationship between human decisions and the will of God.* We are going to center our attention on this subject.

Two Conceptions of Obedience

If we return to what was treated in the previous chapter, we will be able to see two different conceptions of obedience. Of course, there is here some simplification. But even at this stage of the evolution in the changing process of obedience, it is easy for us to see that there are still many manifestations of the merely authoritarian perspective. Moreover, there are even attempts to revive it and to reaffirm it today as the only truly valid one. In pointing out the three phases of the process of change, I consistently utilized the prepositions *from* and *to,* in order to introduce alternative conceptions of obedience. Bringing together the three first terms that begin with the preposition *from* and the other three terms preceded by the preposition *to,* we obtain two paradigms that respectively summarize the two conceptions in question.

Previous Conception of Obedience

Without going too far back in history, we identify, in the course of the first half of this century, a view of obedience that is characterized, among others, by the following aspects:

First, the search for the identification of mission and, as such, for the will of God, upon people as much as upon the apostolic body (the religious community on all levels: local, provincial, and general), was the almost exclusive task of the superior. Only he (or she) was supposed to be under the influence of the Holy Spirit. I am referring, naturally, to the tradition regarding non-capitular obedience.

Second, and as a direct consequence, only the superior developed and made decisions, and this was generally done without a significant consultation, representation, or participation by the others. And I say "significant" because, in reality, rarely—and, in principle, never—all consultative recourse to councillors or assessors was excluded.

Third, decisions made in this way were considered to be the expression of the will of God. In other words, it was presupposed that "God wants what the superior decides." Therefore, the decision had to be respected according to this premise. Motives had to be accepted from this angle, if they were presented at all. In any event, with or without the explicit reasons for the decision, there was nothing left to do than follow it, because "this is what God wants."

In this conception, there is a tacit presupposition. It hardly was made explicit because, in reality, it is indefensible. It implicitly assumes that the decisions of the superior, because they coincide with the will of God, must necessarily be correct, because God never errs. Although never so openly formulated or attempted, at least to this degree of simplification, this presupposition often leads people to confusion in terms of clearly erroneous decisions.

Although proposed during formation or experienced daily by religious, this conception of obedience faced very serious problems. I do not mean to say that these difficulties were not perceived by superiors or their subordinates. What many of us lived for a large part of our religious lives—at least those of us who have been religious for many years—was something very similar to the previously described situation. In the name of obedience and the spirit of faith, we were asked to sacrifice our own judgment and our own way of seeing reality, deferring to so-called "blind obedience," understood and applied from this highly restrictive angle.[2]

Present Conception of Obedience

The following fundamental aspects (among others) can be found in the present theology of religious obedience:

First, the *Christological* focus that unites the mission of the individual within the mission of the religious institute to the continuity of the mission of Jesus Christ, and thereby establishes the meaning of the co-responsibility of all the members in the mission of the apostolic body.

Second, a *theological* focus that mainly proceeds from the revitalization of the theology of the Holy Spirit and from the awareness of the Spirit's activity upon everyone, as much in terms of the individual mission as in the two-way relationship between the person and God and the person and others. Thus, value is placed upon spiritual discernment as the study of this activity of the Spirit on an individual and community level.

Third, an *ecclesiological* focus that, without denying or minimizing what is hierarchical within the Church, highlights the dimensions of subsidiarity and participation.

Fourth, a growing consciousness of the meaning and reality of the *prophetic* dimension of the Church and of religious life. This aspect also functions as a critical and creative factor, questioning and promoting changes in the identification and carrying out of mission.

Fifth, an *anthropological* perception that reveals, in the light of faith and mission, the central place of obedience in the life of the individual and the catalyzing effect that it can and must have in the construction, integration, and interior growth that, in the continual search for the will of God, makes the orientation and profound meaning of life more and more explicit. From the conviction that this aspiration incarnates and manifests the *truth* of a person, there arises the primary reason for mutual human trust and confidence and the possibility for a genuine community among people. Such a community is built upon the common basis of each individual's identification with the ideal of Jesus Christ: to do the will of God is the food and inspiration of life itself.

With these presuppositions, the *life of obedience* is reorganized, keeping in mind:

— that the Holy Spirit speaks to all and through all;
— that we are all in solidarity with and co-responsible for mission and, as such, involved in the making of decisions that concretize that mission on our respective levels;
— that in a religious institute (especially if it is not a capitular one), there are people in positions of authority who constitutionally have the last word in decision making;
— that the decision making process presupposes discernment.

At the same time, right *discernment* necessitates:

— a clear definition of its object and scope;
— a pure and clear intention of wanting to discern (that is, of being led by the Spirit) and not simply to reaffirm or rationalize pre-established tendencies or decisions;
— the best information possible concerning the object of discernment as well as the people or the elements involved in it;
— the definition of the hermeneutic key for the study of reality of people and situations in terms of the conception of mission (social perspective);
— in light of this key to interpretation, the establishment of criteria for the discernment and decision in question, the first of which will be its direct relationship to mission;
— interior freedom constantly asked of the Lord and put into practice by us. Only that freedom makes the process viable and gives it credibility. It alone makes possible the establishment and application of the criteria of discernment. It alone opens people who discern to the direct activity of the Holy Spirit upon them.

Let us do a *rereading* of these conditions for discernment in light of the fundamental aspects of the current conception of obedience as we have stated them previously. We will see that for the actual decision making, in accord with those requirements:

— It is fundamental to have true knowledge of the people for whom the decision is being sought or who are affected by the decision (this means attention to the interior continuity of people's evolution in terms of their history and consistent growth and attention to the apostolic continuity of their mission).
— Consultation must be widened and qualified in order to gain better information necessary for the discernment process itself (this means trust, participation, and decentralization).
— Individuals, whether consulted or not, should furnish, whether requested or spontaneously, the elements and facts that are available to them and that, in their view, may improve the criteria or add to information (this means co-responsibility and active subsidiarity).

Once the process is matured and the decision finally made by those in authority, we may find ourselves basically with two scenarios:

— First scenario: The decision that has been made reflects and truly expresses a consensus. As such, it is able to be accepted by everyone or by the individual or individuals affected by it. There is harmony between those in authority and all others, in terms of the perception of mission and the decision made in view of it. It follows that everyone obeys in unison—those who command and decide in virtue of their role in authority as well as those who are subordinate—fulfilling what everyone believes is the will of God on this specific point of mission. The decision is ready for its implementation.

— Second scenario: It may be that the decision does not reach such a level of consensus and, therefore, carries the possibility of greater or lesser conflict, according to the circumstances. It is this second scenario that I will now try to analyze more closely, in light of what I have called the "current conception of obedience."

Human Decision and the Will of God

First Hypothesis

The lack of consensus in the decision, or the difficulty in accepting it, may stem from the diversity of information about the object of the decision, that is, about the precise knowledge of elements and facts related to persons or things involved in or affected by the decision. In this case, I may disagree with the decision in light of the information at my disposal.

But I can also admit that, although there may have been consultation in the decision-making process, the superior may be in possession of facts that are unknown to me. These facts may be communicated if it is requested, or such a communication may not be possible out of respect for the individuals involved or for some other reason. There is, then, a great deal of *information* involved, but not its interpretation. This may make it easier to accept the decision, although it may not be completely clear to me. Supposing that the superior has done what should be done to obey the mission, seeking the will of the Lord, I also obey this decision that I trust to be within the horizon of that mission.

Second Hypothesis

Everyone, whether or not he or she is a superior, knows the exact same elements and facts. Therefore, the difference is not going to be in the information, but rather in its value and *interpretation*. And this is what may lead me to disagree with the decision.

What normally gives rise to distinct appreciations or interpretations of identical facts is the *hermeneutic key* and the *criteria* which were utilized. Assuming that the superiors as well as the others are motivated by a sincere desire to ascertain the truth, and that every means has been applied to look for what God wants, experience shows that it is very difficult to define and guarantee which is the true interpretation and to give evidence to that fact, especially when many factors are at play.

Let us suppose that the possibility of presenting their point of view, before or during the decision-making process, has been given to those in disagreement with the decision. Once the decision is made, and in the case that potential or effective disagreement persists, there is still room to offer to those in disagreement the possibility of recourse or *representation*, whether to the same authority or to some higher one, presenting the reasons for the disagreement and even offering an alternative interpretation. This can lead, in principle, to a review or even the modification or suspension of the decision already made. Sufficient reasons for this could be, for example, the proof of faults or failings in the discernment process, a poor application of the criteria, the lack of interior freedom at some step; that is, anything that affects *interpretation* in the search for the will of God.

But if, once recourse has been presented and dutifully considered by the one who made the decision, the decision stands, then *the decision must be followed out of obedience.*

It is important to highlight and be very conscious that that acceptance will have to take place:

— not because it may be clearly stated whether the decision is
  right or wrong;
— not because I may finally agree or still disagree with it;
— not because I may be able to say on the level of faith and
  obedience that this decision with which I disagree or eventually concur is the expression of the will of God, for the simple
  reason that the superior has made such a decision;
— *but rather* because, rightly or wrongly, *the will of God passes
  through it* for me or for the community; it passes affirmatively
  and positively when the decision is right, although I may not
  see it, and it passes concessively when the decision is wrong,
  although the superior may not see it or I may not be able to be
  sure of it.

On the one hand, once superiors and subordinates have truth-
fully tried to identify the will of the Lord, everyone is already
obeying in the sense of the apostolic continuity of mission. We can
then say that there is *obedience* here.

On the other hand, there having been a diverse interpretation
of the will of the Lord in this search, I, who hypothetically am not
a superior, accept that the will of God for me passes through this
decision by the one in authority, even in the case when I may not
see that it is identified with the authentic will of God. And here
again, we have true *obedience.*

The *perspective of faith which is inherent to obedience* is affirmed by
the very fact that I do not clearly perceive the will of God in the
decision made and yet I accept and follow that decision because it
is the superior's decision at the end of the described process. In
this sense, that act of obedience might be called "blind," not actually because I may say that it is the will of God what may seem to
me not to be, but rather because, supposing precisely that it may
not be the will of God, I accept it insofar as it manifests the decision of the one who holds the service of authority in the community and, as such, takes the place of God for me.[3]

The profound and difficult living of situations such as this, in
my life or in the spiritual accompaniment of others, backs up a

personal reflection that I wish to share here. In respecting human, limited freedom and thus permitting this decision (if it is mistaken), God may want or allow for something else unknown to us, whether in relation to the person or in relation to the community affected by this decision. And this will only be accepted in peace from a perspective of faith. The person affected by the decision will experience profound suffering, because the decision will be accepted without seeing its ultimate meaning; the same thing will happen to those who are opposed to it, and for the same reason; and those who have made the decision will equally suffer not only because of the difficulty and obscurity of the process used to reach it, but also because of its negative repercussions and because of the suffering it provokes in others.

In all of this, *first*, the attitude of the person or persons affected directly by the decision is very important. Nothing previously stated is abstract or casuistic; indeed, we often find analogous situations in the lives of others or in our own life. Limiting ourselves to very public cases that had international repercussions in their day, we remember for example:

— The case of Fathers Jean Daniélou and Henri de Lubac. Immediately after the publication of the encyclical *Humani generis* by Pius XII, they lost the right to teach theology, although they were eminent theologians. If we look at their reading of the will of God, it certainly does not concur with the penalty that had been imposed on them, but they backed down and accepted the decision, not only later being rehabilitated but also making an inestimable contribution to the Second Vatican Council.[4]

— The case of Father Robert Drinan, Massachusetts Representative in the United States Congress. From his reading of the will of God, backed by his religious superiors and by the local Church, this was his mission and, in fact, he did a lot of good and had much effect. But Pope John Paul II decided that Father Drinan had to resign his post, and he did so despite the tremendous pressure from various groups not to do so.

It would be very easy to multiply the cases. Each one of us knows of them within our own lives and/or in our respective communities. What is important in these situations is not the rebellion against the decision or the explicit or implicit boycott against it, leading to revindication or confrontation. If all of the means of recourse or representation as described in the above-mentioned process have been exhausted, and still the decision was made or held up, we are left only *to obey in the obscurity of faith.*[5]

The question that will surely be raised is the following: What does God want of me in asking for this act of obedience? Rarely does the answer to this question come immediately, but rather it does so in time and with time. It may happen that it may not come in the time that is given us. But our obedience can have an unexpected transcendence for us and for others, a transcendence that only God, and not we, can evaluate. Therefore, the acts of obedience that arise in this context—these specific and possibly rare situations in which we are faced with the difficult, particular, and mysterious experience of truly having to obey—loom at the horizon of faith as an irruption of God in our life: a *gift* that must be accepted and lived in interior peace and in the joy of the spirit, in spite of the intensity of suffering. Was this not the case and the fundamental meaning of Jesus' obedience throughout his life and passion, but particularly on the cross (Phil 2:5–11)?

The new conception of obedience does not eliminate possibilities such as this, nor does it take away their meaning. It frees us, rather, from the inherent perplexity of what previously was asked of us: always to see in the will of the superior the authentic will of God. It offers us an alternative that does not injure obedience and that is the bearer of peace in faith: whatever may be the will of God—that will in the specific case of religious obedience passes by way of the superior's decision—even when this decision may not coincide with what God actually wants, which is something that neither the superior nor I can know with absolute certainty. Yet, as we have seen, what has undergone a deep transformation is the entire conception of obedience, the whole process of decision-making, the full consciousness of what is authority as service in view of mission, and the actual character of relationships between people within the realm of obedience. This whole group of things should contribute to reducing conflictive and paradoxical situations in the life of obedience. They will never eliminate them.

Second, the attitude of the group or community with respect to the person or persons affected by the decision is equally relevant. The group can help them to accept the decision, to value it positively, and to integrate it into their lives. It can lend them fraternal support to face the most difficult consequences of the decision. But, on the contrary, through an attitude of protest or irritation, the group can interiorly disturb the individual and lead him or her to rebellion or deeper suffering. In this way, the decision, which could have been the occasion for crisis (in the technical sense of this word), that is, of discernment and encounter with oneself and with God, of analysis and discovery of new horizons, becomes the cause of sadness, hardheartedness, or depression. What could have been a passage of God through one's life, or an opportunity for maturity and growth, is wiped out and does not reach the possible objective that God might have intended by means of the human decision, independent of whether it was correct or mistaken.

What I am saying here in reference to an individual can be easily said in terms of a community or an entire order or congregation. The intervention of John Paul II with the Society of Jesus (the Jesuits) at the end of 1981, the first of its kind in the entire history of the Society, was accepted by the whole Order in this spirit of obedience, which was and continues to be subordinate to the key question: independent of the rightness or wrongness of this decision, what actually did and does the Lord want of us? How does it affect the concept of our mission? What is God saying to us through this decision? An attitude of exasperation or of rebellion, of open criticism or of radical or covert rejection could have created in the entire Order, and, through it, to wide areas of the Church, an unsustainable situation certainly not desired by God.

The very seriousness of the consequences of the decision-making process should give those in positions of authority, especially in the Church at large and particularly in non-capitular institutes, the awareness of their own task and how it may compromise the destiny of individuals and of mission. All superficiality, all ambiguous and inconsistent criteria, and all negligence with regard to the human and spiritual quality of the discernment involved in decision making is not an irrelevant fact. It is often something irreversible in whole or in part of the chain reaction that its consequences provoke. In the growing awareness of his or her own frailty and limitations, the superior must find the constant need for the interior help of the gift of the Spirit and of fraternal and true recourse to those who can help him or her come to a decision.

Conclusion

Everything that has been said in this chapter is far from the restrictive and tight-fisted view of obedience that reduces it to the antithetical poles of superior and subordinate. On the contrary, it presupposes the radically modified process of decision making in the context of a new conception of obedience, such as has been described in these pages. For the same reason, the radicality of obedience proposed in this chapter does not mean the return to a conception of a mechanical and simplistic obedience, dissociated from the consciousness of power and freedom, of authority, of individual persons, and of communities. Obedience as suggested here, rather, is the affirmation of a free act that demands and implies the totality of the person in all of his or her relationships within the *obediential space*. Any real act of obedience is the living witness and the conscious expression of an option, carried to the unambiguous point of a face-to-face encounter with God on the level of faith and in the light of mission.

Notes

1. See the description of *obediential space* on p. 90.
2. A better study of the sources, especially of certain spiritual traditions in which obedience is a structural element, such as the tradition of Ignatius of Loyola, has demonstrated the distortion or impoverishment that has existed in the later applications of some original intuitions. These are now being rediscovered, not only in their own specific relevance but principally in their mutual connection and interaction. Let me mention just three fundamental aspects of Ignatian obedience, which mostly had been eclipsed or even lost, in spirit as much as in their practical applica-

tions: (1) *personal spiritual discernment,* a key element in the experience of the Spiritual Exercises of Saint Ignatius, was inseparable from his conception of *apostolic obedience,* as directed to individual or communal *mission;* (2) the deep *knowledge* of the subordinates by the superior, as directed to the response of both to the calls and definition of mission, was essential to the Ignatian conception of obedience in terms of the availability and mobility of people who would live apart from the protective characteristics of a conventual and monastic community that could give them structure and support; (3) *representation,* that is, the possibility on the part of the subordinate to manifest to the superior a different point of view and possible dissent before or after a decision in order to bring about a reconsideration of that decision, always allowed people to be at the same time profoundly free and radically obedient. The loss of the original intuition of these three elements, or their distortion in practice, because of a later ascetic conception dissociated from their original spiritual source, converted a rich conception of obedience into something sterile and mechanical. This new prototype, arid and impoverished, so close to what we have termed in this chapter as the "previous conception of obedience," has often been the one known and taught as the tradition of Ignatian obedience. Such a distorted model was reflected often in a mistaken spiritual pedagogy within the Society of Jesus in certain contexts and times, with extensive influence upon numerous religious congregations.

3. It is impossible for me to develop and explore this dimension wherein the superior takes the place of God for me. In fact, it is a fundamental axiom of religious or ecclesial obedience. This is the only way to justify the fact that a human person may renounce the centrality of individual autonomy and obey another human person on the deep level of religious obedience. All authority or power finds its ultimate source in God the Creator. Jesus receives this power from the Father (Mt 28:18) and exercises it in full communion with the will of the Father (Jn 4:34; Mk 14:36), in terms of radical obedience (Heb 5:8; Phil 2:8). Jesus' power and obedience are linked to his mission, which is the proclamation and realization of the kingdom. This power and this obedience pass equally to the Church-community, which perpetuates in the world the presence of Jesus the Lord. Within that community, those who have power are: (a) the community as such, due to the baptism of its members; and (b) those who exercise the service of authority within it, in virtue of special mandates: the apostles and other ministers. Both have power within the perspective of obedience and the continuity of mission, in terms of which this power is conferred upon them and is defined. With respect to this power, thus conferred and defined, both—the members of the community and the

ministers of authority in the community—obey, each in a particular way and according to the service that belongs to each (Lk 10:16; Mt 28:18–20; Jn 21:15–17; Acts 1:21–26; 6:1–7).

4. In a gesture that many interpreted as making amends, both were elevated to cardinal. But this is not important nor does it have anything to do with our problem. I simply state the fact as additional information only.

5. In his acceptance and compliance, in obedience, of the silence imposed on him in 1985 by the Congregation for the Doctrine of the Faith, Father Leonardo Boff, O.F.M. gave us and the whole world, who reacted so vehemently, a notable example of this obedience in the obscurity of faith.

Chapter Eight

Obedience, the Preferential Option for the Poor, and Conscientious Objection

IN THIS chapter, I will continue the reflection upon some aspects of obedience in religious life. Therefore, it should be read in connection with the previous chapters, which are presupposed here.

A New Ecclesial Context

The advent of modern culture is characterized by some structural changes that have modified the entire cultural and social fabric. The evolution of that culture and the wide scope of its consequences throughout history have been highly important to the character of contemporary life. Such consequences have been crucial for the West, which has been the cultural matrix, but owing to the West's gradual expansion, they have been more and more influential upon other regions and other peoples and cultures.

The presence of new forms of rationality, stemming from the natural, mathematical, and social sciences, has profoundly affected the hegemony of philosophical, theological, poetic, literary, and artistic rationality, which prevailed in pre-modern times. The unfolding of those rationalities and its capillary action upon modern life and thought have been mainly manifested in three important phenomena, inseparable among themselves and, by what can be foreseen, irreversible in contemporary reality: the *secularization* of thought and of institutions; cultural, doctrinal, and ethical *pluralism;* and the proliferation and confrontation of *ideologies*.

In this way, the homogeneity of meanings and values that gave

104

unity and relative stability to non-modern cultures and societies has become fragmented. Although this process has greatly advanced and has been boiling for a few centuries in the secular world, the Church has resisted it. For hundreds of years, the Church has defended itself, trying to maintain its *unity* through *uniformity*, particularly in doctrine, liturgy, and discipline.[1] That explains why, on the ecclesiastical scene, many pre-modern forms and models of organization have survived. They have remained untouched for the last five centuries or more, in the same way that the very institutional framework of the Church as a whole has been preserved almost substantially unchanged. Among these forms, *religious life*, in spite of the multiplicity of orders and congregations, was characterized as being a powerful expression of the homogeneity of inspirations in terms of meaning, values, and conceptions. Opposed to the world and in contrast to it, religious life was able to keep intact to a large degree its way of doing things throughout the troubled history of the external world. As outsiders in the world, religious tried though to respond to the needs of the world.

Recapitulating and catalyzing a long process, which had become a flood-tide, from the beginning of this century throughout the history of councils and dogmas, of biblical and liturgical movements, of the new missionary impulse and the apostolate of the laity, the Second Vatican Council was summoned. This Council realized the enormous gap that existed between the Church and the world, due to those centuries of divergent paths.

Beginning with a *re-encounter with itself* (*Lumen Gentium* and other documents) and a *new attitude in its relationships with the contemporary world* (*Gaudium et Spes*), the Church was opened to another style of presence and evangelizing activity that would profoundly affect it. The importance of this Council for the life of the Church, newly situated in the complex context of the present-day world, is very difficult to be rightly evaluated. The Council has been, for the Church, a multi-faceted event of sadness and joy, of hope and confusion, of humiliations and richness, as well as of pastoral and spiritual fruitfulness. The subsequent ecclesial evolution sufficiently reflects its overarching scope and the complexity of its decisions and directions. In the daily life of the people of

God, and at the very root of the institutions of the Church, among which is religious life, the impact of the Council can be better perceived and evaluated. Against this backdrop, we can understand the character of the problem that is the object of this chapter: religious obedience and conscientious objection.

Conscientious Objection

Pluralism and ideological confrontation on the one hand, and, on the other, the discovery of the Church's situation within a world characterized especially by the erosion, if not perversion, of social relationships, have led people—both inside and outside of the Church—to a diversified formation of consciences, as a consequence of the modern fragmentation of meaning and values. This phenomenon was strongly defined and intensified by the stress put on subjectivity and individual autonomy. One of the manifestations of this evolution has been precisely the greater incidence among lay people, clerics, and religious of a profound dissent toward authority positions in the Church and toward situations lived and validated by that Church.

According to this picture, it may happen, and in fact does happen more and more today, that a *religious* may sincerely believe, because of the dictates of his or her own conscience, that a superior's decision cannot be followed and that he or she is morally obligated to choose another position. This is what has been called "conscientious objection."[2] To be sure, we cannot act against our own conscience.

It is obvious that this situation is serious and demands responsibility. The tendentious, superficial, or purely convenient and opportunistic use of the recourse to conscientious objection would be the same as causing religious obedience to fall uncontrollably into disarray or even anarchy.

There are basically two cases in which conscientious objection has a place. The first, and most obvious, is that in which the individual, in view of a superior's decision that objectively does not imply sin, considers it to be sinful due to the formation of his or her own conscience. In this case, to obey would mean to act against one's own conscience and, therefore, to sin. The second case has to do with omission. It would be the lack of a response, estimated by the person to be a serious omission, to an unmistakable call from the Lord, perceived as such, which enters into conflict with a superior's decision or with the official or a reliable interpretation of the constitutions of the institute. This case is more complex than the first, and is more difficult to define.

In both cases, it is important to realize that the formation of conscience about a specific situation demands attention to all of the implied factors which deserve consideration in order to judge the morality of a decision. These factors can be, for example, the good of the Church or of the religious institute—as a whole or in specific aspects—the rights of others or the rights and duties of the particular individual in question, the obligations and values of religious life that have been previously accepted, etc. Only the consideration of reality in its entire context and the non-absolutization of a particular aspect can lead to a good formation of conscience.

Conscientious Objection and the Exercise of Obedience

Let us suppose that the above-mentioned requirements were met and the question was brought before God and was a matter of consultation with individuals who are trustworthy and competent to understand it. If, nonetheless, the problem continues, religious should explain their reasons to their immediate or mediate superiors. These superiors should be ready, clearly and openly, to weigh these reasons with the individual and to examine if, in a particular case, the decision should be upheld or not. If the decision stands, and if the subordinate still does not clearly see how to carry it out in good conscience, it is recommended practically that the problem be submitted to others who are not affected by it, including people apart from the religious institute and, if possible, chosen by common consensus. If, after all of this, a solution is not found which the person believes to be able to follow without being detrimental to his or her conscience, the superior (after consultation with the major superior) will have to come to a resolution that takes into account the good of the individual's conscience as well as the good of other people and the good of the institute, and other possible factors. If similar situations often arise with the same individual, it may be advised to counsel another lifestyle in which that person may serve God and others with greater peace and serenity.

In the first case, but also and especially in the second case of a powerful call from the Lord, it is of utmost importance that the individual, under the direction of some expert, initiate a spiritual discernment that may help him or her to perceive more clearly the will of God, doing away with any doubt or illusion regarding it.[3]

In both cases, it is very important to distinguish between what is intended as the final objective and the possible multiplicity of means on one side, and the instruments that lead to that end on the other side. Conscientious objection, which by definition lies on a profound level of moral choice, is obviously less related to these modes or mediations (which are mutable and may be relativized) and is more concerned with the ends themselves.

I also want to underscore the fact that both cases must always be an occasion of serious reflection for the superior and the other members of the institute. In effect, through a consistent resistance to mediocre conformity with admitted practices that do not leave room for greater generosity, as well as through a new call to overcome routine and to remove immobility, God may use a person or a group of people to point out new paths to an entire congregation or to a provincial or a local community. Therefore, what has previously been said about the formation of conscience and about the need for discernment is as necessary for the subordinate, who must correctly ponder conscientious objection, as it is for the superiors, in order to understand it and act in view of it. Out of negligence or a lack of openness, out of an excessive legalistic radicalization, out of an obstinate defense of institutional or methodological mediations, which may be confused with the true aims of the institute in its mission and charism, the apostolic body on any level may miss a new perspective or the gift of conversion and growth that God is offering in an unforeseeable way. However, this is not meant to generalize and to pretend that in every conscientious objection a special grace may be latent. But it may happen, as much in this case as in other occasions of the relationship within the obediential space, that the *prophetic* dimension may be validly infiltrated through what, at first glance, could be considered conscientious objection by the subordinate or resistance on the part of the superior.

Preferential Option for the Poor and Conscientious Objection

A contextualized study of the Second Vatican Council was done in Latin America by the hierarchical Church in the episcopal assemblies of Medellín (1968) and Puebla (1979). In both, one of the central elements of the analysis of reality in which the Church finds itself in our countries was the evidence of the extreme poverty of the overwhelming majority of our people. This poverty was understood not only as a social phenomenon, episodic and coincidental, but also as the structural and dominant component of reality itself. In other words, poverty is manifested as stemming from the entire tangle of social organization, characterized by violence and oppression, grounded in an imposed model of generalized injustice that is perpetuated in our history. This view is much too evident to be denied. (See Chapter 3.)

In confronting itself in terms of its own mission, that is, the urge to proclaim the kingdom to this type of world, the Church was surprised by a double truth. First, there was the awareness of its past and present participation in this very social organization in which established injustice has been converted into a generative agent of poverty and oppression. Second, there was the awareness of what it has contributed and continues to contribute through its members, methods, and institutions in the maintenance and reproduction of that situation.

The two major consequences stemming from these statements correspond to the two decisive orientations of the Second Vatican Council.[4] In a re-encounter with itself, as related to *Lumen Gentium* and other documents, the Church gathered in Puebla reflects upon itself and projects itself toward the future under the banner of *participation* and *communion*. This is the axis around which revolve all of the Puebla documents and which is the best hermeneutical key for their study, although not the only one. In terms of its

relationships with the modern world through the specific reality of
Latin America—as related to *Gaudium et Spes*—the Church gathered in Puebla makes a preferential option for the poor. These two
poles, intimately united, will be the ones that inspire and penetrate Latin American ecclesial reality and its entire pastoral efforts
of evangelization.

Let us underscore that this option is an initiative of the hierarchy itself and, as such, of those who carry out in the Church of
Latin America the service of authority. Furthermore, this option is
made by the hierarchical body in its highest and most significant
instance here: the Latin American episcopal assembly. This same
option is endorsed by John Paul II in his insistence on the necessity and priority of service to the poor and on the unavoidable link
of the Church to the interests and aspirations of marginated people. The Pope emphasizes communion with the bishops which
must guide this ecclesial commitment, but he leaves no room for
doubt as to his support of it. All of this is very clear in many of his
speeches in Brazil. Limiting ourselves to what is most familiar to
us, let us cite some of them that have also influenced the churches
of other countries:[5] those of Rio de Janeiro, the *favela* of Vidigal,
and CELAM; the workers in the church of Sao Paulo; the builders
of a pluralistic society in the church of Salvador-Bahia; and the
final address to the bishops of Brazil in Fortaleza, as well as the
message to the *Communidades de Base.*

At Puebla, in making its preferential option for the poor, the
Church takes an extraordinarily significant step.[6] It prepares itself
to change its social perspective, the one in which it has remained
for so many past centuries. It takes a new point of departure in its
evangelizing process. It designs and expresses in another way the
idea of its mission. On the one hand, as an ecclesial body, it wants
to be evangelized by those to whom Christ himself showed a
preference. This programmatic attitude leads the Church, as an
institutional body, back to the inspiration of its origins. On the
other hand, in its readiness to look at the world from the reality of
the poor—this is precisely what is meant by the change of *social
perspective*—the Church adopts a new version of its vocation: serving humanity as Jesus Christ, apart from the platform of non-
evangelical power; being yeast and salt of the earth, bearer of light

and instrument of peace; transforming the world, realizing in justice the truth of love.

The Church, and, within it, religious life in Latin America, finds here a clear indication of new perspectives, understood today as inherent to *mission*. Consequently, no religious institute can exempt itself from reviewing, in the light of this option, its own mission and apostolic service in this continent. In this sense, I believe that the preferential option for the poor, as understood according to Puebla, becomes a fundamental element in the formation of our consciences, of all who, superiors or not, want to obey the mission that the Church points out to us. From this perspective, when the commitment to this option collides with a clear rejection on the part of the entire institute or on the part of persons who exercise the service of authority, it could come to be grounds for conscientious objection and to demand consequently the treatment suggested by the first part of this chapter.

The Option for the Poor and Its Mediations

The preferential option for the poor, with the consequent change of social perspective, should be assimilated and realized specifically by the diverse institutes in conformity with the respective and subsidiary character of their charism and mission within the Church. All of the orders and congregations have not been called to express their apostolic service to the people of God in the same way. This expression is differentiated, *first,* in the materiality of what *is done:* catechesis, education, support of popular communities, service to the sick, parish assistance, apostolate through the means of social communication, pastoral care of the youth, etc., each one with its own methods and requirements, with their specific formation and their corresponding destinations. But it is also differentiated on a *deeper level,* according to the *charism* and *spiritual tradition* of the institutes, even when they are dedicated to the identical form of ministry. Therefore, for example, the way of leading a parish or of supporting communities or lay movements will be different depending on whether the leaders proceed from a Franciscan, Augustinian, or Dominican tradition. And the emphasis of retreats or spiritual direction will also be different depending on whether a Benedictine or Jesuit carries it out.

This diversity constitutes a good for the people and a wealth for the Church. The homogeneity of all charismatic inspiration and their reduction to one single charism, in its content and its operative expression, lacks scriptural backing. It would be, furthermore, in contradiction to the historical reality of the Church from its beginnings. Moreover, it would be an unsustainable impoverishment and an actual denial of the freedom of activity by the Holy Spirit and of the concrete responses to the multiplicity of vocations that the Spirit itself raises up. Therefore, in acceptance of and respect to this diversity, and from a clear consciousness of the importance of its maintenance and value, a new situation is created. Faced with the preferential option for the poor within the horizon of mission, religious institutes will have to ask themselves: remaining faithful to our identity, how do we make the change of social perspective that the Church is asking of us effective in our life and in our apostolic activity? How do we incarnate—in life and in action—this preferential option for the poor?

The *response* presupposes a sincere and critical review, in light of this option, of the lifestyles and services of the communities on their various levels—local, provincial, and, eventually, general— to evaluate them, improve them, modify them, reformulate them, or perhaps abandon them. The criterion for carrying it out will come from the conscious and responsible articulation of the very identity of the institute with the new vision of the world from the reality of the poor. Within this perspective, we find specific, complementary, subsidiary, and appropriate responses of our personal and institutional obedience to the mission that the Church proposes for us in this continent. Only thus will the apostolic activity of the Church as a whole, through the diversification of vocations, cover the wide gamut of social reality and will answer the multiple demands on the various fronts of evangelization. Put otherwise, wherever we may be and whatever we may do, we must be fully aware of this positioning of mission that commits us to the poor and places us at the service of building a just society as the Church wishes.

This could not be achieved if everyone were to give the same response. It would be, for example, an objectively indefensible simplification to believe that the only valid response would be the uniform mission of small religious communities in poor neighborhoods, absolutizing the uniqueness of this mediation. It is necessary to keep in mind, furthermore, that until very recently there existed in many institutes, owing to the recruitment of its members or the destination of its work, a true distancing from the world of the poor. From this situation, it may be difficult, and perhaps impossible, to have meaningful insights for a responsible change of social perspective.

The approach to the environment of the poor by means of distinct paths—among which is the possible involvement in that environment by some members who feel called by the Holy Spirit to this task and may fulfill the necessary conditions for it—may make sense in terms of that new perspective that must inform mission, even when this has not previously been a specific practice of the institute. If these individuals are sent and supported by their superiors and their communities, and they maintain a strict communion with their institute, they may be able to transfer to their order or congregation their experience of direct involvement with the poor, thereby helping the institute realistically proceed with its change of social perspective. They may also open the institute to that environment, whether through the presence of its own members or through carrying out tasks there, directly among the poor and starting out of their own situation, in some form of apostolic service. In both cases, it is fundamental that, in the response to mission, the perspective of the option for the poor be articulated with the identity of the institute, that is, with the original inspiration of its charism. This is not necessarily identified with the concrete forms and institutions of its historical activity.

As a consequence of what was just said, we realize we are moving from the level of the basic criterion—the option for the poor—to the realm of its concretization. We start dealing with instruments and means to reach the goal. When the Church's preferential option for the poor is responsibly accepted by the religious congregation, which then commits itself to the search for and application of proper methods in order to implement that option, I do not believe that conscientious objection has to be extended to that actual level of instrumental specification. Such an option can be actualized in different ways within the framework of the institute's mission and consequently has not to pass necessarily through these mediations only. In other words, I believe that the ways in which the option for the poor might be concretized in individuals and communities within the horizon of the institute's mission fall within the normal praxis of the exercise of obedience, along the lines I have outlined in the three previous chapters. These forms do not legitimate a kind of meta-obedience or para-obedience that may grant to those religious, who personally or collectively are directly committed to the poor in some concrete way, an exemption or a full autonomy in view of the initiatives of obedience that come from the institute, to the point of justifying, in unclear situations, the recourse to conscientious objection.[7]

To be more specific, the commitment to a particular group of people who are poor, for example, should not strip religious of their openness to a transfer to another group of people when it may be necessary. Of course, certain conditions would have to be fulfilled, keeping in mind all of the factors implied in a decision of this kind, as we shall see later. Moreover, that commitment should not lead religious to close themselves, on principle, to other forms of service that the institute may ask of them, such as collaboration in formation or participation in religious administration. A religious who is deeply committed to the poor can be of great help to the institute in changing the social perspective of other religious members who are engaged in different services, like schools, hospitals, and pastoral care.

However, the institute as well as the individual or group of people must pay attention, in these cases, to some peculiar aspects of the question that may help establish criteria and direction for action.

The *first* is the involving nature of commitments to popular environments. Once approved and accepted, they become something more than a function from which one may detach oneself at any moment, now or later. The service of a community among the poor requires an effort that is never easy, one of very personal involvement and true communion. Profound communitarian links are established that not always, or rather almost never, are achieved in other areas of life and work, such as the traditional workings of the congregation in its standard institutions.

The *second* is that individuals who accept their presence and service among the poor, in the actual situation of religious life, must necessarily enter into a *two-way process.* On the one hand, they must face a total re-education of themselves, in order to move from a well-defined and economically more favorable environment in which they lived or from where they came—family or religious environment—to a reality that is little or non-structured and poor. Such a setting will be completely new for them and highly demanding if they want to be consistent with their option. On the other hand, there must be a learning process in the understanding of persons and of the community situations to which we are referring, which constitutes an indispensable presupposition for entering into the proper perspective of the poor and to respect their rhythm and identity. This is a necessary condition for walking with the poor without imposition. And it is fundamental in order to allow the poor to be themselves and to become subjects of their own growth, and not mere objects of an extrinsic effort that is foreign to them and their history.

These two directions—the self-education of the involved religious and the religious' involvement in the people's environment—are a process that requires time and close ties and creates deep interdependence between individuals. Moreover, this process is not only the result of a disposition of obedience, that is, from the fact that this mission has been conferred on the religious. At its heart, such a process is, in general, a response in obedience to a call from God and to a personal option that, because of a prompting of the Spirit, matured in prayer, was presented to the institute and received approval and a mandate for it. Furthermore, in the majority of communities involved with the poor, religious serve in the context of a local Church, maintaining much closer ties with it and its pastoral activity than those which arise among religious who serve in institutions belonging to the congregation itself (high schools, hospitals, missions, and so on) and the respective churches in which they work.

The eventual need for a transfer could not be, in these cases, the product of an impromptu action, an almost instantaneous, unilateral decision of the superiors. More than in other areas, what is necessary here is a proper understanding and consideration that keeps in mind this gamut of factors and the two ways mentioned previously. All of this must be valued and discerned in a dialogue filled with trust and characterized by an adult consciousness of co-responsibility in mission. When this profound and interiorly free communion is established, the conditions are created for making delicate decisions, something that must be done in a constructive and non-conflictive climate. The ideal would be that neither the involved religious feel violated or disrespected in his or her decision, which was previously accepted and embraced on the level of obedience, nor the commitment to a specifically poor situation be given a kind of carte blanche that frees and isolates the religious from the entire obediential dynamic of the institute and blocks the freedom of the congregation with regard to the person. In this last case, we could truly ask ourselves if this absolutization of that mediation only could not be some form of becoming rich again. Would it not be the same as defining one's own life once and for all without keeping in mind a reality of which one is also a part? And is this not something that the poor, authentically poor, cannot allow themselves? Pushed by the need to work or to feed their families, the poor are frequently constrained to emigrate, despite the closenesss of ties and commitments to their communities. In the midst of the insecurity and unforeseeability of life, nothing is left but to go from community to community, sharing with the new fellows what was previously received in experience and life and in untiring capacity of self-giving. In all obedience, in life and in mission, a kind of existential poverty is underlying, without which all other ways of being poor are vain or disfigured. This is the poverty of being, the actual, deep poverty that is part of ourselves.[8]

Conclusion

Consciously limiting myself to a rather generic level, I have tried, in the first part of this chapter, briefly to pose the question of conscientious objection and its treatment with relation to the practice of obedience in religious life. In the second part, I have more specifically confronted a possible case of conscientious objection in our reality, touching upon it from the angle of the common mission to which both those in authority and those who are not in authority obey within the institute, consistent with the question posed in Chapter 6. Without going into casuistic polemic, I have tried to show that the attitude of superiors as well as that of all religious, considered individually—all keeping in mind the identity of the institute's charism and mission—is decisive and may contribute to a reciprocal pedagogy in the formation of their consciences. I believe that this is the path for reducing or preventing a possible area of conscientious objection, on the level of principles as well as on the level of mediations.[9]

Returning again to a more generic level, I do not want to finish without alluding, in the perspective of the faith that grounds all obedience, to a very real aspect of our lives. The Lord at times makes us feel an intense call and does not offer us the necessary conditions for giving a response. The Lord does want us to continue living where we are, but from now on beneath the impulse and transforming strength of that inspiration. Father João Bosco Penido Burnier, assassinated a few years ago in Ribeirão das Garças, in Brazil, for more than twenty years asked to be sent as a missionary to the Indians of the Mato Grosso. This was a powerful and constant call in his life, from the time he was my teacher in high school. The superiors knew it, but they asked him first to be secretary to the regional assistant at the Jesuit Curia in Rome, then provincial, and finally novice master for many years in Brazil. He was finally allowed to realize his greater vocation within his own call: to go to the missions. And there he died, some years later, in a martyrdom that consecrated in a few minutes his long inner pilgrimage, in the light and with the strength of a call from God with which he was consistent throughout his life, long before achieving it.

The preferential option for the poor today constitutes an imperious calling for those of us who are the church in Latin America, a calling that we must realize in our activity, whatever may be our service in the Church. To look at the world from the reality and the perspective of the poor perhaps may be the contribution that God expects of us to awaken the same call in the conscience of the worldwide Church. Then we all unite our efforts, not to perpetuate injustice but to live in the hope of building a new society.

to build The Kingdom
reign of God

Notes

1. For a more complete study of this subject, cf. Marcello Azevedo, *Inculturation and the Challenge of Modernity* (Rome: Gregorian University Press, 1982).
2. For a long time, the expression "conscientious objection" was restricted to a religious impediment opposed to military service. In some countries where military service is mandatory, there is official recognition of a young man (or woman) who, in conscience, refuses to enlist when he (or she) is called. In some languages, the expression "conscientious objection" has been reduced exclusively to this case. In other languages, it has been extended to mean other forms of moral impossibility experienced in accord to the dictates of conscience. Before the Council, the extension of this phrase to include religious obedience was not significant. Since then, it has been used more frequently, although not so much as in the 1960s. The XXXI General Congregation of the Society of Jesus (1965–1966) dealt with this question in its decree on obedience.
3. See Marcello Azevedo, "Oração, Discernimento e Decisão" in *Convergência* XVII/155 (September 1982), pp. 398–405; *Oração na Vida: Desafio e Dom* (São Paulo: Ed. Loyola, 1987), pp. 199–207.
4. See Marcello Azevedo, "A Igreja mudou, em que e por quê" in *Temas do Homem na Agenda de Deus* (São Paulo: Ed. Loyola, 1981), pp. 9–26.
5. See Marcello Azevedo, "João Paulo II: As muitas faces da Presença e da Mensagem," in *Temas do Homem na Agenda de Deus* (São Paulo: Ed. Loyola, 1981), pp. 49–57.
6. I have analyzed some aspects of this position of the Church in "Opção pelos pobres e cultura secular" in *Síntese*, no. 26 (1982), pp. 11–26; transcribed in *Convergência*, XVIII (159), January-February 1983, pp. 46–59. See also *Comunidades Eclesiais de Base e Inculturação da Fé* (São Paulo: Ed. Loyola, 1986); ET: *Basic Ecclesial Communities in Brazil: The Challenge of a New Way of Being Church* (Washington, DC: Georgetown University Press, 1987).
7. Experience has demonstrated that, at times, the resistance or lack of consent of the institute to certain demands of concrete mediations does not necessarily mean a non-acceptance of the option for the poor in itself

especially when it is already manifested in other operative sectors. Sometimes, factors that are more universal than the institute or than the individuals in question, as well as other facts relative to the individual or group of persons who asked for this or that mediation, may lead the superiors to deny it, responsibly and without any detriment to their ecclesial conscience. Sometimes it may not be possible for them to manifest in every case the true motive for the negative response so as not to offend or prejudice others. What will probably happen is what was described in the previous chapter.

8. See Chapter 2.

9. As a simple complement, one must keep in mind that, from a strictly technical point of view, it is an anthropological and socio-psychological fact that social relationships between people develop in proportion to the scale of groups. Preferentially horizontal relationships—that is, absence in the practice of authority and a relationship between equals that carries with it a decision-making process that is always or almost always achieved by consensus—may be adequate for small groups and communities that are qualitatively intense from the point of view of interpersonal relationships. In the case of larger groups where the relational quality becomes inevitably unstable and diversified, the explicit service of authority or, at least, the recognition of some form of leadership is practically unavoidable. This is the only way to put into motion a relational paradigm without which the large group—although it may be characterized by good interpersonal relationships and a high degree of participation—would collapse due to a lack of direction or due to operative inadequacy, in the rhythm of decisions, to the demands for action of the group itself. It would be, then, precarious and truly ephemeral to try to transpose the models of relationship and obedience compatible with small groups and communities, which are in principle more homogeneous, to medium-sized or larger groups that are qualitatively more heterogeneous.

Chapter Nine

Fundamental Dimensions of a Religious Community

IN RELIGIOUS life, community is more urgent today than in earlier times. We have been ill-prepared for the type of *community* that we need today. That is why it is undeferrable to create and develop within us the sense and consciousness of community without being content with reducing it to a formula or recipe.

Outlining the Topic

I will not focus on *community* from a sociological point of view, nor am I going to outline any more or less sociologically valid model. The diversity of our *religious communities* is great, as is that of the communities of the Church and the world in which our own communities are inserted. Therefore, it seems to me to be very difficult today to try, as was done many years ago, to present ideal prototypes of community using the methodology of the social sciences.

Nor do I want to adopt a phenomenological standpoint, that is, specific types of religious communities existing today that may appear able to be suggested as models to study and to follow. With my own vision of how many of the various religious communities in Brazil are structured, I would run the risk of highlighting or emphasizing examples or models. Several religious congregations are strongly concerned with the problem: they search and experiment, fully conscious of the difficulty of this effort. Yet, does the religious community, such as it is in the reality of orders and congregations, have sufficient vitality in itself to make renewal possible?

I will highlight what I consider to be indispensable dimensions or elements in any community; I will then focus on the proper character of the religious community.

Solidarity

Let me first state a deep conviction of mine. *Solidarity* between ourselves and with others is perhaps the most basic witness the world expects of us. Among so much division and war, among so many ideological and personal conflicts, *solidarity* is, in a certain way, the only medium for bringing people together in decisive moments, giving them the ability to overcome the walls that separate or divide them.

In the anonymity of today's society, especially of urban society, in the oppression of people by money or its lack, individuals have become so isolated that their great desire is to find *someone* in another person and, above all, to discover that person as a peer, a neighbor with whom it is possible to share. I am not speaking of charity, which is a Christian and evangelical dimension, or of fraternity, but rather of something more elementary: *solidarity*. Without it, no *community* seems to me to be possible, much less the one that the Church desires, a community of communion and participation.

Solidarity exists between people, even among unknown people, independent of the qualifications and relationships they may have. The *individual* is the basic element and cell of every community: family, workplace, club, or social grouping. With even greater reason, the *individual* is the key to *religious community*. Aware of the fact that I will be stressing a common ground, although inevitable, I want to outline three important dimensions in situating the individual in the context of religious community.

The Individual Person

In our communities we need individuals who can express themselves and show themselves to the degree of their own growth, as developed persons, integrated persons, and with great interior unity.

We are going to comment on each of these aspects.

Individuals who can express themselves and show themselves according to the degree of their growth. We often tend to classify uniformly individuals in the human family. We do not see their originality nor do we consider the uniqueness of each person. How often do we force the individuals who make up a group to fit the same mold! We religious today are also falling into this temptation. Because we are by and large middle-aged people, we try to make the younger people adapt to our age, and if they do not, then they are of no use. The possibility of admitting within our communities the expressive, serene, and non-conflictive presence of people with different mentalities and ages, could it not be the only way of guaranteeing the richness of the diverse cycles of life? The young are young, and what they are going to bring to us is the youth of their life, and we have no reason to impose on them the structures of our mature or senile age. We would be suffocating the unique contribution that, as young people, they can give us and that we no longer have. Through the different ages of the children, the family experiences, much more than a religious community, this unavoidable scale of growth.

Developed Persons. When we ask young people today why they choose a particular career—engineering, economics, medicine—they almost always place their answer on a functional level: to do this or that, to achieve a particular thing. But what always, and especially today, is important is *to be* and *to be more.* The full development of individuals in what they do or independent of what they do is one of the greatest tasks that face us in building community. It is impressive to see how individuals with great functional aptitudes are extremely poor when it comes to *being.* It seems undeniable to us that in many of our communities we are depriving human persons precisely of this possibility of openness so that they may develop themselves fully, so that they may *be more.*

How many times do we ourselves, in the midst of the whirlpool of what has been called "personal fulfillment," insatiably seek course after course, degree after degree, spending our life without giving ourselves neither the time nor the opportunity to mature who we are, to reach a certain fullness that is even more in this constant opening to others and for others!

Integrated Persons. Today we are witnesses of the exacerbation of conflict in the world. And the intense information that the means of communication give us constantly places before us the discrepant, the discordant, the abnormal. This makes the extraordinary familiar to us, making us lose sight of what is normal and ordinary. This conflict is reflected and echoed in individuals. Therefore, it is worrisome to see the vast number of religious and laity who, beneath the activity of the most diverse impact and factors, are disintegrated and unbalanced. However, a community would need integrated persons and would need to be itself one of the most active factors in the defense and enrichment of the integration of these same individuals. Without entering into the deep and psychological realm of personality, it seems to me to be basic, for this interior unification that integrates us, to be conscious of who we are and accept it. We must have a very realistic vision of ourselves and of our limitations, although not a static and fixed view, because it is clear that we can improve our qualities and achieve noteworthy expressions of them. Even limitations, in many cases, can be overcome pedagogically and constructively through a persevering and enlightened effort. But in each moment of our lives, considered in itself, we find ourselves with values and limitations, with personal wealth and poverty, in an ongoing and unavoidable tension. The serene attempt to integrate all of this leads to peace, to the inner unity of the person, to tranquility and global balance in one's conception of oneself and of the world. This interior peace and unity are then manifested in gestures, words, glances, and the whole attitude of the person. These are the people who truly do us good, who influence us by who they are, although perhaps they may have little to offer us.

The strength of personal harmony is irresistible in human contact and intercommunication. But this presupposes on our part an immense docility toward ourselves and toward the impacts of life upon us, and it demands the consistency of not trying to sell something for what it is not.

I believe that one of the greatest barriers in the interaction among religious in a community has certainly been that type of anonymous and stratified reserve in which we have been living. We barely know one another, and what we have let be known about us often was who we wanted to be and not who we really were. We offer a false image of ourselves. For the sake of peace, we also accept the false image that others offer of themselves to us.

The mainspring of a community will be found in the mutual transparency of its members, a revelation without any timidity of who we are and an honest and loyal communication of what we are not. This openness demands, certainly, the tumbling of many of the walls we have been building in religious life, several disguises and forms of isolation, all of which is a work of duplicity and formalism that has been killing our capacity for true communication. Those communities that have rediscovered the transparent richness of communication may think what I have just said to be already achieved, and yet it still is daily bread for a great number of religious communities.

The individualistic character, which held so much importance in our cultural and religious formation, has left an indelible mark on our lives. It is a blemish that is hard to erase, and which stands out when we meet available, open, and serving laypeople. Religious who have been liberated from this individualistic perspective today have some extraordinary evangelizing outreach, especially among the young.

In the simple and profound contact and in the critical interaction between people, everyone will realize how decisive others are for us to grow as persons. When we are looking for a real community, this mutually open and generous transparency of gradually growing, well developing, and integrated persons is a necessity. Naturally, I am speaking of an ideal, and a never-easy one at that, but one to which we must lean. The closer we come to it, the better we will achieve community among ourselves. What I am saying is basically valid for every community, for the family, for the workplace, but above all, for *life communities*.

The Religious Community

We are now going to center directly on the *religious community*. Its characteristic and novelty is having its support in *faith*. The religious community must be a community of persons who believe, and they are supposed to believe in such an existential way, by the grace of God, that in fact they join their lives publicly professing this faith and serving the One in whom they believe: God, and specifically, the God of Jesus Christ.

Let us be clear and precise. The religious community is not primarily an environment for people to live together just as good friends or as close relatives in a family-type lifestyle; even less is the religious community a gathering of young men or women before marriage or a group of people who have not been married. Many crises in religious life, especially the most recent ones, have had their origin in a false idea of *community*. An almost magical hope had been placed on it, a hope unaware of the originality of faith that ought to be the foundation of an authentic religious community.

The lack of such a profound faith as the primary dimension of community has indeed emptied and sterilized traditional communities. The religious life of their members survived, thanks to the heroism of a few or to the mediocrity of many: the heroism of those who transcend the situation and overcome it with an intense personal faith, almost always fed by a consciousness of the mission of service to God and to others in this same faith; or the mediocrity of many, who accommodate and even prefer a community or pseudo-community that, in the anonymity of relationships, offers them the alibi of ambiguity.

The religious community as a community of faith must be completely steeped in the experience of God, in contact with God, in "living" God, in the possibility of encountering in God *someone* very personal. Our great problem and risk is to consider faith as something purely rational and intellectual. This also happens in teaching religion. We give doctrinal content and claim that it is or expresses an experience of faith, as if both were interchangeable. This is false. I can know a great deal about faith and yet not have it. Faith, being existential, transcends the simple rational frontier. It encompasses the entire person, in the biblical sense of the term. The believer is the person in his or her totality, with intelligence, heart, will, the fullness of life, everything he or she is. This is a fundamental fact in religious life, which is itself explained by faith and which is exclusively based on it. If we compromise with a vision of a non-existential and inconsistent faith, we end by permeating our life and our apostolic activity with that ambiguity. Then all solid hope of our religious living disappears, the very hope that can face the critical gaze of a technological and rationalized world.

A genuine faith becomes personalized in one who has it and is entirely affected by it. Such a faith grows with the individual existentially. And the person constantly grows with and through the newness of the concrete situations of each day. It is a continual challenge and a difficult test, a vital confrontation between the experience of God and the experience of the world. These two experiences are interrelated, but they often are contradictory in their calls and demands. Precisely for this reason, the growth in faith necessitates a constant critical review of itself. Those of us who have been in religious life for a long time respond today to God in a very different way than we did before. The big mistake on the part of many religious, especially those who adopt a rigid position toward religious life and its forms, is to think of the possibility of freezing in time the actual experience of God and its expressions in the world, above all in religious life.

This is not possible because we are part of this historical world, which is one of constant and accelerated change. Religious life itself underwent remarkable changes throughout history. Eremetical, cenobitic, monastic, mendicant, clerical, devotional, and operative forms of religious life are strikingly different, institutional patterns of the one religious life that truly has been changing throughout the centuries.

Faith in the living God can be nothing else than dynamic, because nothing that lives is static. We believe that God is eternal. But God has spoken and continues to do so in history, not only in the history of salvation that encompasses and transcends immanent human history, but also in the small and particular history of each one of us. Salvation history is repeated and recapitulated within each one of us. We often try to limit God exclusively to the eternal dimension, without accepting that God himself wanted to enter the realm of time, at our side, with Jesus Christ. We force God into a fixed model that, in a certain way, gives us security and quickly settles us. This is a custom-made god who does not question or challenge us, who never leaves us perplexed and flabbergasted, and who does not demand of us the time to assimilate actions and situations that are truly incomprehensible to us. This is a static god, made in our own measure and in our own image and likeness. This god is not God. Only the death of this god will make room for the presence and revelation of the true God.

The God that is presented to us by revelation in the Old and New Testaments does interact, question, challenge, and make demands of his people and those to whom he comes close. This is the great message of Scripture. If we compare the Bible, as an idealized expression of the history of the soul of a people led by the true God, with the literary documents of many other peoples, our attention is drawn to this constant vitality of the internal change of the people chosen as a people.

Moreover, how much is said through the untranslatable, growing experience of God in Abraham and Jacob, and in Moses and David? That experience is of a God who calls them, hits them, slaps them, transforms them, gives life to them, but who, above all, manifests himself to them as always new, always surprising, always unforeseen, and always in terms of the mission for which he chose them together with his people.

The experience of the living God is a difficult one. It is the experience of the God sought in poverty and in the shadow of who we are; it is the experience of the God confronted with the problems of the world that we do not understand, of the God adored in the uncertainty of who the God who really *is* may be; it is the experience of the God of the poor people we are, without any attempt to explain him or to fully understand him, except in the loving disposition of accepting him as he is revealed. Such a rich experience of our God should be the fundamental experience of a religious community. Involved in the world and deeply related to it in order to be at its service, the community will seek to read, day after day, in people, in various situations, and in events (a type of ongoing, living Bible) how to know God more clearly, how to love God more deeply, how to translate here and now God's richness.

I see here a path for personal integration. God makes us happy and leads us to show to the world this intimate joy of being religious, for in this way we do believe in the God who lives. The possibility of experiencing that joy and transmitting it in the dimension of charity, which is the expression of solidarity, allows us to become a religious community. The experience of God in us and the respect for the experience of God in the other gives us a profound humility before our brothers and sisters as well as a sincere openness to them.

God's Rhythm

The sense of God in salvation history and in the history of each person leads us also to discover in faith a great element of life: the rhythm of God. This is something very difficult to express in words and we would need a great deal of time to explore it. But what is certain is that we only discover God's rhythm very slowly.

That is the reason why a possible sociological prototype of community almost never would coincide with the type of community we must seek in religious life. This is precisely what forces us to maintain an immense flexibility in the religious community, properly speaking, because it must be carried out in each person and in the group as a whole by the rhythm of the Spirit. This fact explains why the model of a particular community is never repeated exactly in another, just as the persons who gather in a community are unique. Thus, it is the responsibility of each community to seek and discover, through the power of the Holy Spirit within it, its own life and the rhythm in which it must move. It is superfluous to state the degree of depth that is thereby required and demanded for the experience of God and the growth of each person in faith.

This same experience, when it is *intercommunicated*, is today perhaps the most profound link that makes viable the building up of a religious community. In other times, spiritual communication was very much alive. Should we not value it again much more today, in a world characterized by communication? Sharing the experience of God in us with our brothers and sisters is the almost indispensable complement to the desired participation of our human experience. We should seek as much transparency as possible, while always respecting the unfathomable mystery of each individual and the untranslatable personal depth that can never be totally communicated.

Why have so many attempts at the renewal of community prayer failed? Because we limited ourselves to changing the methods of group vocal prayer or of private and often individualistic prayer, without going through a personal conversion to God and a real openness to others. By not being able to share the experience of God with our brothers and sisters, we then found ourselves without words, or rather, with a heap of formalities, ready-made phrases, and spiritual clichés, so much so that we were ashamed of ourselves. We tried to avoid a deeper communication. We were afraid indeed of unveiling how poor was our own experience of the Lord. We preferred then to speak with uncommitted words, without any true interior echo, or we simply remained silent. That is why an authentic community prayer failed. We converted our prayer into words, trying hard to wrap it in finery.

To build up a real community, we have to intercommunicate our persons as they are related to the experience of God. To achieve this is to lay the very foundation of authentic religious *communities*. Even though each one of us would be working in a different place, with disparate schedules that do not allow for frequent meetings, and although there would be relevant differences among us, we would find in this kind of deep intercommunication the common blood that allows the children of a family to identify themselves as such. But as long as this is not the case, we will continue living together, more or less juxtaposed, more or less coinciding in time and space. In some cases, there may be support in terms of sympathy and friendship, an element that is important and that must be valued by the members of a healthy community. But if the horizon of this friendship does not include the mutual sharing in the friendship of the Lord, we will end by burying the meaning of our own coexistence.

Conclusion

Everything we have said is so difficult—it may even seem unattainable. In fact, it is true that the conscience of many is marked by the stigma of lived arbitrariness and experienced ambiguities, our own quiet inconsistencies and those of others, alienation from the world, the comfortable installation of fixed models, the formalistic slavery to the letter of the texts, but above all the insidious, existential lie in which we often state that we are servants of the Lord and of others, when we know that we limit ourselves to our own service and to that of the group to which we belong.

In spite of it all, in the secular world in which we live, in this historical moment of religious life and of the life of the Church, the revitalization of community as expressed here may perhaps constitute a unique note, a very demanding but profoundly original one, that makes our specific contribution today to the religious life of all times. The experience of God lived as a gift of the Spirit and shared in the transparency with others has significant consequences. It leads us, through the power of the Spirit, to an unshakable hope and to the responsible consciousness that this is our life's mission.

Chapter Ten

The Mission of Evangelization

ALL THROUGH THIS book I have been stressing the central role of *mission* within the full project of religious life. In the light of mission, I tried to present the religious vows in a liberating and inspiring perspective. The starting point for this new chapter is a brief study I did of the 1974 world synod of bishops. This synod was very important and has been relevant ever since to the discussion of the mission of the Church today. A significant result of that synod was Paul VI's apostolic exhortation *Evangelii nuntiandi.*

Some Major Problems of the Church

The synod of bishops that met in Rome in 1974 addressed its central theme—the evangelization of the contemporary world—more from a practical standpoint and through an inductive method than from a theological and doctrinal point of view. It put aside the document prepared previously and studied by a good number of bishops' conferences and began with the direct response of the participating bishops, many of whom spoke personally while others expressed the official view of the conferences of an entire region.

As a result, certain problems emerged as central to the whole Church, even though they were articulated from the viewpoint of local churches throughout the world:

—The great religions, especially in the Eastern regions, where the evangelizing presence of the Church is irrelevant in terms of numbers and influence. This is a problem singularly lived by the Church in Asia.

—The urgency for inculturation and indigenization of the Church, for its definitive disengagement from its affective, cultural, and operative link with the nations that were or continue to be colonizers and with the Western nations. This is a problem acutely felt by the Church in Africa.

—The positive treatment of popular religiosity, a long-lasting and often syncretistic expression of the religious spirit of the simple people. This aspect has often been neglected or even rejected by the Church. More recently, the Church started researching and encouraging popular religiosity, but it was not able as yet to integrate it in an organic effort of evangelization. This is a crucial problem for the Church in Latin America.

—The impotence and lack of preparation by the Church to carry out the evangelization of a secularized society, indifferent to Christian values and to the institutional Church and practically saturated with the theoretical expression of a Christianity that marked and molded it throughout the centuries. This is a serious problem for the European Church, as well as for the Church of North America and for some metropolitan areas in the third world.

—The Church's concern for the programmatic and practical atheism of the communist countries. Evangelization there has been virtually stifled. This is a tragic problem for many churches under communist regimes.

—Finally, the universal problem, known by all, of injustice in the world in all its forms, among which the most scandalous is the oppression of humans by humans and the political-economic domination of the wealthy nations over the poor or developing nations. As a result of the sensitivity to this reality, there arises constantly the presence of the theme of liberation, with diverse emphases according to the distinct regions.

The Image of the Church

How does the Church view itself in terms of its situation in the world? It is not easy to synthesize an answer without falling into the danger of reductionism, but we are going to present highlights of the discussion.

In the synod, the Church appears conscious of its own limitations, a Church that confesses and repents of having overstressed:

—its Western character, which is manifested in the conceptualization of its theology, in its liturgical expression, and in the design of its activity and in its practical behavior with non-Western peoples;

—its conformist and passive compromise with the status quo of social injustice in the world, with which it has not broken ties, in the defense of acquired positions as well as in lacking the persuasive power due to the inconsistency of its own life;

—its juridical and bureaucratic structure, which frequently hinders apostolic life and creativity.

Yet, the Church is also conscious of:

—the urgent need for its internal conversion and for its adaptation and inculturation; faithful to its basic unity, it may consider and assimilate the peculiarity of races, regions, cultures, traditions, pre-existing religions, and other characteristic factors of the peoples that are or come to be part of the Church. There is here a more living consciousness of what the value of particular Churches may mean for the growth of the universal Church.

—the activity of the Holy Spirit, so long obscured in its sensitivity and in the expression of its theology. The Church currently believes in the profound vitality of the Spirit's presence and activity, not as something additional and supplementary but as an internal and life-giving source that is previous, parallel, and subsequent to the entire process of evangelization. The Holy Spirit is presented as a central factor of the all-embracing process of the universe, as much in its path toward evangelization as in the living of that same evangelization.

Priority Tasks and Missions

For the bishops meeting at the synod, it became very clear that:

— Evangelization does not remain extrinsic to the individual nor does it result in a dichotomy, juxtaposing the supernatural effort and the pre-existing natural reality. The practical overcoming of this dichotomy appears in the synod as a late acceptance of a theology that has underscored this fact for more than thirty years.

— Therefore, if evangelization is not to be simply identified with human social liberation, it is also true that it is not opposed to it. On the contrary, in a correct understanding, an integral evangelization is inconceivable without the liberation and human promotion of people, although the latter may come about in a non-integral way without evangelization. In this sense, liberation and human promotion in the light of the Gospel take on a unique character.

In a world marked by great diversity and contrast, it is impossible for the Church to carry out a uniform process of evangelization. The most important consequence of this is the need for exploration of the key elements for the creation and promotion of unity in catholicity. Yet at the same time, the Church has to bear in mind that apostolicity in this unity will be made manifest in non-homogeneous ways, because it will try to accommodate more and more to very diverse people as the receivers of the evangelizing activity. The plurality of concrete involvement in heterogeneous realities through particular churches is necessary for the functional survival of the universal Church in the Catholic expression of communion.

I believe I have given a brief though necessarily limited outline of the teachings of the synod of bishops gathered in Rome in September and October 1974. These teachings still pose a challenge to the Church today. They certainly reveal a Church aware of the complex world in which it lives, a Church that wants to be the continuation in every age of the salvific presence of Jesus Christ. This short summary, which I wrote a few days after the synod, makes us appreciate the richness and fidelity of the synthesis that Paul VI offered us a year later in the outstanding document *Evangelii nuntiandi* (December 8, 1975).

Evangelization and Religious Life

Evangelization

In light of the synod, evangelization is presented as the global task of the Church. The Church's fundamental mission is to renew in the world the meaning and efficacy of the presence of Jesus Christ as God-Man among humanity for the salvation of all people. Evangelization is the process by which the good news of the Gospel is announced to humanity. It is the communication of the Gospel message. It is sharing with people that Jesus Christ has revealed Love to us through the revelation of the Trinity. In communion lived in him, with him, and through him, with the Father and the Holy Spirit, he calls us to love one another and to make present in the world this mystery of communion and love.

Evangelization is achieved above all through the Word, that is, by the transmission of God's self-revelation in and through Jesus Christ. In its understanding of evangelization, the synod again gave priority to the Word over witness, which *Dei Verbum* had highlighted. The balance in this tension between Word and witness is what will certainly allow the Church to value the diversity of apostolic vocations in the world mission of evangelization.

However, evangelization is not limited to announcement. It rather becomes effective and fruitful through the conversion of the one evangelized, that is, through his or her profound transformation, a total surrender to Christ, overcoming, as a human person, every manifestation of selfishness and, as a society, all institutional injustice in any of its expressions. This conversion is what gives evangelization its measure of validity.

Thus, evangelization is not simply an intellectual process, a cultural enrichment by broader knowledge and understanding. Its fullness is only expressed through one's own life, enlightened by the Word in the dimension of knowledge, but made reality in life. One of the serious problems of evangelization today is that most of the Western world and other extensive cultural and geographical areas influenced by it are ill-prepared to welcome this good news. The West received it, transformed it, and for centuries sterilized it through a thoroughgoing philosophical, theological, and socio-political effort, until it became worthless and meaningless for people of today and of the future. The rationalization of the good news emptied the Gospel of its vital content and made of Christianity a system of knowledge and one more religion among many.

Religious Life   who we are

The synod did not speak directly about religious life as a specific apostolic vocation in the Church.[1] Only when emphasizing the presence of women in society and in the Church did it also underscore the role of religious women in the life of the Church and in evangelizing activity. But it did so much more in terms of the need for pastoral agents than as an expression of the sensitivity and understanding of the proper nature of religious life in the Church.[2] It is precisely this aspect that we will now study.

Religious are present on the most diverse fronts of pastoral activity. They are found as much in the clerical type of work (parishes, catechesis, sacraments, and so on) as in environmental pastoral work (education on all levels, health, social assistance and promotion, and so on).

Strictly speaking, what should be the unique and indispensable characteristic of religious life in the work of evangelization? It is *life*, it is *being* religious, a radical *witness* of Gospel life.

Religious life here means the life of those who make public profession in those institutions and communities that are called orders, congregations, or religious institutes, and that are legitimately approved by the Church. We are aware of the distance between what such a life is and what it should be. For the sake of method, it is important to know that we are speaking of this concrete religious life and not of some abstract ideal.

According to *Lumen Gentium*, religious life does not belong to the hierarchical structure of the Church, but rather is a particular way of expressing its holiness. Religious life springs directly from a Christian and Gospel life lived in the world, and not primarily or exclusively from the clerical life, and even less from the life of the hierarchy. Consequently, religious life is closer to the life of the laity than it is to that of the clergy.[3]

Historically, religious life arose in the Church as a critical reminder, charismatic in nature and lovingly addressed to the whole Church, inviting it to remain faithful to the Gospel. Several founders sought only to convert the Church in some fundamental aspect of the Gospel that had been lost: poverty, for example, in the case of Francis of Assisi. Many had no initial intention of founding a congregation, but their intense Gospel life was a sign for their contemporaries and drew followers. Many male founders set aside the priesthood in order to achieve their religious ideal. Some excluded it altogether. Many were not understood by the hierarchical Church of their time. Only the fruitfulness of their lives and the internal power of the Holy Spirit allowed them to overcome significant difficulties.

In the course of time, the official Church recognized religious life. Basically, it is an apostolic life, that is, a life that is lived in the style of the apostles. To reduce apostolic life to pastoral activity is to mutilate it. The apostolate is something inherent to the Christian vocation itself, especially as a consequence of the sacraments of baptism and confirmation. The pastoral activity of the Church, particularly the planned and organized ecclesial pastoral network, is the result of the hierarchical coordination of apostolic vocations in order to achieve specific goals for the good of the people of God. And among these apostolic vocations is that of religious men and women.[4]

The key question can now be asked again: What would be the proper characteristic of evangelization by the religious as such in the Church, as one of the subjects within the global ecclesial task of spreading the Gospel? As religious, they do not evangelize necessarily only with the Word or only with the sacraments. Nor do they do so primarily with their works and institutions, especially in the contemporary world where the supplementary character of these works is either called into question or is voided by the action of the state in the developed countries or even in the underdeveloped countries. In any event, the works are or can be instruments or means of evangelization only to the extent that they are constantly adapted to the needs of the people whom they serve.

But, as religious, they evangelize first and foremost by *being* what they are, whatever may be their way of life and action.[5] And if their life is not evangelizing, they lose their reason for being.

To carry out an effective evangelization in the contemporary world, religious will follow all of the efforts of the Church, making use of methods, plans, and techniques; they will know how to utilize the means of social communication and to value efficient institutions as an apostolic presence in the world. Faithful to their own charism,[6] they have to enter into the pastoral program of the local church in which they find themselves, putting themselves directly at the service of the people of God. These are all vehicles for action or ways of proceeding.

But, fundamentally, religious as such will evangelize to the degree that, through their lives and their being, they again make present in the world, faithfully and radically, Jesus Christ himself.

Jesus Christ the Evangelizer and Religious Life

Jesus Christ the Human Being

Jesus Christ made himself present before all as a human being among humans. The incarnation was the first great step for the evangelization of the world. God, who could have been manifested in a thousand other ways, chose that of becoming human, and the majority of those who knew Jesus or lived historically with him did not recognize him as anything but a man, a full individual, completely involved in the real context of his time. He was a human being, as the Letter to the Hebrews states, like us in all things but sin (4:15).

To be evangelizing, religious life should prepare religious in such a way that they be rich, fully developed, integrated, mature, fulfilled, and happy human people. This demands an authentic effort of conversion to be achieved. Today it is recognized that a particular style of religious life compromised the development of the human reality of religious in their personal dimension, resulting in a significant number of people who are diminished, trauma-tized by interior conflicts, bitter, and at times interiorly destroyed.[7]

Speaking strictly from the point of view of our religious voca-tion, the evangelization of the world must come about through our being and our life. It is important that people recognize us as fully human beings, just as the contemporaries of Jesus recognized him. On this point, a great deal of reflection should be done in terms of the human person as a whole, male as well as female.

The Church, which very soon took on a masculine expression, owing to the cultural situation in which the Eastern and Western world was born and has grown up until very recently, transferred that expression to its entire style of relationship with women in society and in the Church. Religious life was characterized by a unilateral and growing masculinization in a large number of reli-gious foundations: from the inspiration and development of consti-tutions, from spiritual direction and orientation, from its external expression, and from the courses and retreats, to a series of atti-tudes and manifestations in all of its work. The Church and the men in the Church had treated and frequently still continue to treat women religious fundamentally as lesser or inferior people. Throughout the world, women religious, on their part, still accept or seek the tutelage of men, are subordinate to them, and transfer to them many decisions that they could make themselves. A large number of female institutions in the Church are supported implic-itly or explicitly by some men.

It is extremely important today that religious women be fulfilled as women, with all of the wealth of their femininity, and that as such they serve the Church by means of consecrated expression of their feminine human person. The advancement and growth of women does not reside in doing what men do. Nor does it imply that to be themselves women must always move in a separate sphere, doing their own work apart from and in antagonism to men. It is decisive for women not to take men as their model, but rather to recognize, simultaneously and equally with men, their rights and duties, consciously accepted. They will thereby contrib-ute to the process of evangelization, to the simultaneous and inte-grated male-female human effort. They will assume the type of collaboration proper to them, that only they as women can give and that cannot be nor should be taken over by men.[8] With such an integrated perspective, we are very far from some unilateral feminist trends. We are attempting instead an authentic appreciation and discovery of the proper presence of women in the world and in the Church.[9]

Jesus Christ the Man for Others

The majority of his contemporaries recognized Jesus as a human being, yet as an extraordinary and different man, precisely because he lacked any trace of selfishness and was entirely oriented toward others. He was the good man who passed through the world doing good with a boundless love.[10] He was attentive to others. He was someone who stated that it is as important to love one's neighbor as it is to love God.[11] He criticized an entire code of discriminatory behavior[12] and declared everyone equal before God.[13]

To be evangelizing in the style of Christ, the Church will have to undergo a profound conversion.[14] We have built up special ways of being and acting that, supported by the fourth century theology of *fuga mundi*, gradually isolated us from people, although not necessarily from the "world" in the Johannine sense of the term.[15] We made a virtue out of not sharing the content of our life with the vast majority of ordinary people. We gave ourselves a solid and comfortable institutional security, which made us, especially in the countries of the third world, a privileged caste, in a certain way free of the constant crises and problems, privations and conflicts that common people must face daily.

In this way, it may have happened that we led many young religious to a kind of life not comparable to the demanding life of their contemporaries, a life in which they vegetated in our houses, surrounded at times by exquisite life conditions. Is it not true that a large number of religious, old enough to produce, are able to avoid the universal law of work?[16] Is it not amazing that in developed countries and, what is worse, even in the third world countries, religious often live apart from the current demands of work and the pressures of economic reality, with the austerity, discipline, deprivation, difficulties, insecurity, and risk they imply? We are assured of our sustenance; we can exempt ourselves irresponsibly from what is day-to-day life for the people of our large cities. Passivity, a lack of creativity, not having to struggle to survive, made the heroic inspiration of our lives disappear from our horizon. We became stuck in mediocrity and alienated from a competitive world, where those who struggle the hardest survive, where positions are won through contest and kept through competence. It is impressive to see how many religious who have enjoyed exceptional opportunities for study and degrees are cowards in the face of life and consider themselves chronically incapable of tasks that lay people carry out without having had those opportunities of formation and preparation, or that those religious themselves carry out when they leave religious life. The stagnation of some and the lack of preparation of others make many religious institutes a separate caste, incomprehensible to society and the real world in which we live. In almost all congregations there are individuals who are more or less close to people, who suffer and struggle with them, and who ask themselves whether the apostolic body to which they belong is really in the position to evangelize.

Jesus Christ the Prophet

Many people and some of those who lived with Jesus saw in him a perfect human being, a good man who was open to others; but, especially, somebody who had eminently recovered the prophetic dimension, known but almost forgotten in Israel. Jesus knew how to see clearly and to decide; he pointed out errors and denounced the contradictions of the ritualism and Pharisaism that had invaded the religion of his time.[17] He made visible the lack of consistency between discourse and life, and he made his message a source of liberation and internal consistency. He was, above all, the truthful one who restored the primacy of the rights of God.[18]

To evangelize we have to rediscover our prophetic mission in the Church and in the world. Many founders lived this dimension with intensity, questioning the Church from within, with a great love for the Church and out of respect for its rhythm, but living the reality of a pure and Gospel life through the power of the Holy Spirit. It would take too long to explain precisely how the immobility of religious, especially in the last four centuries, led them to characterize themselves by the absence of a critical consciousness, one that should be inspired and developed from the Gospel and that would have allowed them to help the Church in its constant self-purification.[19]

To rediscover the fundamental intuition of our founders as requested by the Church in *Lumen Gentium*, in *Perfectae Caritatis*, in *Ecclesiae Sanctae*, and in *Evangelica Testificatio* certainly means to recapture the prophetic trait of their lives. It means to rediscover the activity of the Spirit of God upon the founder at a particular moment of his or her life and in the life of the Church; it means to go back to the roots, to the Gospel vocation of the Church. All of this will result in a better service of people and of God.

The rediscovery of the fundamental insight of the founder means being able to relate what he or she wrote, the socio-cultural conditions in which he or she lived, to the concrete reality of our own time. More than simply follow our founders,[20] we should continue and constantly update their apostolic insight and work. We should retake the original movement of the Spirit who inspired that man or woman for the evangelical good of the Church, in the present unfolding of history. This would allow us to be faithful, not materially but vocationally, to our founders. It would simplify our life and would make it refer more and more to the Gospel foundation of our charism and not to the occasional and temporal aspects of its expression. Is it not true that up to very recently the Gospel primarily came to many of us through the writings of our founders?

Not a few of our congregations have taken up a serious study, from the historical, sociological, and theological points of view, of the fundamental intuition of the particular founder. This research tries to relate them to the concrete and diversified situations of the world today, as well as to the reality of the post-conciliar Church and of the particular churches whom we serve. Such a process helped the members of our congregations to realize the scope and consequences of all of this for their life. We can now expect to make alive again in the Church the divergent and plural originality of our foundational charisms. We will be sharing with the Church a subsidiary presence of our orders and congregations in service and evangelization, and not a uniform multiplicity of the same models of religious life. The great uniformization of religious institutes that has led us to almost one blueprint only during the last four centuries carried with it the weakening of the original and prophetic strength of our founders. Such a process lost sight of what, precisely through the power of the Spirit, made Francis not be Benedict or Ignatius not be Dominic or Teresa of Avila not be Angela Merici or J.F.F. de Chantal not be Paula Frassinetti,[21] in spite of being inspired by the same Gospel and serving the same Church.[22]

Jesus Christ the Son of God

Finally, some, although certainly very few, recognized Jesus as the Son of God. He himself highlighted the fact that this recognition always meant a decisive inspiration of the Holy Spirit. We can only recognize him as the Son of God, because the Spirit who speaks and acts within us enables us to do so.

To evangelize is to manifest, to realize, to propagate, and to make visible the event of the one good news. And this is not an idea. Liberation and salvation, reconciliation, and communion are an event, a personal reality, the living reality of Jesus Christ, who is the Way, the Truth, and the Life for people of every age.[23] To evangelize is to let humanity and the world know, live, and love this personal reality of Jesus Christ, who revealed himself in history as the Son of God incarnate and who continues to be present in his Church throughout all time.[24]

Evangelization is, therefore, the growing and gradual fulfillment of this Church in the world (*Ad Gentes* 6 and 35). The Church has no meaning if it is not an evangelizing presence in the world. The *entire* Church evangelizes. The whole Church, through all of its members as called to the apostolate in its many different ways, is sent to manifest to the world the graciousness of the divine initiative of salvation made humanly real in Jesus Christ.

Hereby we arrive at the very heart of religious life from the standpoint of evangelization. Today's world lost sight of God and made its own values absolute. Religious men and women, with their own lives and their own ways of looking at and assessing reality, should help people to be aware of the need for transcendence, and for an effort of liberation from sin and death. Most especially, religious should become reliable witnesses, through their deep and existential faith, through their contact with Jesus Christ and their experience of God, to the existence of a personal Someone through whom and in virtue of whom we live this new life, in the search for love, truth, and justice.

This presupposes an intense and profound interior life and a great openness to the activity of the Holy Spirit; it also means a constant attention to the consistency of our life with the Gospel; it demands a deep detachment and disarming. Aware of our radical poverty, we will realize that it is the Holy Spirit who evangelizes through us and by means of us.[25]

Only thus, as it happened with the apostles and with our founders, will we be able to be fruitful Gospel presences in the Church. Only thus will our religious life be truly evangelizing. The rediscovery of the Gospel roots of our religious life is for us, today's religious, whatever may be our original charisms, a number-one and unavoidable task. And this necessitates a profound transformation in all of us of what we are in order to be faithful to what we should be (1 Thes 5:21). And we will not achieve this without a hopeful and humble effort of our own self-evangelization. This self-evangelization presupposes attention to the world in which we live and for which, as Church and in the Church, we live.

Notes

1. Two superiors general—Father Constantine Koser, O.F.M., and Father Pedro Arrupe, S.J.—most closely treated this aspect of religious life as an apostolic vocation in the Church. The expositions of the bishops, in general, excepting the allusions to contemplative life, considered religious life from its operative side, without touching upon its theological nature.

2. Perhaps we could argue that it is one thing only and that we should not drown in dichotomies. In reality, there is a profound unity in the individual whose being is manifested in activity. But undoubtedly

religious life constitutes, in the Church, a proper and defined apostolic vocation. And, as such, it should touch the person at a very deep level, determining thereby his or her particular work as well. Therefore, pastoral activity is not something undifferentiated and uniform for all of the people of God. Even the religious priest who carries out his work in a pastoral setting must be aware of his own religious vocation as combined with his priestly service, two dimensions, however, which have well-differentiated connotations. If one day, for example, the Church were to drop the law of celibacy for priests, this would not in any way affect religious priests, for whom celibacy is something inherent to the very nature of their religious vocation. Lay people also have a singular and defined apostolic identity out of which flows a particular and proper activity. The great error in the current conscientization for pastoral activity is the dominant clerical perspective of it as the most valid form of pastoral expression. In this case, we tend to consider as pastoral activity only that which takes place within the parish-diocese framework: catechesis, sacraments, and the Word. Was it not perhaps this one-sided focus that led many lay people to the sacristy—generous people who desired a greater commitment, offered themselves, but did not find in the official Church any alternative than that of "clericalizing" their actions? The exploration and reevaluation of the various apostolic vocations would result in a wide subsidiarity of the pastoral activity of the entire people of God. The recent theology of the diversification of ministries is a kind of timid breakthrough on the point. I say timid because it is still very much along the line of substituting religious and lay people for priests in roles previously exercised only by the clergy, who today are decreasing in number. We are, then, facing a collaboration that is admittedly reserved and almost paradoxically compulsive-concessive: "because there is no other solution." In reality, a true diversification of ministries (dimension of action) presupposes the conscious rediscovery of the true diversification of apostolic vocations (dimension of being). Theology has a long way to go in order to overcome the current pastoral bottleneck. This is the result of sticking to methods, forms, and goals that were made unviable by today's accelerated transformation of life.

3. See Chapter 1.
4. *Perfectae Caritatis* 1.
5. *Perfectae Caritatis* 1; *Lumen Gentium* 43–47.
6. *Perfectae Caritatis* 1; *Christus Dominus* 33–35.
7. See Chapter 9.
8. See Chapter 11.
9. It is interesting to note how many different so-called feminist

movements, like many statements about the advancement of women in
the media (especially the press and television), tacitly but truly reaffirm
the primacy of men over women. The vengeful and vindictive character,
the mixed and separatist connotation, or the mimetic forms of feminine
affirmation frequently depart from one single reference point: man. In
this way, men continue to be for these movements, acritically and unconfessed, the norm and the constant reference point. The position that we
take here, unfortunately without the time to explore it, tries to integrate
the male and female dimensions of and in humanity and not to isolate or
separate them radically. Therefore, it seems to be a more realistic position, closer to the psychosomatic basic nature of human reality.

10. Acts 10:38.

11. Mk 12:29–31; cf. 1 Jn 4:19–21.

12. Lk 10:30–37; Mt 25:31–40; cf. Gal 3:26–28.

13. Cf. Mt 5:44–48.

14. Cf. Mt 3:8–12; Lk 10:13f; 11:32; Eph 4:17–24.

15. Cf. Jn 17:11; 1 Jn 2:15.

16. I am intentionally treating here, in the context of *mission*, what I
previously stated with regard to *poverty* (see Chapter 2).

17. Mt 23:1–39.

18. Mt 5–7.

19. One characteristic that differentiates a charismatic founder from a
heretic is the respective attitude toward the Church. Both may see just as
clearly the faults or deviations of the Church. The heretic tends to
absolutize the error to correct or the virtue to recover, to the extent of
being willing to sacrifice everything for this objective. The charismatic
founder acts out of love for everything that is the Church, purifying and
sanctifying it from the deviations and limitations inherent to the human
dimension of the Church itself, above all through the shining example of
his or her life.

20. *Perfectae Caritatis* 1–2; cf. *Ecclesiae Sanctae*.

21. Strictly speaking, the great foundational charisms, the ones which
touch upon the very structure of the Gospel, can be considered as specific
apostolic vocations within the global design of that apostolic vocation,
which is in itself religious life in the Church. As a consequence, the same
pastoral activity undertaken by religious of various congregations, by a
Franciscan or by a Benedictine for example, should be colored by the
Gospel reading that characterizes their respective charism. A conscious
effort in this sense leads us to make adequately present in our time the
irruptions of the Holy Spirit throughout the history of the Church in the
person of some saints who have shaken the world. It will also lead us to a

gradual nuancing of pastoral activity, which, on the one hand, will be able to integrate the methodological strength of planning and, on the other hand, the flexible richness of creative and unforeseeable expressions in the life of the Church.

22. Cor 12:4ff, 7–11, 19; Rom 12:6ff.
23. Mt 11:25–27; Lk 10:21–22.
24. Jn 20:30–31; 1 Jn 5:12–13; Jn 14:6–11; Rom 10:15.
25. Jn 15:26–27; Rom 8:2–17.

Chapter Eleven

Women Religious in the Church

THE SUBJECT WE are now going to treat—women religious in the Church—has the advantage of being extremely current and interesting. It touches upon very emotional things and, therefore, does not leave anyone indifferent.

But the disadvantage is that almost every aspect of the question has already been treated. The vast array of studies and research carried out in the last twenty years has produced an extensive bibliography in several languages.

Rather than repeat the historical, philosophical, psychological, anthropological, and theological studies on the subject, which I presuppose and to which I refer, I intend my contribution to be a reflection linked very directly to the concrete life of women religious in the Church.

Much of what follows, therefore, takes its origin in life and experience, in the observation and dialogue with people interested in and sensitive to the subject, and in the critical assimilation of a good part of the vast bibliography available to me.

Religious Life in the Church

One factor that greatly contributed to the isolation of religious life in the Church has been the forgetting of its origins. Religious life came into being as a renewal of Christian life. It sprang up as a desire to return to the Gospel and to incarnate and live the most explicit calls of Christ himself. This challenging Gospel had, in the course of time, been compromised by ambiguities and concessions.

Little by little, religious life was strengthened in the body of the

Church.[1] It came to be considered and presented as the best expression of Christian life, drawing countless people to it. Perhaps many of them came more because of the principle and nature of this kind of life than as a conscious response to a personal vocational call. This resulted, at various times in the Church, in large religious corporations present in the most diverse aspects of the Church's activity and with direct influence on the Christian people. Nevertheless, this influence did not always correspond to a fidelity to the primary demands of the Gospel. On the contrary, not a few historical periods saw a growing deterioration of religious life, which led to serious deviations.[2]

This happened especially in the period between the Middle Ages and the Council of Trent. The Church itself reacted against the weakening of the religious vocation, which had become more of a countersign of the Christian vocation than its expression. With the reform movements after Trent, the viability of the ancient orders was re-established. Nevertheless, during the last four centuries religious life was especially affected by the lack of a theological foundation and by a devotional concept of its purpose. Awareness of the directly evangelical inspiration that is at the root of all religious life was considerably weakened. The growth and renewal of the various institutes was achieved through a largely homogeneous process that often disfigured and emptied the charismatic originality of the founder's inspiration.

Nevertheless, the quality of life and the personal Gospel fidelity of many religious cannot be denied. This is an age that is very rich in expressions of holiness and in missionary initiatives. These were undertaken generously and were characterized by the rising and expansion of many congregations that spread to the most remote corners of the world and fostered the growth of young Churches.

In this way, the implicit or explicit assumption of an intimate relationship between religious life and the radical demand for Gospel fidelity was maintained.[3] From there it was a small step to the subsequent codification of religious life as "a state of perfection." In the mind of the faithful and in the spiritual and juridical literature, the religious vocation is presented as privileged or special, compared to other vocations in the Church.

Theological development, especially in the last thirty years, and particularly in the stage immediately before and after the Second Vatican Council, places religious life and vocation in a wider, more ecclesial context.[4]

The religious vocation is seen as one among other apostolic vocations in the Church, avoiding the qualitative value of better or worse. Strictly speaking, there does not even exist a more or less perfect vocation, as such. Consequently, the term "state of perfection" disappeared, a term that scarcely twenty years before had been the theme of a world congress. Each one is supposed to respond to his or her vocation, to God's concrete call in his or her uniqueness. Given one's response, each person is to live accordingly, in a profound interior consistency. From this point of view, each vocation is a path to God and a way to holiness. Each way has its characteristics and demands, its difficulties, its richness, and its poverty. But what really counts is the intensity of one's fidelity to the Lord's call.

In this conception, religious life as a vocation is very close to the vocation of the believer, to the vocation of the Christian as such, to the vocation of the human person called to live the Gospel in the simplicity of daily life. If the episcopacy and ministerial presbyterate are constituted by their very nature in hierarchical expressions, apart from the common way, the religious vocation stems directly from the normal Christian vocation. From a biblical and theological point of view, we cannot find in it an identity that is so singular that it truly separates and distinguishes it from the basic vocation to fulfill the Gospel.[5] What does characterize it is the desire for and the public commitment to a radical consistency in the response to God's call through Jesus Christ. This call is made explicit in the Gospel and is reiterated day after day in the ongoing confrontation of each person with the real world in which he or she lives.

This is not the time to explore the content of this statement. It is not a doctrine, but is the result of a conscious process of the gradual maturity of many religious throughout their lives. Rather than separating itself or looking for privileged areas within the context of Christian life, our religious vocation strives to affirm and live communally God's *absoluteness, graciousness,* and *total priority.* It calls for an unconditional *openness* to the service of brothers and sisters. Because of this fundamental insight into religious life, we see its original inspiration not in this or that specific Gospel passage, but rather in the irreversible dynamics of the Gospel as a whole.

The path for the incarnation of all this in the life of each person necessarily presupposes the relativization of significant human dimensions that we normally tend to absolutize.[6] Throughout the ages, with its high and low points, its advances and regressions, religious life has taken various forms in an attempt to express that reality. Its great temptation has often been, however, to absolutize these same forms, thus sacrificing to them new calls to a radical consistency.

Consequently, a profound understanding and assimilation of the vocation to religious life in the sense previously explained seems to me to be absolutely necessary and urgent, with incalculable consequences for the re-creation and revitalization of this apostolic vocation among the people of God. If it is understood and lived in this way, religious life is extremely relevant for the Church today and even for a world that has not heard or that has already forgotten the message of the Gospel. The exclusive reduction of religious life to its own ways of carrying out its life and its mission, or to the institutional and mostly clerical methods of pastoral activity, is, at the least, a very partial and narrow vision of its possibilities.[7]

We can say that the hierarchical Church, having ever greater possibilities for action through the bishops' conferences and joint pastoral planning (*pastoral de conjunto*), has not yet discovered and sufficiently valued the dimension of the pastoral presence of lay people. Just as much, we can say that the pastoral presence of religious as religious has not been recognized in its truest sense. The pastoral presence of the laity as well as that of religious still passes inevitably through the expression of the clergy: its language, its way of seeing things, its forms of communication, its words and gestures are adopted.

This accommodation to the cultural universe of the clergy has almost become the condition and the only guarantee that this presence and activity will be accepted. This has led, from a practical and rather unconscious point of view, to an emptying or a lack of appreciation of the apostolic potential of the people of God in their non-clerical expression.

If this is a general difficulty for non-clerics, it is much more so for *women religious as women* and for *women as women religious*. We will deal with this later. It is difficult to treat and understand the situation and the issue of women in religious life without a previous analysis of the deeper and more general aspect of the situation of women in the Church.

Women in the Church

Overcoming the reality and the tradition of his people and of the majority of the peoples of antiquity, Jesus Christ eliminated all of the discriminations regarding the basic aspects of human nature and the rights derived from it. In the Letter to the Galatians (3:26–28) Saint Paul formulates this radical postulate of equality among all people.

Although his preaching was limited to the people of Israel, Jesus sowed seeds of universality in his message (Mt 28:19–20). Christianity is perhaps the only religion that already in its origins explicitly proclaims this universal vocation. Almost all of the other religious expressions existent in the world are basically linked to a people, a race, or a geographical area. Although they may later be spread throughout the world, they retain a significant linkage to their own people and culture. This is the case with Judaism, Islam, and many of the religions of India and the Far East. The general tendency of these religions is to be centered on their adherents. Furthermore, the less elaborated, the more reduced to a place, and the more peculiar they are, the more pervasive and absolute they become in their forms and expressions. This is the case with the tribal religions of Africa or the indigenous religious expressions in America, in the islands of the Pacific, or in Oceania.

Through the preaching of the apostles, especially Paul, the Gospel soon penetrated the pagan environments. Little by little, it was liberated from the exclusivity of its Jewish roots. While it proclaimed its novelty, it also assimilated much cultural baggage from the Greco-Roman world.

Then tendency of today's post-conciliar Church to recognize and accept the *semina Verbi* as present in the most diverse cultures had been forgotten by it for hundreds of years. And yet, that trend can be traced back to the praxis of the primitive and early Church, which incorporated many ways of thinking and acting of the pagan world that were considered to be "naturally Christian truths."[8]

However, once transplanted into a chiefly European-Mediterranean environment, the Church lost this flexibility and freedom in its encounter with other cultures, absolutizing to a certain extent what is conventionally called "Western culture," mainly formed by Semitic, Greek, Roman, and "barbarian" components. This mold, which became quite rigid, shaped the missionary activity of the Church in its proclamation of the Gospel for the following centuries. In this form, the Church widened its frontiers in the age of discovery both in the East—India, Japan, and China—and in the West—the Americas—up to its present growth in Africa. But everywhere, with some rare and memorable exceptions such as Ricci and DeNobili, it ignored cultures, devastated traditions, burned material and spiritual temples and documents, demanded submission to rites and gestures, and imposed models of art and architecture. All this was a demonstration that Western culture had been made absolute, unduly converted into the only vehicle for Christianity and the only bearer of the universal Gospel. Until very recently, fidelity to the Gospel necessarily implied assimilation of Western, or, more exactly, of Mediterranean models.[9]

This fidelity to its Greco-Roman origins and to rabbinic influence crystallized in the Western civilization spread by the Church. This is what made the Church itself, in contradiction to the Gospel principle of the equality of all people, become from the beginning markedly masculine and profoundly discriminatory toward women. Although it is not possible for us to explore this paradoxical element of the Christian attitude, it is worth the trouble to offer some indications that may help us to better understand the perspectives that may be opened today to women in the Church and in religious life.

How can we explain the fact that the Church had not carried into practice the formidable liberating message of the Gospel: that all human beings, as children of God, share in the same dignity and enjoy the same rights? The Church that led its children to accept martyrdom as a witness to their faith was not capable of applying the Gospel that abolished all discrimination based on sex to its own structures as well as those of civil society upon which it exercised a decisive influence.

The example of the way Jesus treated women, in deep contrast to the prejudices of his time, could have encouraged the Church to the realization of this full liberation of half of humanity in the name and through the power of the Gospel. The teaching and praxis of Saint Paul also contributed a great deal to this overcoming of any type of segregation between men and women. But the anti-feminist roots of the Jewish world and of the pagan Greco-Roman world were so strong that Jesus could not carry out himself the content of his preaching.[10] Saint Paul also oscillated between the clear intuition of non-discrimination and the impossibility of putting it into practice, leaving room for a pronounced ambiguity.

The Church, absolutizing precisely this civilization, rooted its anti-feminist attitude on the masculine interpretation of some biblical passages, especially of the second creation account in Genesis and some of the texts from the letters of Saint Paul. It thereby legitimized its impotence to move from the theory of evangelical equality to its practice.

An anti-feminist attitude continued throughout the patristic era and was consolidated in the Church. The support for it was less a specific treatment of the situation of women than the Father's negative consideration of everything referring to the body and the flesh, with the consequent disdain of sexuality. In a patriarchal society, made by and for men, women were seen as the symbol and seat of sexuality. From there springs the age-old identification of man (masculine) with the human person in its fullness, systematically marginalizing women, who were relegated to a merely reproductive function, for pleasure and for work, always at the whim and service of men.

Saint Thomas Aquinas tried to integrate into the sustained ideology of Christian—not evangelical—anti-feminism the inspiration of Saint Augustine and the insufficient biological interpretation of

Aristotle, later eliminated by scientific progress. The equality of men and women was recognized on the level of human nature being both creatures in the image of God. However, the difference and consequent superiority of men was justified by the reality of sexual differentiation.[11]

The modern world and scientific exergesis practically reduced this entire discriminatory argumentation, civil as well as ecclesial, to nothing. But civil society itself found other ways to reaffirm in practice male superiority over women. The Church has multiplied statements recognizing equality. In the Second Vatican Council the Gospel inspiration of this equality was clearly and forcefully underscored.[12] Nevertheless, the Church has not made concrete and real as yet what it believes and proclaims. In today's world, the Church remains one of the last bastions of radical anti-feminism in terms of practice, while paradoxically it is one of the most active defenders of the liberation and promotion of women on the level of principles.[13]

This brief approach to the general question of women in the Church claims only to situate us and offer us a context for the understanding of the more specific aspect of women's religious life in the Church.

Women's Religious Life in the Church

A simple statistical analysis of membership within the Church in the world leaves no doubt as to the significant numerical force of women religious. In the various countries, the average proportion oscillates between one male religious for every three or six female religious. A comparison between male and female superiors general (roughly 200 to 2,000) is also instructive in the respect.

Nevertheless, we can state, without doubt or injustice, that there is a flagrant disproportion between the possibilities that this huge contingent offers and the reality of its contribution. We are not trying to offer an evaluation in terms of the efficacy, but rather in terms of the quality of the presence that would be hoped for. This disproportion is due basically:

—to an unclear definition of the vocational option for many women religious, and at times for religious life as a whole, as a constant factor in the last thirty or forty years, which is the period of time that interests us here;

—to the neutralization (based on structural circumstances of feminine religious life) of many of the natural values and qualities of its members, truncating individual growth;

—to the systematic refusal, until recently, to carry on a solid intellectual and cultural formation of women religious, who were kept on notoriously inferior levels of education (with the significant exception of women religious in the United States since the 1950s);

—to the lack of a regular and consistent program of professional formation and preparation for tasks to be fulfilled. Having thus been sent out without proper preparation, sisters often experienced negative consequences for themselves, for people, and for the mission;

—to the lack of concern for a serious theological, biblical, and ecclesiological basis for religious life; this led to building consecrated life upon spiritual, moral, and customary elements only;

—to the exclusive and individualist focus on one's own perfection and salvation, a trend that generated pietistic and quietistic attitudes on the one hand, and conflicts on the other;

—to an accentuated lack of information about the world, its problems, evolution, and transformation, all of which are factors that necessarily influence religious life but from which religious tried unrealistically to remain distant and sheltered.

As a result, the secular masculinization of feminine religious life seems to be a constant with deep repercussions. This is a phenomenon that runs parallel to the markedly masculine configuration of the Church. This characteristic has been manifested basically:

—in the origins of several female institutes, founded either directly by a man or by a woman who was strongly influenced by a man; in the conception of religious life thus born, masculine elements or focuses would almost always prevail, in spite of the intent to be freed from them;

—in the legislative codifications and developments of the various female congregations; many of them were not only inspired by male constitutions, but they often limited themselves to transcribing them with a minimum of adaptation, or they copied them unaware of the feminine aspects to be highlighted or integrated, having recourse in this process only to masculine expertise;

—in the dispositions, spiritual orientations, exercises and retreats, courses and studies, the strong masculine presence has often been accepted acritically and, on occasion, subserviently;

—in the appointment of persons as well as in the administration of goods, a strong influence of the masculine branch of the congregation was apparent, leading to the same operative methods, the same investments, and identical administrative criteria;

—in the configuration of daily life, from habits or dress (characterized by the preoccupation of asexualizing women) to the internal customs of convents and communities, in which very feminine values were sacrificed in the name of masculinely conceived asceticism;

—as a consequence of the above, there was a docile submission to male dictates, independent of whatever may have been their origin (spiritual director, superiors general and provincials, bishops, and so on). This was due not to the motivation of women religious, but to the authority of the words of the individual man; what was said by a man was considered of more value than the same thing said by a woman.

What is at fault here is not actually the masculine collaboration and male participation in all this, but rather the servitude to it on the part of women religious and their quiet acceptance of unilateral masculine trends when women's religious life is the point in question.

Because of men, that explicit or implicit attitude of Western civilization was maintained in the Church, an attitude that takes for granted and even institutionalizes the passivity and subordination of women, in this case, of women religious. This has been basically translated:

—in the acritical and indiscriminate acceptance of dominant
and exclusive male influence upon the way of being and acting, of thinking, and of behaving of women religious;

—in the subtle, tacit, and unconfessed scorn of women, and of
women religious in particular, thinking of them as less valuable people without significant qualifications or talents;

—in a superior, paternalistic, and pseudo-affectionate behavior
that is manifested, on the one hand, in attention, diminu-
tives, clichés, and sweetened positions, and, on the other
hand, in impositive demands, hard and authoritarian attitudes, and refined forms of oppression and humiliation, if
not ostensible contempt;

—in an ongoing conviction of the minority status of women
religious, of their innate inability to decide, administrate, and
carry out a relevant task themselves. That is the reason for
the aberration, even in our day, of the administration by
bishops and dioceses of the material goods of women religious, without giving them adequate information or asking
their opinion as to what to do with what is theirs;

—in an absence of recognition and appreciation of their advice.
This is translated into the lack of participation of women in
the ecclesiastical decisions for the entire people of God, even
when the specific level of female religious life is directly involved. This is also manifested in the benevolent admission
of female presence by using women only for practical tasks
that are domestic or bureaucratic;

—in the utilization of the services of women religious without
granting them professional status. Therefore, there is the in-
veterate abuse of using women religious for housework or
pastoral action as free or cheap labor, without contract or
remuneration and without realizing what their congregations
have invested in them. After many years of service and no
longer capable, because of age or illness, to produce, women
religious are returned to their congregations without any
guaranteed income or social security because this aspect of
the problem has not been considered;

—in the still currently held misconception of the cloister as a
repulsive place, giving many contemplative convents the sad

image of being rather an expression of ecclesial marginal-
ization of women.

Even if almost everything we have just said still exists, more or
less intensely, it still cannot be denied that an important change is
taking place that is due fundamentally:

— to the growing consciousness of women, and of women religious in particular, of the need for their own growth;
— to the gradual development and the cultural, social, and
professional improvement of women religious in several congregations;
— to the theoretical evolution of the Church itself with regard to
women, above all after the Second Vatican Council;
— to the inevitable evolution of the Church's praxis in view of
the growing lack of male ministers and of their replacement
by women, especially women religious, who were until recently inadmissible.

This new attitude, which moves from chronic disregard to
wholesome value, does not always necessarily result in a correct
evangelical conception of the equality of men and women. Rather,
there are various indices that allow us to see a current return to
masculine rule. This is manifested:

— in the compulsive generalization of substitution. Women religious, who could not even approach the altar, suddenly are
morally pressured to set aside everything they previously did
and to assume, as the only valid form of pastoral work, the
care of parishes, catechetical directorship, and aid in the bureaucratic functions of diocesan and parish offices; in a word,
they substitute for the lack of priests;
— in the manipulation of working groups, often ideological and
even political, in which the men think and the women carry
out the consequences. Implicitly or explicitly, the men launch
ideas or programs, frequently without realistic basis, and try
to be sheltered from their more radical consequences; but they
cannot stop the unleashed process in women religious who,
more effectively involved, are willing to sacrifice everything;
— in the discussion about identity. To make women religious

more available, an ideology is invented of the incompatibility between the vocation of availability for the entire Church (the basic inspiration of international congregations) and the specific and committed involvement in a particular Church. This gives rise to insurmountable difficulties, from the development of agenda and schedule to the diversity of apostolic directions between the congregation and the diocese. This process rapidly leads to a tension that affects religious commitment. The consequence is a conflict that leads to a gradual disaffection for the congregation, if not a juridical separation from it. There is a big mistake, though, in thinking that by depriving women religious of their supply ship (the religious congregation), the diocese will have sufficient means to sustain them spiritually for a long time. With a few exceptions, which do exist, the loss of women religious to their congregations often leads, for a more or less extended period of time, to their loss to the local church.

—in the laudatory, symbolic, and mystical stylization of women, whom God would have created with a particular nature and with a specific noble vocation to represent in the human race the spirit and capacity of the gift of themselves, of generosity, of acceptance, and, as such, of continuing to accept, in humility and resignation, the fact that only men are charged with carrying out the business of the world and of the Church.

Women Religious as Women in the Church

Religious life is charismatic by nature. That is how it was born. That is how it was in the beginning of a great many congregations. In general, the founders had a powerful consciousness of the need for the strength of the spirit and for the primacy of the internal law of charity that had to be lived and embraced. The growth of the initial group led them, frequently against their will, to legislate, codify, and express in disciplinary terms what, in reality, is nothing more than a demonstration of realism.

Canonical legislation was superimposed on this internal legislation of the institutes. Especially after the Canon Law of 1917—but practically since the Council of Trent—the Code made many religious institutes quite uniform, despite very diverse origins and inspirations. The result was the extension of that uniformity to formation and to mission. The new Code of Canon Law (1983) offers a different perspective and leaves more room for the particular charismatic expression of each institute; this will allow the consciousness of the complementary significance of diverse religious families to develop in the Church.

Religious, however, responding to the invitation of the Second Vatican Council and, more specifically, to the "motu proprio" *Ecclesiae Sanctae*, of a return to the original inspiration of their own founders, will also have to avoid the temptation to codify everything in terms of what is prescribed, leaving a wide margin for the actual expression of the inspiration of their founders, abstracting from the social circumstances of time, individual, culture, or place.

Only in this way will religious life again be a fruitful source in the Church for the distinct presences of the Holy Spirit, without reducing itself to being the rear-guard or vanguard of pastoral efforts. The almost exclusive conception of religious life as of institutional bodies specialized for specific tasks has only the *activity* of religious in mind, forgetting their *being*, which is supposed to be their actual contribution to the Church. The consequence of it is that the attempt to codify and legislate continually and primarily falls on their behavior and conduct, losing in this legislative process the original inspiration of their religious life itself.

The relevance granted to this dimension leads many bishops, as we have already said, to see religious exclusively through the prism of their practical dedication to operative needs in the diocese, parish, sometimes still in terms of their educational or hospital work and, more recently, in terms of substituting women religious for the lack of clergy. This reductionism leads to a substantial loss of basic elements of the meaning, character, and nature of religious life in the Church. What we are saying could also be applied, in a certain sense, to the activity of the Vatican Congregation for Religious. Religious often conform their way of being to the dispositions of the Congregation because of its authority and the character of its task. Yet the Congregation, by its very nature and purpose, is involved much more in the functional, juridical, legal, and operative aspects of religious life. It is up to each institute to investigate and define the very core of religious life in terms of its process and evolution, the historical and actual configuration of the charism. Unless it becomes an immense consolidation of religious institutes, the Congregation for Religious cannot have, or pretend to have, the tools or the full charismatic competence for this mission. The risk of taking it on directly, becoming a substitute for the charismatic instances of the various institutes, would lead to a gradual impoverishment of religious life and to an extrapolation of the very character of the Congregation and the specific nature of its service.

In terms of female religious life, we can affirm that its effective renewal is strictly linked to the evolution of women religious themselves as *women*. The question of women religious cannot be dissociated from the global question of women in the Church and in the world, which has been previously treated in this chapter. As for women religious, I would like to outline here some specific aspects of that question.

The Community Dimension

Since we have lived for so long outside of the normal situations of the daily life of people, this often gives us true caricatures of life in our communities. Adults, who in the world would be mothers in families capable of responding to others at home or at the workplace and of facing very difficult situations and responsibilities, are the object among us of an almost maternal solicitude and of a treatment worthy of children.

While many industrial presidents, state leaders, professors, and high-level researchers reach these posts at thirty-five or forty years of age, we do not consider our people at that age to be truly mature enough to carry out far-reaching tasks. In general, we consider people of this age to be the "young ones" in our communities and, as a logical consequence, the age of maturity is put back until fifty-five or sixty years of age.

Along the same lines, it is worth looking at the many communities in which authority is so centralized that it makes adult people, often very qualified, depend on permissions to achieve what makes common sense. There is a true genocide of the personal power of decision making. This process of exacerbated centralization makes any kind of personal decision, even the most elementary, impossible without recourse to the superior. Today, this may seem to be an outdated observation, but experience shows that the fact itself is still frequent and common. We cannot even change the style and objectives of formation in many congregations. We continue statically to form people who are going to live in a dynamic and demanding reality, one facing unforeseen and accelerated changes that demand personality and rapid decisions.

To expect, however, to have everyone decide everything is another frequent anomaly in religious communities that try to overcome the previous situation. In the name of the democratization of obedience, the consultation with the grassroots, and the use of slogans taken out of context, absurd situations take place. The result is superficial decisions, lacking knowledge or sufficient study of the question or, in other cases, such slowness that no decision is ever reached. It leads to games of shirking responsibility and to the inevitable backtracking of decisions in a world in which important matters are decided in a short period of time.

A good many communities and religious institutes today suffer anachronistic pathologies for the simple reason that, in spite of radical changes in rather superficial areas, they follow principles that belong to another time and another culture. This leads to dead-end streets and kills the vocational perspective of young people who do not and cannot accept a life whose structural expression is in deep discord with the rhythm of history.

The Vocational Dimension

This vocational problem carries with it today a challenge that deserves special study and that, in my view, is closely related to the consciousness of the need for the evolution of women religious as women of their time.

Young people today have more and more autonomy due to their involvement in professional work that, together with salary, gives them a certain economic independence from their families. The growing access of women to the university gives today's young women a wide and extensive cultural wealth, a sense of the scope of things. This makes these young women demanding and critical. Young women feel liberated and have overcome their inhibitions before people, colleagues, superiors, men, and tasks.

We could enumerate other suggestive characteristics. To limit ourselves to these three indicators, certainly few but common enough among the urban female youth of almost all of the countries of the world, we can conclude that these young women will have difficulty entering communities deficient in these respects. The valid counterpart in elements and values that religious life could offer them and that they are seeking so often is frequently neutralized by the premature elimination of a healthy autonomy, by the lack of cultural environment and critical sense, and by a formation that sterilizes all creativity. The young woman of today cannot encourage herself to commit her life to something that tries to perpetuate an age-old, worn-out image of women.

We immediately understand the almost insuperable challenge posed by young women in developed urban and metropolitan areas. We are faced with a double solution that has no future:

— In first world countries, with few vocations, the practice of importing religious has developed. This consists in bringing young religious women from India, Korea, and Vietnam, and a few from Latin America, to Europe to sustain works that would have otherwise been abandoned. This is the primacy of work over person, which often tries to justify itself on the pretext of the individual's qualifications.

— In developing countries, with a stratified social structure that is not homogeneous in terms of culture and resources, there is an attempt to gain vocations from the countryside, from the very simple people and from "traditional" families. Young women, docile and uneducated, are led to work in metropolitan areas, on the pretext of their advancement.

Because of its frequency, particularly in more established and sheltered communities, we cannot pass over the rejection of a rejuvenation of the chain of command. In the end, this is the subtle rejection of the young person for the simple reason of being young. This is a type of vocational contraception, whose motivation coincides with the selfish attitude of some childless homes.

Life is to be lived so that no one will disturb it. Communities, some more active and others resigned, consciously approach their end or wait as if they had an incurable disease. This phenomenon is more serious and sensitive when there is a keen awareness of the need for significant changes and when there is a lack of strength or will to accomplish them.

Perspectives

Faced with everything we have been saying, it may be possible to present some specific perspectives for the direction of feminine religious life in the Church and in the world, precisely in this phase of transition.

A first aspect would be the discovery and exploration of the ontological-theological reality of the masculine-feminine. This points to the conviction that there is a profound unity and equality in human nature, which is fully realized in each one of the two ways of existing sexually: male and female.

The evangelical expression of this reality leads us to recognize the scope of the liberating message of Jesus Christ concerning the equality of rights between man and woman.

Historical analysis shows us the secular inconsistency of civil society and Christianity in the effective and practical concretion of this equality, allowing us to see their mutual influence. On the one hand, Christianity, while still under the influence of rabbinic Semitism, assimilated the elements of Greco-Roman civilization, thus giving rise to the so-called Western civilization. This was absolutized by the Church and Christian society in its patriarchal and anti-feminist model. On the other hand, civil society in the modern world, already disconnected from Christianity on the level of faith, is still greatly influenced by Christianity in the cultural development and growth of its anti-feminist stand. In both present-day Christianity and civil society, the belief about the equality of rights between men and women is affirmed in principle. But we realize the inconsistent persistence of sexual discrimination in practice through a male domination, although it is subtly disguised.

Faced with this, what perspectives are offered to these hundreds of thousands of women religious in the Church? We will try to outline some views:

The liberation of women from their age-long subordination to men, in the world as well as in the Church, will not be possible without a parallel liberation of men from their dominating and hegemonic pretension. There is, then, a common task that can only be fulfilled in an integrated way, and never in terms of conflict and vindication. The radicality of the conflictive attitude is precisely what determines the intrinsic fragility of some so-called "feminist" movements.

Feminine religious life, so deeply marked by its secular path under masculine, dominant, and unilateral influence, cannot perceive its own liberation without a previous replanting of feminine reality of the women who live as religious. We are faced with a mission of enormous timeliness, the realization of which affects women religious in the very heart of their being and opens to them new and unsuspected perspectives in the missionary aspects of their work.

The discovery and practical realization of the reality of women, in their full equality of rights with men, offers the opportunity to religious, as women, to awaken in others of their own sex the consciousness of their dignity and the scope of their rights. This can make them see in the past, but above all in the present, the most diverse forms of male domination, from a merely instrumental glorification and sublimation to an erotic-sentimental, functional exploitation that continues to keep women enclosed in a patriarchal society.

The consequences of this attitude could be the overcoming of two disfiguring points, which today as much as before continue to vitiate the correct understanding of male-female relationships.

First, one should not try to masculinize women in order to free and advance them. This is one of the most frequent errors of some "feminist" movements, for which men continue to be, in fact, the norm to which women must conform. Along the same lines, we are not dealing with isolating men from women in the name of the latter's liberation. On the contrary, what is important and fundamental is the effective recognition of differences, leading women to freely accept men as different and at the same time being consistently conscious of feminine identity and dignity. This carries with it the possibility of an integrated and subsidiary collaboration in which the whole human person acts, in complete equality, through the different realities of male and female.[14]

Second, the traditional dichotomy of tasks, based on the distinction of the sexes, reserving some for men and some for women, must not be perpetuated. What is important is to awaken the sense of responsibility in both sexes, allowing each one to assume responsibility according to his or her particular character. This presupposes a comprehensive recasting of perspectives and objectives, as much on the level of education as in the area of work and the carrying out of public activities, in the world and in the Church.[15]

Against this backdrop, women, especially women religious, may realize that the world built, directed, and dominated for thousands of years by men is in our day at its highest point of material development:

— due to technological-scientific rationalization, a key to efficiency that in many ways is the source of advantages and well-being, but also of trauma and conflict;

— due to the control and projection of all this through a rigid and sophisticated bureaucratic structure.

In both cases there is a loss of values related to affectivity and spontaneity. There is a lack of personalization and a quasi-institutionalization of anonymity. Human beings are programmed, computerized, and manipulated in their opinions by the mass media, directed for propaganda toward consumerism and endless profit. The institutionalization of the dehumanizing process is practically at the peak of the highest material progress ever achieved by humanity. This type of erosion of what is human has its counterpart in the ecological problem affecting the entire globe: human beings who are lost and unbalanced as human persons cause aggression and mortally wound nature that surrounds them.

There is here an immense task that awaits women in general and women religious in particular: to change the quality of life and to find the path for a true and globally human civilization.

The simple consciousness of this task could rejuvenate so many communities and institutes of women religious who are ready to give up their works, which time has made inappropriate or obsolete. The mere functional self-understanding of women religious does not allow them to forget that they possess in their own reality as women a reserve of human wealth, "a reserve of love that will cause the city of men to fall, the hard, selfish, avaricious, and lying city of men," as stated by E. Mounier.

> Human nature has practically no limits in its perspectives for the future. The impact of the contribution of women will have no reason to adjust itself necessarily to what may be thought of feminine qualities, but rather it is up to women to find for themselves the paths for a new incarnated activity in still undiscovered ways that lead to human fulfillment. It is, then, a true cultural revolution, not a revolution of women. It is a global and pacifist revolution that is directed toward the radical modification of the secular relationship of the two halves of humanity to cause the human to emerge in its totality.[16]

Pope John XXIII saw in the advancement of women one of the most important "signs of the times." The contribution of women religious to the humanization of the world and of the Church, as was said previously, will be nothing less than the actual translation of the Gospel message today. It will be a return to the original Christian idea about women, a vision that men managed to suffocate. The women of today, especially women religious, already free, at least theoretically, from the weight of a masculine Western civilization, are being called to incarnate that freedom and equality in practical life and thereby to achieve a conquest of our time for the Church and for the world.

Notes

1. On religious life, see the key work of J.M.R. Tillard, O.P., *Devant Dieu et pour les hommes. Le projet des religieux* (Cerf, 1974).
2. Cf. R. Hostie, *Vie et mort des Ordres Religieux* (Desclée, 1972), a more psycho-sociological than theological focus, very suggestive for an historical vision of the vicissitudes of religious life throughout the ages.
3. Cf. Tillard, pp. 193–196.
4. Cf. Tillard, the entire chapter "Le projet religieux dans le mystère

de l'Eglise," pp. 281–351. Cf. *Perfectae Caritatis* and Paul VI's apostolic exhortation *Evangelica Testificatio*.

5. Cf. Tillard, the entire chapter "Le projet de la vie religieuse et l'Ecriture," pp. 135–196, and Chapter 1 above.

6. See Chapters 2 to 8.

7. See Chapters 1 and 10.

8. *Ad Gentes*, 11; Gal 5:22–23; Medellín, VI, pp. 5–6. Cf statement of the African bishops in the world synod of bishops on evangelization in 1974. Cf. *L'Osservatore Romano* and *La Documentation Catholique* on the Synod and *Pro Mundi Vita*, especially volumes 33 and 36.

9. It is interesting to note the conclusion of Hostie, *op cit.*, in his last chapter on the strong geographical concentration of the foundations of religious institutes, more than half of which originated in France and Spain, and the consequent repercussions on evangelization. On the same subject, see Marcello Azevedo, *Inculturation and the Challenge of Modernity* (Rome; Gregorian University Press, 1982).

10. One of the more consistent and mysterious traces of the human reality of the Word incarnate, Jesus Christ, is this acceptance of the human limitation, in time and history, of the gradual fulfillment of timeless truths. Thus, for example, his preaching, limited to the lost sheep of the house of Israel only, of the universal mystery of salvation.

11. Cf. K.E. Borresen, *Subordination et équivalence. Nature et role de la femme d'après Augustin et St. Thomas d'Aquin* (Oslo: Universittsforlaget and Paris: Mame, 1968).

12. *Gaudium et Spes*, 29.

13. I am deliberately omitting the recently studied question of the ministries and ordination of women. I am doing so because of the character of this book, which precisely stresses the distinction between religious life and ordained ministry. See Chapter 1.

14. When we say the whole person, we mean the human nature/person as such. In almost all neo-Latin languages and also in English, we do not have a word that corresponds to the German *Mensch*, which precisely expresses human totality, as much the man (*Mann*) as the woman (*Frau*).

15. The dichotomy of tasks is one of the greatest vices of almost all civilizations and cultures. Domestically as well as professionally, there are still immense walls to overcome, in spite of all that has been gained by women's access to the university, to research, and to technology, as well as the domestic revolution that brought with it electrical household appliances.

16. Aubert, *op. cit.*, p. 146.

EPILOGUE

I END THESE pages very conscious of not having treated, except briefly, some questions that are nevertheless important for religious life today. There is no doubt that there are many others that should have been considered. I am limiting myself to these reflections that I now conclude. They were born of life. They emerged from situations and questions that groups of religious, here and there in my life, formulated and continue to formulate, in search of a better understanding of their vocation. They arose, above all, from the specific and simple background of my own life.

This book was not meant to be a sample of knowledge and erudition. It is instead a reaction to the pulse of life. And, in life, it is more important to be open to working, learning, and sharing than it is to pretend to know and to teach. In the ongoing school of history and of the strained day-to-day reality, in the living together with my brothers and sisters in vocation, as well as in the encounter with people who live other vocations, there matured a mutual listening and a dialogue that are translated as service to God and neighbor, to the Church, and to religious life. That is where these convictions were brought together in the light of faith.

Widening this dialogue, I entrust this English edition, which has been greatly reworked, to my new readers. It deals with the heart of our life and specific vocation, which must be more realistic and more challenging in its personal and communal involvement with the Church and the world. Perhaps the book will not lead to finding ready-made answers or to sowing complete certainty. It is enough, however, that it be judged to have awakened a great love for this vocation that consecrates our life for service and for mission. I would like it to have contributed to a greater fidelity to the truth that liberates. More decisive than the theology of religious life is religious *life* itself. Theology is done in terms of life. And only life, in the end, can judge the value and scope of any theology.

There may be, today, more theologians and fewer prophets, witnesses, and mystics. But these are the ones who actually give direction to history and make it advance. Accepting them and keeping them among us, walking with them, amid the contradictions of history and of our own lives, we will be able to forge ahead in joy and in gratitude, singing, dancing, and praising, to the encounter with the Lord who lives now and forever.

APPENDICES

Preface to the First Brazilian Edition

"What has been well thought out is expressed clearly" (Boileau).

I AM GOING to begin the prologue of this book by speaking of its author in order to underscore some of the ideas in his work. Father Marcello de Carvalho Azevedo, a Jesuit, born in Belo Horizonte in the state of Minas Gerais in Brazil, was elected president of the National Brazilian Conference of Religious Men and Women (CRB)—a full-time job—for three consecutive terms (in 1968, 1971, and 1974). During his first and second terms, and for part of the third, he had to face very difficult situations, in which he demonstrated himself to be a tenacious and untiring person, highly respected and competent in evaluating risk and in proposing solutions. He responded to each challenge with an ever more penetrating consciousness of new realities. He placed the CRB at the crossing of historical forces. He discovered the point of least resistance, the exact fulcrum. His success at overcoming enormous financial and economic difficulties reflected his extraordinary efficiency in administration, without falling behind in the development of theological foundations or guidelines that were to inspire and support an authentic plan for the renewal of religious life. Throughout those nine years, Father Azevedo's ecclesial and secular training created, for those who were fortunate to work with him, the image of a man of great knowledge who deals with complex problems in a comprehensive way, respects

the rhythms of people, accepts suggestions, searches for synthe-
ses, sets priorities, and makes decisions.

In this book, Father Marcello manifests what he has received
from both nature and the Lord, and which he has cultivated: the
gift of speaking and writing clearly, the natural consequence of an
equally logical and clear thinking. This concise and convincing
clarity leads him to repeat, sometimes in new and diverse ways
and with suggestive nuances, the same idea in different chapters,
giving the reader the creative and dynamic impression of being the
one who is discovering some new aspect, some unknown facet of
the question that was still insufficiently perceived or tasted. This
repetition does not sound like a tautology or pleonastic redun-
dancy. It rather has the merit of profoundly recording the author's
reasoning and communication. No one would dare to say that the
repetition of the *leit motif* in the movements of a symphony lessens
it or empties it of meaning because it is executed with different
instruments, distinct tones, dissonant chords, as an aria or as a
chorus, in royal auditoriums or in humble rooms; instead, all of
this enriches and consecrates it.

Throughout these pages, the reader will discover Father Marcello's act of faith in the ongoing actuality of religious life within a
wide ecclesial context and intuition, despite the precariousness of
every human attempt to stifle with fixed images this manifestation
of the Spirit or of wanting to establish criteria that are incompatible
with the pervasive and rapid mobility of life. We must therefore
anticipate this life and build it with far-reaching perspectives, living the present as an imminent future, as an immediate goal of
ongoing hope.

As the reading continues, there is a review of all the elements and
premises that belong to the harmonious structure of a substantial
theology of religious life, developed with a post-conciliar mentality
and with a new examination and systematic analysis of religious
life: its origins, vocation, mission, identity, charism, prophecy, juridical codification, community, institution, structure, rule, poverty, chastity, obedience, liberation, sign, counter-sign, and so on.
These pages contain an important part of the author's ideas about
religious life that should form part of our existential language.

The life of religious has been complicated in the last few years precisely because these men and women were not able to understand what was basic to all of our problems. Dealing with only one part of the reality, we thought we were touching upon its totality. Father Marcello helps to identify, define, and point out what is fundamental, what is true, that is, "to attain in our life the full and radical realization of following Jesus Christ, which means to embrace the totality of the Gospel plan." The book is an attempt to create this mentality. The characteristic of religious life must be "the desire for a radical consistency in the quality of the response to God's call made flesh in Jesus Christ, made explicit in the Gospels, and reiterated day after day in the continual confrontation with the total reality in which each person finds himself or herself."

May the Lord, in his ever-renewed goodness, make it possible that the reading of this book shorten the distance between what is thought and what is said, between what is desired and what is accomplished. Consistency, righteousness, and critical consciousness are absolutely central and determining underpinnings of religious life. In confidence, from someone who has worked shoulder to shoulder for seven years with Father Marcello: The insights that make up this book have not been written and made public in haste. Rather, they have been gradually discovered, meditated upon, matured, experienced, prayed over, and internalized with such an intensity that they would become part of the author's life and an inspiration for all of our lives.

The only justification for a work is its rootedness in reality, and this is the greatest value of *Vocation for Mission: The Challenge of Religious Life Today.* Books like this one are not to be read only; they have to be lived.

Rio de Janeiro, June 13, 1977
  Rev. Marcos de Lima, S.D.B.
  Director, *Convergência* and Publicações CRB

Preface to the Second Brazilian Edition

THE National Brazilian Conference of Religious Men and Women (CRB), in 1977, published the first edition—five thousand copies—of this book by Father Marcello de Carvalho Azevedo, S.J. Having totally depleted our stock and having a significant backlog of orders, the CRB publishes this second edition, which in reality is a simple reprinting.

Schopenhauer distinguished two types of writers: those who write to write and those who do so in order to say something. I believe that Father Marcello belongs to the latter category. The speed with which the first edition was exhausted says much for men and women religious in Brazil. As such, it becomes necessary to reread and recapture what is said between the lines in these pages, which lack any trace of the ambiguous statements of simple pragmatism. The pragmatic focus is reduced to offering a "philosophy" of action, without leading to the support of some basic principles. Moreover, an exclusive and undiscerning pragmatism is the same as a denial or sterilization of those same principles. Lacking a solid foundation, they become ineffectual because the merely practical focus only has immediate interest. It loses sight of the wider picture, isolating itself from the context. It is immaturity that suggests fad; and fad is as passing as the seasons.

This work by Father Marcello is part, however, of the efforts of Brazilian religious to uncover the basics, without deviating from their path amid the cloud of options that represents an oscillation between a lack of conviction and deviations or fatal flaws. One

176

cannot rationalize positions that reality must undo. As an ecclesial phenomenon, religious life has a future to the degree that individuals and groups create authentic conditions to think and to act as a whole, synchronizing the ongoing postulates of the Gospel with the demands of the current march of history. It is to be open to the signs of the times, to read the signs of God. It is to establish a balance between prophecy and the charism of the religious vocation. It is to discover God's path in the intricate jungle of human events. It is to link life to the Gospel, and not to the episodic and temporal aspects of its expression.

No ancient or anachronistic spirit can persist when beginning the path of an unavoidable evolution. But it demands synchronization, that is, the effort to be compatible and convergent, to have clear ideas and critical sense, to penetrate the marrow of questions, even when it would be easier to discuss generalities and to decide later. Life is complex and is lived amid accelerated change. Great events unfold in a short time. That is precisely the crisis, that is, the inability of people and institutions to face the multitude of diverse and unforeseen vital manifestations.

The Religious Conference of Brazil, in reprinting this book by Father Marcello de Carvalho Azevedo, S.J., is reaffirmed in its conviction that only the essence of religious life—the absolute priority of God, with a consequent relativization of all the rest—will make it possible to bring everything together in a stable manner. To step boldly upon this terrain of healthy consistency is to be led by a deep sense of hope.

Rio de Janeiro, October 7, 1979
  Rev. Marcos de Lima, S.D.B.
  Director, *Convergência* and Publicações CRB

Author's Preface to the Third Brazilian Edition

BY THE END of 1978, the five thousand copies of the first edition of this book, which appeared in July 1977, had been sold. The second edition, with the same number of copies and without any revision of the text, appeared at the end of 1979, with no copies available by July 1981. Given the rising number of requests, the CRB requested a third edition. I asked for a period of time for reflection because there were at least two points to consider.

First, the fast pace of change in the world and the Church and, consequently, of religious life in our day may cause even a recent book to be quickly outdated. The criterion for a new edition cannot be reduced to reader demand only; one must also take into account the author's responsibility for the content, the timeliness, and the manner of presenting what is communicated in that book.

Second, the meeting at Puebla, in 1979, marked a milestone of such importance for our ecclesial life that it prevents the reissue of any previous writing in the field without first revising it in the light of Puebla's criteria and orientations.

These two major points, and other less weighty concerns (although just as far-reaching), prompted me to revise and reanalyze the book in detail. I am happy to respond now to the interest of the readers and, confirming the judgment of the CRB, I give the green light to a third edition. I believe that not only the book's message but also the perspectives and manner of treating that message maintain their validity. I think that it will continue to be useful for religious in their effort to and concern with examining and incarnating their vocation and mission in the context of the Church and the world, especially in Brazil, as was the case with the two previous editions.

Consequently, I have revised the material published in 1977 and 1979. In the present edition, I have taken out the chapter on "Non-Communication in the Communication of Religions" since this was treated more broadly in another work.[1] I have included two other chapters that enrich the book because of their close ties with the central theme—the vocation and mission of religious life. These two chapters relate to concrete situations that many religious institutes are presently living. The first is a reflection on some *fundamental dimensions of a religious community,* a subject that has been little developed previously. The second is entitled: *Vocations: Impasse or Challenge?* I wrote it in October 1981, for the December 1981 issue of *Convêrgencia.* There I treat a current and difficult problem, one that is on the minds of many people. [Editor's Note: Because of its specific Brazilian character, the chapter on vocations is not included in this English edition.]

To say that the content of this third edition still seems to be valid does not mean I am unaware of its limitations and incompleteness. I am thinking especially of the abundant bibliography that appeared in Brazil, between 1978 and 1981, as preparation for, or commentary on, Puebla. A great deal of the content of these publications by various authors is very close to or has a profound relationship with what I develop here. In many of these publications I recognize the traces of a particular stage, present in the themes of the general assemblies of the CRB in 1977 and 1980. This stage was characterized by a questioning of the *praxis* and the *practices of religious life* in the Church and in society. Recently, this was also the central focus of the works of the Theological Reflection Team of the CRB, which celebrated the tenth anniversary of its fruitful existence in 1981. This view will help specify the themes and perspectives that are foundational in this book.

On the subject of *poverty,* for example, there has been the growing consciousness in the Brazilian church of the need to change its *social perspectives.*[2] The result has been its *preferential option for the poor* in a creative, fanning-out process with many aspects. At the same time, this has influenced the makeup of the apostolic mission of religious men and women, as well as their initial and ongoing formation programs. Obviously, the thematization of religious poverty today would be incomplete if it did not incorporate all the richness of reflection and life that for us is the ecclesial reality of recent times.

In terms of religious *obedience*, one aspect to explore is the relationship between the central meaning of obedience for vocation and mission, as I have outlined it here, and the growing consciousness and experience of pluralism in the Church and in the world. These two constellations, the mutual interaction of which is fundamental for a lucid comprehension and implementation of obedience today, point to a third, and no less sensitive and complex, component—that is, the ever widening and responsible participation of religious in the decision-making process on distinct levels. Such a problem is posed not only for religious institutions, but also for the wider ecclesial context: the presence and participation of lay people in the life and options of the Church as a whole. The study of that third dimension of obedience would not be possible here without excessively lengthening the text, and stretching a part of the book out of proportion. But this is precisely one of the points requiring further exploration.

The question of evangelization, conceived in a world determined by modern and contemporary culture, has been more amply treated from wider perspectives in a new work to which I refer the reader.[3]

The subject of *religious community* is discussed here in terms of a very specific aspect that appears to me to be central and decisive. There are, nevertheless, many others that should not be forgotten. How can one ignore, or at least minimize, for example, the increasing impact of the emerging basic ecclesial communities (BECs) on the life of the Church and, consequently, on religious institutes in Brazil? The extensive bibliography on these basic communities reveals various origins and orientations, and it is of unequal quality. Yet we have the existential experience of many individual religious as well as of whole communities derived from their presence and their participation in the basic ecclesial communities. To treat this subject here would have led us very far astray from our actual theme. However, anyone who wants to complete the study of religious communities in the context of many local churches in Brazil has to be conscious of the importance of BECs.[4]

In reviewing the various chapters of this book, which chronologically reflect a significant and decisive phase of religious life in the Church, I have realized the great advances achieved during these past few years. What becomes evident is religious life's dynamism in its articulation with ecclesial life. The greater openness and flexibility of the Church and religious institutes to renewal in regard to more immediate and accidental questions is evident. It is also apparent—and understandably so—that perplexity and resistance, vacillation and rigidity, are the reactions in other more complex questions whose impact is necessarily more profound. This is clear, for example, with reference to the subject of formation, evangelization, or women religious. In spite of everything that has evolved in these areas and has been experienced and written about them, many points remain unclear. Almost all of us are faced with difficult choices. On the one hand, some irrelevant and outdated aspects of our life are frequently considered as decisive elements for religious mission and formation. On the other hand, many crucial factors and urgent ecclesial demands are neglected or looked at superficially. Furthermore, we often ignore or relativize meanings and values that are indispensable for religious life in any time or place. As Father Marcos de Lima said in the preface to the first edition, "Our religious life has been complicated in the last few years precisely by our inability to capture what was basic in the complex whole of our problems."

The desire to serve and to help my brothers and sisters in searching for the fundamental traits of our religious vocation and mission with greater clarity and interior freedom, in love and fidelity to the Lord, moves me to approve of the printing of this third edition. This book springs from life and is rooted in life. It is indeed much more an expression of life than an enlightened elaboration of thought.

Through the power of the Holy Spirit within us, may this book contribute to our service of God and of our brothers and sisters in the joy of the vocation to which we have been called by the grace of this same Spirit.

Rio de Janeiro, January 1, 1982
Solemnity of Mary, the Mother of God
    Fr. Marcello de Carvalho Azevedo, S.J.

Notes

1. See Marcello Azevedo, *Modernidade e Cristianismo: o desafio à inculturação* (São Paulo: Ed. Loyola, 1981); ET: *Inculturation and the Challenges of Modernity* (Rome: Gregorian University Press, 1982). The complete text of "Non-Communication in the Communication of Religions," omitted in this third edition, can be found in the two previous ones. It was originally part of a collaborative work, *Comunicação e Incomunicação no Brasil* (São Paulo: Ed. Loyola, 1976), and was also published in *Síntese*, Nova Fase III, no. 7 (April-June 1976), pp. 27–41.

2. By *social perspective* I mean the standpoint or the vantage point from which I perceive, analyze, and interpret some reality, or from which I act upon it. *Social perspective*—sometimes also called *social location*—is a concept of the sociology of knowledge, an epistemological and methodological concept. *Social perspective* should not be confounded with *social class*, a sociological and political concept and/or empirical reality, or with *social position*, the stand of a person within his or her class or society, a concept or reality of a sociological nature as well. People can have the same social position or belong to the same social class, and yet have different social perspectives. We all have our *social perspective*, which is the guiding thread of our "praxis." The term *praxis* does not mean simply "doing" or "action." Nor is it practice, the opposite of theory. Praxis is a concrete form of involvement in history, involving *awareness* of two things: that history is something carried out in time, and that it is the result of human action *deriving from concrete choices*. Thus, praxis is the conscious doing of history, and Christian praxis is the fleshing out of faith's historical implications in actual life. One's *social perspective* is a decisive factor for one's *praxis*. The new sensitivity to the reality of poverty in the world is at the root of the Church's change of social perspective and praxis in Latin America after Medellín and Puebla.

3. See Azevedo, *Inculturation and the Challenges of Modernity*.

4. For a broad treatment of the BECs, see Marcello Azevedo, *Comuni-*

dades Eclesiais de Base e Inculturação da Fé (São Paulo: Ed. Loyola, 1986); ET: *Basic Ecclesial Communities in Brazil: The Challenge of a New Way of Being Church* (Washington, D.C.: Georgetown University Press, 1987). This book has also been translated into French (*Communautês Ecclésiales de Base. L'énjeu d'une nouvelle manière d'etre Eglise* [Paris: Ed. du Centurion, 1986]), and into Spanish (*Comunidades Eclesiales de Base. Alcance y desafío de un modo nuevo de ser Iglesia* [Madrid: Soc. Educ. Atenas, 1986]).

Author's Preface to the Fourth Brazilian Edition

MULTIPLE EDITIONS of a book are published not because everything within it has been said once and for all. Rather, a book survives multiple editions—which are not simple reprintings—because the author is faced with a difficult discernment each time: what to keep, what to cut, what to amplify, and how to reformulate what can no longer be expressed as it was before. It is this process that determines a book's survival. Each edition is a kind of new creation; it is faithful to the first inspiration but open to new realities. As in life, we grow and are transformed without ceasing to be what we are. This is also true in this fourth edition. It was worked and reworked. It offers, I believe, an even richer and more mature text than in the preceding editions.

It benefits, first of all, from a wider audience which raised new sensitivities and demands. After the third Brazilian edition was published in 1982, *Os Religiosos: Vocação e Missão* was published in Italian (1983), in Spanish (1985), and in French (1985). The English, German, and Polish translations are being prepared. The development of each edition and the personal revision of the translations allowed the author a critical review that is reflected in this fourth edition, which includes a new chapter on poverty and three on obedience. The chapters were rearranged more organically: identity of the religious vocation, the vows, the community, mission, women religious, and new vocations. Each one had its formulation carefully scrutinized. I took into consideration the suggestions, questions, reactions, and comments of readers and other people who were exposed to the book through courses, workshops, and seminars.

A new edition should also pass through the sieve and the test of new situations. From the publication of the third edition in 1983 to the end of 1984, when the printing was exhausted, three relevant facts concerning religious life had to be considered in the light of a fourth edition: the promulgation of the new Code of Canon Law (1983); the apostolic exhortation *Redemptionis Donum* of Pope John Paul II, on "Religious Consecration in the Light of the Mystery of the Redemption" (1984); and, for the majority of religious institutes, the end of the lengthy process of the revision or redevelopment of their respective constitutions and their approval by the Holy See. Each of these three factors had an immediate impact on the life of religious orders and congregations and cannot be absent from the preparation of this fourth edition. To say this is to define the history and scope of this new publication. To call attention to this fact is one of the functions of a preface.

I have always insisted that this is not an erudite or academic work. It is an existential book, born of life lived and tested from day to day. That is the reason for the absence of citations, the lack of concern for justifying what is said by the authority of Scripture, tradition, or the documents of the magisterium on its various levels. There is, however, an echo of all this and it would be easy to provide an abundance of references for my statements. I have not done this here, just as I did not do it in the previous editions. Yet, I judged it to be an aid to the reader to place in the margins—in the first chapter on the identity of religious vocation—a few references to the new Code of Canon Law.

I hope that those who have read the previous editions, as well as new readers, may find in this fourth edition a stimulus to love the vocation to which we were called, and an impulse to grow in that vocation, through the power of the Spirit. At an interview and roundtable discussion, organized in Paris by Editions du Centurion for the launching of the French edition in May 1985, I found myself surrounded by twelve journalists, most of them lay men and women, who had previously read the book. I was surprised at their interest in the subject and its presentation in this book. Moreover, I was pleased with the unanimous observation of the lay journalists: "This book is written for religious men and women . . . but it has done great good for us lay people. It helped us to better understand religious life . . . to grasp the meaning and the challenges of our own vocation as lay people . . . to comprehend the complementarity and the necessity for mutual interaction and support among the various vocations within the Church."

July 31, 1985
Feast of Saint Ignatius of Loyola
  Marcello de Carvalho Azevedo, S.J.

ABOUT THE AUTHOR

MARCELLO AZEVEDO was born in Belo-Horizonte, State of Minas Gerais, in Brazil. He holds a Master's degree in Philosophy from the Jesuit School of Philosophy in São Paulo, Brazil; a Master's degree in Cultural Anthropology from The New School for Social Research, in New York, N.Y, USA; a Licentiate in Theology (M.Div.) from the Jesuit School of Theology, in Frankfurt/Main, West Germany, where he was ordained a priest. His doctoral programs in Philosophy, Theology and Missiology were completed at the Pontifical Gregorian University in Rome, Italy, from which he holds a Doctorate in Missiology. He regularly teaches in the Department of Missiology at the Gregorian University four months every other year.

Father Azevedo was Director of Studies at the Pontifical Brazilian College in Rome, Provincial of one of the Jesuit Provinces in Brazil, and an elected member of the 31st and 33rd General Congregations of the Society of Jesus (1965–6/1983). He was the National President and full-time Executive Director of the Brazilian National Conference of Religious men and women (CRB) for three consecutive terms (1968–1977).

He is currently a Senior Member and Research Fellow at the Center John XXIII for Social Research and Action, in Rio de Janeiro. Fluent in Portuguese, English, French, Spanish, Italian and German, he has been often invited as a speaker or panelist to several international meetings and conferences in various countries. In the last few years he has taught as a visiting professor at the Washington Theological Union, in Silver Spring, MD, at the Centre Sèvres d'Études Supérieures in Paris, France, and at the University of Santa Ursula, in Rio de Janeiro. For five consecutive years he was a Research Fellow at the Woodstock Theological Center, Georgetown University, Washington, D.C.

He is the author of seven books published in Brazil and in Europe, some of which were translated into various languages. He published several articles on theological, philosophical and cultural anthropological subjects in Brazilian, European and American journals.

[May 1988]

HEROINES OF
MODERN RELIGION

MAUD BALLINGTON BOOTH

HEROINES OF
MODERN RELIGION

EDITED BY
WARREN DUNHAM FOSTER

ILLUSTRATED

Essay Index Reprint Series

BOOKS FOR LIBRARIES PRESS
FREEPORT, NEW YORK

First Published 1913
Reprinted 1970

STANDARD BOOK NUMBER:
8369-1572-0

LIBRARY OF CONGRESS CATALOG CARD NUMBER:
77-107700

PRINTED IN THE UNITED STATES OF AMERICA

PREFACE

A preface is supposed to be an acknowledgment to those whose help has made possible the book. This preface, then, must first of all thank those enthusiastic readers whose appreciation of the first volume of the Modern Heroine Series gave the editor the enthusiasm which has made the preparation of this book so pleasant a task. To girls such as the one who in a village in the Georgia pinelands found in "Heroines of Modern Progress," not the account of what ten brilliant women had done for womanhood and the race, but the statement of what she herself wanted to do and, God helping her, would do; to women such as the one who by the sweep of the story of how ten high souled pioneers had blazed new paths for all womanhood was carried far beyond the loneliness and hardship of her own heroic pioneering upon a Montana homestead; to men like the New England pastor who caught compelling inspiration from what Mrs. Ellen M. Henrotin, Honorary President of the General Federation of Women's Clubs, in her introduction to "Heroines of Modern Progress," calls the development of "the woman from the mere mother of the family to the mother of the group and so to the 'World Mother' of to-day"—to them and others like them is due the credit for whatever excellence these ten biographies may have. And

And how great has been that progress! How vividly is pictured the sweep of three hundred years when one sees Anne Hutchinson standing alone at the bar of the General Court of the Massachusetts Bay Colony about to be banished because she believed in salvation by faith instead of by works, and Maud Ballington Booth, in whose life faith and works found perfect union, standing before the mellowing criminals at Sing Sing to hold out to them the promise of regeneration here and now and in the world to come.

Because of the diversity of mind, method and creed of the ten women, the editor felt that by intrusting to different writers the different biographies he would secure a sympathetic but critically just treatment that would otherwise be impossible. All of these religious leaders, however, rise so far above the limitations of prejudice and creed that their glowing lives are part of the heritage of the race. For no sect or cause, does the author of any chapter or the editor of the series hold a brief; the women are always women, interesting as such as well as for what they have done to make life brighter for all of us.

The editor cannot give too warm praise to the six men and women who have labored with him in the effort to make each biography a vivid and true picture of one woman who has helped all of us enter into a fuller spiritual life and to make the ten biographies a vivid and true picture of the contribution of all modern woman-

the several authors are the first to acknowledge
this indebtedness.

To tell the stories of the representative
women who, luminous as examples of personal
sanctification and whole-souled ministry, have
brought numberless men and women into a
more harmonious relation with their Maker, is
the purpose of this book. Fittingly, the first
volume of the series, "Heroines of Modern
Progress," pictured the lives of ten women
representative of the whole, well-rounded feminine endeavor to make this world of ours a
better one in which to live. Fittingly also, this,
the second volume of the series, is devoted to
ten women who made vital contribution to the
development and application of religious
thought. How faint is the line between the
two groups is shown by the life of Hannah
Whitall Smith, who, as "mother confessor" to
the women of the first group and a member of
the second, binds the two volumes together.

In deciding upon the subjects for this volume, the editor was again embarrassed by the
number of women whose personalities and efforts were so far-reaching that they deserved
inclusion. So typical and so diverse, however,
have been the spiritual and social achievements
of the ten women chosen that the editor hopes
that this volume will in truth serve as a record
of the religious progress of the last three centuries. How unified and closely knit is the
story of that progress is shown by the chrono-
logical conspectus at the end of the book.

hood to the cause of religious progress. By painstaking care, by loyalty to the work as a whole, by patience with the criticisms, just and unjust, of those experts to whom this work was submitted, by kindly deference to the editor's insistent demands for the certainty of accuracy in facts that are incidental as well as in those that are essential, by . . . but the qualities by the exercise of which the collaborators won the editor's admiration are too numerous to catalogue.

WARREN DUNHAM FOSTER.

Boston, Massachusetts, September 1, 1913.

TABLE OF CONTENTS

CHAPTER   PAGE

   I   ANNE HUTCHINSON 1
          Anne Elizabeth Jenkins

  II   SUSANNAH WESLEY 23
          William Horton Foster

 III   ELIZABETH ANN SETON 57
          R. V. Trevel

  IV   LUCRETIA MOTT 88
          Anne Elizabeth Jenkins

   V   FANNY CROSBY 115
          Woodman Bradbury

  VI   SISTER DORA 134
          Gertrude Leslie Mumford

 VII   HANNAH WHITALL SMITH 160
          William Horton Foster

VIII   FRANCES RIDLEY HAVERGAL 179
          Woodman Bradbury

  IX   RAMABAI DONGRE MEDHAVI 196
          John Claire Minot

   X   MAUD BALLINGTON BOOTH 222
          R. V. Trevel

       BIBLIOGRAPHY 258

ILLUSTRATIONS

Maud Ballington Booth . . . . . *Frontispiece*

FACING
PAGE

Susannah Wesley 24

Elizabeth Ann Seton 58

Lucretia Mott 88

Fanny Crosby 116

Sister Dora 134

Hannah Whitall Smith 160

Frances Ridley Havergal 180

Ramabai Dongre Medhavi 196

Heroines of Modern Religion

CHAPTER I

'ANNE HUTCHINSON

BY ANNE ELIZABETH JENKINS

AMONG the records of the life of Anne Hutchinson, no account is found which pictures her as a little girl. It would seem as though the Puritans in their stern outlook on life made no place for childhood with its sunny irresponsibility, and so never had the interest nor curiosity to inquire into that of the woman who was the storm center of one of their most bitter religious controversies. It would be interesting to know whether or not the little 'Anne had her childish longings and searchings for God, and whether her quick wit and ready repartee were developed by friendly sparrings with her father and her playmates. What of the childish personality that developed into the bright, intelligent, courageous woman of later years? It is possible only to speculate, however, about these early days in Lincolnshire. The grimly spirited controversy which she started in Boston has turned the searchlight so full upon the three years of her preachings and discussions there, that what came before and after is in the shadow.

We know that she was born in 1590 in Lincolnshire, and that her father, William Marbury, was a preacher—first in her birthplace and later in London. This fact would lead us to suppose that Anne was early trained in religion and doctrine. Since the family was in good position there Anne was of gentle descent.

When she came to America in 1634 she was already married to William Hutchinson, a man of good estate who had lived at Alfred in the same shire with the Marburys. Almost nothing is recorded of this man except that he remained faithful to his wife through her persecutions. Governor Winthrop says of him that he was a man of very mild temper and weak parts and was wholly guided by his wife. Although Governor Winthrop was a man of upright and noble nature, he was thoroughly human, and it could hardly be expected that he would look at the Hutchinson family with an unprejudiced eye.

What Mrs. Hutchinson called her revelations was the cause of their leaving England. For some time before their departure she had had "inward struggles" and "flashings of convictions" that told her, she thought, that the only preachers who were acceptable to God were her brother-in-law, John Wheelright; and John Cotton. When these two clergymen decided to sail for America the revelation came to Mrs. Hutchinson to follow them. Either her hus-

band shared her convictions in regard to these
ministers or else he loved his wife sufficiently
to be willing to follow her into the new country, regardless of his own views—in any case
he accompanied her to America. It is not
probable that she had formulated very definitely her religious opinions before she left
England but she held firmly to the belief that
God spoke to her as directly as He did to
Abraham or the prophets, and she must have
been fairly certain of the "covenant of grace"
which she afterwards maintained so fervently.
That she gave vent to "peculiar opinions" on
board the ship *Griffin* coming over, is testified
to by a fellow passenger, a Mr. Symmes, who
was so disturbed by her views that, upon land-
ing, he hurried to the authorities to report her
lack of orthodoxy. His accusations against
Mrs. Hutchinson had enough weight with the
church to prevent her immediate admission to
membership. Her husband was accepted but
she was kept waiting for some time.

In a realm very different from that of
theological discussion she began to attract notice almost immediately. Her many acts of
simple kindness endeared her to the women of
the colony. Whenever there was sickness she
gave of her time and her sympathy until she
became greatly beloved among her own sex.
Her mind was full of her religious convictions,
and so it was but natural that she should speak
of them to the sick whom she was tending. It
is easy to picture her sitting beside the bed of

a young mother and talking eloquently of the
spirit of God in our hearts, while she cared for
the baby which she had just helped bring into
the world. It is easy to understand, too, how
the young mother would eagerly drink in what
she had to say—because it was less stern and
severe than the preachings which she heard at
the bare meeting house of the town.

This pleasant picture of Mrs. Hutchinson,
the kind friend and neighbor, is very different
from the one which her enemies painted.
Thomas Welde describes her as a woman "of
haughty and fierce carriage, of nimble wit and
active spirit and a very voluble tongue, more
bold than a man though in understanding and
judgment inferior to many women." Since it
is hard to imagine a woman of haughty and
fierce carriage caring so tenderly for the weak
and helpless, it is well to remember in reading
this description that it was written by a man
who bitterly hated the woman of whom he
wrote. That no description of her physical
personality has come down to us is a strange
fact. It would seem as if she could not have
been a woman of any distinctive outward
beauty or physical charm, or some hint of this
attractiveness would have crept into the records of her life. Yet history tells us that the
women of her family had for years been noted
for their exceptional comeliness. Unfortunately the contemporary accounts of her are
for the most part the work of her enemies.
Governor Winthrop, however, who would be a

fairer antagonist than Welde, describes her as having a bold spirit and ready wit. There must have been a lovable side to Anne Hutchinson for it is said that no one who was once her friend ever became her enemy. Even Cotton, who repudiated her teachings, remained friendly to her.

These doctrines and opinions which Mrs. Hutchinson expressed to her women friends—and later to both sexes—spread very rapidly. The women began to meet at her house, and before the authorities realized what was happening, some eighty or one hundred women were gathering every week to discuss and uphold the doctrines of antinomianism, and their beliefs had converted practically the whole Boston Church.

In order to understand the events which followed it is necessary to consider two things—first, the social situation in Boston in 1637 and second, the doctrine of antinomianism.

It was just seventeen years since the Pilgrim Fathers had landed in America. The spirit of desperate sincerity and seriousness which they brought with them to the new country was still strong in the breasts of the colonists of New England. Their lives were full of privation and hardship and they had little time for anything but work and prayer. Religion was the food and comfort of their souls—"the food which ate up all the attachments and remembrances of home, all their regrets at leaving it, very many if not all of their baser passions."

They had little time for relaxation or amusement. The few hours left them after their daily labor were given to prayer or religious discussions. The Bible was about their only literature. There were no libraries, no newspapers, no daily mail, no clubs, no gatherings merely social. All the people were prophets. The greatest stress was laid upon merely formal observances. The church services were hours long. People went about with solemn faces, and sanctimonious air, and filled their conversation with scriptural phrases. Everywhere it was the letter of the law which was emphasized. In such an atmosphere as this the gatherings at Mrs. Hutchinson's home were oases in the desert to women who "kept silence in the churches" and were barred from the discussional gatherings. They were the only social events of the season and as such they became exceedingly popular.

And now as to what Mrs. Hutchinson discussed with these women—the opinions which she advanced.

Antinomianism was no new doctrine. It had been preached in Judea, in Germany, in England. In its essence it was merely opposition to legalism; Christ, not Moses; the spirit, not the letter. The Antinomians spoke of this choice as the "covenant of grace," as opposed to that of works. They said: "Just because you observe the letter of the law is no proof that you are good in your heart—your good works may be mere outward show. The vital thing is to secure a state of heart which will make evidence of holiness." They did not advise the discontinuance of good works, but warned against making clean merely the outside of the platter.

Their own idea was that of the Master who denounced the scribes and Pharisees for their observances which were merely outward. Unfortunately, however, it was perverted to mean "there is no necessity for good works—the true believer can do nothing that is sinful." The result of this perversion was, in Europe, a series of outrages committed in the name of religion. The Massachusetts people knew of these and felt that they must carefully guard against any such excesses. The colonists had good reason to be forehanded; they had been reported as having swarmed to America to find elbow room for fanaticism, and since exaggerated accounts of the disorder were at once sent back to England, every disturbance endangered their charter. Hence they were especially loath to have the doctrines of Antinomianism taught in their midst, but they did not realize its alarming spread until practically all the Boston Church, including Governor Vane himself, had come under the "covenant of grace—not of works," and were the devoted followers and warm supporters of Mrs. Hutchinson.

It is difficult for the twentieth century reader to understand the situation in Boston at this time. It must be remembered that politics and

religion were so closely related that one could
not be affected without touching the other.

The meetings at Mrs. Hutchinson's which
had originally been devoted to emphasizing
what Mr. Cotton was preaching—the "covenant of grace"—gradually began to be devoted
largely to the criticism of the sermons of every
other minister in the colony. The assertion
was that they were preaching a covenant of
works. Now this accusation was stinging; the
Puritans had revolted from the Church of England because outward observances had to a
large measure replaced spirituality. So to be
accused of setting up a new covenant of works
was irritating in the extreme. Unfortunately
about this time Mrs. Hutchinson began to lose
her grip upon herself and upon good sense.
She and her followers manifested more and
more the "holier than thou" attitude.

They attended the services of first one
church and then another for the sole purpose
of criticising the sermons. There came to be
certain pastors under whom they refused to
sit. Whenever Pastor Wilson preached, Mrs.
Hutchinson and her followers left the meeting
house. They frequently sent letters to clergymen whom they accused of being under the
covenant of works.

After a while the followers of Mrs. Hutchinson began to distort her teachings, just as
Antinomianism had been distorted in Europe.
In America, however, few excesses resulted
from this perversion. They declared that good

works were unnecessary to those who were under the covenant of grace—that is to those who
were certain of the spirit of God in their hearts.
Then they went so far as to say that good
works were a mark of Cain; upright men,
especially all the ministers except Wheelright
and Cotton, simply because of their uprightness
fell under the suspicion of lack of grace.   An
example of the perversion of Mrs. Hutchinson's
doctrine is in Captain Underhill.   He averred
that he had ''lain under a spirit of bondage in
a legal way five years and could get no assurance until at length as he was taking a pipe
of tobacco the spirit sent him an absolute promise of free grace with such assurance and joy
as he never since doubted of his good estate;
neither should he though he should fall into
sin.''   And resting serenely on this assurance
of grace, the captain continued to indulge in
the grossest immoralities!   It is in no way fair
to blame Mrs. Hutchinson for these excesses or
distortions.   She was powerless to control
them, and she herself lived always an upright
life—full of good works.   Yet it is clear that
the doctrine of covenant by grace and not by
works was one which gave dangerous loopholes
to the would-be sinner and enormous possibilities to the hair-splitting brethren.   The Biblical warning, ''Faith without works is dead,''
seems never to have loomed into the vision of
our Bible-reading forefathers of that day.   No
one thought of joining the two rival covenants
to form a complete whole, and so the strife

grew more and more bitter. Children playing
together asked each other: ''Is your father under a covenant of grace or a covenant of
works?''; the assessments of rates and the dis-
tribution of town lots were affected by the same
question, and affairs reached a climax when the
military forces of the colony mustered for the
campaign against the Pequots were ready to
shirk the service because they suspected their
chaplain of being under a covenant of works!
The rival forces were divided into two distinct
groups. On the one side was Mrs. Hutchinson,
Wheelright, Vane and Cotton—although he deserted them toward the end of the struggle—;
on the other, Winthrop and every minister in
the colony outside of Boston. Poor souls,
their lives had been made miserable for them;
their uprightness had been made a subject of
suspicion, their orthodoxy and soundness had
been challenged and their congregations had
been diminished.

Finally they met, six hundred and thirty-
seven of them, and agreed to put all lectures
aside for three weeks until the controversy
should be settled. They held a synod, at which
they first attacked Mr. Wheelright on the
charge of heresy. The assembled ministers
found him guilty as he denied nothing—only
affirmed his views the more stoutly. When the
decision of the synod was made public a storm
of dissent went up and a protest against this
judgment was sent to the Great and General
Court. The Court would not receive it. As

Wheelright refused to retract anything he had said, he was arrested. He had been convicted of heresy—that most serious of all offenses in this church-state—and there was no escape from the logical consequence, punishment by its civil arm. Accordingly he was convicted. He immediately appealed to King Charles but his appeal was ignored. Sentence was, however, suspended until the next session of the General Court when it was ordered enforced and Wheelright was driven out of the Colony.

The Court had put its hand to the plow and would not turn back. What was heresy and treason in the preacher Wheelright was no less in Mrs. Hutchinson. She was regarded as the instigator of the whole trouble. The next step was to eject Vane from the governorship and substitute Winthrop. Vane sailed for England and the report spread that he intended to obtain help for Mrs. Hutchinson at the English Court. Almost to a man her own church organization was staunchly supporting Mrs. Hutchinson but feeling ran higher and higher until at last she was called for trial.

She was tried before the Great and General Court of Massachusetts, the dignified legislative body of the commonwealth, which has retained its formal name to this day. It was no ordinary court of law—it was an assembly of delegate freemen from all Massachusetts Bay Colony. From the decisions of this Court there was no appeal except to the king across the water and, as in the Wheelright case, such appeal was not always allowed. There were other magistrates, men of local authority, but the Great and General Court was the embodied will of the Puritan Colony. To this tribunal was Mrs. Hutchinson summoned.

The identity of Church and State was absolute. There were no freemen except church members, no tests of citizenship except adherence to the creed. It was not a question of Church *and* State; the Church *was* the State; literally as well as figuratively violence to the creed was treason to the State. Heresy and sedition were synonymous. Therefore when 'Anne Hutchinson taught her heresies, if heresies they were, she offended the State and to the State she must answer. It was not Anne Hutchinson, however, who was on trial. It was religious freedom that stood before the bar. With Roger Williams and the Quakers, she answered in her person for the spirit of toleration and charity in creed and doctrine. But with them she suffered. Not yet was Massachusetts ready for the larger faith of later years.

All the magistrates and assistants of the upper house took part in the trial. Endicott was there and Bradstreet, Harlakenden, Stoughton and Nowell, with Governor Winthrop in the chair. And there, too, was every clergyman in the colony, smarting under the implications which Mrs. Hutchinson had placed upon him. Cotton by now had gone over to the enemy, though he later defended Mrs.

Hutchinson in court. Before this august body this woman of unchallenged piety and of high excellence of character was held to account, for maintaining certain theological opinions. She was kept standing until her evident bodily infirmity obtained the privilege of sitting. Governor Winthrop, although he could not accuse her of a single offense which would subject her to court punishment, heaped censures upon her. She had "defamed ministers," had "maintained meetings at her house not comely in the sight of God nor fitting for her sex;" "though the synod had denounced them she had persisted in holding them." After this denunciation Mrs. Hutchinson quietly replied:

"I am called here to answer before you, but I hear no things to my charge."

Governor: "I have told you some already and more I can tell you."

Mrs. Hutchinson: "Name one, sir."

Governor: "Have I not named some already?"

Mrs. Hutchinson: "What have I said or done?"

Then she was accused of having defamed the characters of the clergymen.

Throughout the trial Mrs. Hutchinson showed herself keen and quick, well poised and utterly fearless. The accusers vaguely wandered on: "They had heard that she had said," "it was reported that this was so." Invariably she would answer, "I pray, sir, prove it that I said they preached nothing but a covenant of

works," and they had no proof. Apparently
the greater part of the controversy rested on
misinterpretations of the opinions of Mrs. Hutchinson. That she had privately made impulsive criticisms of some of the clergymen is
doubtless true, but that she had publicly defamed their lives, they could not prove. To
every statement which they made came back
that steady "Prove this then, sir, that you say
I did."

When the first group of charges fell because
of lack of definite proof, Mrs. Hutchinson with
saneness and courage boldly anticipated any
further accusations by deliberately restating
and defending her obnoxious doctrines. Possibly she hoped by shifting the attack to confuse her enemies. Possibly she hoped in the
more purely theological aspects of the controversy to enlist new friends. Possibly she
foresaw the certain result and rushed to meet
it. At any rate she made no secret of her
tenets and boldly defended them.

She claimed to have communion directly with
God and not necessarily through the Scriptures.
Blasphemy! She claimed to have revelations
and defended them. She spoke of those which
had led her to accept Cotton and Wheelright as
the true ministers of God, and to follow them
to America, saying that she would be delivered
now from all danger and risk by God as was
Daniel in the lion's den. The glowing style of
her language and the boldness of her address
led one of the ministers to suggest that she was

rather an antitype of the lions than of Daniel. She said in part: "I bless the Lord who hath let me see which was the clear ministry and which was the wrong. Since that time I confess I have been more choice and he hath led me to distinguish between the voice of my beloved and the voice of Moses, the voice of John the Baptist and the voice of anti-Christ, for all those voices are spoken of in Scripture. Now if you do condemn me for speaking what in my conscience I know to be truth, I must commit myself unto the Lord."

Mr. Nowell: "How do you know that that was the spirit?"

Mrs. Hutchinson: "How did Abraham know that it was God that bid him offer his son, being a breach of the sixth commandment."

Deputy Governor: "By an immediate voice."

Mrs. Hutchinson: "So to me by an immediate revelation!"

Deputy Governor: "How! An immediate revelation!"

Mrs. Hutchinson: "By the voice of His own spirit to my soul." "But now having seen Him which is invisible, I fear not what man can do to me."

Governor Winthrop: "Daniel was delivered by a miracle; do you think to be delivered so too?"

Mrs. Hutchinson: "I do here speak it before the Court. I look that the Lord should deliver me by His providence."

After a long trial, which makes tiresome enough reading, and which seems to us an absurd haggling over definitions and terms, the governor declared:

"The groundwork of her revelations is the immediate revelation of the spirit and not by the ministry of the word, and that is the means by which she hath abused the country that they should look for revelations and not turn to the ministry of the word."

The Court replied: "We all consent with you."

Governor: "Ey! it is most desperate enthusiasm in the world for nothing but a word comes to her mind and then an application is made which is nothing to the purpose and this is her revelations when it is impossible but that the word and the spirit should speak the same thing. The Court hath already declared themselves satisfied concerning the things you hear concerning the troublesomeness of her spirit and the danger of her course amongst us, which is not to be suffered. Therefore, if it is the mind of the Court that she shall be banished out of our liberties and imprisoned till she be sent away, let them raise their hands."

All but three hands went up.

"Those that are contrary minded hold up yours."

Only Mr. Coddington and Mr. Colburn responded. They maintained, not that the defendant was in the right, but that the Court had no jurisdiction over her offense.

Governor: "Mrs. Hutchinson, the sentence of the Court you hear is that you are banished from out of our jurisdiction as being a woman not fit for our society and are to be imprisoned till the Court shall send you away."

Mrs. Hutchinson: "I desire to know wherefore I am banished."

Governor: "Say no more. The Court knows wherefore and is satisfied."

The trial was no trial, but rather a mockery of justice. The witnesses in her behalf were browbeaten and silenced in disregard of all fairness, and she herself was badgered and insulted. It was a bare-faced inquisitorial proceeding.

After this parody on justice was ended, Mrs. Hutchinson was imprisoned in the house of Welde's brother, Joseph, in Roxbury, where she was allowed to see only her most intimate friends. Here she was constantly importuned by the zealous minister, Welde, to recant her false views. During her imprisonment she was very melancholy but became more of an oracle than ever.

In the spring the church at Boston drew up a list of heretical opinions which they claimed she held and confronted her with them. She listened patiently and answered each accusation with a modest and pertinent reply, but refused to recant. She was solemnly admonished by the church, and recalled for a second examination. By now she was wearied by this constant nagging. Some things she recanted

—and she acknowledged faults of temper, of speech and of conduct. She also owned that her revelations in court were rash and groundless and she desired the prayers of the church in her behalf. Yet she maintained that she had the liberty to keep her own convictions. These concessions she placed in writing, but the church decided that they were not direct enough, and were subject to misinterpretations. The elders accused her of lying; she denied the accusations. In spite of her denial the sentence of excommunication was pronounced against her:

"Therefore, in the name of the Lord Jesus Christ and in the name of the Church, I do not only pronounce you worthy to be cast out but I do cast you out; and in the name of Christ I do deliver you up to Satan that you may learn no more to blaspheme, to seduce, and to lie, and I do account you from this time forth to be a heathen and a publican and so to be held of all the brethren and sisters of this congregation and of others; therefore, I command you in the name of Christ Jesus and of this church as a leper to withdraw yourself out of the congregation."

When, in obedience to his command, Anne Hutchinson—the outcast—moved through the awe-struck throng, her devoted friend and follower, Mary Dyer, rose and walked by her side and the two passed out together. As they went forth one standing at the meeting-house door said to Mrs. Hutchinson:

"The Lord sanctify this unto you."

"The Lord judgeth not as man judgeth,"
she replied. "Better to be cast out of the
church than to deny Christ."

Our forefathers doubtless believed this
odious act of persecution to be a political necessity. Moreover, Mrs. Hutchinson had probably tried their patience with her methods of
procedure. Excuse, however, is scant.

Mrs. Hutchinson sought refuge in Rhode Island where the colonists were assured of freedom of religious thought. Her family, with
the exception of her married son, accompanied
her, and she continued to exhort and teach even
in her new home. The ministers of New England could not leave her at peace, but sent
delegates to remonstrate once again with her.
It seems that these "godly" men took the occasion to pry into her family life for we read
that her husband defended her as a "dear
saint" and "servant of God." The testimony
of the one who lived closest to her ought to be
worth more than that of her antagonists.

In 1642 this faithful companion died. Soon
after his death, Mrs. Hutchinson left Rhode
Island and went to Long Island, probably to
Pelham Neck on the border of what is now
called Hutchinson River.

For a woman of such rare mental powers
and gentle descent as Anne Hutchinson to have
left the civilized society of Rhode Island to
bury herself and her family in the wilderness,
must have required remarkable elevation of

purpose and physical daring. But among men she had met with bitter persecution and injustice and it is quite probable that she was glad to leave this all behind her, and that she looked forward to years of quiet communion with the God who had been so constantly in her thoughts.

Scarcely were they settled in their new home when Governor Kieft by his treachery and inhumanity aroused the fury of the native Indians. Whereupon they resolved to exterminate the Dutch and all connected with them. An army of fifteen hundred warriors swept over Long Island. Everywhere was seen the blaze of bonfires, and the war whoops of the savages sent terror to the hearts of the settlers. One of these hideous mornings, so the account runs, an Indian came to the door of Mrs. Hutchinson's log cabin, professing friendship, but when he discovered the defenseless condition of the household he returned and butchered all but the youngest daughter, Susan, who was taken prisoner and remained in captivity four years. When she was finally released she knew no language but the Indian.

The news of Mrs. Hutchinson's death was received in New England as an evidence of her guilt. It was taken for granted that God was punishing her, and doubtless many ministers made her the subject of that week's sermons. Even previously a superstition, which to the modern mind is almost inconceivable, began to attach significance to every misfortune which

befell the followers of Mrs. Hutchinson. A
poor barber, called hastily to perform a den-
tist's office, becomes bewildered in a storm of
snow between Roxbury and Boston and is
frozen to death. Presently it is remembered
that he had been a theological adherent of Mrs.
Hutchinson.

Welde makes note of her death and adds: "I
never heard that the Indians in those parts did
ever before this commit the like outrage upon
any one family or families and therefore God's
hand is the more apparently seen herein to put
this wofull woman to her and those belonging
to her an unheard of heavie example of their
cruelty above all others."

It is difficult to obtain an unprejudiced judgment of Anne Hutchinson. She seems to have
been either despised or adored. Pictures given
by her enemies have already been presented.
Eugene Lawrence, an ardent admirer, says:
"Anne Hutchinson had so delicate a spiritual
organization that the future world was ever
more real to her than the present—wealth, lux-
ury, ease had for her no charm. She lived in
the universe rather than in the world. The
common joys of life, domestic ease, refined society and material splendor, she cast aside with
disdain. Truth was fairer to her than dia-
monds and liberty of speech and thought to
luxurious chambers and downy rest. . . .
The lonely hut by Hutchinson River was her
palace and her temple rather than the comfortable dwelling she possessed in Massachusetts

Bay. . . . Her life was as spotless as her doctrines—she was an example of the purity she taught. The faithful looked upon her with wonder, delight, and love. An angel seemed to have descended upon them—a spotless spirit was once more found upon the earth."

This eulogy is of course exaggerated. She herself acknowledges faults of temper and of speech, but the few vital facts which have come down prove that she was fired with enthusiasm for God, and that she courageously and unceasingly, if perhaps frantically and unwisely, poured out the truths which were in her heart. They also prove that her life was full of good deeds. Thus in her own life, she combined the "covenant of grace" and the "covenant of works." For these reasons, though the questions she raised have ceased to interest, she is truly a heroine of religion.

CHAPTER II

SUSANNAH WESLEY

BY WILLIAM HORTON FOSTER

ONE day in 1701, the year before the death of William Third of England, Samuel Wesley, rector of Epworth parish, in his domestic worship, voiced his customary prayer for the king. For thirteen years this had been his daily habit, and he had never noticed until this morning that Susannah, his wife, did not supply the dutiful "Amen!" which responded to every other petition. When he remonstrated with her somewhat tartly for this breach of churchly decorum, he learned to his surprise that she had never said "Amen!" to that prayer and that she never would. Church-woman as she was, defender of Protestantism as was William of Orange, she had never regarded him as the rightful monarch and she would never recognize him as king.

The complacent rector could hardly believe his ears. He remembered the year of the silent revolution which had placed William and Mary upon the throne. He remembered that day in the same year which had marked his marriage with the beautiful Susannah Annesley. All his married life until now had run parallel with the

23

reign of the king. To be told that all these
years the wife of his heart had been denying the
very foundations of his political faith, even of
the State itself, was indeed almost beyond belief.

Yet this attitude was significant of Susannah.
For all this time, in the daily intimacy of the
home, she had pursued her even way. If she
could not yield technical allegiance to King William, the point was unimportant, let it pass!
If she could not subscribe to all the details of
her husband's political belief, she could still
glorify the office of wife and mother. Careless
of non-essentials, she knew the eternal realities.
For thirteen years she had been indifferent to
the determination of the point of doctrine involved in William's crowning; all these years
she had been enacting the rôle of wife and
mother—the maker of a home.

For over forty years longer she continued the
chief actor in this drama—of Epworth Parish
it might well be called—and without her character, the play would never have been enacted.
Here there is a touch of comedy, there a bit
of melodrama, occasionally a hint of farce; but
always dominant and overwhelming, the tragedy of the smothering commonplace. And out
of this drama, of which Susannah Wesley was
the dominating figure, grew a new religious
faith that in all the Anglo-Saxon world revital-
ized religion.

January 20, 1669, in Spital Yard, a narrow
court in London, was born Susannah Annesley,

SUSANNAH WESLEY

the youngest of twenty-five children. July 23, 1742, in an abandoned London gun foundry, converted into a combination dwelling and meeting house for her preacher son John, Susannah Wesley died. The span of her life witnessed a new quickening of religious thought, the culmination of the renaissance and the reformation which had gone before. It was possibly greater than either, for it was a renaissance *of* the reformation; it was a new birth of the spiritual life of England. In this movement two names stand conspicuous, the two Wesleys—John, the organizer and founder, and Charles, the pious minstrel of the new life. What these two teachers of the new ideas of spiritual equality were, they owed directly and specifically to the counsels and training of their mother. She was not only the mother of the Wesleys but the mother of Methodism.

In her girlhood, Susannah witnessed the dying embers of a fire of persecution of the nonconformists which had burned as steadily if not so fiercely as any which had gone before. The "Act of Uniformity," of 1662, required every clergyman to declare his "unfeigned assent to all and everything contained and prescribed in the Book of Common Prayer." On St. Bartholomew's day, when the act went into effect, over two thousand ministers bade farewell to their weeping congregations. Exemplary in their lives, educated and eloquent, they were "guilty of no crime, save that they did not dare to worship God according to other men's con-

sciences!'' They were forbidden to live within
five miles of any place where they had
preached; they were forbidden to teach any
school, public or private. Nor were they the
only sufferers. Worshipers who attended any
other than the established form or even received
the dissenting ministers in their homes were
heavily fined or imprisoned or transported.
The enforcement of the acts was committed to
the king's soldiery; the prisons and even the
gallows were crowded with those who took counsel alone with their conscience. Over five thousand, it is said, died in prison. The other St.
Bartholomew's day exacted scarcely a heavier
toll.

In such an England, was Susannah Annesley
born. To such steadfastness and courage was
she as well as her future husband, Samuel Wesley, an heir. For not only was Samuel Annesley, her father, driven by the Act from the
wealthy living of St. Giles in London, but Samuel Wesley's father, John Westley—Samuel
was the first to spell his name without the
t—was forced to leave the parish of Whitchurch, a little village of Dorsetshire. The dignified London rector only his friends among the
nobility saved from physical violence. Not
more resolute in his convictions but more militant in his faith, John Westley, however, knew
no peace after the fateful twenty-third of
August. He was driven from his lowly pulpit
at Whitchurch; successive orders forced him
from village to village. His body was too frail

long to withstand this grim religious warfare, and when he was but a young man he died. His father, Bartholomew, much more violent in speech and action than his son, easily withstood the fierce struggle brought about by persecution, but was crushed by John's death and survived him only a short time.

Such was the heritage which met and blended in the lives of Susannah Annesley and Samuel Wesley. Yet strangely enough the two lines of descent were apparently reversed. Samuel Annesley seems to have been reproduced in Samuel Wesley, while all the grim steadfastness of the Westleys—father and son—seems to have been transmuted into a still finer metal in the resolute soul of Susannah.

In November, 1662, a few months after his father John Westley had been ejected from Whitchurch, Samuel Wesley was born. Because of the death of his father before the lad was ready for the university, dissenting friends cared for his education. For five years, he met in daily intimacy the best men of the new creed. Always ready of wit and agile in mind, he had a trick for rhyme and lampoon; his varied talents he utilized, not always too delicately, in the controversial literature of the day. His counselors regarded him as one of the most hopeful of the future ministers of their faith although he had no particularly deep experiences of his own and was content passively to take his theology with his instruction from his father's friends.

After five years or so, however, there was a
silent revolution in Samuel Wesley's life as
vital to him as was the revolution of 1688 to the
English nation. The causes of this complete
overturn of his religious beliefs are somewhat
obscure, but it is certain that the young girl,
afterwards his wife, profoundly influenced him.
After the penalties of the Act of Uniformity
had been suspended in 1672, Dr. Annesley took
the ministry of a dissenting church in London.
His hospitable door welcomed all who knocked,
and they were many; for not only was the good
doctor genial and hearty but his flock numbered
a full score of attractive daughters. Young
Samuel was a favorite guest. He came and
came again, perhaps because he found the
clergyman's conversation edifying or perhaps
because the beautiful Susannah was a delightful
companion. One constant topic of conversation
was the all-absorbing question of religious conformity. Together they came to doubt the
righteousness of the dissension, and together
they abandoned the creed of their fathers and
returned to the church of authority.

When the young dissenter came to his new
beliefs, he allowed no time for his courage to
ooze away. To avoid the reproaches of his
relatives and friends, he arose early one August
morning, and trudged afoot to Oxford there to
prepare for the regular ministry. His leaving
was not dishonorable, however; from a legacy
he repaid the loans of his father's friends and
of necessity entered Exeter College as a servi-

tor with but a few shillings in his pocket.
Formerly his life had been comfortable but now
to his lot fell the blacking of boots, the serving
of meals and the menial services of a valet.
With such work he earned his keep and, aided
by his literary labors, he managed to exist, so
well, in fact, that five years later when he took
his final degree he was eight pounds richer than
when he entered. He hastened at once to London, was ordained a deacon and, later, priest.
The year 1688 or possibly 1689, saw him settled
as a curate, and married to his young girl friend
Susannah, now just turned eighteen.

While her lover was doing the work of a servant in Oxford, Susannah was growing up
among cultured companions. In all minds, ecclesiastical discussions held first place. "Before I was full thirteen," Susannah says, "I
had drawn up an account of the whole transac-
tion, under which I had included the main of
the controversy between them [the dissenters]
and the Established Church, as far as it had
come to my knowledge." She was "early ini-
tiated and instructed in the first principles of
the Christian religion," and had a "good example in parents, and in several of the family."
In girlhood she "received from the heart the
form of doctrine" from her father's lips.
When asked by one of her children for a rule
as to diversions she replied that her own rule
as a girl was never to spend more time per day
in worldly pleasures than she was willing to
spend in private devotions.

With all her interest in religious dogma, however, Susannah was a normal, hearty English
girl. All twenty of the Annesley girls were
fun-loving and comely. Her sister Judith was
painted by Sir Peter Lely, and Elizabeth's
charm of face and figure have been minutely
told. Yet one who knew them well says:
"Beautiful as Miss Elizabeth Annesley appears, she was far from being as beautiful as
Mrs. Wesley." Moreover, Susannah early
showed that all-embracing motherliness that
later enabled her to sustain her husband and
family under the most trying circumstances and
to build all three of her clergyman-sons into
greatness. In a letter she says: "What then
is love? or how shall we describe its strange
mysterious essence? It is—I do not know
what! A powerful something! Source of our
joy and grief! Felt and experienced by every
one, and yet unknown to all! Nor shall we ever
comprehend what it is, till we are united to our
First Principle, and there read its wondrous
nature in the clear mirror of uncreated Love;
till which time it is best to rest satisfied with
such apprehensions of its essence as we can col-
lect from our observations of its effects and
properties; for other knowledge of it in our
present state is too high and too wonderful for
us; neither can we attain unto it." Her own
wife-love and mother-love accomplished the
wonder of reawakening the religious life of the
English speaking people because, built upon the
foundation of a trained mind and infinite pa-

tience, it was all-embracing and united to the
great "First Principle."

For two years after the marriage, the young
curate and his bride lived in lodgings in London. Here the first child, Samuel, was born.
Mrs. Wesley managed the small income so well
that the family kept out of debt. As an author
the young husband more than fulfilled the
promise of his earlier years; he was long the
chief contributor to the *Athenian Gazette* which
numbered among its writers many of the first
men of the nation—DeFoe and Swift among
others. Because he added both to his reputation and his income, he fixed upon himself the
writing habit from which he never recovered!
More unfortunately still, he never overcame his
passion for versifying; upon the slightest occasion he fell into fluent rhyme.

His preliminary service as a curate in London lasted until 1690 when he received the rectory of South Ormsby, a little village in Lincolnshire. This first preferment began a life-long
struggle for advancement. A rector had no
way of bettering his condition except to make
friends with the members of the nobility who
had the rectorates as absolute gifts. Samuel
Wesley's was no mean spirit but he joined with
the rest in soliciting the favor of his superiors
in rank. For forty years he was hoping against
hope that My Lord This or My Lady That would
help him to a more lucrative parish. Poems
were his chief method of approach, and as regu-

larly as a new poem appeared he hopefully
dedicated it to some new patron. Still he
stayed on in his modest rectory, in his own
words "wasting in sighs the uncomfortable
day." His meter, however, is no more accurate
than the fact, for he wasted no time in sighs
or otherwise. He did his daily task of admoni-
tion and counsel. Indeed his sense of duty was
so rigid that it mattered little to him upon whom
the earned reproof fell. This thorough-going
honesty always stood in the way of his material
progress. The rectorate of South Ormsby he
lost because he would not wink at the vices of
the man who had the gift of the living. At another time, he condemned a wealthy offender to
stand for three successive Sabbaths on the damp
mud floor in the center of the church, without
shoes or stockings, bareheaded, wrapped in a
white sheet, doing penance. A poorer par-
ishioner who had been guilty of the same offense he let off with a fine and then paid the
fine himself.

For seven years the family lived in South
Ormsby. The church itself was attractive
enough but the rectory "a mean hut composed
of reeds and clay." Here there were fifty
pounds a year to live upon "and one child additional per annum." Yet no one complained.
Each newcomer was welcomed, the thrifty wife
made a little food fill many mouths, and the
rector wrote poems and pamphlets more busily
than ever. His "Life of Christ," a metrical
work of some nine thousand lines, a mingled

work of genius and dullness, helped keep the
wolf from the door.

In all these years, as well as the years that
were to follow, his wife had need of all her
thrift. Her life from marriage to death is a
constant struggle against weakness and poverty. One disaster followed another so drearily
that a less thoroughly equipped woman would
soon have despaired. The hourly tragedy of
the lack of food and clothing, the burden of an
ever increasing family of children—her nineteen were all born within a period of twenty
years—wrecked neither her courage nor her
resourcefulness. Her meager income rivals
the widow's cruse of oil. Possibly a later inspired historian will see the daily food afforded
Susannah as clearly given from God as was the
oil of the widow of Zarephath.

This courage is dominant throughout her life.
She never gave up; she never yielded even to
actual disease. She did the work to be done, no
matter what her condition of body or mind.
Her son John wrote long afterward of the calm
serenity with which his mother "transacted
business, wrote letters, and conversed, surrounded by her thirteen children." She was a
quietly practical woman who, having much to do,
found time to do everything by dint of methodi-
cal industry. Yet while she was ordering her
kitchen, she was training her children. Their
times of going to rest, rising in the morning,
dressing, eating, learning, and exercising, she
managed by rule, which was never suffered to

be broken, unless in case of sickness. From the
fifth year of Samuel's life to the completion of
the home education of Kezia, her nineteenth
and last child, she enforced a daily routine
which made the home an actual school. Six
hours a day for twenty years, she taught her
children and taught them so well that they
were all really educated. They were brought
to a "regular course of sleeping" by laying
them in their cradle awake, rocking them to
sleep, and constantly rocking them until they
awakened. "When turned a year old, they were
taught to fear the rod, and to cry softly, by
which means they escaped abundance of correction which they might otherwise have had."
"As soon as they were grown pretty strong,
they were confined to three meals a day."
They were allowed to eat and drink as much as
they would, but not to call for anything. "If
they wanted aught they whispered to the maid
who attended them who came and spoke to me."
"If they asked aught of the servants in the
kitchen they were certainly beat, and the servants severely reprimanded."

Her system of moral instruction was equally
definite. "I take such a proportion of time,"
she writes, "as I can best spare every night to
discourse with each child by itself, on something
that relates to its principal concerns. On Mon-
day, I talk with Molly; on Tuesday, with Hetty;
Wednesday, with Nancy; Thursday, with
Jacky; Friday, with Patty; Saturday, with

Charles; and with Emilia and Sukey together on Sunday.''

To form their minds aright, she considered her first task to be to ''conquer their will and bring them to an obedient temper. To inform the understanding is a work of time, and must with children proceed by slow degrees as they are able to bear it; but the subjecting the will is a thing that must be done at once and the sooner the better.''

In the success of her home school, patience was the chief ingredient. When the rector once visited the schoolroom, he observed his school-mistress wife repeat one statement to one of her children twenty times.

''I wonder at your patience; you have told that child twenty times the same thing.''

''If I had satisfied myself by mentioning it only nineteen times, I should have lost all my labor,'' she replied. ''It was the twentieth time that crowned it.''

Notwithstanding both system and patience, there were difficulties in the ordering of the school-household. Jacky in particular was stubborn. Before assenting to anything, he would insist that it be reasoned out to his satisfaction. Charles, less than five years younger, was frail from his birth; but once fairly started into boyhood, his lively daring caused his mother endless anxiety for both his physical and spiritual well-being. The thought of to-day does not agree to all of her pedagogic pre-

cepts but it does credit her thoroughness, her
conscientiousness, and above all, her devotion
to her ideals of duty. Although many of her
theories were harsh they were softened in practice. Each child from Samuel to Kezia accorded her a devotion that could not have been
given her had she not been essentially gentle
in soul. A rivalry existed among the daughters
as to who was the mother's favorite, and to
Martha was generally given that honor. She
replied: "What my sisters call partiality was
what they might all have enjoyed if they had
wished it; which was permission to sit in my
mother's chamber when discouraged, to listen
to her conversation with others and to hear her
remarks on things and books out of school
hours."

Mrs. Wesley's education of her children was
not a purely juvenile task, undertaken prepara-
tory to the work of the schoolmaster who might
later succeed her. She conceived her duty toward each child as stretching from birth until
death. With constant counsel, she followed her
sons' courses through college and into the ministry. Her advice was not simply on questions
of personal conduct but on questions arising out
of their studies and work. To John she wrote
while he was at Oxford: "Dear Jacky:—I was
glad to hear you got safe to Oxford, and would
have told you so sooner had I been at liberty
from pain of body, and other severer trials not
convenient to mention. . . . Our nature is frail;
our passions strong; our wills biased; and our

security, generally speaking, consists much more certainly in avoiding great temptations than in conquering them. . . . Our Lord directed his disciples when they were persecuted in one city to flee into another; and they who refuse to do it when it is in their power, lead themselves into temptation and tempt God.'' Her devotion took not the form alone of endearments—although those intimate touches abound —but a brooding watchfulness that never relaxed. In a letter to Susannah her daughter she starts thus: ''Dear Sukey,—Since our misfortunes have separated us from each other, and we can no longer enjoy the opportunities we once had of conversing together, I can no other way discharge the duty of a parent, or comply with my inclination of doing you all the good I can, but by writing. You know very well how I love you. I love your body; and do earnestly beseech almighty God to bless it with health and all things necessary for its comfort and support in this world.''

She had, indeed, a passion for motherhood! The motherhood which held the world's first born babe in its arms and voiced the cry which has sung in every other mother's heart, ''I have gotten me a man child from the Lord!'' was hers. The motherhood which keeps all these things and ponders them in her heart, was hers. The universal motherhood which runs from age to age, was hers. To Eve and Mary and in like degree to every mother everywhere came the divinest thing ever revealed—motherhood. And in Susannah Wesley it shone bright. It dedicated to the service of God her firstborn before he had seen the light. It took her life and offered it a daily recurring sacrifice to the prosaic duties of the home.

While the Wesleys lived at South Ormsby, Dr. Annesley, the father of Mrs. Wesley, died. Her feeling toward him was one of peculiar devotion and there was an intimacy in their relationship which not even her change of belief had affected. Her intense affection survived his death with scarcely diminished ardor. As long as she lived, he had to her mind but changed his outward form, and she was fully persuaded that he was constantly near her and conversing with her. This deep sense of an almost literal "communion of saints" she transmitted to her sons, and John and Charles both repeatedly asserted their belief in the nearness of the departed.

This feeling was perhaps strengthened by certain peculiar happenings in the rectory at Epworth, the Wesleys' later home. For years they heard mysterious noises and weird rappings which became so frequent that the ghostly visitant assumed in the household a place secure if not welcome and answered to the name Old Jeffrey given him by the children. He seemed to be attached to certain of the household rather than to others and was particularly devoted to Mrs. Wesley. The four girls, Emilia, Susannah, Mehetabel, and Anne, were the first in the family who observed Jeffrey's attentions, and when they reported them to their parents, the father smiled, thinking it all a trick, and the practical mother at once thought of rats. A little later both parents were convinced of the genuineness of the manifestations. None of the rector's incantations worried the ghost but he paid instant obedience to Mrs. Wesley's request not to disturb her from five to six in the morning. To the children Old Jeffrey was a great joke. They enjoyed each new experience and eagerly awaited each new prank of their thoroughly disreputable guest. To the rector Old Jeffrey was a puzzling problem; he was decidedly a Jacobite in politics and expressed a violent antipathy to prayers for the reigning monarch.

Whatever may have been the explanation of Old Jeffrey, the whole family was convinced of his reality. Believing strongly in buried treasure, practical Samuel wrote from school advising digging in the garden at the point where Jeffrey had appeared. John and Charles joined their mother in thinking him to be a comfortable messenger from the dead. In connection with Old Jeffrey, Mrs. Wesley said, "I am rather inclined to think there would be frequent intercourse between good spirits and us, did not our deep lapse into sensuality prevent it." This mysticism colored much of her thought, and in varying forms and degrees gave to John and Charles new points of view which in turn affected their thought and largely influenced the doctrines of the sect they founded.

It was in 1697 that the rectory of Epworth was conferred upon Samuel Wesley, directly from the Crown. It was probably given him at the request of Queen Mary, to whom he had dedicated his metrical *Life of Christ*. The parsonage itself consisted of "five baies, built all of timber and plaister, and covered all with straw thache, the whole building being contrived into three stories, and disposed into seven chief rooms; namely, a kitchinge, a hall, a parlor, a butterie, and three large upper rooms; besydes some others of common use; and also a little garden impailed, between the stone wall and the south." The "home-stall or scite of the parsonage . . ." contained "by estimation, three acres." There "was one barn of six baies, built all of timber and clay walls, and covered with straw thache; and outshotts about it, and free house therebye." Then came "one dovecoate of timber and plaister," covered with the usual "straw thache" and finally one "hempkiln, that hath been useaelie occupied for the parsonage ground, adjoyning upon the south." The living, nominally worth some two hundred pounds a year, would probably have supported the Wesleys in comfort had not the poetical rector tried to farm.

Dr. Wesley's poetry occasionally produced revenue; but the qualities necessary to poetry stood in the way of agricultural success. Other rectors had always rented the clerical lands at Epworth but Dr. Wesley insisted upon cultivating his fields himself. He borrowed the capital necessary for stock and equipment and bravely set out as a gentleman farmer. With a fine flush of poetical enthusiasm he saw a vision of rural peace and comfort, of his spiritual and literary labors set off against a serene background of pleasant fields and bounteous harvests, the fruits of his own honest industry. Though uncomplaining as always, Mrs. Wesley shrank from the prospect. "He is not fit for worldly business," wrote her brother on one occasion. "That I assent to," she replied, "and must own I was mistaken when I did think him fit for it. My own experience hath since convinced me that he is one of those who, our Savior saith, 'are not so wise in their generation as the children of this world.'"

With these rosy hopes but with such sad lack of needed training—he had no knowledge of farming other than the verse-loving student would gain in a London lodging—did Samuel Wesley enter upon his new life at Epworth. The annual interest charge he incurred proved a heavy tax and from his burden of debt he never escaped. The house, in comparison with the one at South Ormsby, was a palace, and life would have been comfortable indeed had the financial stress been a little lighter. Yet the one upon whom the burden fell the heaviest— Susannah Wesley—did her day's work without complaint. In the many privations she endured she saw but the disciplines which made for her spiritual development. Once in her diary she records: "Though man is born to trouble, yet

I believe there is scarce a man to be found upon
earth but, take the whole course of his life, hath
more mercies than afflictions, and much more
pleasure than pain. I am sure it has been so in
my case. . . . And these very sufferings have,
by the blessing of God, been of excellent use, and
proved the most proper means of reclaiming
me from a vain conversation; insomuch that I
cannot say I had better have been without this
affliction, this disease, this loss, want, contempt
or reproach. All my sufferings, by the admir-
able management of Omnipotent Goodness, have
concurred to promote my spiritual and eternal
good. . . . Glory be to Thee, O Lord!"

For over forty years the rectory at Epworth
was her home. It would be a veritable catalogue of ships to recount the regular, almost
daily hardships through which she passed.

"Tell me, Mrs. Wesley," Archbishop Sharp
once asked, "whether you ever really wanted
bread?" "My Lord," she replied, "I will
freely own to your Grace that, strictly speaking, I never did want bread; but I had so
much care to get it before it was eat, and to
pay for it after, as has often made it very un-
pleasant to me; and I think to have bread on
such terms is the next degree of wretchedness
to having none at all." In 1701 when Susannah and the rector pooled their funds to send
for coals, all they could muster was five shillings. Twenty-five years later they had but
five pounds for the family support from May-
day until after harvest. Emilia, the oldest

daughter, her great comfort, knew better than anyone else what pains her mother had to bear. She many times declared her mother's weakness and poor health came not only from her ever recurring maternity but as much from the simple lack of proper food and clothing. Yet the courage of the mother never faltered.

The continual charities of the open-hearted rector were another reason why Mrs. Wesley needed her abounding patience. Whether the Wesleys themselves had enough to eat or not the rector always gave freely of his time and means to the service of others. For seven successive winters he journeyed to the convocations of his church in London as the representative of the clergy of his diocese. He was expected in return for this honor, if honor it was, to pay his own expenses.

Nor was poverty alone all the family had to bear. Samuel Wesley was a pronounced Tory. His uncompromising morality had already alienated some of his most influential parishioners; he had visited severe punishment upon offenses too often condoned by a softer virtue. He was none too popular at the best. When the Whigs came into control of the government they speedily cut off several of his few perquisites, and all the accumulated rancor of his enemies seized this occasion for attack. He was insulted; he was robbed of his due in tithes and revenues; twice he suffered from the incendiary; mobs surrounded his house and with drums and guns made night hideous, and at last he

was arrested for a debt of thirty pounds and
thrown into the debtors' prison of Lincoln
castle. Here he was held for over three months
until his friends could arrange his debts and
effect his release. In all the attacks upon him,
he never forgot his personal dignity nor his
dignity as an ambassador of heaven, but no
sooner was he within the walls of the debtors'
prison—a debtors' jail of the England of the
eighteenth century, be it remembered!—than he
exclaimed: "Now I am at rest, for I am come to
the haven where I've long expected to be! . . .
A jail is a paradise in comparison of the life
I led before I came hither." He realized the
seriousness of his predicament but like many
another man who has long struggled under an
impending calamity, he welcomed the actual
blow as more endurable than the suspense. "I
hope to rise again, as I have always done when
at the lowest," he writes; "and I think I can
not be much lower now." His first thought
after he entered his cell, was for his wife and
children; his next for the unfortunate poor
about him. He saw in his imprisonment an opportunity for usefulness. Only two days after
his arrival he writes: "I don't despair of doing some good here—and so long I sha'n't quite
lose the end of living—and it may be do more
in this new parish than in my old one; for I
have leave to read prayers every morning and
evening here in the prison and to preach once
a Sunday. I am getting acquainted with my
brother jail birds as fast as I can."

The rector had good reason to worry about his family at home. Life in the parsonage was one continual struggle. Susannah's dairy was the sole support, and one night an enemy of the vicar's stabbed her cows. Her chief solicitude, however, was lest her husband might be in greater straits for food than were she and the children. All she could do was to send him her wedding ring, the only jewelry she had, but he promptly returned it.

After his release, his friends advised him to leave Epworth. He refused. These are his reasons, as he gave them to the Archbishop of York: "I confess I am not of that mind, because I may yet do some good there, and 'tis like a coward to desert my post because the enemy fire thick upon me. They have only wounded me yet, and, I believe, can't kill me." Upon his return the enemy fired upon him more thickly than ever. The climax came when his house was burned to the ground and the family but barely escaped with their lives.

This last fire at Epworth—this was the second attempt—is to every Methodist the pillar of fire which speaks a special providence for his church. For John Wesley, then a young child, was left for lost in the building after his agonized father had been repeatedly beaten back by the flames. As the rector, kneeling in prayer in an outer passage, commended to God the soul of the lad, whom he thought surely doomed, kindly neighbors formed a human pyramid which was the means of the lad's rescue. To

John, the mystic, that prayer always seemed
to be the divine seal on a peculiar and exalted
mission for which he had been miraculously preserved. His tombstone he ordered to be inscribed, ''A brand plucked out of the burning.''
In the rescue his mother saw an equal miracle.
She encouraged John's belief in his great destiny and fostered his high hope. ''What shall
I render unto the Lord for his mercies? The
little unworthy praise that I can offer is so mean
and contemptible an offering, that I am even
ashamed to tender it. But, Lord, accept it for
the sake of Christ, and pardon the deficiency of
the sacrifice. I would offer thee myself, and all
that thou hast given me; and I would resolve
—O give me grace to do it!—that the residue of
my life shall be all devoted to thy service. And
I do intend to be more particularly careful of
the soul of this child, that thou hast so merci-
fully provided for, than ever I have been; that
I may endeavor to instill into his mind the
principles of thy true religion and virtue.
Lord, give me grace to do it sincerely and prudently; and bless my attempts with good success.'' The answer to this prayer was Methodism.

On the night of the fire, when the agonized
rector finally realized that wife and children
were all safe, he gathered them about him in the
garden. He was told that all his property was
lost. ''What care I,'' he said. ''I have my
children and dear wife. These are riches

enough. Come, neighbors, let us give thanks to
God for his blessings.''

Possibly the hardest blow to the rector was
the loss of his library. His were scholarly
tastes, and his library for that day was by no
means poor. With what pains and sacrifice it
had been gathered, he alone knew. Only two
bits of charred paper escaped the flames. One
was a copy of the only hymn written by Samuel
Wesley now found in the Methodist hymnal,
''Behold the Saviour of Mankind,'' and the
other a fragment of his beloved Polyglot Bible
with only a sentence legible: ''Sell all thou
hast. Take up thy cross, and follow me.''

From this fire, the family fortunes never recovered. The rebuilding of the house plunged
Dr. Wesley deeper into debt. And the new rectory was never decently furnished. The rector,
generously impractical as ever, that he ''might
do what became him, and leave the living better than he found it'' undertook to plant mul-
berry trees, cherry trees, and pear trees in the
garden, and walnut trees ''in the adjoining
croft.'' Within doors, Susannah once more
gathered her children together. She rigidly
enforced the reforms made necessary by their
separation during the rebuilding of the house,
restored domestic discipline, and vigorously resumed the painstaking processes of education.

The aggressiveness of the rector's enemies
seemed to have spent itself with the last fire.
A revulsion of feeling set in, and for the re-

mainder of his life at Epworth he took comfort
in the friendship and loyalty of his parishioners.
Susannah's routine was unchanged. Although
Samuel had gone away to the university long
before the last fire at Epworth—all events in
the Wesley history date from that memorable
fire—Kezia, the nineteenth and youngest, was
born thirteen months after. With children always in the nursery and in the schoolroom,
Susannah's hands were always full. However
it was the spiritual welfare of her children—
present and absent—that concerned her most.

"I have a great and just desire that all your
sisters and brothers should be saved as well as
you," she once wrote to Samuel, "but I must
own I think my concern for you is much the
greatest. What, you, my son, you, who was once
the son of my extremest sorrow, in your birth
and in your infancy, who is now the son of my
tenderest love, my friend, in whom is my inexpressible delight, my future hope of happiness in this world, for whom I weep and pray
in my retirements from the world, when no
mortal knows the agonies of my soul on your
account, no eye sees my tears, which are only
beheld by that Father of Spirits of whom I so
importunately beg grace for you that I hope I
may at least be heard—is it possible that you
should be damned?   O that it were impossible!
Indeed I think I could almost wish myself ac-
cursed, so I were sure of your salvation. But
still I hope, still I would fain persuade myself
that a child for whom so many prayers have

been offered to Heaven will not at last miscarry." To the severe religious thought of her day, salvation was the aim and end of existence. It was a matter for agonized striving. This very striving, however, made men, real men. Considering the Wesleys she made great, what must have been the strength of her striving?

How this essential salvation was to be obtained, was a matter that she insisted upon settling for herself. During the winter of 1712, when the rector was absent in London upon one of his regular "convocation" visitations, she was dissatisfied with the teachings of his curate. Accordingly early one Sunday evening she gathered her children and her servants in her ample kitchen, read the best sermon she could find in print, read prayers, and gave general religious instruction. Another night, the father of one of the servants came, and then a neighbor, and then another until some fifty were listening to her. Overflowing the house, they adjourned to the large barn. Soon the outraged curate, tired of empty benches, was complaining to his absent rector that Mrs. Wesley was conducting that thing horrid to ecclesiastical ears, a "conventicle." Many scores were week by week gathering with her, he said, to the great scandal of the church and surrounding clergy. The equally outraged rector wrote hastily reproving her not only for the damage she would do his reputation, set as he was in high position, but also for the unseemliness of a woman's speaking in public. She replied in very vigorous words: "And where is the harm of this? If I and my children went a visiting on Sunday nights, or if we admitted of impertinent visits, as too many do who think themselves good Christians, perhaps it would be thought no scandalous practice, though in truth it would be so. Therefore, why any should reflect upon you, let your station be what it will, because your wife endeavors to draw people to the church, and to restrain them by reading and other persuasions from their profanation of God's most holy day, I cannot conceive. But if any should be so mad as to do it, I wish you would not regard it. For my part, I value no censure on this account. I have long since shook hands with the world, and I heartily wish I had never given them more reason to speak against me."

She concluded her letter with the wifely rejoinder that if as rector he should *order* her to discontinue the service, she would obey the constituted authority of the church. Nothing less than a command, she said, would suffice; for her reason would never be satisfied with his arguments. Needless to say neither her husband nor her rector carried the discussion further.

For twenty-three years longer, their life at Epworth continued unbroken; then the rector died. Thought of his wife and daughters to be left unprovided for embittered the months of his illness. He asked Samuel and John and Charles in turn to take the rectory so that the family would have at least a home. When one

after the other they declined, he saw no further
way in which he himself could shape their future
and was at last content to leave their care where
it had always been, in the hands of Providence.
As his death approached, his simple trust and
faith grew even stronger. Again and again he
exclaimed: "The inward witness, son, the inward witness; *that* is the proof, the strongest
proof of Christianity!" To his youngest son
he said: "Be steady! The Christian faith will
surely revive in this kingdom. You shall see
it, though I shall not." As the flame of the
rector's life flickered and then burned out, his
son John read the last prayers for the dying.
So Samuel Wesley left Epworth rectory, where
for thirty-nine years he had suffered and toiled.

Seven years later the son—even then the
wonder of England—who had committed to
Heaven the soul of his dying father was denied
the use of his father's church. From the tomb
of his father he preached, night after night
under the open sky, to the men and women of
Epworth, to a congregation which covered all
the hillside. As hundreds responded to his
preaching—preaching which brought religion
out of the closet and made it vital for all men
—he remembered his mother's "conventicle"
when as a lad of eight he had heard her preach
to these same neighbors; he remembered also
the last words of his father, "The inward witness, son, the inward witness!" These two
ideas, the simple congregation of worshipers
and the witness of the spirit, were the cardinal

doctrines of John Wesley's new faith; these
two cardinal doctrines found their birth in the
rectory at Epworth.

In these seven years after her husband's
death, Susannah lived in the homes of her children. John and Charles envied Samuel his
greater ability to do for her; Charles wrote him:
"Let the Society give her what they please,
she must be still, in some degree, burdensome
to you, as she calls it. How do I envy you that
glorious burden, and wish I could share it with
you! You must put me in some way of getting
a little money, that I may do something in this
shipwreck of the family, though it be no more
than furnishing a plank."

Hardly had she lost her husband when she
was called upon to part with her two youngest
sons who sailed for America in the full flush
of youthful missionary zeal. Feeble as she
was when she parted with them, she never expected to see them again. Yet she sent them
away with her blessing: "Had I twenty sons I
should rejoice that they were all so employed,
though I should never see them more."

Months later when broken in health and
spirits, they returned from their unsuccessful
journey, as naturally as when they had been
lads, they returned for comfort to their mother.

The next parting was for all time. In 1739
she had returned to London, an aged widow;
fifty years before she had left it in the happy
fullness of early married life. All her twenty-
five brothers and sisters were dead; of her own

children but nine survived. Then Samuel died,
Samuel her firstborn and always best beloved,
with whom she had expected to spend what life
remained to her. He had amply repaid his
mother's affection; to the lads John and
Charles he had been a second father. Bitter
as was her loss, she wrote to Charles with characteristic courage: "Your brother was exceed-
ing dear to me in his life; and perhaps I have
erred in loving him too well. I once thought it
impossible for me to bear his loss; but none
know what they can bear till they are tried.
He is now at rest, and would not now return to
earth to gain the world. Why then should I
mourn?"

Although always in sympathy personally
with his brothers, Samuel, long before his death,
had been startled by these lads adventuring into a new faith and a new creed. At last he had
pled with them in a very agony of concern for
their spiritual life. But to their mother, their
progress was as natural as the unfolding of a
flower. As her years grew shorter, her mind
harked back to the earlier faith of her girlhood,
of her own father's comfortable faith and
genial hope. She remembered her own "conventicle" in the kitchen at Epworth and so was
not frightened at the thousands who gathered
in the fields and lanes to listen to her eloquent
sons. When John became the acknowledged
head of Oxford Methodists he sent her an account of their work and the sneering opposition
to it. She replied: "I heartily join with your

small Society in all their pious and charitable actions, which are intended for God's glory. . . . May you still, in such good works, go on and prosper! Though absent in body, I am present with you in spirit; and daily recommend and commit you all to Divine Providence."

She did not content herself, however, with mere sympathy. Her constructive advice played no small part in shaping the new doctrines as one by one they were developed in John's mind. Always practical-minded she aided materially in keeping the new creed "with feet on the earth" while its "head was in the clouds." For instance, when John returned from an evangelistic tour and found that a layman had been preaching, although in no fashion ordained, it was her gentle remonstrance which held his indignation in check and saved to the new church one of its most distinctive features—the lay preacher.

"Thomas Maxfield has turned preacher, I find," said John.

"John," said his mother, "take care what you do with respect to that young man; for he is as surely called of God to preach as you are. Examine what have been the fruits of his preaching and hear him yourself."

Concerning her son's own preaching, her influence was in the right direction. "Suffer now a word of advice," she wrote him. "However curious you may be in searching into the nature or in distinguishing the properties of the passions or the virtues of human kind, for your own private satisfaction, be very cautious in giving nice distinctions in public assemblies; for it does not answer the true end of preaching, which is to mend men's lives, and not to fill their heads with unprofitable speculations. And after all is said, every affection of the soul is better known by experience than any description that can be given of it. An honest man will more easily apprehend what is meant by being zealous for God and against sin when he hears what are the proper ties and effects of true zeal, than the most accurate definition of its essence.''

This excellent advice, she reënforced with the statement:

''I have often wondered that men should be so vain as to amuse themselves by searching into the decrees of God, which no human wit can fathom; and do not rather employ their time and their prowess in working out their salvation and making their own calling and election sure. Such studies tend more to confound than inform the understanding, and young people had best let them alone.''

As she had helped the rector at Epworth she now helped her two sons in London. In literal fact as well as in the maternity that enfolded her sons, she was the mother of Methodism.

The new faith grew. As she saw the disciples of her sons number into the thousands, she quietly watched the sands in her own glass run lower and lower. As she saw all England

quickened into a new spiritual life, her own
religious life softened and deepened. As she
saw John and Charles and their followers
awaken dead consciences, she now centered in
them all the hopes and longings of the long line
of pious forebears. In the souls of her young
preacher sons she saw caught all the greatness
of spirit of the Wesleys and the Annesleys who
had gone before.

An old foundry at Moorfields had been fitted
up as a church and dwelling for John and his
helpers. Here Mrs. Wesley came on the last
short stage of her journey. Here she died in
July 1742. The same son who had read the
prayer for the dying as her husband breathed
his last read for her the same comforting words
of victory.

Her last request was: "Children as soon as
I am released, sing a psalm of praise to God!"
As they had honored her in life, so they obeyed
her in death. Gathered about her bedside they
forced back their grief as the anthem of her release and of their love swelled to triumphant
notes. And well might the anthem be triumphant, for Susannah Wesley had so played her
mother-part in the drama of Epworth Parish
that she gave to the world—not to Methodists
alone—a new freedom of large faith, a new
democracy of vital religion, and a new intimacy
with God.

CHAPTER III

ELIZABETH ANN SETON

BY R. V. TREVEL

ELIZABETH ANN BAYLEY, who became
Mrs. William Magee Seton, was an American Episcopalian gentlewoman. It was very
much owing to the distinction and influence of
her family that Mrs. Seton's conversion to the
Church of Rome was of high advantage to it
during its beginnings in the United States.
Her birth date of 1774 fixes her as a contemporary of Mr. Washington Irving and Captain
Fenimore Cooper, whom she knew, although she
did not live so long as these other New Yorkers.
Her pen was as gifted, too, in its way as theirs;
but Mrs. Seton wrote little for general publication, notwithstanding the thirteen volumes
of her correspondence and reminiscences which
are treasured in the mother-house of the religious community which she founded at Emmitsburg in Maryland. Of translations, Mother
Seton made one of the life of St. Vincent de
Paul, whose life so resembles her own though
two centuries and an ocean separate them, and
made several others of religious works also
French. She was guided in her pathway curi-
ously much by French minds, and also by mem-

bers of a notable family of Italy, devout people whose friendship was brought her by her husband. Moreover, in part she was French by birth.

The Huguenot family of the Lecomtes, or Lecontes, came to American shores in the eighteenth century, and, establishing themselves on Long Island Sound, they applied the name of their Bay of Biscay castle to the spot, calling it New Rochelle. A son of an English family of position in the County of Norfolk, who came likewise to the colony of New York in the same generation, married a Miss Leconte. One of the sons of this marriage was Richard Bayley, who became eminent in New York City as a distinguished physician and a citizen of fine character. Dr. Bayley married Miss Catharine Charlton, daughter of an Episcopalian clergyman of Staten Island; and they had three daughters, Mary, Elizabeth (the subject of this chapter), and Catharine. The young mother did not survive the Revolution, the drama of which was then playing on the stage of New York; and only two years later the infant Catharine died. "I sat alone," Elizabeth records in her *Remembrances,* "on the step of the doorway, looking at the clouds, while my little sister Catharine lay in her coffin. They asked me, 'Did I not cry when Kitty was dead?' 'No,' I said, 'because Kitty was gone up to Heaven; I wish I could go too, with Mamma.'"
Gazing at the clouds and at the stars, in de-

ELIZABETH ANN SETON

light and piety, was a habit, almost a pastime, with Elizabeth all her life.

Dr. Bayley now married a Miss Barclay, the property of whose family included the present Barclay Street.   Little is related of the second Mrs. Bayley except that Elizabeth quickly became attached to her—and to her half-brothers and sisters as they were born.   More notable was the close companionship which formed between the child and her father.   When she first began to learn her letters, and to work her sampler, the schoolmistress was a somnolent old person, and the little girl when she saw her father in the street on his professional visits would slip out and kiss him undiscovered. This is the only irregularity in which Dr. Bayley indulged his daughter; he saw that her nature was noble, and studied to moderate and perfect her sensitiveness and ardor into a balanced character.

The windows of Dr. Bayley's house looked across the Battery, and Bowling Green, which were shaded parks, and out upon the harbor where the family saw with friendly eyes King George's men-of-war.   When Washington had been forced to evacuate the city, and Sir Guy Carleton held it with his troops, Dr. Bayley and this commander became intimates; the doctor, a royalist, served as a surgeon in Carleton's army. But in 1783, when Elizabeth was nine years old, there came a week when the British soldiers grew busy and marched day after day down to

the boats, and melted away from New York.
Instead of their red flag a new one streamed
from the poles. A majestic tall gentleman,
whom Elizabeth saw riding with Governor Clin-
ton, who now ruled the city, asked him, she was
told, if New York would make the best capital
for the country; but both the Colony, or the
State as now it was called, and the city decided
against this, and so General Washington took
up his first presidency in Philadelphia.

Dr. Bayley, with public spirit, conformed to
the new government, and soon served it as the
health-officer of the port of New York. He
was also made the first professor of anatomy
in Columbia College. When in 1788 he went
to England, to read further in his profession,
Elizabeth went to the Westchester County
home of her father's family. Even though only
fourteen she had met society, as young women
then did early, and was already admired by the
other sex, by William Seton among others.
Elizabeth was accomplished, too, and bright
and charming always, in company or companionship; but she cared least for this side of existence, even thus young. By preference, she
went alone. She read St. Thomas à Kempis'
Imitation of Christ, read the poets Milton
and Thomson, read these books beside her constant Bible, which had been her favorite book
since she was seven. She was once surprised on
the high rocks of an icy hilltop in winter, where
she was singing hymns with face upturned to
the sky. The story seems that of a wild spirit,

but the maid was anything but wild; she was rather simply pure and purely religious, one who perceived God in all the aspects of nature. In her own words: ''I took joy in God that He was my Father. This thought gave me pleasure in everything, coarse, rough, smooth, or easy, and made me always gay,''—gay, for oftenest in her most precious book she turned to the joyous Psalms. On the beach she would sometimes walk reciting her hymns at night. If Elizabeth had known any Roman Catholics her dawning asceticism might have been explained, but there were but a handful of Roman Catholics in the State, and they were regarded with horror probably by herself as by others. Perhaps she took some of her promptings from her reading of history in her father's library. Her Guardian Angel, in whose spiritual existence she believed, was her only censor among the books; the doctor, a freethinker, was accustomed to let her pore over whatsoever volumes she would, and Rousseau and Voltaire, whose works she perused, did her no harm.

After Dr. Bayley returned from abroad and the family was united again, Elizabeth, in the brilliancy and beauty of her growing youth, shone in the inner circle of fashionable New York. She was gracefully slight. Miss Sadlier speaks of her brilliant black eyes; and her French biographer, Madame de Barberey, describes them as large and brown, full of tender light, and correctly traces a delicate strength in the pure features. Undoubtedly these eyes, so

brightly soft, were derived with the innocent
sparkle of her spirit from her Huguenot grand-
mother.   In the beautiful profile of a miniature
the tresses are curling and dark, the complex-
ion evidently pale; the line of the nose would
be straight but for an outward curve ever so
slight.   The whole features wear both a woman's fair charm and the light of a mind.

The gaieties of her season as a belle far from
absorbed her.   Visions of a higher, more earnest life haunted her; she wished that there were
monasteries of holy men in America, and convents of consecrated virgins among whom she
might cast her lot and pass her life in the service and praise of God.   As there were no such
institutions on Manhattan Island, Elizabeth
persuaded "the friend of her soul," Rebecca
Seton, to visit the sick and poor with her.   The
two young girls grew to be familiar figures on
the streets, as they carried their baskets of
good things; they were called the protestant
sisters of charity.

The Seton mansion on Stone Street was one
of the most princely in New York.   Equally
hospitable was Mr. Seton's "Craigdon," his
Bloomingdale country-seat, about six miles up
the Hudson, its wooded acres covering the western slopes of the island, beginning at a point
about where Grant's tomb now is.   Mr. Seton's
interests were in iron manufacturing in New
Jersey, and in shipping; his agents in Italy
were the Filicchi Brothers, distinguished Ital-
ians who knew such Americans as John Adams,

Jefferson and Charles Carroll. His son William had spent some years abroad, a part of the time in the business house of the Filicchi. In 1791 William was in New York, however, for so he dated a letter to his brother in which he says: "It is currently reported and generally believed that I am to be married to Miss Bayley." The ardent manner in which this letter goes on to forget its dignified beginning leaves little doubt of the current reports, and history has left none. William Seton and Elizabeth Bayley were married in St. Paul's Church by their Bishop, Dr. Prevoost, on January 25, 1794. Few and brief, however were the years of happiness which followed for her, for Elizabeth Seton's life was to be a sorrowful one.

Her father was no more devoted to her than the elder Seton promptly became. Because of her responsive intelligence the old merchant took her into his intimacy more than he did his own daughters, who were motherless and many. With her he discussed the disasters to his ships, for those were troubled days when first the French Revolution and then Bonaparte was disturbing the peace of Europe, and no cargo was safe on the seas. Young Seton was forced to travel much; once he wrote to his bride from Philadelphia: "I showed my friends your miniature, and many agreeable things were said for which I felt greatly flattered, but let them know that the artist, although a Frenchman, had not at all flattered *you*." The italics are the lover's. Their first child, Anna, was born in May, 1795. On the very next year, however, a shadow fell—her husband began to fail in health. The embarrassment of the large Seton affairs also increased. These cares were partly countervailed by the successive birth of Elizabeth's William, Richard, Rebecca and Catharine. In 1798, however, the head of the family died, unable longer to sustain the failure of his fortune. His death threw the whole disorganized business upon the shoulders of his consumptive son; or rather it should be said, upon William and his beautiful wife, for her clear judgment proved valuable in the tangled business.

Another blow fell upon young Mrs. Seton when she was twenty-six. It is strange to think of yellow fever year after year in New York, but in the early days of the last century sanitary engineering was most rudimentary. Dr. Bayley, who as health-officer was established at his quarantine station on Staten Island, fought the disease nobly and ably. In 1801 he contracted it. His daughter's distraction was not only from fear of his death but concerning his salvation. As he was dying she won from him some expression of Christian belief; but, not satisfied, she caught up her infant Catharine and offered her life to God for the saving of her father's soul! Possibly in the intensity of her filial and religious feeling Elizabeth meant to promise a mortal sacrifice such as those of the oldest Hebrew days. If so, the frenzy duly passed; but indeed Catharine's life was devoted to God as promised, for she died at ninety as the Mother Superior of the Sisters of Charity of Mount St. Vincent on the Hudson, one of the largest communities descended from the one her mother founded in Maryland.

In 1803 the Setons hoped to improve Mr. Seton's health by a sea voyage, and, taking Anna their eldest child with them, they sailed for Italy on the packet *Shepherdess*. The voyage did the invalid no good; and at the end of it, on account of the yellow fever at New York, they were not permitted to land at Leghorn; for a month the passengers were quarantined, almost imprisoned, in a lazaretto. Mr. Seton's old friend Filippo Filicchi, who came from his home in Umbria to meet the party, found them a sad group behind the pest-house grating. It was largely through the efforts of Signor Filicchi and his brother Antonio that the Americans were finally released and allowed to proceed to Pisa. Their friends were worthy successors of the great Italian merchants of the Middle Ages, and were indeed true Christian gentlemen. But not all the kindness of the Filicchi and the sleepless devotion of his wife could save the sick man. Mrs. Seton again, as at her father's death, endeavored to bring the sufferer to religious thoughts and prayer; although reared in the Episcopal Church, he had never been devout. She had the sad happiness of his responding. As soon as her grief and weakness allowed the use of a pen, she wrote to Rebecca: "I often asked him when he could not speak, 'Do you feel, my love, that you are going to your Redeemer?' and he motioned 'yes,' with a look of peace. At a quarter past seven, on Tuesday morning, December 27, his soul was released, and mine from a struggle worse than death.'' Such was Elizabeth Seton's Christmas. Her husband's body was conveyed to Leghorn, and buried in the protestant cemetery in the presence of all the Americans and English then there.

As soon as Mrs. Seton could rest and recover strength after her loss, Signora Amabilia Filicchi begged her to accompany her to Florence on a visit to relatives who lived in the palace of the Medici. In Florence Elizabeth's friend took her to the chapel of La Sanctissima Annunziata. "A heavy curtain," she wrote to Rebecca, "hung at the entrance; we raised it and my eyes were struck with the sight of hundreds kneeling; but the gloom of the chapel, lighted only by wax tapers on the altar and a small window at the top, darkened with green silk, made every object at first appear very indistinct, while that kind of soft and distant music which lifts the minds to a foretaste of heavenly pleasures, called up in an instant every dear and tender idea of my soul, and forgetting Signora Amabilia's company, and all the surrounding scenes, I sank on my knees in the first place I found vacant and shed a torrent of tears at the recollection of how long I had been a stranger in the house of my God, and the accumulated sorrow that had separated

me from it." And while the mass was being
said Elizabeth Seton repeated all that she could
remember of the service of her own church—
which was to be hers little longer. From the
time of her entering the Florentine chapel she
began to entertain the question whether its religion was not the true one and the Anglican
faith mistaken. She resisted and dispelled the
idea, but it always returned. Being sincere
Roman Catholics themselves, the Filicchi encouraged her questionings. Moreover, the
members of this patrician family impressed
her with the beauty of their religion by the per-
petual presence of it in their lives. But one
day Antonio provoked the widow to say, with a
touch of her old archness: "O my, sir, if there
is but one faith, and nobody pleases God without it, where are all the good people that die
out of it?"

"I don't know," answered Filicchi; "that depends on what light of faith they have received.
But I know where people go who *can* know the
right faith by praying and inquiring for it and
yet do neither!"

"Much as to say, sir," returned Mrs. Seton,
"you want me to pray and inquire, and be of
your faith?"

"Yes, pray and inquire," Filicchi repeated
earnestly. "That is all I ask of you."

Soon after, at a mass in the beautiful church
of Our Lady of Monte Nero her next neighbor
was a cynical young English tourist who at the
moment of the elevation ventured to whisper to

her with a sneer, ''This is what they call their
'Real Presence.' '' The American lady sank
on her knees in disgust at the stranger's blasphemy and in sympathy with the worshipers.
That stanza of Pope's ran in her mind:

''If I am right, Thy grace impart,
    Still in the right to stay;
If I am wrong, oh, teach my heart
    To find the better way.''

What most appealed to Mrs. Seton in Italian
religious life was that one was able to go to
mass every day.   She so yearned for every
possible sharing of the Lord's Supper that
when she was at home in New York it was her
habit to hurry from one communion table to
that in another church each Sunday, because
the Episcopal churches did not celebrate the
communion through the week.

In February, 1804, the widow, with Annina,
as she now called her daughter, turned homeward.   Again they embarked in the *Shepherdess,* but it collided with another vessel, and had
to put back for repairs.   It may well seem
that Providence intended to sanctify Elizabeth
Seton through tribulation: now Annina took
the dread scarlet fever, and as soon as Annina
was up the mother contracted the disease herself.   When they were able to travel, however,
the chivalrous friendship of Antonio Filicchi
decided him to accompany Mrs. Seton to New
York.   In April they started on their voyage
in the *Flamingo* and sailed up the Narrows on

the first of June. The very month after her
arrival she lost her nearest and dearest friend,
her sister-in-law Rebecca, in whose charge Mrs.
Seton's younger children had lived during her
stay abroad.

There followed now a year of intellectual
anguish. Mrs. Seton wavered between the
faith of her fathers and that of Rome. Signor
Filicchi remained in America for some time,
doing all he could to win this devout spirit to
his Church. Elizabeth often and seriously discussed the question of the true religion with her
rector, the distinguished Mr. Hobart; but he
convinced her of nothing in saying that "the
sumptuous and splendid worship of Italy will
not, I am sure, withdraw your affections from
the simple and affecting worship of Trinity
Church." Mrs. Seton was more and more realizing, on the contrary, that the richer worship
was gaining all her religious affections. The
members of her family and her connections
stormed at her or met her coldly, according to
their natures, but Mrs. Seton was undisturbed
and sought only the approbation of her God.
At last convinced that she was being led by the
hand of God, Mrs. Seton was received into the
Church of Rome on Ash Wednesday in March,
1805, by Father Matthew O'Brien, in St.
Peter's Church in Barclay Street. The step deprived her of almost every former friend. It
isolated her, practically without means of support, in the city of her birth where her family
were among the rulers.

In passing, one cannot but question whether, if there had been Episcopal sisterhoods in her time, she would not have entered one of their orders and remained in the faith in which she was born. It is very possible that she would; the Episcopal was the faith of her fathers and it would naturally have had the loyalty of inheritance. Yet her imagination was so commanding—while spontaneous and vivid—that even had there been an Anglican order for her to enter, she might still have been captivated into some cloister of the most imaginative religion that has flowered from the New Testament.

The elder Mr. Seton, it must be understood, had left Elizabeth's husband little but his ruin. It was necessary for Elizabeth to give up the Stone Street mansion, and she moved into a cottage about a mile and a half out of town, evidently somewhere between the Union and Madison Squares of to-day. Signor Filicchi begged her to draw on his agent for pecuniary means; indeed the two Italian gentlemen served Mrs. Seton in this way almost throughout her career. She always accepted their kindness with a similar generous simplicity; there was less of the personal than of religious in the giving and receiving of their funds. At this time Elizabeth thought of winning an income by teaching. She joined a well-mannered English Roman Catholic, a Mr. White, who, with his wife, was about to open a school for boys. It is amazing now over a century later to know

what happened. New York was so prejudiced
against the Church of Rome that people would
not send their sons to this school conducted by
three of that faith, and it had to close. Mrs.
Seton endeavored to secure a place as a teacher
in the boarding school of the Reverend Mr.
Harris, Curate of St. Mark's Episcopal Church
in the Bowery, but he did not dare to give the
post to the gentle applicant. He did agree,
however, to send some of his pupils to board
with her. Mrs. Seton rented two adjoining
houses in Stuyvesant's Lane, but the parents
at once removed their children from the school,
lest any contact with a Roman Catholic should
poison their Christianity. The persecuted
woman had to give up her boarding house.
Only the repeal of the law saved her from pros-
ecution for breaking the act against the conduct
of schools by members of her faith. The talk
excited by Mrs. Seton's conversion was probably the cause of a riotous demonstration
against St. Peter's Roman Catholic Church.
She meekly suffered, but what was to be done?

Elizabeth thought now of teaching in some
convent in Canada where her church was well
established. At the advice of her friends Bishop
Carroll and Father William Louis du Bourg
she decided instead to go to Baltimore to teach
a girls' school there. Mrs. Seton sold "Craigdon" and all its chattels with joy, such was her
relief to leave the hostile faces in her own New
York. She and her daughters reached Baltimore on Corpus Christi, 1808; and her boys

who, through the generosity of the Filicchi had
been at Georgetown College on the Potomac, entered St. Mary's College of Baltimore, a Sulpitian institution of which Dr. du Bourg was the
president. Under his direction she opened a
school next to the Chapel of St. Mary's Seminary. Thus at last in friendly Baltimore she
met peace and happiness; her greatest joy was
that she could now practice her religion as fully
and freely as she wished. Not only were there
noble priests in Baltimore, but also cultivated
women of her new faith, such as Madame
Fournier, the sister of Father du Bourg. A
number of these distinguished leaders of the
church were great Frenchmen who had been
storm-tossed to our American shores by
the Revolution which had shipwrecked their
France; such of them as du Bourg and Matig-
non; Flaget and Nagot; David, Dubois, Bruti,
and Duhamel; and Bishop Cheverus of Boston
believed that she was "destined for the accomplishment of a considerable work in the United
States."

In friendly Baltimore, the school flourished;
as many girls came as it could accommodate.
In 1808 an incident occurred which hinted a possibility that Mrs. Seton had desired for many
years. To her who had worn a crucifix from
her childhood, and longed for a conventual life
ever since, the dream now seemed to be turning into a plan.

Father Badad, the spiritual director of the
school, on a visit to Philadelphia, met there a

Mr. O'Conway who told him that he had a daughter, Cecilia, who desired to take the veil, but he regretted that she would have to go to Europe to accomplish her purpose. Father Badad, after a moment's reflection, replied: "I believe that Miss O'Conway will not have to leave the United States. There is a holy widow in Baltimore whose virtue is the wonder of all who know her; she wishes to lead the retired life of self-sacrifice and good works, and something may come of it if these two ladies should correspond and meet." Cecilia O'Conway did go to Baltimore and was welcomed by Mrs. Seton. Thus in the little Paca Street schoolhouse something in the nature of a community was formed between these two, with the approval and blessing of Bishop Carroll and the priesthood. The original purpose was to teach poor Roman Catholic children.

News of the movement speedily brought further applicants to share in it, among them Maria Murphy, niece of the Philadelphia philanthropist, Matthew Carey, and several young girls of Baltimore and other places in its region. In spite of the cruelty of New York towards Elizabeth Seton, her church had grown rapidly there; it sent two candidates for membership. Baltimore furnished two more. Then, later still, two of Elizabeth's sisters-in-law, Cecilia and Harriet Seton, who loved and admired her, came to join her. In truth, Cecilia —"sweet, merry Cis," as Mrs. Seton called her —had pined for her in sickness in New York, and had half run away to Baltimore followed by Harriet. Father du Bourg was appointed as the ecclesiastical superior of the new community, and Mrs. Seton was elected and consecrated as its superioress. The name adopted was that of the Sisterhood of St. Joseph. One evening soon after, conversing with her sisters, Mother Seton suddenly burst into tears, and, falling on her knees, remained long in that position confessing the most humiliating actions of her life; until, with hands extended to Heaven, she exclaimed in prayer: "My gracious God! Thou knowest my unfitness for this task. I who by my sins have so often crucified Thee, I blush with shame and confusion. How can I teach others, who know so little myself, and am so miserable and imperfect!"

This new American order patterned as closely as possible after the organization of the French Sisters or Daughters of Charity founded by St. Vincent de Paul. The Sisters of St. Joseph adopted a habit very much like the dress which Mrs. Seton had worn ever since her widowhood, one that she had copied from the costume of some nuns in Italy. The cap was of white muslin—later changed to black—with a crimped border, and the gown of flowing black with a short cape.

With all the pupils in residence besides these Sisters, the Paca Street premises were outgrown. One morning, after receiving the holy communion, Mother Seton observed a student from the neighboring seminary kneeling in

front of her; he was a young Virginian of some
fortune, and the superioress exclaimed to herself: "Oh, if he would buy some land for our
sisters, and build a little house for us!" She
later found Mr. Cooper was entertaining the
same thought at the time; he did donate a thousand dollars for the purchase of land for an institution for the Sisters. The place chosen was
selected largely at the instance of Father Jean
Dubois, later the Bishop of New York, who now
became associated with Mother Seton in the direction of her community. A friend of de
Lafayette's, he was a spirited Parisian priest
who had refused to compromise with the French
National Assembly. Bishop Carroll had assigned him to the spiritual charge of north-
western Maryland, a frontier country in which
Frederick, Emmitsburg, Hagerstown, and
Westminster were the principal settlements.
He built the first Roman Catholic church at
Frederick. Knowing that district, Father Dubois showed the bishop a grand and solitary
valley near Emmitsburg in the Blue Ridge; two
miles up one mountain, perched the College of
Mount St. Mary, a branch of the Baltimore St.
Mary's Seminary over which Father du Bourg
presided. Here a site was purchased for the
building of the first American sisterhood.

An Indian legend, which sprang up in this
part of Father Dubois' wilderness, makes the
choice of a location seem most happy. Miss
Sadlier relates the story of this fair, wooded
plain, where the magnolia and thorn-apple

breathed and bloomed in an inspiring mountain world:

"Nearly two centuries before, when Maryland was first colonized, one of the Jesuit missionaries, in quest of Indian tribes to whom he might make known the glad tidings of Salvation, toiled up the hills and traversed the trackless forests, until he reached this valley, and preached the Word of God to the red men whom he found there. Like all the Maryland Indians, whose passions were never roused by the injustices that their race met with in other English colonies, they received the black-robe with respect, and accepted the true faith. Dark Puritan days afterwards came to Maryland, and the tribe lost their beloved Father; but one, at least, among them, never forgot his teachings, and faithfully practiced his religion, as far as he could do so. This was a chief of rank and power amongst his people. He had a special devotion to Our Blessed Lady, and used to say his beads many times a day, often wishing as he did so, in his simple, child-like faith, that he might have the happiness of beholding her. The years went by, and the chief grew old and feeble, but ever told his beads and wished his wish. At length, one summer day, as he tilled the field, murmuring the while his 'Hail Marys,' a beautiful gracious lady, clad in flowing robes stood before him, and told him that she was the Blessed Virgin whom he had so longed to see. 'Know,' she continued, 'that in this field where you have for so many years prayed to me, I

shall one day gather many virgins, who will
sound continually the praises of God.' The
beautiful vision then faded, leaving the old
chief filled with happiness.'' Elizabeth Seton
led her mild Sisters here as if in fulfillment of
this vision.

The first party left Baltimore with Mother
Seton on June 21, 1808, to prepare for the coming of the rest.   The distance was fifty miles.
The gentle group traveled in primitive fashion,
with a huge canvas-covered wagon such as in
the middle of the century was to cross the
prairies to California for earthly gold; generally all walked, excepting Cecilia Seton, who
was frail and ill, though happy, and rested as
well as she might in the crude jolting vehicle.
The mother in her diary says playfully: ''The
ducks and pigs came out to meet us, and the
geese stretched their necks in mute demand to
know if we were one of their sort, to which
we gave assent.''

After several days' pilgrimage they reached
their domain, then hardly more than a bare
clearing a half-mile from the sparse Emmitsburg village.   The coming struggle, lightly born
though it was, would have seemed lighter if
they could have seen arise before them the
present group of stately buildings which they
were founding that day.   But as it was, they
were met by little more than hardship.   As the
Flemming farmhouse, which was being refitted
for their occupation, was not ready, Father Dubois gave up his house to them.   It was a tiny

structure of only two rooms, but Mother Seton and her young companions were so glad to have arrived and to find themselves in their mountain temple that they made light of all their severe discomforts.

The status of Harriet Seton was different from that of the rest. Although of course sympathetic with her friends, she had not yet become a Roman Catholic. She was there really as a companion to watch over her sick sister, Cecilia. But how many of those who seem to be last shall be first. In the first months of Emmitsburg was enacted the closing scene of this young girl's tragedy. She was engaged to Mrs. Seton's half-brother, Barclay Bayley, to whom she was warmly attached, and it was her intention as soon as Cecilia was perfectly well again to return to New York to marry him. In the healthful mountain air Cecilia grew stronger, happy in her religion and in Mrs. Seton. But Harriet lingered on, held there by the happiness of the sisters in all their labor and their rites. She waited wistfully about Father Dubois' church when they had entered it. All in the church wore something that she did not, but she wore something on the ribbon around her neck that they did not. She would kiss it. Could she doubt its worth? The comparison between her miniature of her lover and the crucifix was inevitable. She felt herself yielding to the sweet, potent attraction of the ancient church; yet her heart with girlish truth long fought for the absent one, her lover.

It was in vain, for after a sharp struggle she found herself the lover only of Christ, and she adopted the Roman form of His service. In the warmth of her fervor she so spent and exposed herself in nursing the sick that she contracted a mortal disease herself. So lately the flower of fashion in New York, Harriet Seton laid her young form down in the first grave that was dug for the Sisterhood of St. Joseph. This was in the December of 1809. Cecilia followed to lie beside her only four months after.

One day, soon after their coming, when Mother Seton and her companions had been walking about their property and inspecting the progress on their new house, the superioress said: "Nothing is lacking save the place of our final repose on earth. Let us choose where that shall be." Harriet Seton had sat down to rest beneath an oak. "See my place!" she exclaimed. And she threw an apple against the tree and caught it on the rebound. It was in that spot that they buried her and her sister so soon after; and adjoining their graves the general cemetery of the congregation was laid out.

These deaths show the early want and struggle of the Sisterhood. Even in the rebuilt Flemming cottage the household conditions were little improved, if at all. This building, named the "Stone House," consisted only of an undivided interior with a garret above; and even this space was further limited by a little oratory which Father du Bourg, who came from Baltimore, set apart at one end, with its altar at which he held the first mass for the infant community. Mrs. Seton appointed Sister Kitty Mullen as housekeeper; Sister Rose as Mother's assistant; Sister Cecilia as secretary and school sister; Sister Sally as procuratrix, washer and baker. The Sisters all cooked in turn, and helped in the washing. They primitively washed in the stream, some distance away in the valley, for the dwelling had no "modern conveniences." Sister Rose White has described the routine:

"The Sisters rose at five o'clock. Prayer, meditation, and recital of a third part of the Rosary occupied them till a quarter to seven. At seven they assembled in the little oratory recess to hear Mass celebrated by Father Dubois, and after Mass they recited the second part of the Rosary. They breakfasted at nine. Then, after an act of adoration to the Sacred Heart, they separated to employ themselves in the discharge of their several duties, such as nursing and other neighborhood visiting as well as work indoors. At a quarter to twelve they gave some moments to examination of conscience, to adoration, and to reading of the New Testament. During dinner at noon one of the Sisters read aloud some pages of Holy Scripture, to which the others listened in reflection. After dinner there was recreation until two o'clock. Reading of the *Imitation* and work filled the time from then until five, when they made a visit to the Blessed Sacrament and recited another third of the Rosary. At seven they had supper, followed by recreation until half-past eight. The day terminated with short spiritual reading and prayer. It was a life tending to the fulfillment of the Apostle's counsel: 'Pray without ceasing; all that you do, do for the love of Jesus Christ.' " Mother Seton was so constant "in her fervour and mortification" that her juniors imitated her with love and reverence.

The Sisters went to mass on Sundays up to the church on the mountain near the college. They waded the brook which crossed their forest path, until Father Dubois observed the wetness of their feet and had a horse sent down to them. The Sisters in their turn assumed the care of the church altar, washing its linens, and one or another of them took the part of organist through the chanting of the psalms and canticles. It was a weekly pastime on fine Sundays to climb the mountain after mass to a half-sheltered dell of rocks which they called their "grotto." From this eminence they had a magnificent sweep of mountain view. The valley, nesting the village and their little habitation, stretched away in beauty beneath their eyes. To such women as these the sublime scenery woke no feelings so much as adoration of its Creator and gratitude to Him. Up here Elizabeth Seton often recited the canticle of the three children in the fiery furnace, that prayer which calls upon all things to bless and

glorify God, their parent. They spread their
luncheon here, the mother and the rest conversing gaily, for they were ever the lightest-
hearted of ascetics. Afterwards they climbed
or read or talked, until the notes of the distant
church bell rose softly to their ears and called
them down to the vespers which ended the one
recreation of their week.

The principal objects of Mother Seton's order
were always two: the teaching of children and
the saving of souls. No doubt the two purposes
were considered as different forms of the same
thing. The congregation was to subsist by
teaching, but at the start it was so poor that
it had almost no means. Their few pupils
brought their numbers up to sixteen; with the
help of the meager payments for tuition and
board, they were barely able to house and feed
themselves. The Sisters gave the pupils far
better food than they had themselves; the community members could afford neither butter,
milk, nor coffee; for long seasons they had nothing better than bread made of the coarsest
grain and a pitiful tea brewed from molasses
and carrot-roots. Mother Seton's watch was
the only timepiece. They had no looking-glass
and no glass in their windows, only a few slats
nailed across the latter, through which the snow
came freely in. It is less wonder that Harriet
and Cecilia Seton succumbed under such circumstances than that their Sisters survived.

When Mr. Carroll, who had now become Archbishop Carroll, had visited the establishment,

he wrote back to Mother Seton: "I cannot think with calmness of your situation for the winter, for I learn from Father du Bourg that your new house cannot receive you until the beginning of the year, and certainly that is no time for a removal. I have confidence that in spite of my fears you will at least preserve your lives under your present diminutive shelter, inconvenient and open to all winds as it is." It is evident that the Archdiocese was poor itself, or Archbishop Carroll must have sent some relief as well as his sympathy to the Emmitsburg Sisters. Mr. Cooper, who had purchased the land for the Sisterhood, was now a student at the college on the mountain, and he often came down to serve with Father Dubois at mass in the Sisters' tiny chapel.

It is amazing how much the Sisters accomplished in their crowded little abode, and almost without income—teaching poor children, visiting the sick and attending their own, spinning, weaving, knitting, and making clothes for the poor. Their own clothes were in such condition that Bishop Cheverus of Boston, observing one particularly tattered Sister, inquired if she were doing a penance. Mother Seton only smiled. More prosperous days followed. By 1810 the Stone House was filled to overflowing, and in February, as soon as it was possible, the community moved into its larger building. Now for the first time St. Joseph's Sisterhood thrived. Numerous were the candidates for admission to the community and the school. Sis-

ter Elizabeth Boyle, one who was admitted at
this time, came, like the superioress, of a distinguished Episcopalian family. Thirty-six
years later she became the first mother of the
New York community.

From the first it had been manifest that the
rule of St. Vincent de Paul, which Mother Seton
was so anxious to follow, must be modified in
certain respects. That rule looks to the education of the poor and their assistance in other
ways, and in France, where the Daughters of
Charity follow it, they are relieved of self-sup-
port by their endowments. At the same time,
in Europe there are numerous schools for the
daughters of the well-to-do, but such establish-
ments were few in the United States at the beginning of the nineteenth century. Therefore,
instead of confining their efforts to the education
of poor children, the St. Joseph's Sisters
changed their plan so as to allow themselves
to take girls to school whose parents could pay
for their tuition and so in part bear the expenses of the community. Thus in 1812 the St.
Vincent rule, duly modified, was adopted for a
probationary year. In the next year the Sisterhood finally ratified the rules and each Sister
took her first unconditional vows—vows which
bind the votaress for a twelvemonth, when she
might renew them or not. In 1813, eighteen
Sisters first pronounced the determinate vows
and thus formally became the first American
Sisters of Charity. At last, Mother Seton's
order was firmly and formally established.

Also in 1813 the novitiate of the community was formed, with Sister Catharine Mullen as the mistress of novices. From the Emmitsburg Community as thus organized have sprung either directly or indirectly almost all the Roman Catholic sisterhoods now in the United States. The mother community at Emmitsburg has remained the largest house. Its greatest daughter community is that of Mount Saint Vincent on the Hudson, which in turn has mothered houses in New Jersey and Canada and elsewhere. At the time of Elizabeth Seton's death at forty-seven her spirit had already borne and reared twenty-one communities in the East; and now they have spread into nearly every State. They have taken the form of orphan asylums, hospitals, free schools, and boarding schools. In the governance of these schools she allowed no *espionnage,* no watching of the pupils to "catch" them in misdoings. The only punishment permitted by Mother Seton was, when necessary, to require the refactory pupil to sit on a bench before a crucifix; there always sooner or later the child would melt, and come and confess her fault, when she would be kissed upon the forehead and sent away happy. It is no wonder that a ruler of so smiling an authority was so beloved.

In 1819 a question arose as to Mother Seton's reëlection. The rules forbade more than two successive terms, and Mother Seton herself objected to her own reëlection; she had already served twice and an illness had weakened her.

The community, however, would not entertain the thought of having any other superior. Archbishop Carroll referred the problem to a council of Sulpitian priests. As the dignitaries sustained the Sisters in setting aside the rule in this matter, Mother Seton meekly obeyed, with the remark, however, that it was an election of the dead. In two years' time she did lapse away in consumption, in 1821. At Emmitsburg in a bare room one reads in silence this inscription:

HERE, NEAR THIS DOOR, BY THE FIRE-PLACE, ON A POOR, LOWLY COUCH, DIED OUR CHERISHED AND SAINTED MOTHER SETON, ON THE 4TH OF JANUARY, 1821. SHE DIED IN POVERTY, BUT RICH IN FAITH, AND GOOD WORKS.

Her body reposes in a Gothic tomb of white marble in the center of the cemetery. Cardinal Gibbons in 1880 urged that steps be taken towards her canonization, and the question of naming her a saint is still pending in the Vatican in Rome. And well may she be canonized, for her life was rich not alone in religious exaltation but in that saintship of service which has pronounced its benediction upon suffering everywhere. Founder of the Sisters of Charity she was, but her work did not stop there. The devotion of her Sisters has found its counterpart in other faiths and creeds. Wherever there is sorrow there is woman's compassion

buoyed by woman's faith. And the language
of this compassion is the same whether it issues
from lips framed in the close black bonnet of
the Deaconess or the snowy wimple of the Sister
of Charity.

CHAPTER IV

LUCRETIA MOTT

BY ANNE ELIZABETH JENKINS

"LUCRETIA MOTT was as much above the average woman as Abraham Lincoln above the average man."

After her death, this tribute was paid to Mrs. Mott by a friend, and when one follows the eighty-seven years of her life, so rich in good works, so steadfastly modeled after high ideals, he cannot but feel that the tribute was earned.

She was born on the third of the "First Month," in the year 1793, on the island of Nantucket where her ancestors had lived since its first settlement by white men. Her father, Thomas Coffin, although a sailor from boyhood, was a man of refinement and of unusually studious habits. Her mother, Anna Folger Coffin, is described as a woman of great energy, keen wit and unfailing good sense. They were members of the Society of Friends as their fathers and grandfathers had been before them, and Lucretia was carefully trained in the beliefs and daily observances of this society. She wore the sober costume of the Friends, she attended the meetings, and was taught to seek the Divine Guidance in all the problems of her childish

LUCRETIA MOTT

world. She believed that she was wayward and used to pray earnestly over her hasty temper, but in later life she wrote of herself: "I always loved the good and in childhood tried to do right."

Very little is told about that childhood. Here and there, a word throws the light for a moment on the little girl. She was "high-spirited," "ingenuous," "quick-tempered," "impatient of stupidity," "active," "warm-hearted," "a spit-fire," "a tease," yet she was the little mother of a family of five whenever Mrs. Coffin made her necessary trips to the mainland; she was the trusted messenger, sent on all the important errands; and she had learned to sit without drowsiness or restlessness during the Friends' meetings. Much may be inferred from these few words. They give the record of a battle for self-discipline, fought and won by a little girl under twelve years of age. They do not show, however, that she had any sense of the artistic. Her attempts at singing frequently called from her mother the remark: "Oh, Lucretia, if thee was as far out of town as thee is out of tune, thee wouldn't get home to-night;" and once, in later years, when a friend called her attention to a beautiful view she said: "Yes, it *is* beautiful now that thou points it out, but I should not have noticed it."

While Lucretia was a girl, Mrs. Coffin earned a scanty living, during the long absences of her husband on his cruises, by keeping a little shop for the sale of East Indian goods. As the leading industries of Nantucket were whale-fishing and East Indian trading, which kept the men away from home much of the time, the women had much opportunity to prove their efficiency in business as well as domestic affairs. Many a Nantucket woman carried on her husband's business during his voyages, besides doing the milking, churning, carding, spinning, weaving, scouring, cooking and mending demanded by her own department of the family partnership. It was small wonder, then, that Lucretia never for a moment looked upon women as the weaker sex. Many years later she said with vigor, at a woman's rights convention: "The cause is dear to my heart. . . . I grew up so thoroughly imbued with woman's rights that it was the most important question of my life from a very early day."

This simple, wholesome life formed Lucretia's habits. Although she did not live on the island after her twelfth year, she always cherished its traditions and "Nantucket way" was the way of her household to the very end. One of the most winning Nantucket customs was that of drawing the chairs in the front parlor into a sociable circle around the fire, so that when the guests came in from tea, they found them ready for the evening's conversation. This had been little Lucretia's task, and long after her girlhood, she sometimes slipped away from the tea-table and, feeble as she was, pushed the chairs into the old hospitable circle. Her grandchildren all remember her saying when

they were together in the parlor: "Move up—
come forward. Do come more into a circle."

It was after a most unfortunate experience
that Captain Coffin gave up his sea-faring life
and moved his family to Boston. At first the
children attended a private school, but afterwards the father sent them to the public schools
of the district "to mingle with all classes without distinction." The child profited by this
contact for she wrote later that it gave her a
"feeling of sympathy for the patient and struggling poor."

When she was thirteen years old, Lucretia
was sent, with a younger sister, to the Friends'
Boarding school at Nine Partners, New York.
Here they remained for two years without going
home, for the journey was too expensive to be
undertaken. The school experience was, on the
whole, a happy one, though the fair-minded Lucretia sometimes rebelled at what seemed to
her the unreasonable severity of the discipline.
It was especially hard for her to see others punished and once when one of the boys—a favorite
of hers—was confined in a dark closet, on bread
and water, she and her sister contrived to get
into the boys' side of the house in order to tuck
under the door bread liberally buttered.

One of the favorite amusements of the board-
ing-school girls was to play meeting. At one of
these meetings, they considered a case of violation of the "Discipline" and Lucretia and another girl were appointed to visit the offender
and to report to the society. This report

they drawled as follows: "Friends, we have
visited Tabitha Field—and—we labored with
her—and we think—we mellowed her—some."

James Mott, who afterwards became Lucretia's husband, was a teacher, at this time, in the
boys' department of the school. His sister
Sarah was Lucretia's favorite friend and the
three often met at his home.

When Lucretia was only fifteen, she was
made an assistant teacher in the school, and,
at the end of a year, was promoted to the position of a regular teacher. As teachers, James
and Lucretia were frequently thrown together
and soon fell deeply in love. They were the
exact complement of each other. "He was tall
with sandy hair, kind, blue eyes and a shy, grave
manner; she was short in stature, dark-haired,
impulsive and vivacious in manner and quick in
her movements. He enjoyed nothing so much
as silence; she nothing more than talking; he
was likely to become depressed and discouraged; she . . . was a sunbeam of happiness.
His was the gentler and more yielding disposition; hers the indomitable energy and resolution, which in a less disciplined character might
have been willfulness." Even at this age—17
—Lucretia's nature contained the elements of
spiritual fervor which later developed so beau-
tifully and blossomed into a life devoted to the
service of mankind.

The engagement was approved by both families. James accepted a place in Thomas Coffin's new business. After a few months, he was

able to declare their intention of marriage before the monthly meeting, as is the custom of
the Friends, and on the tenth of Fourth month,
1811, in the Pine Street Meeting House, their
marriage was solemnized, according to the order
of Friends "with a gravity and weight becoming the occasion." James was almost twenty-
three and Lucretia a little past eighteen. The
wish of James' mother that "each succeeding
day" might bring "an increase of pure, tran-
quil contentment" was perfectly fulfilled
through fifty-seven years of married life.
Their friend Robert Collier said of it, many
years later: "It was the most perfect wedded
life to be found on earth. They were both of a
most beautiful presence . . . both free to take
their own way as such fine souls always are and
yet their lives were so perfectly one that neither
of them led or followed the other, so far as one
could observe, by the breadth of a line."

The first years of their married life were
years of financial strain, during which it was
necessary to exercise the most rigid economy.
When Captain Coffin's business became insufficient to support two families, James began to
look about for a place for himself. Since a
little daughter had come to them, there were
now three mouths to feed. After two or three
unsuccessful attempts to establish himself, he
finally, in 1817, entered the employ of John
Large, of Philadelphia, at a salary of seven
hundred and fifty dollars, with the promise of
one thousand dollars before the year was out.

Lucretia opened a small school, which was successful.

Just at this time an event occurred which was one of the moving influences in Lucretia's life. It was the loss of their second child, a boy of rare promise. In her grief, Lucretia turned to her religion for comfort and was finally moved to express herself in Friends' meeting. Long years afterwards, when asked how she became a preacher in the Society, she said that "grief at the dear boy's death" turned her mind that way and "after a small beginning, meeting with sympathy and encouragement the rest was gradual and easy."

When Mrs. Mott entered the ministry, the Society of Friends was, to outward appearances, a united body, but it was known among the leaders that there was trouble brewing, the trouble which later resulted in the "Separation." Lucretia, who was always more interested in principles than dogmas, took no part in the controversy at first, but her well-known sympathy with Elias Hicks, who later headed the unorthodox party, made her an object of suspicion among the orthodox Friends. One day two women elders called on her. They sat a few moments in silence and then said that they had sometimes been unable to agree wholly to the views she advanced and that they had been particularly tried with an expression used by her in meeting on the previous First day. They could not remember the sentence but it ended with "notions of Christ." Mrs. Mott repeated

the entire sentence: "Men are to be judged by
their likeness to Christ rather than by their
notions of Christ." Was that it? It was.
Then she quietly informed them that it was a
quotation from their honored William Penn!
The Friends sat in silence a few moments and
then rose and left the house. What else could
they do?

It is unnecessary to go into the details of this
religious controversy. It is enough to know, in
this connection, that the liberal party which was
afterwards called the "Hicksite," claimed the
right of private judgment and individual opinion in opposition to a dogmatic settling of all
religious questions, and that James and Lucretia Mott sympathized with this party. In 1827,
during the week of the yearly meeting, a large
number of Friends gathered to discuss the question. The result was that the two parties
agreed to separate. The Hicksites "went out"
and began to hold meetings of their own.
James Mott "went out" with them. For some
time Lucretia was undecided what to do. She
had dear friends in both divisions, and the situation was much as a liberal minded Friend
summed it up: "For the short distance you
propose to move, it seems scarcely worth while
to get up." After about a month, however, she
took the step, and never afterwards regretted
it.

This division in the Society of Friends reflected the general spirit of questioning among
the churches. Channing's heresy was becoming

orthodoxy in the face of the bolder utterances of Theodore Parker. Everywhere there was a breaking away from dogma.

With church theologies, the Motts were always out of sympathy. "The more my attention is directed to a studied theology and systematized Divinity, the more deeply do I deplore its effect on the mind and character," Mrs. Mott wrote.

And again: "By what right does Orthodoxy give the invidious name of Infidel . . . to those who dissent from its cherished opinions? . . . I am not troubled with difficulties about the Bible. I love the truths of the Bible. I love the Bible because it contains so many truths; but I was never educated to love the errors of the Bible." Mrs. Mott searched always for the spirit of the teachings of the Bible and never was confined to its letter. "The bold figurative language of that book [the Bible] . . . should be taken in its most spiritual sense," she said.

When asked once how she reconciled herself to the statements in the old testament in regard to the Lord's commanding his children to go to war, she answered that she did not believe that God ever authorized or sanctioned war in any age or any nation. "I can more easily believe that man is fallible than that God is changeable." Again she said: "The error of the assumption of human depravity and a vicarious offering is so fatal to human progress that I should be unfaithful to my conviction did I not attempt to controvert this creed and to uphold truth as of all acceptation, rather than *authority* for truth." At a memorable meeting she made the statement that all the leading reforms of the age had sprung, not from dogmas but "from the individual soul of man."

The religion of Lucretia Mott went hand in hand with progress. She had no use for the narrow sectarianism that set itself against each forward step taken by the world's thinkers. She believed that the human mind is capable of being perfected and that religion must accomplish this emancipation.

Between 1822 and 1830 four more children had been born to Mr. and Mrs. Mott—the second daughter, Martha, came in 1818. Yet in spite of the fact that there was now a family of eight for which to provide and although Mrs. Mott, twelve years before, had given up her school, with its contribution to the family purse, Mr. Mott, in 1830, made the tremendous financial sacrifice of retiring from the cotton business because it depended on slave labor.

The question of slavery, which was the burning one of the hour, had borne itself in upon the consciousness and the conscience of Lucretia Mott. In her protests against it, she antedated even Garrison, and from the time of the separation, she pled "in season and out of season for immediate emancipation." When in 1833, the American Anti-Slavery Society held its third decennial meeting in Philadelphia, to demand "immediate, not gradual emancipation," she was there as a spectator and re-

sponded to the invitation to speak. The service
she rendered the convention was most important. When the delegates learned that two influential men who had been invited to preside at
the meetings had declined for prudential reasons, the convention wavered. At that critical
moment, Mrs. Mott rose, and with a vigor that
carried conviction, reminded her hearers that
right principles are stronger than great names.

"If our principles are right, why should we
be cowards?" she said.

She took her seat amid cries of "Go on," and
not another word was spoken in favor of delay.

Immediately after this convention, the Philadelphia Female Anti-Slavery Society was
formed. Lucretia Mott became one of its members, and later its president. Her activity
brought down upon her the persecution of the
Society of Friends which was taking no position in regard to the slavery question and was
averse to having one of its members so prominent an Abolitionist. The Friends tried again
and again to find grounds for dismissing Mrs.
Mott from their membership but she gave them
no adequate reason. This persecution, which
followed her for many years, was a source of
great grief to Mrs. Mott, whose friendly nature
reached out naturally for approbation. That
she followed the course which seemed right to
her in spite of the consequences is a proof of
her splendid moral courage.

The stand which the Motts took upon Abolition brought them into many stirring scenes.

In 1838 Lucretia Mott was one of the women
who calmly prosecuted the business of the Anti-
Slavery Convention of American Women, in
Pennsylvania Hall, unmoved by the hoots and
yells of the mob which surrounded the building and hurled stones through the windows.
And that night, after the burning of the hall,
she and her husband, with a few friends, sat
quietly in their parlor awaiting a threatened
attack by the same rioters, whose savage cries
they could hear, coming closer and closer. The
attack was averted, but Lucretia Mott showed
that for the sake of her principles she was
ready fearlessly to meet even violence.

When speaking of the outrage of the burning
of Pennsylvania Hall, Dr. Channing said:
"In that crowd was Lucretia Mott, that beautiful example of womanhood. Who that has
heard the tones of her voice, and looked on the
mild radiance of her benign and intelligent
countenance can endure the thought that
such a woman was driven by a mob from
the spot to which she had gone, as she reli-
giously believed, on a mission of Christian sympathy?"

On another occasion, when the annual meeting of the Anti-Slavery Society of New York
was broken up by a mob, some of the speakers
in leaving the hall were roughly handled by the
rowdies. When Mrs. Mott noticed this disorder, she asked the gentleman who was escorting
her, to go to the help of some of the women who
were timid.

"But who will take care of you?" he said.

"This man," she answered, quietly laying her hand on the arm of one of the roughest of the mob, "he will see me safe through."

The ruffian responded to this gentle appeal to his manhood and helped her to a place of safety.

In 1839 the British and Foreign Anti-Slavery Society of London called a general conference, to commence June 12, 1840, to confer as to the best means of hastening the extinction of the slave trade. Since the Massachusetts and Pennsylvania Anti-Slavery Societies had by this time admitted women to equal membership with men—although after a quarrel which divided the societies—they responded by sending both male and female delegates to the convention. Among these delegates were James and Lucretia Mott, and a woman whose name has become famous in the woman's rights cause, Elizabeth Cady Stanton.*

The trip would have been an impossibility to the Motts, owing to financial difficulties, if a friend had not sent them a generous gift of money. This gift they accepted in the spirit in which it was sent, since the cause of Abolition was so dear to their hearts that they were eager to forward it. This evidence of friendship was very sweet to Lucretia Mott, for friends were growing fewer and fewer as she became more and more devoted to the anti-slavery cause. Her health was much broken at this time, and

* See *Heroines of Modern Progress*, p. 67.

her husband welcomed the sea voyage, hoping
that it might put new vigor into her frail body.

Mrs. Mott carried to London with her a "minute" from the Monthly Meeting to which she
belonged, which stated that she was an approved minister, in good standing with the Society of Friends, but the orthodox Friends, who
had so persistently carried on their persecution
of her in America, took pains to write over to
England to warn their "brethren" of the heretic who was shortly to come to them. Consequently abroad she was the object of much petty
persecution of the kind that at home had so
annoyed her. One young Quaker, who had
pointedly left her out of his invitations on a
number of occasions, said to her: "Thou must
excuse me, Lucretia, for not inviting thee with
the rest, but I fear thy influence on my children."

But a greater disappointment than this re-
ception at the hands of the Friends awaited
Mrs. Mott in London. The news came to the
Motts that no women were to be admitted as
delegates to the convention. Garrison himself felt so outraged at this decision that he refused to take his seat in the convention. He
could not forget that Lucretia Mott was the
first woman to give him the right hand of fel-
lowship when he came out of prison.

The effort to seat women was led on the first
day of the meeting by Wendell Phillips, whose
wife was delegated by the Massachusetts Society. An excited discussion followed, which

continued several hours. Then the question was decided in the negative by a rather large majority because the admission of women was "contrary to precedent," and would make the convention "ridiculous." William Ashurst pointed out to them the inconsistency of calling a *world's* convention to abolish slavery and at its opening hour depriving half the world of their liberty.

This act of unfairness and discourtesy Mrs. Mott mentions briefly in her diary. In one place she says: "The Friends present were nearly all opposed to women's admission. We were told that the secret of it was that our coming had been announced in London Yearly Meeting and that they were put on their guard against us as not of their faith." William Howlitt attributed their exclusion wholly to the fact that they were looked upon by the Friends as heretics. He writes to Mrs. Mott: "What a miserable spectacle is this! The 'World's Convention' converting itself into the fag-end of the Yearly Meeting of the Society of Friends. . . . The convention has not merely insulted you, but those who sent you. It has testified that the men of America are at least far ahead of us in their opinion of the discretion and usefulness of women."

Mrs. Mott's keen sense of humor never failed her, even in the most discouraging conditions. She jots down in her diary: "The World's Convention . . . assembled with such guests as they chose to invite. We were kindly admitted

behind the bar.'' And again: ''Nathaniel
Calvin then for the first time sallied forth to
our bar saying: 'Now if the spirit moves you
to speak on this subject—you will be *allowed*
to say what you wish.' Out of the abundance of
a full heart and an indignant spirit here might
words have been uttered!''

On the last day of the convention the women
were honored by seats downstairs so that they
could hold conference with those who chose
to go to them. A protest against their exclusion was offered. Mrs. Mott says of it:
''Calvin boldly and impudently moved that it
be laid on the table. William Scabs made excellent closing remarks that although on some
subjects they had had conflicting sentiments di-
viding them as distinct as the billows, yet he
believed there was unity enough in our common
cause to make us again 'as the sea,' and so the
Convention closed!''

In an account of the World's Convention,
Richard D. Webb of Dublin says: ''The middle of the front seat of the ladies' own portion
of the hall was the usual seat of *one* who was
certainly one of the most remarkable women of
the whole assembly. . . . Nobody doubted that
Lucretia Mott was the lioness of the Convention.''

And again in speaking of the exclusion of the
women delegates, he says: ''We shall not discuss the question here . . . but we shall take
the liberty to express our wish that half the
temper, fullness of mind, warmth of heart, di-

rectness of utterance, facility of elucidation and
vivacity of manner which distinguished Lucretia Mott had been the gift of nine-tenths of the
gentlemen who raised their voices . . . for our
edification.''

Expressions of indignant sympathy from
Harriet Martineau, Daniel O'Connor, and a few
other friends, helped Mrs. Mott through this
period of heart-sickness. Chief among these
friends was Elizabeth Cady Stanton, whom they
met for the first time in London.* Mrs. Stanton writes: ''Mrs. Mott was to me an entirely
new revelation of womanhood.'' ''I found in
this new friend a woman emancipated from all
faith in man-made creeds. . . . Nothing was
too sacred for her to question as to its rightful-
ness in principle and practice. 'Truth for authority, not authority for Truth, was . . . the
motto of her life.' ''

From London, the Motts made a hurried trip
through Ireland and Scotland, where Mrs.
Mott preached. The persecution by the orthodox Friends followed them even here, but they
found friends who extended to them courtesy
and kindness.

After their return to America, the Motts continued their life of useful activity. They attended the Anti-Slavery meetings; Lucretia
preached as before, and their house was the
gathering place for a large family and circle of
friends. A few quotations from her letters will
show that her preaching and club work did not

* See *Heroines of Modern Progress*, p. 68.

make Mrs. Mott neglect her housewifely duties.
She writes:

"With all this traveling and reading, I find
time to darn the stockings, and attend somewhat to a family numbering from ten to twenty
every day." "I prepared mince for forty pies,
doing every part myself, even to meat chop-
ping, picked over lots of apples, stewed a
quantity, chopped some more and made apple
pudding." "Early in the morning before
quite light I assorted the ironed clothes and
mended stockings." "We had nine or ten
friends lodging with us" and "some forty or
fifty at meals daily."

This entertaining was done in the simplest
manner, for Mrs. Mott was extremely frugal
—through years of necessity, although her husband was now prospering in business and they
were beyond want.

To keep open house became the habit of her
lifetime, so much so that she found herself in
an amusing situation, once, when she was visiting a granddaughter. The house was small
and the family large. Mrs. Mott went up to
Boston to meeting and was expected home, with
her husband, to a family dinner. However,
after the meeting a young gentleman and lady
from England presented letters of introduction
to her and she became greatly interested in
them. When the time came for her to take her
train, she impulsively asked them to go home
with her to dine. They accepted at once, and
she also invited William Garrison, his son, and

her sister Martha. When they had left the cars, Mrs. Mott, who began to realize what consternation their arrival might produce, hurried on ahead to break the news to the hostess. With pretended dismay, but with a good deal of amusement, she said to her granddaughter: "What *will* thou say to me! I've asked Lord and Lady Amberly and William Lloyd Garrison out here to dine, and Aunt Martha and William with them. They are all just coming up the hill."

It was at home, surrounded by a host of loyal admirers, that Mr. and Mrs. Mott found happiness, although the attacks from the Friends grew more and more bitter. Titled foreigners, scholars, politicians, preachers and reformers met at their board, where, after the meal was over and the table cleared, the sweet-faced hostess washed up the silver and glass, while she joined in the conversation of her guests.

But these guests were not always those who were their social equals. Many a ragged, hungry outcast crept to their door and went away fed and clothed, and no hunted fugitive from slavery was ever turned away. Their granddaughter describes an instance of this sort. They were all sitting in the parlor one evening when they heard the angry rumble of a mob. Experience had taught them what to expect; a slave was being pursued.

"With the natural impulse for protection he rushed to the well known refuge—the house of

James and Lucretia Mott.'' James Mott, then a white-haired man, opened the door. The slave dashed in, and without stopping, ran through the house and out of the back gate. James Mott stood at the door confronting the angry mob, when someone threw a brick at him. The brick hit the door jamb behind him, and this bore for many a day the mark of the misdirected fury.

At the trial of the Passmore Williams case, Mrs. Mott was in attendance to give sympathy and support to the slave Jane Johnson, and when the poor soul was taken from the Court and driven hastily away, Mrs. Mott sat with her in the carriage.

In the year 1848, around the tea-table of a common friend, the first woman's rights convention was planned, by Lucretia Mott, Elizabeth Cady Stanton and Mary Ann McClintock.* Back in London, during the world's convention, as they walked slowly home together at the end of the first day's session, Mrs. Mott and Mrs. Stanton conceived the idea of a woman's rights convention. Eight years of active work in the cause of Abolition had given these women courage to start this new crusade and had fully convinced them of the crying need for it. The convention was held in Seneca Falls, New York, July 19 and 20. The Declaration of Sentiments drawn up at this convention demanded all that even the most radical friends of the movement have since claimed.

* See *Heroines of Modern Progress*, p. 72.

Other conventions followed in various parts of New York, Ohio, Massachusetts, Indiana and Pennsylvania, and for twenty years, Mr. and Mrs. Mott gave the movement their generous support.

In one of her discourses, called "Woman," Mrs. Mott defends her position by reference to the Bible: "The laws given on Mount Sinai for the government of man and woman were equal and the precepts of Jesus make no distinction. Those who read the Scriptures and judge for themselves, not resting satisfied with the perverted application of the text, do not find the distinction that theology and ecclesiastical authorities have made in the condition of the sexes." And for all her work, whether for the emancipation of woman or for that of the negroes, there is this background of religion.

During the winter of 1856, it became apparent to her family that Mrs. Mott was no longer strong enough to bear the strain of housekeeping in the city. She was worn out with entertaining so much and with the constant drain on her sympathy and strength made by friends, public duties and private charities. Her granddaughter says: "It seemed as if she could not call an hour of the day her own; all sorts of people came to her with their affairs and no one appeared to realize that she might have affairs of her own."

So "Three-thirty-eight," the city house, was sold, and a little farmhouse eight miles out of Philadelphia on the Old York Road, opposite

Oak Farm, where some of her family already lived, was bought.

A final gathering of the clan was arranged, a last meeting before the doors which had always stood open to them should close for good. A series of nonsense verses written to celebrate the event was greeted with shouts of laughter, but for most of those who were present, it would have been quite as easy to cry as to laugh. The verses began:

> Who wearied of the world's renown,
> And sought a useful life to crown
> By selling off his house in town?
>   James Mott.

> Who was it that the sale decreed
> And urged him on to do the deed,
> And wished to close the terms with speed?
>   Lucretia!

And ended with:

> Who constantly will ring the bell,
> And ask if they will please to tell
> Where Mrs. Mott has gone to dwell?
>   The beggars.

> And who will miss, for months at least,
> That place for rest for man and beast
> From North and South and West and East?
>   Everybody.

In the spring of 1857 Mr. and Mrs. Mott moved to the new house, where they spent the remainder of their lives. The house was a sunny old place, surrounded by maple and oak trees. From this haven, Mr. and Mrs. Mott ventured out into the city or nearby villages for meetings, conventions and a certain amount of necessary shopping. They usually drove in a neat square covered wagon built for two.

Mrs. Mott always did her shopping at the small, out-of-the-way stores, though she paid more for her purchases and had often to go long distances to get them. One anecdote is told of her in connection with this custom. She bought a child's high chair and had it put on to the cars. At her usual stopping place, a mere shed, the chair was put off. Contrary to custom, no carriage met her, and there was no one in sight. Since she was afraid to leave the chair, she said to herself, with a little laugh, "It is not heavy," took off her bonnet, tied the strings together, hung it over her arm, and, placing the chair upside down on her head, walked across the fields to her house, nearly a quarter of a mile away!

She was always very unwilling to receive attention, and whenever her family remonstrated with her for going about so much alone, and offered to accompany her she would say: "No, thank thee, I do not want anyone. There is always somebody to help me in and out of cars and the conductors are very kind."

We may be sure that there was always someone to help this dear Quaker gentlewoman with her radiant look. One friend said of her at this time: "Her face became like that of a transfigured saint."

Sometimes the Motts would spend days away from home at the trial of a fugitive slave. It is said that the effect of her presence was potent. One of the lawyers in the Dangerfield trial, when he was asked some years later how he dared to change his political opinions, responded: "Do you think there is anything I dare not do after facing Lucretia Mott in that court room and knowing she wished me in hell?"

When there were no meetings or conventions James and Lucretia spent happy days at "Roadside." In the middle of the library, opposite the Franklin stove, stood her rocking chair and her two-shelved table covered with books, papers and writing materials, never disturbed by any hands but her own. Every morning she sat here, after her regular work was done, first to glance over the newspaper, and then to write letters or to read. She read a great deal, but could never enjoy a book alone, if it really interested her. If her husband was out, she would step to the foot of the stairs and call for some member of the family to come down to share the pleasure with her. There was usually someone near at hand, for Mr. and Mrs. Mott had not lived alone since the early days of their married life.

On the tenth of Fourth Month, 1861, James and Lucretia Mott celebrated their golden wedding. Children, grandchildren, and one tiny great-grandchild were present, and the wedding certificate, now yellow with age, was brought out and read aloud. The family noticed that a portion of the parchment had been torn away. Then Mrs. Mott was forced to admit that her hand had performed the desecration. Years before she had torn off the corner, because she needed some parchment with which to mend a battle-door for one of the children! This practical act was quite in accordance with the nature of the little woman who could drive for hours through the most lovely scenery without looking up from her knitting.

Mrs. Mott was always fragile, but her health at this time seemed failing. She wrote to her sister: "My day seems at times to be nearly over; but I shall patch up and mean to live as long as I can."

During the stirring days of the Civil War, Mrs. Mott was torn between her sympathy with Abolition and her condemnation of war. Her heart rejoiced when the great struggle was over and the negro had received his freedom. The close of the war meant also the end of the persecution which Mrs. Mott had endured for so many years. With the surrender at Appomattox Court House, peace came into the ranks of the Friends. Some of those who had been most bitter in their feeling toward Mrs. Mott had died, and now that emancipation was an accomplished fact, all of the Friends were inclined to believe that they had always favored it. In spite of the loss of several who were dear to them, the life of the Motts was full of

quiet happiness. They had lived to see their
work appreciated.

This serene companionship came to an end
in 1868. On the day before their wedding anniversary, James Mott passed quietly away in a
peaceful sleep; so peaceful that his wife did
not recognize it as death. Worn with the
night's watching, she laid her head beside his
on the pillow and slept too.

Her sister Martha, in writing to a friend,
concerning Lucretia said: "Though much
broken by the heavy affliction that has come to
her . . . she has borne the stroke better than
was feared."

She took up her life again with patient brav-
ery and tried to fulfill her duties, but the sense
of desolation remained with her to the end.

She continued to attend the yearly meetings
of the Friends, and woman's rights conventions. She was often invited to speak at these
and other meetings, where her presence was
looked upon as a benediction. At the centen-
nial anniversary of the old Pennsylvania Abolition Society she received a real ovation.
After one or two speeches had been made, the
president said:

"I propose now to present to you one of the
most venerable and noble of the American
women, whose voice for forty years has been
heard and has tenderly touched many noble
hearts. Age has dimmed her eye and weakened
her voice, but her heart, like the heart of a wise

man and a wise woman is yet young.   I present
to you Lucretia Mott.''

As she stepped forward, the vast audience
rose with tumultuous applause, cheering and
waving hats and handkerchiefs.   One who was
present said that the scene could never be forgotten; the frail little woman with a heavenly
inspiration beaming from her face, standing
there, motionless, waiting for the profound silence which followed.

She lived twelve years after her husband's
death, and then, on the evening of the eleventh
of Eleventh Month, after an illness of a week,
she quietly went to join him.

The funeral service was simple and impressive.   At the burying ground several thousand
people were gathered to pay the last act of
friendship to her who had been a friend to so
many.   With the exception of a few words by
Dr. Henry T. Childs, everything was conducted
in profound silence.   As all were standing by
the open grave, a low voice impulsively said:

''Will no one say anything?''

Another responded: ''Who can speak?
The preacher is dead.''

CHAPTER V

FANNY CROSBY

BY WOODMAN BRADBURY

THE name of Fanny Crosby (Mrs. Frances Jane Van Alstyne) is bound up with the evangelism of the last half century. To hear her name is to think of gospel songs and to remember pleasantly the blind poet who wrote "Blessed Assurance," "Rescue the Perishing" and "Saved by Grace." Yet few, even of those who are especially interested in gospel hymnody, realize the extent of her work. Her chief publishers possess five thousand five hundred of her hymns; and inasmuch as she declares that she must have written at least half as many more, she has the astonishing number of eight thousand religious poems to her credit!

"Hymns rarely have any serious value as poetry," said the late Professor Goldwin Smith. "There is nothing in them on which the creative imagination can be exercised. Hymns can be little more than the incense of a worshiping soul." Most critical readers will agree with Professor Smith; and if his dictum is true of the work of such great figures in Christian hymnody as Isaac Watts, James Montgomery and Charles Wesley, it applies with yet more truth to the prolific effusions of Miss Crosby. Great poetry her work is not. She is not sufficiently gifted to produce it on any theme, apart from the limitations of hymn-writing. A great facility in rhyming and expressing the emotions of the Christian heart in regular rhythm which can be set to music is hers in marked degree. More for herself than this, she does not claim. But hers is "the worshiping soul" and her hymns are "the incense" which she, and countless thousands of devout worshipers with her, offer to the God and Father of our Lord Jesus Christ.

Fanny Crosby was born in the little village of Southeast, Putnam County, New York, on March 24, 1820. Six weeks later she lost her eyesight. Her eyes became inflamed; Mr. Crosby called in a local physician who applied hot poultices, with the result that the baby's vision was destroyed. The popular indignation when this malpractice became known flamed so hot that the ill-educated doctor hurriedly left town for parts unknown. Fanny, herself, however, as she grew into girlhood, harbored no trace of resentment against him. She accepted her lot cheerfully, as a part of the will of God for her. Her natural buoyancy of disposition reënforced her Christian faith.

"Blindness," she wrote in later life, "can not keep the sunlight of hope from the trustful soul. One of the easiest resolves that I formed in my young and joyous heart was to leave all care to yesterday, and to believe that

FANNY CROSBY

the morning would bring forth its own peculiar
joy.'' A wise and fruitful resolve!

Much of this elasticity of nature was doubtless due to her splendid ancestry. Fanny
Crosby was well born. She can trace the two
lines of her ancestry back to the earliest New
England stock. Her mother, who was also a
Crosby, was descended from Simon Crosby
who came to Boston in 1635 and was one of the
founders of Harvard College, from which his
son, Thomas, was graduated in 1653. Fanny's
great-grandfather, Isaac Crosby, was the father
of nineteen children. One of them was born
while he was serving in the Revolutionary
Army; whereupon he asked for a furlough on
the ground that he had many children at home
and ''hadn't ever seen one of them.'' The furlough was immediately granted. The records
do not say whether, on his return to the army,
he confessed in what sense his words were true.
If he had the sensitive conscience of his de-
scendant, he doubtless did.

Fanny Crosby came naturally therefore by
a sense of humor and a playful spirit. She
was full of fun, joined the other children in
play, and was likely to be deep in any mis-
chief that was going on. Taking the description of natural objects from her young companions, imagination made them as plain to her
as sight did to them. She would leap over stone
walls, play tag, climb trees with the agility of
a cat, and ride the colts bareback across the
fields. This vivid imagination was made pos-

sible by senses of hearing and touch unusually
graphic. Sounds of nature, for instance, were
always a "feast" to her.

When a very little girl, a lamb was given to
her as a playmate. They soon became inseparable friends. The lamb grew, however, as
lambs will, and family necessities were insistent
then, as now, though "the high cost of living"
was not thought of. One day the lamb was
missing; the next, the dinner table supported
a savory roast on which the attention of all
was ravenously centered. Not so, the little
girl; she put two and two together and refused
to eat the cannibalistic meat or to receive comfort of her elders. In a day or two her tears
were dried; but when a neighbor offered her
another lamb for a pet, she refused it. The
pain of losing outweighed the joy of possessing.
The child had not grown to the wise philosophy:

> 'Tis better to have loved and lost
> Than never to have loved at all.

For solace, Fanny turned to the rose garden
which she had always loved. She was allowed
to pick whatever roses she wanted except from
a certain white rose bush "in the midst of the
garden." She would probably never have
yielded to temptation by herself; but when her
companions asked her for a white rose, she
picked one for them. Her aunt saw her do it;
and later in the day, she called Fanny and asked
her if she had picked a white rose. Promptly

came the answer, "No," although the child had
never told an untruth before. The aunt took
down the Bible and read the story of Ananias
and Sapphira, without note or comment. But
Fanny learned her life-long lesson that day.

At this period of her life, she began to learn
Bible verses. Thereby her memory, which
throughout life has been remarkable, was
trained, and the foundation laid for her knowledge of the Bible, which was of such inestimable
advantage to her as a hymn-writer. When
there were competitions in reciting Bible verses
either at home or at school, she was always
victor. Evening after evening at twilight, she
would sit on a favorite big brown rock and
drink in the sounds of birds, crickets and the
near-by waterfall, imagining the hues of the sky
and softly repeating to herself all the verses
of the Bible that came to her well stocked mind.
The scene is a prophecy of the Christian poet
that she became.

Although the little girl herself, probably because she did not know the poignancy of contrast, did not fret because of her sightlessness,
Mrs. Crosby could not endure the thought of
her daughter's blindness, if a cure could be
effected. So a journey was planned to New
York City to consult the great specialist, Dr.
Valentine Mott. It was an adventurous journey
to reach the Hudson River; then a trip of several days in the sailboat, where the mother was
seasick and little Frances played with the captain and the crew who sang songs and spun

"yarns." A young man and his cow were fellow passengers on the boat, the former too full of whiskey and the latter of milk. The drunken owner refused to milk the cow; but the captain ordered it done while the man's attention was diverted, and Mrs. Crosby, now happily recovered from her seasickness, made a custard which all on board pronounced very good!

Thus, after a journey more fraught with incident and excitement than would now-a-days be crowded into a trip across the continent, they arrived in New York; and after a few days' rest, presented themselves to the renowned physician for his examination and verdict. "My child," he said, in tones memorable for their kindness, "you can never be made to see!" The loving mother was grief-stricken, but not so the child. Life had brought her much joy already; would not yet fuller joy come with the years? She could not but look forward with anticipation and courage. In that mood was born her first poem, written when she was eight years old:

> Oh! what a happy soul I am!
>   Although I cannot see,
> I am resolved that in this world
>   Contented I will be.
> How many blessings I enjoy
>   That other people don't!
> To weep and sigh because I'm blind
>   I cannot nor I won't.

If the reader smiles at the expressions, he must admire at least the sentiment.

To gain an education now became her consuming ambition. Her father had died when
she was less than a year old, and the family
resources were meager. At the age of fifteen,
she was admitted to the New York Institute for
the Blind and a new chapter in her life was
begun. She did all she could to show her appreciation of the opportunities of this school.
Because of her flow of spirits and ready companionship she became a favorite among her
blind companions. Her skill in versifying
seemed remarkable to her mates who nearly succeeded in turning her head with their praise.
A wise teacher, seeing this danger, called her
to his office and gave her wholesome truth about
her poetry and herself. "Fanny, shun a flat-
terer as you would a viper," he concluded.

Among the chief advantages in this school
was the opportunity to meet distinguished
people. Visitors from foreign lands and American notables paid visits to the Institute and
were introduced to the students. William Cul-
len Bryant read his poems, Horace Greeley was
a frequent visitor, President Polk made a
pleasant impression, and Gen. Winfield Scott
caused a great flurry of excitement. Miss
Crosby particularly liked Henry Clay; his voice
was so sonorous and persuasive. For a time,
the superintendent had a young assistant whom
teachers and pupils learned to admire for his
ability and strong sincerity. His name was
Grover Cleveland; and as they followed his
brilliant career from step to step, no one of

them was surprised that he should become the President of the United States.

Less pleasant to record was the breaking out of cholera in the Institute. The epidemic raged fiercely in the city, and the hoarse cry: "Bring out your dead!" sounded grimly in the night hours. Many of the blind caught the infection and died. Miss Crosby herself had the initial symptoms one afternoon. Bravely she kept the news to herself, took the medicine, practiced the precautions which had been enjoined, committed herself to God,—and woke in the morning to find herself perfectly well! Those were dreadful days and left their scar upon the memory of those who passed through them.

After seven years of student life, Miss Crosby was graduated from the Institute, to return to it afterwards as teacher for eleven years, from 1847 to 1858. In 1844, she launched her first volume of verse, under the title, *The Blind Girl and Other Poems*. Many of these poems were autobiographical. Others were the addresses in poetic form with which she had greeted famous visitors to the Institute. *Monterey and Other Poems* followed in 1849. On the year of her marriage, 1858, she published *A Wreath of Columbia's Flowers*.

The most significant occurrence in this period of her life was her conversion. Religious she had been from childhood up, but not until she was thirty-one years of age did she have that vital assurance of Christ's love and God's pardon that she called her conversion. One night

in a vivid dream, a warm friend of hers, who
seemed to be dying, asked her, "Will you meet
me in heaven?" It did not matter to find, on
waking, that the friend was in sound health.
The question had set her to thinking deeply.
Shortly after she and her companions were
singing, "Alas! and did my Saviour bleed" and
and as they came to the line, "Here, Lord, I
give myself away," she definitely offered herself to God and a flood of light and joy ensued.
She joined the Old John Street Methodist
church. This experience became determinative
of her inner life, of her lifework, and of the
sentiment of her hymns.

Fanny Crosby was married to Mr. Alexander
Van Alstyne in 1858. Like herself, he was
blind and had been a teacher in the Institute
for the Blind. He was musical, also, and their
united lives made harmony for forty-four years,
until his death in 1902. At his wish, she continued to write under her maiden name by which
she was already becoming widely known.

At the time of her marriage, Fanny Crosby
was well started on what proved to be her life-
career, that of producing religious verse. In
1851, Mr. George F. Root, important in the development of music in America, wrote an air
for which he needed words. She supplied them
so acceptably that they collaborated in about
sixty songs. All of these had a wide circula-
tion and some became the most successful songs
of the period. Among them were "There's
music in the air," *Hazel Dell, Rosalie, the*

Prairie Flower, and *Bird of the North,* all sweet, sentimental songs warmly beloved a generation ago and popular now.

Four years later *The Flower Queen* was produced by them jointly. One day Mr. Root would tell in prose what he wanted the various flowers to say and hum the melody he had in mind; the next day Miss Crosby would have those sentiments expressed in rhyme, to fit the given melody. *The Flower Queen* was the first American cantata and was frequently produced in widely separated parts of the country. It gave popularity both to author and composer. Mr. Root's fame was still further enhanced by his war songs and Sunday school music.

Another composer with whom she was early thrown in contact was William B. Bradbury. He was a prolific composer for the Sunday school, a devout man who believed in consecrating his talent to religious uses. Such tunes as *Woodworth* ("Just as I am"), *Rest* ("Asleep in Jesus"), "Sweet Hour of Prayer," and "He leadeth me," are a worthy contribution to American hymnology and will preserve his name for many generations. Others like "Jesus, like a Shepherd lead us," "Even me," "The Solid Rock," were immensely popular in their day. Bradbury was a connecting link between the choral style of Greatorex and Lowell Mason on the one hand and the ballad style in sacred music which so soon became popular under the name of gospel songs.

When Mr. Bradbury was introduced to Miss

Crosby, he was deeply impressed with her work. "I am surprised beyond measure," he said, "and as long as I have a publishing house, you will always have work." He had long desired such words as Miss Crosby could write. This promise was fulfilled, and her connection with the firm ran for more than forty years. Mr. Bradbury himself, however, did not long survive. When he died, in 1868, his last words to her were, "Take up my life-work where I lay it down." At his funeral there was sung the first hymn they had done together, speeding his spirit to the land

> Where the fields are robed in beauty
> And the sunlight never dies.

Though their joint work was so short, she became warmly attached to Mr. Bradbury; and thirty years after his death she said to a namesake of his: "Of all my friends, I loved him the best. When I get to heaven I am going to ask first for William B. Bradbury."

In these early years, she worked much for Philip Phillips, the singing evangelist, whose songs were collected in *The Singing Pilgrim*. At one time he gave her a commission for forty hymns. These she did one by one, storing them all in her mind till all the forty were ready; not until then was the amanuensis called in. Not one of them was put on paper until all were done. As a feat of memory, that is truly remarkable, almost incredible. Later she repeated the feat, furnishing him with nearly as many more not one of which was committed to writing until all were finished.

Another of her collaborators was the Reverend Robert Lowry; to his music she wrote one of her most inspired hymns—"All the Way my Saviour leads me." The spirit of trustfulness and joyous resignation in the poem, is aptly conveyed by the music as well.

With Mrs. E. L. Knapp, she has twice collaborated most successfully. "Nearer the Cross, my Heart can say" and the world-famous "Blessed Assurance" are their joint work. The latter was written after Mrs. Knapp had played the melody over several times, asking what it "meant" to Miss Crosby. "It means *this!*" was the answer; and thus the spirit of the music was caught and put into language. "Blessed Assurance" has been particularly welcome in camp and on the march, although all of Miss Crosby's songs, with their warm sentiment and well-marked rhythm, have been very helpful among soldiers—and sailors, as well. The Soldier's Christian Association of the British Army has made constant use of them. During the South African war, many times when a group of soldiers would pass another, the salutation would be "Four-nine-four, boys," and the response would invariably be, "Six further on!" The key to these watchwords is found in the fact that number 494 in *Sacred Songs and Solos* is "God be with you till we

meet again"; and "six further on" is number
500, "Blessed Assurance, Jesus is mine."

Much work as compelling as that done with
Mrs. Knapp, Miss Crosby accomplished in collaboration with William H. Doane. To mention
such lines as "Pass me not, O Gentle Saviour,"
"Rescue the Perishing," "I am Thine, O
Lord," "Jesus Keep me near the Cross," "To
the Work, to the Work," and "Safe in the
Arms of Jesus," is to realize the extent of the
popular debt to both of these partners. The
composition of the last named hymn is characteristic of Miss Crosby's readiness of achievement. Mr. Doane burst into her room on April
30, 1868, and said, "There are just forty
minutes before my train leaves for Cincinnati.
Here is a melody. Can you write words for
it?" Twenty minutes passed in silence broken
only by the ticking of the clock, Mr. Doane waiting, Miss Crosby thinking. Then she turned
round to him. "It is all done," she said, and
dictated her verses. He caught his train, bearing with him words that were destined to bring
comfort to thousands of people.

"Safe in the Arms of Jesus" became popular
with great rapidity. That this hymn gave more
peace and satisfaction to mothers who had lost
their children than any other was the statement
made by Dr. John Hall, the pastor of the Fifth
Avenue Presbyterian church, New York. It has
also been useful in causing repentance and a
change of life. This incident, reported to Miss

Crosby, is typical: "John," said a dying mother, looking up at him through tearful eyes, "sing to me once more 'Safe in the Arms of Jesus.'" The young man choked. "Mother," he said, "I can't sing that song. It would be a lie; I am not safe and I can not sing a lie." It is not surprising to know that that confession of his need led him to Christ.

This was one of the first of the gospel hymns to be transcribed into foreign languages. "Once when laboring in London, I went to Basel, Switzerland, for a few days' rest," said Mr. Ira D. Sankey. "The evening I got there I heard under my window the most beautiful volume of song. I looked out and saw about fifty people, who were singing 'Safe in the Arms of Jesus' in their own language. I recognized the tune and spoke to them through an interpreter. The next evening I held a song service in an old French church in that city. The church was packed with people and many stood outside on the street."

Mr. Sankey figures in another typical incident. In 1894, when Miss Crosby was at Northfield, she was asked to make an address. At first she demurred, but finally consented and closed her remarks with the verses, "Some day the silver cord will break." The audience was much moved; and an English reporter who was present took down her hymn and published it in his London newspaper. Some time later, Mr. Sankey, who himself has successfully set some of her poems to music, saw the paper, cut

out the verses and handed them to Mr. George
C. Stebbins to be set to music. The inspiration
came; and soon the world was singing,
"Saved by Grace." A dramatic illustration of
the effect of this hymn once surprised the staid
worshipers of Christ Episcopal Church, Alle-
gheny, Pennsylvania. In the midst of a Sunday morning service, a quietly dressed young
woman of intellectual face arose and proceeded
rapidly and eloquently to tell of her conversion. As a little girl, she had attended Sunday
school there; had married young and been
drawn into a life of vanity, frivolity and world-
liness; and had been brought back to God by
hearing "Saved by Grace" sung at an out-door
meeting. The congregation, at first a bit
shocked, was visibly impressed with this narra-
tion; and the rector, descending from the chan-
cel, took the speaker's hand, welcoming her return.

Very different from the religious atmosphere
of Northfield were the surroundings which gave
rise to another of Miss Crosby's great hymns.
When Miss Crosby was visiting a mission in
one of the worst slums of New York, her sym-
pathies were kindled and the yearning of her
heart found expression in "Rescue the Perishing"—a hymn which has become indispensable
in rescue work of all sorts. Not only did Mr.
Moody find it useful, but also temperance
workers like Frances E. Willard and Francis
Murphy. A drunken man, unshaven and dirty,
staggered into this very mission one stormy

night. After the audience had sung "Rescue the Perishing," the leader used illustrations drawn from his life as a soldier. At the meeting's close, this man walked unsteadily up to the front and asked:

"When were you in that company you spoke of?"

"Why, all through the war," said the leader.

"Do you remember the battle of Shiloh?"

"Perfectly."

"Do you remember your captain's name?"

"Yes, his name was Hamilton."

"You are right! I am that man! I was your captain. Look at me to-day and see what a wreck I am. Can you save your old captain?"

He was saved that night and was soon helped by some of his former friends to get a respectable position, where his changed life bore eloquent testimony to the power of the gospel.

Of another sort was a man in Sussex, England, who owes equally much to this hymn. "I believe I can attribute my conversion, through the grace of God, to one verse of that precious hymn, 'Rescue the Perishing,'" he says. "I was far away from my Saviour and living without a Christian hope. I was fond, however, of singing hymns, and one day I came across this beautiful piece; and when I had sung the words,

Down in the human heart, crushed by the Tempter,
  Feelings lie buried that grace can restore;
Touched by a loving heart, wakened by kindness,
  Chords that were broken will vibrate once more,

I fell upon my knees and gave my heart to the Lord Jesus Christ. From that hour I have followed Him who, through this verse, touched my heart and made it vibrate with His praises ever since.''

Can work done so rapidly as was Miss Crosby's, and turned out in such profusion be of the highest quality? Undoubtedly not. Most of Fanny Crosby's work is ephemeral. Much of it has already passed into oblivion and much of the remainder will pass away sooner or later. The church hymn-books designed for formal public worship do not contain her verses. She recognized the fact that so large an output would lower the value of her name; and her eight thousand hymns have appeared under a hundred or so different pseudonyms! If the reader comes across the names of Rose Atherton, Florence Booth, Ella Dale, Frances Hope, Ruth Harmon, Victoria Frances, let him pay mental homage to Fanny Crosby; and he will be surprised to learn that the same homage is due when he sees the names of James Apple, James Black, Rian J. Sterling, W. Robert Lindsay, and others. Her achievement, be it noted in passing, is all the greater because she made such a valuable contribution to religious progress with hymns many of which were not of the highest merit.

So large is the progeny of her brain that it is little cause for wonder that the mother can not remember all her children. One morning the congregation at Northfield sang with much gusto, "Hide me, O my Saviour." Miss Crosby, who was sitting on the platform, liked it and turned to Mr. Stebbins to inquire the authorship. But the meeting was breaking up and in the confusion he made no answer. The same hymn was sung in the afternoon and again she asked Mr. Stebbins the author's name. After making sure that she was in earnest, he answered, "You are the guilty one!" For once, the wonderful memory had failed.

The theology of all these hymns is uniformly evangelical. Their author believes humanity to be sinful and in need of salvation; and she magnifies the love of God, the grace of Christ and the power of the Holy Spirit. The beauty of faith and of peace is painted in alluring tints and the glories of heaven described in glowing imagery drawn from Revelation. Every one of her hymns gives one aspect of the ever-fresh gospel. The central truth of her message in song is, "God so loved the world that He gave His only begotten Son, that whosoever believeth in Him should not perish but have everlasting life." Thus her songs form an appropriate atmosphere for evangelistic preaching: they produce conviction of sin and conversion. Of their far-reaching influence, only eternity can give the details.

Fanny Crosby has "tasted and seen that the Lord is good" and desires others to enjoy the same bountiful feast. Shut in from the distracting sights of the outer world, she has seen deeply into eternal truth and has put that truth into verse that has influenced countless thousands of lives.   Over fifty million copies of her gospel songs have been sold.   During the last years of her life, Frances Ridley Havergal kept up a correspondence with Fanny Crosby, though they never met.

In these lines of Miss Havergal is admiration of Miss Crosby for her spiritual insight, her resignation and her consecration:

Sweet blind singer over the sea,
Tuneful and jubilant, how can it be
That the songs of gladness, which float so far
As if they fell from an evening star,
Are the notes of one who may never see
"Visible music" of flower and tree?

.   .   .   .

How can she sing in the dark like this?
What is her fountain of light and bliss?

.   .   .   .

Her heart can see, her heart can see!
Well may she sing so joyously!
For the King himself, in His tender grace,
Hath shown her the brightness of His face.

.   .   .   .

Dear blind sister over the sea!
An English heart goes forth to thee.
We are linked by a cable of faith and song,
Flashing bright sympathy swift along;
One in the east and one in the west,
Singing for Him whom our souls love best!
Sister, what will our meeting be,
When our hearts shall sing and our eyes shall see?

CHAPTER VI

SISTER DORA

BY GERTRUDE LESLIE MUMFORD

OCCASIONALLY in searching for the development of great natures one finds that from their very faults, from the very temperamental obstacles against which they struggle, spring the sources of their greatness. So it was with Dorothy Wyndlow Pattison, with a will so strong that, although it often brought her into difficulties, it enabled her successfully to struggle through difficulties that would have overwhelmed a woman less determined. The very characteristic that sometimes became a stumbling block to her feet more often proved to be the means of the fulfillment of her aspirations.

Dorothy Pattison, born January 16, 1832, in the little village of Hauxwell, near Richmond, in the North Riding of Yorkshire, was the eleventh child of a family of twelve. Her father was Reverend Mark James Pattison, a man who "walked with God." From him she inherited her shapely figure, while from her mother, the daughter of a Richmond banker, came her beauty of feature and coloring so much admired. As a child Dorothy was very

SISTER DORA

delicate—a fact that kept her from regular
lessons.

Her knowledge she picked up in scraps which
she eagerly stored away in her retentive mind.
In her childhood, as in her later life, she was
quick to grasp a situation; her powers of observation later stood her in good stead in the
hospital ward. Among the country people she
had the reputation of being a quiet child but
it was due to the fact that she was not sufficiently robust to throw herself into active
sports. Delicate or not, she wes by nature
both mischievous and strong-wil.ed, the leader
in many escapades.

Upon one occasion she and one of her sisters
had new Sunday bonnets which they did not
like. In vain they pleaded not to wear them;
the decree had gone forth that the bonnets must be worn out. At last Dorothy's
chance appeared in a pouring rainstorm which
came up one day when Mr. and Mrs. Pattison
were out. "Quick!" cried Dorothy to her sister, "here is our chance for getting rid of the
bonnets." On went the bonnets, and the children's heads were thrust out of the window
until the distasteful headgear was completely
ruined. When Sunday came, the two children
appeared with no bonnets. Upon being sent
for them they returned, confident and cheerful,
with the wrecks upon their heads. "Why,
mamma, we can't wear those," said Dorothy.
But they did, not only for that day but for
many a day afterwards!

In the parish, she was a general favorite.
The Pattisons, as a family, were both charitable and hospitable towards their poor neighbors, and Dorothy shared with her sisters the
work of carrying aid to the cottagers. The
girls saved their pocket money and turned and
remade their old dresses so that by spending
less for clothes they might have more money
to give. Sometimes when they were seated at
the dinner table with the keen appetites of normal children after a morning in the open air, a
remark of the rector that poor So-and-So must
be faring badly as Bill was out of work again
would cause them to pack their own hearty dinner in a basket and take it to the suffering
family, while they themselves dined on bread
and cheese. They delighted to give, not only
material things, but their time and practical
sympathy. Once, when Dorothy was abroad,
a schoolboy in the village became very sick
with rheumatic fever. His one longing was to
live to see "Miss Dora" again. On the day on
which she returned he listened intently and long
before anyone else could hear the carriage
wheels he cried, "There she is," and waited
with what patience he could command. He
was not disappointed; at once she became his
nurse and remained with him until he died.

As she grew older she outgrew the delicacy
that had characterized her as a child, and with
her newly-acquired strength she felt the need
of action. Outdoor games and driving but most
of all vigorous cross-country riding, she made

an outlet for her overflowing energy. She became a daring rider, followed the hounds with
keen enjoyment, and cantered alone across the
solitary moors.

At twenty, she was a picture of health, with
a personal beauty that was obvious to the dull-
est eye. As she came back from a cross-country gallop, with brown curls loosened, and the
delicate color of her cheeks heightened by the
sharp country wind, she was a picture at which
all turned to look. To physical strength and
beauty were united high animal spirits and a
sense of humor, which, always sparkling out
through her merry brown eyes, were to keep
her sweet and strong through the trials of the
years before her.

But the energy that caused her, when phys-
ically able, as a child to tear vigorously
through the house in strenuous games with her
brothers and sisters, and, later, to enjoy so
much a wild gallop upon a horse's back, now
demanded some definite work upon which to
spend its powers. A passive acceptance of life
was foreign to her nature. She longed to be
out and doing. Florence Nightingale's* work
in the Crimean war roused all her enthusiasm.
She begged her father to let her go out to
Scutari as a nurse, but upon his refusal she
acquiesced with outward quietness. She
slighted none of her duties, in the home or in
the village, and spent much of her time in nursing her invalid mother. Sometimes she visited

* See Chapter V, page 120, *Heroines of Modern Progress.*

her oldest brother, Mark, at Redcar. When she was twenty-nine, her mother died, and thus Dorothy's chief work in the home was taken away from her.

At Choatham, near Redcar where she visited her brother, was an order of nursing sisters— the Sisterhood of the Good Samaritans. There they had established a convalescent hospital, and they devoted themselves to relieving the sickness of the poor of that neighborhood. In their example, Dorothy thought she had found the solution for her unsatisfied craving for a life of worth-while activity. Her father, however, was opposed to the idea of her entering the sisterhood; so for the time she gave it up. But she could not longer remain idle in comfort. Just at this time she saw an advertisement for a lady to take charge of the village school at Little Woolston, on the borders of Buckinghamshire, and in October, 1861, much against the wishes of her father, she left home to become a teacher.

Here she threw herself into the labors of a parish schoolmistress, but far in excess of her duties. She not only taught the children, but she visited them in their homes, nursed them when they were sick, played with them when they were well, told them wonderful stories, and in return was fervently loved by them. Nor did she stop there; her work extended to the poor and sick of the whole parish. If she was lonely, living by herself in a tiny cottage with no servant except an old woman who came

in occasionally to scrub, she only threw herself
harder into the work. Indeed, she probably
overworked, and a neglected cold soon brought
on an attack of pleurisy. When she grew a
little better she was sent to Redcar to con-
valesce; the associations there roused in her
all the longings for a definite and settled life
work—longings that had been steadily growing
within her. This time her willfulness would
brook no opposition; against the combined
wishes of the members of her family, in the
autumn of 1864, she became a sister of the order of the Good Samaritans.

The Sisterhood of the Good Samaritans is
what is termed a "secular" order affiliated with
the Church of England. That is, it is a working order whose members are bound by no
vows except one of a definite term of obedience
to their pastor and to the "mother superior"
appointed by him. To this order, then,
Dorothy Pattison, henceforth Sister Dora,
brought her burning ardor for work. Here she
was put through a severe training, which, while
distasteful to her at the time, undoubtedly not
only made her proficient in the mechanical part
of her profession but gave her lessons in self-
control. She learned to make beds and to
cook; at first, when those in charge pulled to
pieces the beds she had just made, she would
sit down and cry for discouragement, but in the
end her good sense conquered and she quickly
learned to adopt the approved methods. A
large part of her time was spent in a small

cottage hospital in North Ormesbury, where she worked sometimes with another sister but often alone. On January 5, 1865, she writes from Ormesbury to a friend in Little Woolston: "I have been ordered off to the hospital to-day, and am sitting up to-night with a poor man who is suffering from concussion of the brain; and he alarms me by getting up and trying to get away, and he is insensible [*i. e.* not himself], so that it is useless speaking to him. It is so cold that, though sitting over the fire, I am shivering. I have put a blister on my patient. I hope, when it takes effect, there will be an improvement. I hope he won't die, for I am the only Sister here; the others have gone for their holiday."

She stayed at North Ormesbury until the early part of 1865, when she was sent to Walsall, in South Staffordshire, to assist in the work of a small cottage hospital there.

Walsall is an industrial town in the coal and iron district near Birmingham, on the outskirts of the "Black Country." By day it is sordid and dingy, but at night it glows with an awful splendor. The same smelting furnaces whose smoke daily blackens the landscape, at night glare through the darkness with a malignant flaming red positively infernal. The smelting furnaces and the coalpits furnished work for most of the men in town. Accidents were numerous and medical aid was scarce; a hospital of some sort where the wounded could be taken for immediate treatment became a necessity. Accordingly, in 1863, a cottage hospital of four beds was established under the charge of Sister Mary of the Good Samaritans. By the time it was a year old the number of beds had increased to fourteen. Hither, in 1865, Sister Mary having fallen ill, came Sister Dora, as head of the hospital. Immediately after her arrival she caught smallpox from some of the outpatients and for a time was very ill. She was put in a small room whose window faced the street. At that time the little hospital was the victim of much opposition and even petty persecution from the very people it was there to help. Stones and mud were thrown at the window of the room where Sister Dora lay sick. Soon after her recovery, as she passed a crowd of roughs, one exclaimed: "There goes one of those Sisters of *Misery!*" At the same time he threw a stone which cut her forehead. A short time later, the very fellow was badly hurt in a coalpit accident and was brought to the hospital, where Sister Dora nursed him with particular care. One day, when he had nearly recovered, she discovered him silently crying, and presently he penitently blurted out the whole story. To his surprise, he learned that Sister Dora had recognized him when he was brought in. This was his first experience with the Christian ideal of returning good for evil.

In April 1865, she was recalled to Choatham for a short time. Here the restraint and decorum imposed by the Sisterhood sometimes proved too much for her lively spirits. One day a donkey with the reputation of upsetting everybody was brought to the door of the home. "Oh, let me ride him," cried Sister Dora. "He won't kick me off." Tying her bonnet strings a little more tightly than usual, with her black skirts tucked up carefully around her, she mounted the beast and managed to stick for a while despite his most frantic efforts to throw her. It was a clash of two stubborn wills, but the brute strength of the donkey finally won and Sister Dora in spite of her proud boast was ignominiously thrown. She did penance for this prank, however, because for some days her knees were so bruised and swollen that they were very painful to kneel on. She had had her fun, however, and bore the pain in silence rather than confess her undignified behavior to the mother superior.

It must not be supposed that her irrepressible spirits were always thus in evidence. Just before coming to Walsall she had passed through the crisis of her religious life. She had never lost her sense of the nearness of God and a firm belief in the efficacy of prayer, but her intellectual judgment had become distorted. For a time her intelligence balked at believing the authenticity of the Scriptures and her attitude might well have been summed up "Lord, I believe; help Thou my unbelief." During this time she was aided and strengthened by Reverend Richard Twigg, rector of St. John's,

Wednesbury, to whose church for early communion she walked almost every Sunday morning. Large-hearted, large-minded, his life a living example of his faith, he steadied and held Sister Dora as no one else could. Among all the people she met during her stay in Walsall, Mr. Twigg was the one who, more than anyone else, was destined to help her most when she needed help. She emerged from this inner trial, however, with her whole being centered around a deep personal love of her Saviour, Jesus Christ. Later she was to be tested and it was this sincere devotion to her Lord that brought her out triumphant.

Her always strong desire to help others was reënforced by the inward peace and sense of love she now felt. She had inherited a comparatively large income but she spent it chiefly on others; her own wants were very simple. Work and prayer seemed to be the two rules of her life and it would be hard to say which predominated.

It was this spirit that she carried with her back to Walsall after her second brief stay at Choatham. There she took up her work again quietly and unobtrusively. For a long time the prosperous and healthy hardly knew of her. Only in the slums, in the back allies where ignorance and dirt fought a winning fight against health, she was known by those whom she sought out—those so miserable that they would not, even for relief, obtrude themselves at the hospital. It is no wonder that they

learned to love her who healed their bodies
even as she prayed for their souls. So she
moved in and out among them, in all kinds of
weather, at all hours, never considering herself—indeed throwing herself into her work
with such impetuous eagerness that in 1866 she
had a serious illness; for three weeks her life
was in danger. Then the people of Walsall
found out what Sister Dora meant to the
town. The hospital was besieged with in-
quiries, and she herself always felt that her
recovery was due to the prayers of the congregation of St. John's, Wednesbury, where
she attended church.

The usefulness of the hospital increased
steadily, and under her adequate care, gave
great relief to the community. The small,
fourteen-bed building soon proved to be insufficient. Always poorly ventilated, it became so
impregnated with infection that wounds refused
to heal, and case after case was sent away un-
cured. The committee in charge resolved to
build one larger and better. In this undertaking they not only had Sister Dora's approval
but, to a great extent, her financial aid, and
thanks to her assistance the new hospital was
ready for occupancy in 1868. It was situated
on a hill, with good ventilation, and had twenty-
eight beds with room for more if needed. Just
as patients and nurses were well settled in their
new quarters, a smallpox epidemic broke out.
Sister Dora's efforts were now redoubled.
Every minute that she could spare from her

hospital duties she spent nursing the victims in their homes. Often she would be the only one in the house besides the sick person. One night she found a man dying with "blackpox" —smallpox in its most virulent form. There was no light in the house but a small candle-end; so giving a neighbor some money she asked her to get a light of some sort. The woman did not come back; as the miserable bit of candle flickered down, the dying man raised himself, saying: "Sister, do not leave me before I die." She took him in her arms, and in total darkness she sat on through the long night even after he had died, until the dawn came.

In course of time the epidemic was over, and work settled down to its accustomed routine. From the beginning of her hospital career Sister Dora had determined to become an efficient surgical nurse. The old surgeon of the hospital, seeing her cool and sensible courage, had taught her as much as he could. She undertook more and more of the minor cases and gradually came to set all the fractures. She was an advocate of conservative surgery and invariably voted against amputation if there seemed even a chance of saving the limb. One night a young man was brought in whose arm had been caught in his machine and so badly torn and twisted that the physician declared it must be amputated immediately. Sister Dora's sympathy was aroused by the young fellow's groan of despair. He turned from the doctor to her kindly face and implored her to save him. She examined the wound attentively; the young workman's face showed that he had led a clean and wholesome life. She told the doctor she thought she could save the arm. He replied flatly that amputation was necessary, and refused to have another thing to do with the case. On her own responsibility, Sister Dora undertook to save the arm. After three weeks of tense anxiety on her part, she called the physician and showed him the arm progressing rapidly towards its old time usefulness. With pride the surgeon who had taught her brought the hospital staff to show them what might be done. The patient thereafter went by the name of "Sister's Arm."

Sister Dora had been doing all the nursing, the wardwork, and sometimes even the cooking, but the work had increased so much that she was now obliged to have help. Accordingly, with the consent of the committee, she took a small number of "lady-pupils" to teach the rudiments of nursing. As a teacher she was not wholly successful; she was rather impatient, preferring to do the task herself than to go through the tedious process of showing others how to do it. The difficulty was that she did not have the power of organizing the efforts of others, and her own personality was so great that it had overshadowed all lesser endeavors. "The main lesson which her lady-pupils carried away from Walsall, was not how to dress wounds or how to bandage, or even how to manage a hospital on the most popular as well as on the most economical method, but rather the mighty results which the motive power of love towards God, and for His sake, towards mankind, might enable one single woman to effect."

A great deal of her work was done for children, with whom she was an especial favorite. Often she would carry the littlest one around on one arm, while she made beds, prepared medicine, or did other hospital work. To the fretful she would say, "Don't you cry; Sister's got you!" Burns were perhaps the commonest cases which the hospital had to treat. Children were brought almost frantic with terror and pain. When such a case came in, she would drop whatever work was in hand and bend all her energies to soothing the frightened child. After she had calmed the small sufferer she would dress the wounds. If the child was plainly dying she would tell it in a simple way about Jesus, the children's friend, until the child died peacefully and happily, as did one nine year old girl whose last words were: "When you come to heaven, Sister, I'll meet you at the gates with a bunch of flowers."

Thus, simply, she talked to the children of Christ. Unless for some definite purpose, however, she never talked about her religion to strangers, but when occasion arose she was not afraid to bear witness to her faith. Once, when she was riding in the third class carriage of a train, four or five drunken men got on at one of the way stations. At last Sister Dora

could bear their foul language no longer; rising
to her full height—a commanding figure in her
plain black dress and little white bonnet—she
said: "I will not hear the Master whom I
serve spoken of in this way." One of them
dragged her to her seat and bade her keep still.
Having made her protest she wisely saw the
folly of any further action. When she got out
at her station, however, one of the men came
up to her and bade her shake hands for she was
"a rare plucky one!"

In this and in many other instances she was
"plucky" with the courage that comes from
faith. Her creed was that of the Church of
England, but she had a broad tolerance for all
sects; indeed she often confessed a liking for
slightly "sensational" religion. She attended
with keen interest a Moody and Sankey revival
and afterwards used their hymn book in her
hospital. The Oxford Movement, which had
stirred all England during her childhood, left
her undisturbed. She felt no need of ritual in
her worship, and, on the whole, was perhaps a
little scornful of it. The Bible was her constant companion, a marked copy being always
with her; a "lady-pupil" who came upon her
while she was quietly reading it describes her
expression as "unearthly."

And now came the test of Sister Dora's faith.
A gentleman connected with the hospital wished
to marry her. He was a man of great intellectual power, but lacked one vital possession—
the Christian faith. Although Sister Dora was

attracted to him personally, she felt that it
would be wrong for her to marry a professed
unbeliever. Mr. Twigg of St. John's, who had
helped her before, came to her aid again.
There could be but one decision: she put away
this earthly love that she might better attain
to the heavenly. The strain, however, combined with her continuous hard work proved
almost too much for her. One day she fainted
while making up a bed in the ward and for a
month was dangerously ill. During this illness
perhaps no inquiry was more typical than that
of the man nicknamed "Sister's Arm." Each
Sunday morning he walked eleven miles to the
hospital, pulled the bell with a hard jerk and
said to the maid, "How's Sister?" Then he
would say, "Tell her that's *her* arm that rang
the bell," and walk the eleven miles back.

One day, after she had been ill a month, she
heard there was to be a serious operation performed that morning. When the doctors were
ready to operate Sister Dora appeared in her
old place, and from that time resumed her work
with increased vigor. A picture given by one
of the "lady-pupils" of the daily hospital
routine shows Sister Dora down in the wards
at half-past eight in the morning, making beds,
giving the patients their breakfast, reading
prayers, doing the regular routine of the wards
—"the bright sunshiny way she always worked,
with a smile and a pleasant word for everyone,
was in itself a medicine of the best kind"—
dressing wounds, caring for the out-patients,

serving the patients' dinner—which she herself always carved—prayers again, for the
nurses and servants this time, and seeing out-
patients until it was time for the afternoon
tea.

As the hospital was small, there was necessarily a large number of out-patients, for only
those who could not be treated otherwise were
admitted to the wards. One day a woman came
in with a gash in her head caused by a drunken
husband. As Sister Dora was bandaging it
the woman broke out fiercely against her husband. She would not stand his abuse any
longer, she declared. She was going to have
him arrested that very day. "Do you really
mean it?" asked Sister Dora. "Indeed I do,"
said her patient. Whereupon Sister Dora took
off the bandage she had just put on and bound
the broken head up again much more elabo-
rately than before. "Why did you do that?"
asked a curious "lady-pupil" later. "Oh,"
said Sister Dora, her eyes twinkling, "I thought
if she did have him arrested the judge would
give him another month on account of that second bandage." Such incidents as this en-
livened somewhat the rather dreary work of
the day.

After the nurses' tea, about half-past five or
six was the pleasantest part of the day, for
then she talked cheerily to each patient or else
someone would play the harmonium and they
would all sing hymns. To quote one of the
pupils: "Nobody had ever seen such a woman

as this before, so beautiful, so good, so tender-hearted, so strong and so gentle, so full of fun and humor, and of sympathy for broken hearts as well as for every other kind of fracture, and the best friend that many of these poor maimed men had ever known." Then wounds would be dressed for the night, the patients given their supper; after she finished her round of duties she would always read evening prayers for the patients. It did not matter to her that many of them were asleep. In her own words: "The prayers go up for them all the same." This was the record of a day's routine in her hospital—now truly hers, for in 1874 relations were finally and completely severed between Sister Dora and the Sisterhood of the Good Samaritans. What she said to a friend who was engaging for her a servant for the hospital best expresses her ideal for it: "Tell her this is not an ordinary house, or even hospital; I want her to understand that all who serve here, in whatever capacity, ought to have one rule, *love for God,* and then I need not say love for their work. I wish we could use and really mean the word *Maison-Dieu.*"

She was a great believer in prayer and many a man has awakened at night to find her kneeling by his bed quietly praying for him. It has been said of a certain great surgeon who has recently died that before he performed any operation he paused for a moment's prayer. Of Sister Dora it is true that before attending to any wound she first prayed that, through her

as the instrument, God in his loving kindness
would effect a cure. She had a great respect
for the presence of death, and the doctor's assistants no longer smoked and jested at post-
mortem examinations when she was present.
On all practical subjects connected with the
hospital she brought to bear her great intellect,
and to the committees she was the final authority, and in all contentions, it was Sister Dora,
who, calm and clear-sighted, settled the difficulties.

A word must be said of the two missions that
were held while she was at Walsall. The first
was in 1873. These "missions" of the Church
of England are a form of evangelistic "revival
meetings." It is a special effort, concentrated
through a week or two of powerful appeal, to
quicken spiritually those within the church and
to bring those outside to a knowledge of the
love of God and of his power to save sinners.
On the second night of this first mission, Sister
Dora went out into the streets to bring in those
who would not come by themselves, and entered
the church with thirty or forty in her train.
The second mission was held in 1876, and she
prepared to work for it more earnestly than
for the first.

With her as guide, two of the clergy went into
the worst parts of Walsall. One night the
whole company in a saloon, including fifteen or
twenty hardened women, went down on their
knees while she prayed aloud for these "brothers and sisters." While the mission lasted,

Sister Dora and one clergyman held midnight
services in a little hall in the heart of the slums,
and even after the mission ended Sister Dora
continued its work under her own direction.
A short service was held late every Sunday
night and she would go out personally into the
homes of these dissolute men and women and
bring them to the service. In all this there was
an element of risk, of positive danger, but a
rough, "Shut up, you fool—it's Sister Dora,"
was enough to forestall any violence.

The year preceding this last mission had been
marked by a second outbreak of smallpox in
Walsall. After the last epidemic the city authorities built an epidemic hospital on the outskirts of the town. The difficulty now was to
get the people to go to it. They would rather
die at home, they said, and those whose relatives
were stricken concealed them. Sister Dora,
seeing that the spread of the disease was unavoidable under the circumstances, wrote to the
authorities that she would nurse the smallpox
patients. Thus the difficulty was overcome, for
people knew that where Sister Dora was they
could trust their relatives. So she dropped
her own work and went to take up that of the
epidemic hospital, knowing that she herself
might take the disease, and with a firmly-fixed
presentiment that she might not return alive.

The only help she could get at this hospital
was from an old porter—who would often get
drunk and go off for the night—and two old
women from the workhouse. In a letter she

says: "I came and opened the smallpox hospital on Saturday. It was spreading in the town, and no one could be found to come; also the people could not be persuaded to come until they heard I was here. . . . [For help], I have got two 'critters' from the workhouse; one is so helpless, I have to do work for her, and the other sits up at nights so can do no more. . . . They [the patients] are all so pleased to have me here. I had such a nice Sunday. God's blessing seems very much on the place. I spoke to them. . . . Oh, that I had Mr. Twigg's power to help souls! I know you will all pray for me that, living or dying, I may glorify Him. You must not fret for me." Later she writes: "I rejoice that He has permitted one so unworthy to work for Him; and oh, if He should think me fit to lay down my life for Him, rejoice, rejoice at so great a privilege. My heart is running over with thankfulness, and as I toil on I seem to hear the still small voice, 'Ye did it unto Me.' . . . Oh, don't talk about my life. If you knew it you would be down on your knees crying for mercy for me, a sinner." "I do miss my Sundays. . . . If it were not for the thought 'where two or three are gathered together, *there* am *I* in the midst,' I do not know what I should do. . . . I think I may almost say it is a closer walk with God. With the pestilence all around you cannot help living each day as if it were your last. There has come that peace which the world cannot give. If I had a wish, it would be that He would count me worthy to

lay down my life for Him.'' To her patients at
her own hospital she writes, after having remembered each one personally: ''Have you
been singing to-day? You must sing particularly 'Safe in the arms of Jesus,' * and think of
me. Living or dying, I am His. Oh, my children, you all love me for the very little I do
for you; but, oh, if you would only think what
Jesus has done, and is doing for you, your
hearts would soon be full of love for Him, and
you would all choose Him for your Master.
Now, whilst you are on your beds, read and
study His life; see the road He went, and follow Him. I know you all want to go to heaven,
but wishing will not get you there. You *must*
choose *now* in this life; you cannot choose here-
after when you die. That great multitude St.
John saw round the throne *had* washed their
robes and made them white in the blood of the
Lamb, which was shed for each one of you.
God loves you; I know it, by His letting you get
hurt and bringing you to the hospital. 'As
many as I *love*, I rebuke and *chasten.*' Think
over these things my dear children. Your
mother is thinking of you and praying for you.
And if it please God you should never see her
again, will you make up your minds to walk in
the narrow way, so that we may all meet in the
green fields above? May God bring you all
safe there is the earnest prayer of your faithful
friend, Sister Dora.''

* For the account of the origin of this hymn, see Chapter
V, page 127.

After six months of this steady and confining service, in spite of her presentiment, she returned to them and resumed her work quietly. Just two months after her return in October, 1875, there was an explosion of one of the smelting furnaces. Eleven men fearfully burned by molten metal, were carried to the hospital, which turned out all but its worst cases to make room for them. Night and day, for ten days Sister Dora worked, cutting away the clothing that would adhere to the burnt flesh, bandaging wounds, and giving what little relief was possible. Many people came to offer their help but could not endure the terrible sights and odor. This accident gave the hospital its death-blow—it had become fatally infected, and the committee finally determined to pull it down and build a larger new one. In the meantime they fitted up a small house in Bridgeman Street as a temporary hospital.

In this temporary hospital during the winter of 1876-7, Sister Dora began to notice in herself a weakness foreign to her perfect health. Always strong, she had been in the habit of picking up her patients or carrying a dead body without particular effort. Although now only with increased effort, she continued her heavy work until the trouble grew so that she was forced to consult a doctor. There, in the doctor's office, she entered the outskirts of the valley of the shadow. Although she had concealed her illness up to the last possible moment, she had begun then to feel the inroads of a malignant cancer.

All through that winter she worked with a frenzy that brought remonstrances from her friends. In addition to her work in the hospital, at night she carried on the evangelism in the slums which she had begun at the time of the second mission. She was enabled "to see the image of God, defiled and darkened though it might be, impressed upon every living soul, to feel her kinship with it, to lay her hand, not upon the defilements and impurity, but through the means of her infinite love and tenderness, upon the one spot yet capable of being healed, thus kindling the faintest spark into a living flame." On Christmas 1877 (her last) she invited all her old patients to a dinner which she provided. She worked steadily until June when an outbreak of typhoid in the temporary hospital caused its closing, and Sister Dora had an unexpected holiday.

As soon as she was able to leave she visited her nieces in the Isle of Man. From there she went to Paris, and in September was in London studying the treatment of wounds under Professor Lister. All this time she was bearing alone her own rapidly increasing burden. On October 8 she returned to Walsall where the hospital committee, hearing of her serious illness, hired a small house for her. Her condition was such that her doctor gave her about a fortnight to live, and on October 10 she wrote to a friend: "It is *hopeless* (I use that word merely technically) so they don't tease me with medicines and remedies, and there is no fluctuation of hopes and fears. I have not a care; it is all sunshine. God has taken away the fear of death, and all sorrow at parting with life."

On November 4, the new hospital was opened "in the name of Sister Dora," a silver key having been sent to her by the committee with the request that she give it to the Mayor and "thus empower him to open the new building *in her name.*" Where to find her successor had been one of her greatest anxieties, and on December 6 it was happily removed. Sister Ellen, a complete stranger to Sister Dora and to Walsall, offered her services for the hospital. Sister Dora realized that here was the right person, and gave herself up to the relief of being waited on by her. Her release came December 24, 1878. When they could do no more for her she bade them leave her, crying, "I have lived alone; let me die alone." And so she died—alone save for Him in Whose service she had spent her life —"not grudgingly or of necessity" but cheerfully and willingly.

Her funeral was attended by all Walsall. By a strange coincidence there were at the same time the funerals of four paupers. Their cortéges arrived first and filled the little chapel so that Sister Dora's coffin was left on the porch. The church service was read over the five at once—as one of the nurses said: "Just as Sister Dora would have wished—not to be divided, even in death, from the poor people she loved so well." The police were useless to keep the people out of the cemetery, but it was a quiet, reverent crowd that stood, every man with his hat off, while the beautiful service at the grave was read. Rich and poor, clergy and laymen, bishops and the lowest of them she had worked to help, all united in paying to her this last loving tribute.

Her personality still colors Walsall. Among all the monuments proposed for her the one that the working people most desired was not the home for convalescents that she herself wanted to establish, but a statue of her, so that she would be tangibly present to their children and their children's children. As one humble workman said: "Why, nobody knows better than I do that *we* sha'n't forget her—no danger of that; but *I* want her to be there, so that when strangers come to the place and see her standing up, they shall ask us, 'Who's that?' and then we shall say, *'Who's* that? Why, that's *our* Sister Dora.' "

She stands there now, a beautiful statue, yet not simply a thing of cold stone, but rather a vital personality—*their* Sister Dora.

CHAPTER VII

HANNAH WHITALL SMITH

BY WILLIAM HORTON FOSTER

IN the early seventies of the last century Hannah Whitall Smith was sitting in her rooms in London reading the news from home—America. She read how a band of women, inspired only by their motherhood, had gone singing through the streets of Ohio towns, how they had prayed in saloons for the victims of drink. She read of the wonderful spread of the movement into the "organized motherhood" of the Women's Christian Temperance Union, as its great president later called it. She was stirred by the narrative and as she herself said "sitting before an English fire in our London house, I joined that crusade." All her later life she had been a student of the Bible and a teacher of its truth. With the coming of this new expression of woman's love for "God and home and native land," she received a new commission to teach, to teach soul culture to thousands of women who should themselves in turn pass on her message. These militant missionaries of personal purity soon saw their message must be preached and taught as an organized body of truth. As the movement grew into an organized propaganda,

HANNAH WHITALL SMITH

Mrs. Smith was its chief spiritual counselor.
To the moral earnestness of these heroines of a
new crusade she gave point and head. Their
new evangelism was hers to mold and direct.
What was her fitting for this task?

"John M. Whitall was the best loved man in
Philadelphia," said one of his friends to his
daughter Hannah. And yet John M. Whitall
was a Quaker and wore a long gray coat and a
broad brimmed hat. Humor, however, had been
his from boyhood. Those who knew him as a
lad used to say that he was at once the most
provoking and the best beloved boy in all their
circle. After his father lost most of his money
all the boys were left to shift for themselves.
John chose the sea, and at sixteen "signed" as
the proverbial cabin boy. Good seaman as he
soon became, he was a still stauncher Quaker.
In 1823, when he was just twenty-three years
old, he writes: "While at home from my fifth
voyage I believed it right to adopt the plain
dress and language of Friends. While under
the conviction of its being right, and fearing I
should lose my situation if I did so, I met with
Samuel Battle, Sr., who, without knowing the
distressed state of my mind, told me, if I was
faithful to what I felt to be right, the Lord
would make a way for me where there seemed
no way; which He did, giving me favor in the
sight of my employer, much to my comfort.
Hearing of a ship as needing a chief mate, I
borrowed a plain coat of my friend, James Cox,

my own not being ready, and called to see the
captain, telling him I could not 'Mr.' and 'Sir'
him as was common. To which he replied
kindly that it would only be a nine day's wonder,
and at once engaged me as first mate. Thus
my prayer was answered and a way made for
me where I saw no way. Praised forever be
the name of the Lord.'' Eight years after he
first shipped, he became captain of the largest
merchantman sailing out of Philadelphia; five
years of profitable voyages enabled him to
settle ashore when but thirty. The energy
which had driven his merchantmen from coast
to coast was equally efficient in the less strenuous adventuring on land. In time his firm became the largest manufacturer of their wares
—clear glass—in the world. Yet they never
made glasses for strong drink of any kind.

With all his earnestness of purpose he had
too much humor to be a fanatic. His daughter
writes: ''I remember well the fun we sometimes had, after we were grown up, over his in-
genious methods of extracting himself from difficulty when he did not know the first name of
any one. He used to substitute for 'Mr.' or
'Mrs.' the word 'Cummishilamus,' and would
say, for instance, 'Cummishilamus Coleman'
said or did so and so. When, however, he had
to write the address on a letter, he could not of
course use this word and then he would turn to
one of us and say, with a merry twinkle of his
dear eyes,—'Come, Han, thee has no scruples,

so thee may write the 'Mr.' or 'Mrs.' on this letter!"

This staid Philadelphia family lived in an atmosphere of sunshine. The daughter writes: "I remember well how, when my childhood's sky would be all darkened by some heavy childish affliction, a cheery 'Well, Broadie,' in his hearty voice, or some little passing joke spoken with a roguish twinkle of his loving grey eyes, would clear my sky in a moment, and make life all sunshine again. And, even when I was older, his power to cheer grew no less, and it was quite my habit, whenever I found myself down in the depths, to put myself somewhere in his way, with the certainty that even a moment's peep at his strong cheery face would lift me out. I can even remember that, in his absence, the sight and feel of his dear old overcoat would somehow brighten everything, and send me off encouraged to be braver and stronger."

The father did more than drive the clouds away; he prevented them from forming. Hannah says: "One of the much amused young people of the present day said to me once: 'It seems to me you did not have many amusements when you were young.' 'We did not need to,' was my prompt reply. 'We had my father and my mother and they were all the amusements we needed. They made our lives all sunshine.' I wish I could give to others the vivid picture I have of their inexpressible delightfulness.

We knew, down to the very bottom of our hearts, that they were on our side against the whole world, and would be our champions in every time of need. No one could oppress us, neither playmates, nor friends, nor enemies, not even our teachers (those paid oppressors of childhood, as we felt all teachers to be), nor any one the whole world over, without having to reckon with those dear champions at home; and the certain conviction of this, surrounded us with such a panoply of defence, that nothing had power to trouble us overmuch. 'We will tell father,' or 'we will tell mother,' was our unfailing resource and consolation in every sorrow. In fact, so sure was I of their championship, that when ever any of my friends or school fellows were in trouble, I used to say, 'O well come home with me and let us tell my father and mother;' feeling sure that that dear father and mother could set the whole world straight, if the chance were only given them. And when the answer would come as it often did, 'Oh, that would be of no use, for your father and mother cannot do everything,' I would say, with a profound pity for their ignorance, 'Ah, you do not know my father and mother.' "

In her girlhood such was Hannah Whitall's conception of fatherhood and motherhood. It was but the shortest step for her theology to clothe her idea of God with the love her earthly father daily typified. As she grew into womanhood and the bloom of her spirit deep-

ened, it only sweetened her perception of the
divine. Her confidence in her father John M.
Whitall was no more serene than her confidence in her Heavenly Father. She knew that
He could set the whole world right, if the
chance were only given Him. Whether her
message was the little four leaved tract signed
"H. W. S." you have seen tucked in your
mother's work basket among the stockings waiting to be mended, or whether it came to Frances E. Willard and J. Ellen Foster in the
Women's Christian Temperance Union, or to
Margaret Bright Lucas or Lady Henry Somerset in the British Women's Temperance Association, it was the same as the message of her
girlhood to her girlhood's friends, "Oh, well,
never mind; come home with me and let us tell
my Father." If the response was not as perfect as her longing heart might wish, she had
the same loving pity in her thought, "Ah, you
do not know my Father!" All her life her
mission was to discover to others their own
souls. And she, mother confessor to womanhood—to the Anglo-Saxon womanhood * that
was fighting out a dozen reforms besides temperance—could do this divine thing, for she had
taken counsel with her own soul and had
searched its depths. The history of her life is
a record of that exploration. The material
facts of birth and death, of love and marriage,

* See *Heroines of Modern Progress*, by Elmer C. Adams
and Warren Dunham Foster.

of children and home, of private life and public career, are but the date lines of this diary of a soul.

This radiant family life—the family life that made it possible for Hannah Whitall Smith to be the chaplain of the great social movements— is all the more vividly projected because of its drab Quaker background. Hannah's ancestors had left England for America to seek the freedom denied them at home. They brought with them a sober earnestness, a repressive creed which fostered introspection. The "perceptible guidance of the Holy Spirit" was their sole rule of conduct. They taught no doctrine or dogma and regarded even the Bible itself inferior in authority to the voice of God speaking in the heart. They thought Sunday school or Bible classes a sort of "creaturely activity" which belonged only to the "world's people." They permitted no prayers; Hannah could not repeat the Lord's Prayer until she was a woman grown. Quakers could not but believe themselves God's own people, set apart for some peculiar work. Their's was in fact a religious aristocracy; this view may have been narrow but it gave a real dignity to life and its duties.

From the Quaker principles of her home, Hannah as a girl once suffered in a peculiarly feminine way. One day her mother came home from meeting and announced to the girls that she felt that the long fringes on certain white china crêpe shawls, the delight of their hearts, were too "gay" for "Friends' children." "I

can see it all to-day," wrote Hannah when she
was seventy years old, "as she carefully spread
the shawls out on a large table, and laid a yard
stick along the fringe at what she considered
was the right length, and proceeded to cut off
all the lovely beautiful extra lengths. It was
like cutting into our very vitals, and I remember
well how we pleaded and pleaded that the fatal
yardstick might be slipped down just a little
further. Our great fear was that our fringes
would be cut shorter than the fringes of similar
shawls that had been purchased at the same time
for our most intimate friends, Hannah and Jane
Scull, who were a little gayer than ourselves.
To have their fringes, even so much as the tenth
of an inch longer than ours, seemed to us a
catastrophe not to be borne."

Another catastrophe was to follow. "The
shape of sleeve that was considered plain in my
day was what are called leg-of-mutton sleeves,
and sleeves of all our dresses were of this orthodox leg-of-mutton shape. But some benign influence, what it was we never understood, induced our mother one spring to let us have our
sleeves made a little in the fashion, which happened at that time to be what was called bishop
sleeves, full at both the shoulder and wrist.
The fashion was for very large and full
'bishops' and ours were tiny little ones, but
they were real 'bishops' and our pride in them
was immense. The dresses were our new
spring school dresses, of a brown and white
striped print, calico we called it. They were

finished while the weather was still very wintry-like, but so great was our desire to show off our fashionable sleeves to the astonished world, that nothing would do but we must put them on and go for a long walk without any coats; and no two prouder little girls were abroad in the whole world that morning than Hannah and Sally Whitall, as they walked along the streets of Philadelphia in their fashionable attire.   I remember our younger sister Mary wanted to go with us, but her sleeves were still leg-of-mutton, and we felt it would take from the full effect, if one member of our party should display the despised sleeves, and we made her walk on the opposite side of the way.   I can see her longing glances across the street now, as she admired our glory from afar.   However, she had her revenge not long after, for ruffled pantalets coming down to the feet, had come into fashion, and as our mother was making her a new set, they were made long and ruffled, while we still had to wear our plain hemmed ones, not showing below our dresses.   And this time she also went out to walk to show her new panties, but, kinder than we had been, she invited us to accompany her.   I am sorry to say, however, that the old Adam in us resented her favored condition so strongly, that we refused to walk on the same side of the street with her, and scornfully crossed over to the other side, leaving her to walk alone, with all the glory taken out of her beautiful ruffled pantalets by our cruel scorn and unkindness.''

No clouds more serious than these darkened the skies of her girlhood. "Truly my life has been one fairy scene of sunshine and of flowers," she wrote at sixteen, and later, "There is a continual clapping of hands and shouting of joyful voices in my heart, and every breath feels almost as if it must terminate in a smile of happiness. Mother says I laugh too much, but the laugh is in me, and will come out, and I cannot help it."

Back of the laugh in the young girl's heart was an overwhelming desire to be good, somehow, but how she did not know nor care. For years she was content to await the "leadings of the Spirit,"—guide of all good Quakers. Until she was sixteen she hardly knew that she had a soul, she says; then began her long search after God. In 1848 there came a rush of new thoughts and hopes and wonderings. She realized the greatness of the universe and began to question the complete absorption and self-withdrawal of her Quaker faith. Her chief concern was to win God to her side; she conceived Him as some magnificent but rather selfish power indifferent to her or actually engaged against her. To find out God—that was the passion which slowly but certainly took possession of her life and gripped it for the three score years and more which were to come. From this time onward her diary is one long record of agonized wrestlings. She has no help from friends or even her beloved parents; their Quaker reserve, their respect for the dignity of the individual soul, forbade. To her diary she says: ". . . far worse than all, I could not feel as if I really loved God. It is dreadful. What shall I do? I must repent, I must love my Heavenly Father, or I shall be eternally ruined. But I cannot do it of myself; God alone can help me, and I know not how to pray. O, what shall I do? Where shall I go? It is said 'Ask and ye shall receive.' But I cannot become really righteous until I repent, and I cannot repent."

Her Quaker education forced her to refer all her longing questions to the "inner light." Patiently she waited. She firmly believed that only when God should reveal Himself to her soul, could she come really to know Him. Her early teaching inevitably turned her mind inward, upon her own feelings and emotions. What God had said in the Bible seemed of not nearly so much authority as what He might say to her own heart. "I have no recollection of ever for a moment going to the Scriptures for instruction," she says. "The 'inward voice' was to be our sole teacher. And for me at that time the inward voice meant only my own feelings and my own emotions. As there is absolutely nothing more unreliable and unmanageable than one's inward feelings, it is no wonder that I was plunged into a hopeless struggle . . . I talked about my 'Saviour' as I called Him, but I never for a moment even so much as imagined that He could or would save me unless I could make myself worthy to be saved; and as this worthiness was mostly I believed, a matter of inward pious emotions, I had no thought but to try somehow to get up these emotions.'' Fortunately for the young girl, her natural joyousness delivered her from this morbid state of false religion. Her diary despairingly records: ''So often have I entered into a covenant to serve Him wholly and entirely, with fervour of spirit, but when the impression of my hours of retirement has nearly faded and the temptations of the world have assailed me, I have yielded, and have forgotten my high and holy calling through fear of the world's dread laugh and through the love of sin. O that I could do otherwise! The mercy of God will some day be exhausted, and where will I be then? I dare not think.'' After writing these tragic words, as if her religious exercises were over, she would go to bed quite happily and sleep the sleep of the just without a moment of wakeful anxiety, and would arise the next morning full of the joys of a new day, forgetting all the miseries recorded the night before.

Thus the daily struggle went on. Until she was married at nineteen she was tossed back and forth between the natural joyousness of her nature and the emotions born of morbid self-searching. Her marriage with Robert Pearsall Smith and the new and wider interests to which she was introduced turned her attention in other directions and for a time her religious emotions and feelings sank into the background. Hannah Whitall had been happy in her parents;

she was equally happy in her husband and, later, in their children. The Quaker spirit which respected each soul's individual integrity characterized the new family life as it had the old. Her questionings continued, however, and she still anxiously awaited an emotional baptism which in some mysterious way should supply her from within with the light which could only come from without. Finally her distress became so great that she gave over her struggle and let loose her grasp on the faith she had. In 1855 her diary under the ominous heading "The Eclipse of Faith," records: "I . . . have been cognizant of an actual and rapid mental growth. I pass from one phase of experience to another, leave behind me one standing place after another, and am now—where? Oh, Christ, that I indeed knew where! . . . An inevitable chain of reasoning on free will has loosened every foothold, and I know not where to rest, if indeed there *is* any rest. Without any apprehension on my part of the result, thoughts and reasonings have been slowly gathering around my faith, and dashing themselves against it, until at last, with a sudden shock, it has fallen; and I am lost!" Her reasoning tells her God is neither omnipotent, omniscient, or a God of justice. She concludes, "There is no escape! A thousand questions rush in on every side! I am a sceptic!"

After this maze of questioning, however, came relief. At the death of her daughter Nelly, Mrs. Smith's reason saw the little girl's soul

going out into a universe without God but her
motherhood refused to accept the dictum of her
skepticism. One day soon after, however, in
a prosaic noonday meeting held for business
men in the heart of the city her reason caught,
as in a flash of insight, the *fact* of God. There
was no spasm of emotion; the restful conviction
came to her that God was a fact and that she
must seek to know Him. All her life so far she
had been seeking to find herself; she had sought
in her heart for those attributes which might
lead God to find her. Now she realized that her
business was to find out God, to get acquainted
with this new Being the fact of whose existence
she had just grasped. She says: "It was not
that I felt myself to be a sinner needing salvation, or that I was troubled about my future destiny. It was not a personal question at all. It
was simply and only that I had become aware of
God, and that I felt I could not rest until I
should know Him. I might be good or I might
be bad; I might be going to Heaven or I might
be going to hell—these things were outside the
question. All I wanted was to become acquainted with the God of whom I had suddenly
become aware."

Where should she find Him? Nothing in her
life so far had given her any clew to the search.
"I concluded that probably the Bible was the
book I needed. 'This book,' I said to myself,
'professes to teach us about God. . . . I will
see if it can teach me anything.' " For over
fifty years from the day she began this search

the volume was always with her. At first she was fearful she would soon exhaust the book, it was so small. But as she studied her fear changed to prayer for added days and years in which to study. In finding God she had found herself. Her experience was not a gift or attainment or a conversion, even; it was a discovery. So great to her was the value of her discovery that she was filled with amazement that she had "lived so long in a world that contained the Bible and never had found all this before. Why had nobody ever told me? How could people, who had found it out, have kept such a marvelous piece of good news to themselves? Certainly I could not keep it to myself, and I determined that no one whom I could reach should be left a day in ignorance, as far as I could help it. I began to buttonhole everybody, pulling them into corners and behind doors to tell them of the wonderful and delightful things I had discovered in the Bible about the salvation through the Lord Jesus Christ. It seemed to me the most magnificent piece of good news that any human being had ever had to tell, and I gloried in telling it."

The story of what she found in this wonderful Bible would be a liberal course in theology. Yet it was not a theology so much for those out of Christ entirely as for the great mass of formal Christians who accepted, honestly enough, the theory of salvation, but persistently refused to accept the fact of salvation. Because of her Quaker training she had had no doctrinal training, and all that she was learning came in a blaze of illumination. Theological terms were unknown to her; she took the Gospel in a simple common-sense way and taught it as simply.

Hers was a simple faith. It was not so simple, however, as the one she passed on to her little daughter. One day she noticed her little daughter Mary lying on a bridge crossing a brook on their estate, eagerly watching a tin cup she had lowered into the water. She was patiently waiting for the fish to jump in; she had prayed to God for a fish, she explained to her mother, and of course one would jump in as the answer to her petition. After her mother had showed her how to prepare a hook and line and bait, she left the child alone. In a few minutes Mary came running in with her fish, exclaiming to her mother: "Oh, mamma, I see; worms is Heavenly Father's way!"

Heavenly Father's way was the way of the Smith family. Placid but sincere was the life of this household, as it had been of the Whitall home. Mrs. Smith, from one happy year's end to another, studied the Bible. As quickly as she discovered a new phase of this fact of God she felt compelled to pass it on to others. By voice and pen she spread the good news she had found. She and her husband—for he had come with her into the same fresh inspiration— carried their joint work into England where it soon came to be as much a part of English religious life as it was of American. Wherever

the English language was read, her books and
tracts found their way. Everywhere the result
was the same; she brought Christians to the
deeper possibilities of the Christian life. Early
in the organization of the Woman's Christian
Temperance Union, she began to teach those
women, women who were themselves teaching a
world to be pure. Later she performed the
same service for the members of the English
branch of the international organization.* In
the National Woman's Christian Temperance
Union she for a time was Superintendent of the
Evangelical Department but whether in official
capacity or not she was always preparing Bible
studies and readings—Scripture lessons that
strengthened and deepened the religious background of that great crusade. While her tracts
were going by the hundreds of thousands to encourage the rank and file of the white-ribbon
army, her home was the sanctuary to which the
generals came for spiritual rest, where they re-
created the spiritual exaltation without which
they could not have given point nor head to the
on-sweeping movement.

Thus Hannah Whitall Smith became the high
priestess of Anglo-Saxon womanhood, organized and embattled as it never had been before.
She became the high priestess solely because
she had found her own soul, and, through finding
it, had found the fact of God. The story of her

* For accounts of the Women's Christian Temperance
Union, see the biography of Frances Willard, page 215, and of
J. Ellen Foster, page 245, *Heroines of Modern Progress.*

life is the record of her state of mind; had that
record been different, the record of the worldwide woman's campaign for social purity and
justice would not be what it is.

Mrs. Smith's later years were filled with in-
validism. She was finally confined to her room
and at last to her chair. Her last written message, a card sent broadcast to her friends, is
as sunny as the course of her life: "I felt a
great desire, during the season of Christmas
and New Year's greetings to send one myself
to all the friends whom I love so much, but
owing to my difficulty in writing, it seemed impossible. In one of my wakeful hours at night,
however, on the first day of the New Year, it
suddenly came to me that I might send a cir-
cular greeting for 1911 to all of you which would
embody the substance of what I would love to
say to each one individually, had I but the
strength to do so.

". . . I am living with my son and my two
grand-daughters in a beautiful home on the
banks of the Thames, not far from Oxford.
. . . I could not ask for a lovelier refuge in
which to pass the last years of my life, nor for
better company. . . . My old activities have all
had to be laid aside, and I am only waiting and
longing for the blessed call to my heavenly
home. But I am glad to tell you that I am very
happy and contented in my narrowed life, and
with my lessening capabilities, and can say,
'Thy will be done' to my divine Master from
the very bottom of my heart.''

So she died, April 30, 1911, saying to her divine Master, "Thy will be done." And this is what she says of that divine Master: "I had found that God, just alone, without anything else, was enough. Even the comfort of His promises paled before the comfort of Himself. What difference did it make if I could not find a promise to fit my case? I had found the Promiser, and He was infinitely more than all His promises.

"I remember well how, when I was a child and found myself in any trouble or perplexity, the coming in of my father or mother upon the scene would always bring me immediate relief. The moment I heard the voice of one of them calling my name, that very moment every burden dropped off and every fear vanished. I had got my father or my mother, and what more could I need? It was their simple presence that did it. They did not need to stand up and make a string of promises for my relief, nor detail to me the plans of deliverance. The mere fact of their presence was all the assurance I required that everything now would be all right, for me—must in fact, be all right, because they were my parents and I was their child. And how much more true must all this be in regard to our Heavenly Father, who has all wisdom and all power, and whose very name is the God of Love."

CHAPTER VIII

FRANCES RIDLEY HAVERGAL

BY WOODMAN BRADBURY

THE songs of a nation are as important as its laws; and the hymns of the church have had as great influence on its life and doctrine as the decrees of councils or the systems of theologians.

For nearly two generations, Christian people have been singing:

> Take my life and let it be
> Consecrated, Lord, to Thee.

Can any one measure the influence of this one hymn upon the lives of those who have loved it and sung it?

Its origin is interestingly significant. Miss Havergal, the author, was invited to a house party of five days in London. There were ten in the party, some unconverted to Christ, and some of the Christians "not rejoicing." Now, personal joy in the Lord, the bubbling of an ever-flowing fountain of peace, was to Miss Havergal so constant and precious an experience that she wished all to share it. Accordingly, her heart went out toward them all; and

she prayed, "Lord, give me all in this house."
She adds, "And He just *did*.   Before I left the
house, every one had got a blessing."   They
had all come to Jesus and believed His promises; "and so coming, so believing, they found
rest unto their souls.   They found, too, that His
word was true and that His taking away our
sins was a reality."   That night, she was too
happy to sleep.   A deep joy possessed her.   "I
passed most of the night in renewal of my consecration; and these little couplets formed themselves and chimed in my heart one after the
other till they finished with 'ever, only, *all* for
Thee.' "   Surely that which is born in such an
experience is endowed with vitality and pre-
destined of God for real accomplishment.

Frances Ridley Havergal was born at Astley,
Worcestershire, England, December 14, 1836,
and died at Caswell Bay, Swansea, South Wales,
June 3, 1879, in the forty-third year of her life.
She was a bright and winsome child, precocious
in affection as well as in intellect.   At the age
of seven she wrote verses.   Soon after, she became a linguist; she acquired mastery of
French, German and Italian and of Latin,
Greek and Hebrew—of the last two that she
might better understand the Bible.   To the
study of the Scriptures all her powers of schol-
arship and intuition were bent, as a look into her
annotated and underlined Bible would show and
as a study of her hymns would abundantly testify.   During her visits to Wales, she learned

FRANCES RIDLEY HAVERGAL.

enough Welsh to enable her to take part in worship.

Her conversion was thorough and, as is generally the case, profoundly influenced her theology. As a child she felt herself a sinner, and this feeling was intensified at her mother's death, which occurred when Frances was only eleven years old. At fourteen, Diana, her room-mate at school, "found peace," and cried out to her friend: "Oh, Fanny, dearest Fanny, the blessing has come to me at last. Jesus has forgiven me, I know. He is my Saviour and I am so happy. He is such a Saviour as I never imagined, so good, so loving. Only come to Him and He will receive you." Thus encouraged and exhorted, Frances assiduously sought the Saviour till she finally could "trust," and that surrender brought assurance that her sins were forgiven. In successive stages throughout her life this assurance deepened.

Later, when she was sent away to a boarding school in Germany, she was surrounded by a hundred and ten girls who shared neither her experience nor her aspirations. Her personal religion was too vital a thing for them to understand. A lesser nature might have succumbed, but she found that nipping atmosphere "very bracing" to her Christian life. She wrote home, "I must walk worthy of my calling."

The formal seal upon this "calling" occurred after her return to England, when she was seventeen years old. Of her experience as she

stood before the altar at Worcester Cathedral
she writes: "My feelings when his [the
bishop's] hands were placed on my head I can
not describe. When the words, 'Defend, O
Lord, this Thy child with Thy heavenly grace,
that she may continue thine forever, and daily
increase in Thy Holy Spirit more and more,
until she come into Thy everlasting Kingdom'
were solemnly pronounced, if ever my heart followed a prayer it did then, if ever it thrilled with
earnest longing not unmixed with joy, it did at
the words, 'Thine forever.' "

This deep, sacred experience found expression in a stanza of self-dedication, written on
the day of her confirmation, July 17, 1854:

THINE FOREVER

Oh! "Thine for ever," what a blessed thing
    To be forever His who died for me!
My Saviour, all my life Thy praise I'll sing,
    Nor cease my song throughout eternity.

She always kept the anniversary of her confirmation as a day of retirement and prayer;
often she then renewed her pledges in verse as
the following stanza, written but two years before her death shows:

Only for Jesus! Lord, keep it for ever,
    Sealed on the heart and engraved on the life!
Pulse of all gladness, and nerve of endeavor,
    Secret of rest, and the strength of our strife!

The vows solemnly taken in youth thereafter ruled her life. She lived for her Saviour. Her friends and acquaintances could not but feel her complete consecration. A teacher wrote of her: "What imprinted the stamp of nobility upon her whole being and influenced all her opinions was her true piety, and the deep reverence she had for her Lord and Saviour whose example penetrated her young life through and through."

This piety of hers, however, had nothing dark and dismal about it. Upon a visit to Ireland when she was but twenty years old, Miss Havergal left this impression upon an Irish school girl: "Five o'clock P. M. was the hour appointed for the girls to arrive at the Lodge. We were in a great state of delight at the thought of seeing 'the little English lady.' In a few seconds Miss Frances, caroling like a bird, flashed into the room. Flashed! Yes, I say the word advisedly, flashed in like a burst of sunshine, like a hillside breeze, and stood before us, her fair sunny curls falling around her shoulders, her bright eyes dancing, and her fresh sweet voice ringing through the room. I shall never forget that afternoon, never! I sat perfectly spellbound as she sang chant and hymn with marvelous sweetness, and then played two or three pieces of Handel which thrilled me through and through. She finished with singing her father's tune (Hobah) to 'The Church of our Fathers.' She shook hands with each, and said with a merry laugh: 'The next time I come to Ireland, we must get up a little singing class and you must all sing with me.' As we walked home, one and another said: 'O, isn't she lovely? and doesn't she sing like a born angel!' 'I love her, I do; and I'd follow her every step of the way back to England if I could!' ''

Looking through the eyes of this enthusiastic Irish girl, is it hard to guess why throughout her life Miss Havergal radiated Christian happiness? She was indeed an accomplished musician; she played the pianoforte with skill, sang with charm, and composed. Her friends delighted to hear her interpret the great masters, especially Handel, Beethoven and Mendelssohn, much of whose work she knew by heart. Her playing of Beethoven's *Moonlight Sonata* was unforgettable. Even the great Hiller said she had decided talent.

This musical taste and ability she inherited from her father, the Reverend William Henry Havergal, M. A., a devout rector. He composed cathedral services and many hundred chants and tunes, and several sacred songs, the profits of which were always devoted to various forms of benevolence and missions, and the repair of churches. A cathedral service in A won him a prize medal and a second gold medal came for his anthem, *Give Thanks*. His home life with his six children, of whom Frances was the youngest, was ideal. Frances, like her father, delighted in making religious use of her musical talent. "Literal singing for Jesus is to me, somehow, the most personal and direct commission I hold from my beloved Master. Every line in my little poem, 'Singing for Jesus,' is from personal experience."

She became increasingly interested in the great cause of temperance, in which there was then an even greater need than to-day for earnest work. Hospital visitation, foreign missions, Sunday school work for boys, and gospel work among sailors enlisted her coöperation and in these practical ways her religion found expression. She was greatly interested in the religious possibilities of the Young Women's Christian Association, and was a zealous worker in it. It is little wonder that a life of such devoutness should be marked by trust, praise, and spiritual insight. "A disappointment," she said, "is His appointment." " 'Thy will be done' is not a sigh but a song." Later in life, she wrote to a friend: "I have been so happy lately, and the words 'Thou hast put gladness in my heart' I can use, as true of my own case."

Her happiness was not dimmed by the fact that her health was never robust and ailments came with increasing frequency. Her last illness was brought on by an exertion characteristic of her whole life. She had promised to meet some men and boys on the river bank; and though the day proved to be very damp, she went with her Bible and temperance book, held the meeting, and returned wet and chilly with the rain and sea-mist. Though feeling poorly, she insisted on going to communion the following day, and rode back on a donkey, attended by quite a procession of people. Her donkey boy recalls that Miss Frances told him, "I had better leave the devil's side and get on the safe side; that Jesus Christ's was the winning side; that He loved us and was calling us, and wouldn't I choose Him for my Captain?" Arriving at home, Miss Havergal ran in for her book and the boy signed the pledge on the saddle. A young sailor, also, W. Llewellyn by name, seemed interested. He was going to sea the next day. Miss Havergal dragged herself to the cottage to speak with him. He signed the pledge and his last letter, written from Brazil, states that he has faithfully kept it. This was the last time Miss Havergal's feet were

Swift and beautiful for Thee.

These exertions caused her to take to her bed.

Her illness took a sudden turn for the worse. She seemed to divine what the end would be. When suffering the most, she whispered, "It's home the faster." Later, she said to her sister, "God's will is delicious; He makes no mistakes."

The vicar of Swansea hurried to her bedside. "Is Jesus with you now?" he asked. "Of course he is!" was the reply; "it is splendid! I thought He would have left me here a long while; but He is *so* good to take me now. Tell

—— that God's promises are all true, and the Lord Jesus is a good big foundation to rest upon. Ask Mr. A—— to speak *plainly* about Jesus; I want all young ministers to be faithful ambassadors, and win souls. . . . Oh, I want all of you to speak *bright,* BRIGHT words about Jesus, oh, do, *do!* It is all perfect peace. I am only waiting for Jesus to take me in.'' A sharp spasm ensued, after which she sank back, folded her hands on her breast and said: "There, now it's all over. Blessed rest!" Those who looked on in awe said that her death was almost a visible meeting with her King. Her countenance lighted up as if she were already talking to Him, a glorious radiance on her face. Then, as her brother was praying, her spirit fled away.

In forming an estimate of the value of Miss Havergal's life for posterity, first place must be given to her hymns. It is by these that she, "though dead, yet speaketh." Fifty of them are now found in common use in English-speaking countries. One will readily recall familiar lines, such as "I gave my life for thee," "Lord, speak to me that I may speak," "Tell it out among the heathen," "O Saviour, precious Saviour," "True-hearted, whole-hearted." Still other hymns have won immortality, such as "Our yet unfinished story," "I could not do without Thee," "I am trusting Thee, Lord Jesus," "Thou art coming, O my Saviour." If this list seems large it is an evidence of the magnitude of her life-task. If, on the contrary, it seems incomplete, and lovers of her work wonder at the omission of their favorites from the list, this fact too, is evidence of the quality and permanence of her contribution to hymnology.

These hymns first saw the light in a very humble way. Intimate friends urged their publication, and they were printed as leaflets or ornamental cards. Their success was immediate and they were scattered by the tens of thousands. With their message of gospel cheer, they reached humble homes in all parts of the world; afterwards they were gathered into inexpensive booklets. It was not till 1869 that a collection of her poems was published under the title *The Ministry of Song. Under the Surface* followed in 1874, *Life Mosaics* in 1879; and other volumes appeared posthumously, through the devotion of a sister.

The origin of "I gave my life for thee" shows the spontaneity of all her work. Miss Havergal was visiting in Germany in 1858; and coming in weary, one afternoon, her eye rested on an *Ecce Homo*. It was such a picture of the suffering Saviour as touched the heart of Count Zinzendorf in 1719 and made a missionary of him. Whether the experience of the great Moravian was in Miss Havergal's mind or not, the motto beneath the picture, *"Hoc feci pro te; quid facis pro me?"* touched her emotions, and she rapidly wrote the hymn upon a bit of paper. But it seemed poor to her, and she started to throw it into the open fire.

Something restrained her, however, and she put it, crumpled and singed, into her pocket. Soon after, she read it to an old saint in an almshouse who was much helped by it. She was encouraged to print it, and it met with wide favor. Her father composed a tune for it, *Baca,* and it was widely sung. The tune by P. P. Bliss is generally used in the United States, although many musicians have composed for it; but it remained for Barnby's genius to wed the hymn to perfect music, in his *St. Olave.* It was the hearing of three of her hymns sung at church, among them *Baca,* which led Miss Havergal to note the wide influence of religious music and to resolve to concentrate her energies upon its production for her Master.

"Tell it out among the heathen that the Lord is King" followed much later in her career. It was born on a snowy Sunday morning in 1872 when Miss Havergal's ill health debarred her from going to church. Her friends, on returning from service, were surprised to find her at the piano, a new hymn already written in her hand. In explanation, she said that she was following the church service in her room when a sentence from the prayer book struck her attention. "What a splendid first line!" she thought, and so the hymn came. It was popularized by Mr. Sankey in a tune of his own composition.

Miss Havergal always felt that her poems were "given" to her from above. "Writing is *praying* with me, for I never seem to write even a verse by myself and feel like a little child writing what is dictated.'' In 1874, she wrote to a friend: "The Master has not put a chest of poetic gold into my possession and said, 'Now use it as you like!' but He keeps the gold and gives it to me piece by piece just when He will and as much as He will and no more.''

More of her theory of hymn writing she gives in the introduction to her book *Specimen-Glasses*. She calls them "flowers," and continues: "Far-wafted fragrance, exquisite workmanship, delicate and striking beauty of form and color, stores of hidden honey, are not the only points of comparison. There should be in every such flower incorruptible seed, which may spring up in the heart of many a gatherer, blossoming there in the beauty of holiness, and bearing fruit unto life eternal. . . . Some hymns are true amaranths, and never die, rather gaining than losing the power of their fragrance and loveliness as years and even centuries pass on.''

Later on, in this same book, she writes an illuminating comment on the hymns of Charlotte Elliott which not only is inherently true but also applies perfectly to Miss Havergal herself. "Her hymns are all heart-work, and whether written in first, second or third person, we feel that she has lived every line; and that is why they touch other lives so magnetically. . . . It may take many a year of living to produce a hymn which comes to the surface in a flash of thought.''

Work of this quality naturally is attractive to the musicians of the highest skill; and Miss Havergal's verse has been set to music by some of the best composers of the nineteenth century. Among them can be mentioned Gounod, Blumenthal, Randegger, Pinsuti, Dykes and Abt.

With her poetic gift went also, as a most fitting companion, an unusual appreciation of music. As a little girl she noted that the cuckoo's song which was a major third in May became a minor third in June. "Music," she wrote, "seems the only universal language understood by men of every age and tongue, and by the angels too. It is an alphabet of the language of heaven, though not any more equal to it than an A B C book is to Milton." Again: "On no form of the beautiful is 'passing away' so engraven as on music. In 'passing away' lies its very essence. The most exquisite passage, if lingered on, loses its very existence as well as beauty; the time, the motion, is the life, the actual notes only a dead letter without it; while to *hold* it is simply an inherent impossibility." This is philosophic criticism of rare order. She was equally sensitive to the esthetic and spiritual side of music. "To me the overture to the [Mendelssohn] *Lobgesang* is a vision of Christian life, with its own peculiar struggles and sorrows as well as joys. It is the sixth, seventh and eighth chapter of Romans in essence. The mingling of twilight yearnings, ever pressing *onward,* with calm and trustful praise, ever pressing *upward,* is an almost unbearably true echo of the heart; the *andante religioso* is the still, mellow glow of light at eventide, to which one looks forward; then I go just one step farther and find a fore-echo of the eternal song in the burst of vocal praise, after the long tension of the voiceless overture.''

Miss Havergal's hymns echo her theology; it was warmly evangelical and deeply subjective. If it were to be criticised at all, it would be for its lack of the social emphasis now so common in Christian thinking. Moreover, to one whose experience has not been so deep as hers, she seems over-intense. The writer remembers the repugnance he felt as a boy to some of the sentiments he found in *Kept for the Master's Use*. He had a feeling that a college song was all right on occasion and revolted against the pietism which would ''sing''

Always, only, for my King.

It seemed an undue renunciation of innocent pleasures, a false demarcation between the world and the church, the secular and the Christian. This fact is noted here simply for the enlightenment of those who may have felt the same way, as if Miss Havergal were

A creature quite too bright and good
For human nature's daily food,

to alter Wordsworth for this purpose!

This feeling, however, does an injustice to

Miss Havergal. There was no cant about her. There was absolutely none of the holier-than-thou in her relations with others. She was simple, unaffected, genuine, true. She lived higher up on the mountain-side of Christian experience than most mortals; but she beckoned to all who dwelt below and bore consistent witness to the quality of life up there.

Her life has been seized upon by ardent sectarians of different schools to illustrate their pet theories of "sinless perfection," of "second blessing," and the like; but her experience was far too large and genuine to fit into any molds so narrow and irregular. Her career illustrated not a second blessing but a score of blessings; it was a running commentary on the text: "Grow in grace and in the knowledge of Jesus." "You know something of how He can 'come,' " she once wrote, "but do you think you have reached the end of His gracious comings?" She was a little suspicious of a too-easy consecration. "There is always a danger that just because we say 'all' we practically fall shorter than if we said 'some' but said it very definitely."

Sanity, reasonableness, a sunny, human temper, a sense of humor, marked her work as well as her life and kept her from flying off on any tangent. Greater than her music, greater than her hymns was the person herself. Her religious life was pure, deep, constant. She fed upon her Bible. All her work is pervaded by its teachings. In one poem of sixty-four lines,

the writer has counted one hundred and eleven
references to the Christian Scriptures! One
is not surprised, therefore, at her spiritual development. To her nearest and dearest she was
the embodiment of her own words:

The fullness of His blessing encompasseth our way;
The fullness of His promises crowns every brightening
    day;
The fullness of His glory is beaming from above,
While more and more we realize the fullness of His
    love.

Thus, through devotional poetry and music,
her intense life sings happiness into Christian
hearts. Her middle name, Ridley, was given
her in memory of the great Oxford martyr of
the sixteenth century; did she not bear it
worthily? Hers was the living sacrifice, daily
laid on the altar, a service of reason and persuasion. Reverend James Davidson says:
"She carved out a niche which she alone could
fill. Simply and sweetly she sang the love of
God and His way of salvation. . . . She lives
and speaks in every line of her poetry. Her
poems are permeated with the fragrance of her
passionate love of Jesus."

After Miss Havergal's death, a sum of
money amounting to nineteen hundred pounds
was raised as a memorial to her, to be
used for supporting native Bible women in
India and circulating her books. Her life
is her best memorial, however, just as, in
turn, it is a memorial of her Saviour's power

to save from sin and enrich the life of
the believer. Her body was buried in a quiet
English churchyard, and the stone bears this
verse: "The blood of Jesus Christ His Son
cleanseth us from all sin." No Scripture could
be more fitting for her whose life was so truly
redeemed and whose influence is still a redeem-
ing force.

God's singer! In a land
Of alien thought and language thou didst sing
The songs of Zion; now before thy King,
    Blest singer, thou dost stand!

Thine earthly singing o'er—
Thy singing sweet and strong and glad and wise—
Thou art, among the choir of paradise
    A singer evermore.

CHAPTER IX

RAMABAI DONGRE MEDHAVI

BY JOHN CLAIR MINOT

IN the religious system of the Hindu nation there is a goddess Rama whose name signifies "brightness" or "light." It was singularly appropriate that Ananta Shastri, a learned Brahman, and his young wife Lakshmibai, gave the name of this goddess to the child who was born to them in 1858 in the jungle of Gungamal. There was little enough of brightness in the lives of the parents to be sure, but the little daughter, Ramabai, has lived to become a light that has pierced the sinister shadows which thickly envelop the womanhood of India. The work that she has established, made possible by the strength and beauty of her womanhood, has become a far-shining beacon to lead her sisters from the ignorance and superstition that have kept them in cruel darkness through many centuries.

Of the numerous agencies, whether of native origin or resulting from the missionary spirit of England and America, which are seeking to free the women of India from the heavy bondage of the religious law and social customs of their race, none is to be rated higher in its practical methods or its far reaching influences,

RAMABAI

than that of which Ramabai has been the head
and heart since she returned to India from
America in 1889. The secular home and school
in Poona for high-caste child widows and the
Christian home and industrial farm school at
Kedgaum, thirty-four miles distant, have done
a work for thousands which is beyond meas-
urement by human standards. And the women
whom she has saved from death and trained
for useful lives are taking the lead in the
emancipation and Christianization of the
women of India.

Ramabai had an unusual heritage for the
work to which she has given her life. Her
father was of the ancient Mahratta race—a race
of conquerors—which has played a remarkable
part in Indian history. From him she received the pluck, the perseverance, the independence, the forcefulness, and in general the
strength of character that she has needed every
day since her girlhood in the jungle. Though
an orthodox Hindu and a strict adherent to
caste and other religious rules, he in his own
way was a reformer. He believed, for example, that women had a right to an education, and he practiced what he preached by
teaching his child wife to read, to write and to
understand sacred literature. This liberality
was such an open disregard of the cherished
traditions of the country and aroused such a
storm of protest from his family that he was
forced to take his wife far away to a solitary
home in the forest.

The wife, who became the mother of three children of whom Ramabai was the youngest, was given to him in marriage in a way that well illustrates conditions in India. One day Ananta, while bathing in the sacred river, Godavery, met a striking looking pilgrim, who was likewise engaged. They fell to talking, and after a few preliminaries, the pilgrim offered his daughter, then only nine years old, to the strange Brahman pundit, as his wife. The offer was accepted and the marriage ceremony was performed the next day. Thus Lakshmibai Dongre became the wife of Ananta Shastri and never saw her parents again, but her lot proved far happier than that of most of the millions of child brides of India.

The thatched hut to which Ananta Shastri took his girl wife, and where Ramabai was born a dozen years later, was in a dense forest on top of a peak of the Western Ghats. There the scholarly Brahman was able to study in peace, to educate his wife as he pleased, and to worship the gods of his faith far from the turmoil of the world. From his rice fields and cocoanut plantations near his old home, he received an income sufficient for his needs. It chanced, however, that the mountain top was the object of sacred pilgrimages and he deemed it a religious duty to entertain all the pilgrims who came there. After a dozen years of this hospitality, it had to cease because his resources were utterly exhausted.

Thereupon with his wife and three children,

Ananta Shastri left the mountain home and
for the rest of his life was himself a religious
pilgrim, wandering from one end of India to
the other. At this time Ramabai was a baby
of six months; she was brought from the mountain top to the plains in a little basket of cane.
Her earliest memory, she relates, and, indeed,
all the memories of her girlhood and young
womanhood, are associated with traveling—
traveling from one city or village to another,
often shelterless and hungry, visiting shrines
and temples, worshiping images of the Hindu
gods, and always reading aloud, either in the
temples and public places, or in the shade by
the roadside.

Of this period of her life, Ramabai writes as
follows: "The reading of the Puranas served
a double purpose; the first and foremost was
that of getting rid of sin, and of earning merit
in order to obtain Moksha, or liberation from
a lower existence. The other purpose was to
earn an honest living, without begging.

"The readers of Puranas—Puranikas as
they are called—are the popular and public
preachers of religion among the Hindus. They
sit in some prominent places, in temple halls,
or under the trees, or on the banks of rivers
and tanks, with their manuscript books in their
hands, and read the Puranas in a loud voice
with intonation, so that the passers-by, or
visitors of the temple may hear. The text,
being in the Sanskrit language, is not understood by the hearers. The Puranikas are not

obliged to explain it to them. They may or
may not explain it as they choose. And sometimes when it is translated and explained, the
Puranika takes great pains to make his speech
as popular as he can, by telling greatly exaggerated or untrue stories. This is not considered sin, since it is done to attract common
people's attention, that they may hear the
sacred sound, the names of the gods, and some
of their deeds, and be purified by this means.
When the Puranika reads Puranas, the hearers,
who are sure to come and sit around him for
a few moments at least, generally give him presents. The Puranika continues to read, paying
no attention to what the hearers do or say.
They come and go at their choice.

"When they come, the religious ones among
them prostrate themselves before him and worship him and the book, offering flowers, fruits,
sweetmeats, garments, money and other things.
It is supposed that this act brings a great deal
of merit to the giver, and the person who receives does not incur any sin. If a hearer does
not give presents to the Puranika, he loses all
the merit which he may have earned by good
acts. The presents may not be very expensive
ones; a handful of rice or other grains, a pice,
or even a few cowries, which are used as an ex-
change of pice—64 cowrie shells are equal to
one pice—are quite acceptable. A flower, or
even a petal of a flower, or a leaf of any good
sacred tree, is acceptable to the gods. But the
offerer knows well that his store of merit will

be according to what he gives, and he tries to be as generous as he can. So the Puranika gets all that he needs by reading Puranas in public places.''

Thus passed year after year. When Ramabai was about eight years old her education began at the hands of her mother, and it continued with system and thoroughness until she was fifteen. Never until she left India, did she attend school. She learned to speak half a dozen tongues and gained a wonderful knowledge of the Sanskrit language and literature. English language and literature, however, was excluded from her education, for it was a firm belief of her faith that to come in contact with English people, or even to learn their language, was to lose caste and all hope of future happiness.

Although he was a loyal Brahman in many respects, her father refused to follow the custom of giving his little daughter in marriage when she became nine years old. Largely on account of this refusal and because of his advanced views on the education of women, he was virtually ostracized by those of his caste in his last years when he became feeble and blind. Ramabai loved and honored her father, but she revered the memory of her mother, as a teacher, no less than in the intimate relation of motherhood. When she published her remarkable book *The High-Caste Hindu Woman* in Boston in 1887 she dedicated it ''to the memory of my beloved mother, Lakshmibai Dongre, whose sweet influence and able instruction have been the light and guide of my life."

The awful famine season of 1874 broke up the family group. Within a few months of each other, the father, mother and older sister all died of starvation. The brother and Ramabai, who was then sixteen, somehow managed to live, and continued to lead the only life that they had known. The brother and sister, being high-caste, were too proud to do menial work, and their education, which was mainly in the sacred literature of the Hindus, offered them no practical way to earn a living. So they wandered from place to place, studying, worshiping, and reading in public places. In the three years following the death of their parents and sister, they walked more than four thousand miles, and suffered many privations. Much of the time they had no shelter except the free lodgings for the poor, which are common to pilgrims and travelers of all except the low castes.

During this period, Ramabai's faith in the religion of her ancestors grew weaker and weaker. She saw that the fulfillment of the hard conditions laid down in the sacred books did not bring the promised rewards. Obedience to the rules of the gods brought no favor or recognition. Worship, according to the rites she had been taught, left in her soul an ever unsatisfied hunger. It was in this restless spiritual mood, that she and her brother arrived in Calcutta in 1878. In the twelve

months that they remained there, during her
twentieth year, her exceptional mental attainments won for her the recognition of the wise
men of her race—and she took her first steps
towards the acceptance of Christianity.

So rare a thing in India is an educated
woman that the fame of Ramabai had reached
the ears of the pundits, or learned men, of Calcutta. By giving her an education, had not her
father, a high-caste Brahman, defied social customs and religious teachings? Had not she
been equally bold—she who had read the sacred
writings in public, and lectured in many towns
in behalf of education and other privileges for
the women of India? So they summoned her
before them, heard her story, and gave her a
long and searching examination. It was a
severe test; but she did not flinch. Her self-
possession and modesty, her mastery of languages and literature, her logic in defending
her rights as a woman, completely won the
learned men from their conservatism and their
prejudice against her. They accorded her
frank praise instead of the censure that she
had expected; in recognition of her merit they
publicly conferred upon her the title of *Sar-
asvati*, Goddess of Wisdom. From that time
this title has often been added to her name, and
even more frequently the title Pundita has been
prefixed. Not only has she become known the
world over as "the Pundita Ramabai," but she
is frequently referred to as "the Pundita," so
absolutely preëminent for her learning and

wisdom is she among all the millions of native
women of India.

About this same time, she and her brother
accepted an invitation to attend a social gathering of Christians. There they met people of
their own caste who had been converted to
Christianity. At first they were shocked to see
Brahmans talking and eating with the English
men and women. So crude was Ramabai's
idea of Christian worship that she thought the
people were paying homage to their chairs
when they knelt before them to pray. A copy
of the Bible in Sanskrit was given her, and she
took it home with her. "I tried to read it, but
did not understand," she writes. "The language was so different that at first I thought it
a waste of time to read it. But I have never
parted with it since that time."

As she studied and lectured in Calcutta, new
thoughts woke in her heart and a new longing
filled her life. Suddenly her beloved brother
died, and she was alone and almost friendless
in a country where women are wholly depend-
ent upon their male relatives. But among her
friends was a young Bengali lawyer, Bipin
Bihari Medhavi, a graduate of the Calcutta
University. He had studied in a mission
school and like Ramabai he had thrown aside
the old belief, but had not joined the Christians. He sympathized with the liberal views
of the Pundita and with her unselfish plans, as
dimly formed, for helping the women of her
race. That he was of a lower caste than hers

—of the fourth, or Shundra caste—would have
been an insuperable barrier between them in
spite of his high character and attainments
had she still been of the faith in which she was
reared. But she had definitely abandoned that
faith, and when they knew they loved each other
they were at once married. This was in 1880,
a few months after the brother's death, when
she was in her twenty-second year. Had not
her father sacrificed his own caste standing for
the sake of her education and happiness, she
would have been given in marriage at the age
of nine.

For nearly two years Ramabai knew a happy
home life, of which the supreme happiness was
the birth of a daughter who was named Manorama,—"heart's joy." Then her husband died
suddenly of the cholera; with her baby she faced
the world alone again—this time belonging to
the most unhappy class of all the unhappy
women of India, a sonless widow. To add to
her lonely desolation, her relatives and former
friends had only contempt for her because she
had married out of her caste. Their complaint
was not so much that she had married a man
of inferior caste as that she had married out of
her own caste, for her husband had likewise
suffered for marrying her—though he was of
the fourth caste and she of the highest. Even
his own brother had not dared to write to him
for fear of losing caste—and the loss of caste
means to the Hindu millions of reincarnations
before it can be regained.

For some time before the death of her husband the purpose had been forming in the heart of Ramabai to devote her life to improving the condition of the women of India; in this unselfish ambition her husband had fully sympathized. In her travels from one end of the country to the other, during the years since her infancy, it had been her privilege as a Brahman to have free access to the homes of the high-caste Hindus. Her soul revolted at the cruelties to which she saw the women subjected by the social custom and religious regulations of her people. If the miserable lot of the child wife filled her with pity, she was far more deeply moved by the harder fate of the child widow, who, more especially if she has borne no son, becomes a pitiable outcast, reviled, abused and shunned by her husband's relatives and by the whole community. Once the child widows of India commonly found release from their miserable existence, and as they believed, a prompt admission to heaven, by suicide on the funeral pyres of their husbands. This terrible custom, called the rite of *suttee*, has been forbidden by British law since 1829, but has nevertheless been practiced in many instances in later years.

Throughout India widowhood is regarded as the punishment for crimes committed by the woman in her previous existence on the earth. Disobedience or disloyalty to the husband are the crimes punished in the present birth by widowhood, according to the Hindu conception.

If the widow is a mother of sons the social mistreatment and hatred of which she is the object are greatly lessened by the fact that she has brought superior beings into the world; yet she is looked upon as a sinner without hope of happiness in this life or the next one. The widow who is the mother of girls is much worse off, particularly if her daughters have not been given in marriage during the life of her husband. But it is upon the child-widow and the childless girl widow that falls the greatest abuse—from her own family as well as from the community. She is considered the great criminal upon whom the judgment of the gods has been pronounced.

The young widow is at once stripped of all her ornaments, of her bright garments and all the little things that she has loved to have on her person or near her. The cruelty of this deprivation lies in the fact that from earliest childhood she has been the slave of her own petty interests, and the passionate lover of ornaments and self adornment. In many cases, too, her head is shaved of the wealth of long and glossy hair which nature has given her. The only clothing left her is a single coarse garment. She is closely confined to the dark part of the house and often as strictly guarded as though she were a prisoner. The object of all this humiliation is to punish and mortify her, and to keep her from improper or indiscreet acts that would bring disgrace on the family name.

Nor is this all; the widow is allowed but one meal during the twenty-four hours; she must never take part in family feasts or jubilees; she must not even show herself to people on auspicious occasions. A Hindu thinks it highly unlucky to see a widow early in the morning, and will cover her with curses if so seen. A prospective traveler will postpone his journey if his path is crossed by a widow at the time of his departure. The name *rand* by which she is generally known is a term of bitter contempt. There is scarcely a day in which she is not beaten, or abused as the cause of her husband's death by his relatives and neighbors. If her husband has no relatives she goes back to live with her own people. Although then she has somewhat less to suffer, custom and religious faith have a stronger hold upon her parents than parental love. She is closely confined, forbidden to associate with anybody outside of the immediate family and watched with great concern, lest she bring further disgrace upon the family. Her life is empty of pleasure or hope; she cannot look forward to another marriage; she is simply a curse to herself and to society.

If she runs away, what is her fate? No respectable family, even of a lower caste, will have her for a servant. She has no art or trade by which she can earn an honest living. She has nothing but the single garment that she wears. The only alternatives are suicide or— a hideous life-in-death. For untold centuries, millions of the child widows of India have been driven to this fate.

Before Ramabai herself had been forced into this most unhappy class of all unhappy India, she had decided to take active measure for the relief of widows. Her husband and she were planning to establish, on a small scale, a refuge and school in their own home when his sudden death put an end to the project. Her determination to carry on the work on which she had set her heart was unaltered, however, and she determined to do what she could, by lecturing and personal appeals, to start a general agitation for the emancipation and education of women. She left Calcutta and went to Poona where she remained about a year. There, among the people of her own race, she was received with kindness and given help and encouragement. She founded a society, the special object of which was to discourage child marriage, and in this connection, before a British commission, she gave evidence that made much of a stir in England.

As Ramabai was now studying the English language, she frequently met the European missionaries. From them, little by little, she learned the great truths of Christianity, and the seed that had been left by that chance visit to a mission in Calcutta, before her marriage, began to take root. Yet she was slow in accepting the Christian religion as her own in place of the inherited faith that she had definitely abandoned years ago. Her husband had not taken kindly to her acquaintance with the missionaries in Calcutta, and had forbidden them to come to his house. Many years later, in discussing her first leaning toward Christianity, Ramabai wrote: "I do not know what would have happened had my husband lived much longer."

It was through her growing friendship with the missionaries at Poona that Ramabai realized her own lack of preparation and training for the work she hoped to do in India. Consequently, after many misgivings, she decided to go to England to study. This decision meant crossing the sea, the "black water" of which all Hindus have a religious horror; only the impulse of her high purpose enabled her to take the step that meant the turning point of her life—and, no doubt, of the woman-life of all India. Early in 1883, accompanied by her baby daughter, she made the journey and went directly to St. Mary's Home, an institution of the English church, at Wantage. There the sisters, one of whom she had known in Poona, gave her a warm welcome and a most favorable opportunity to pursue her studies in both secular and religious subjects. As soon as she had mastered the English language, she was appointed professor of Sanskrit in Cheltenham Female College, where, in addition to her teaching, she studied the sciences, English literature, higher mathematics and Greek.

Soon after her arrival in England, the sisters of St. Mary's took Ramabai for a time to a branch of their home in London where she watched their rescue work for the unfortunate women of the great metropolis. The results there showed her, if more evidence was needed, the great vital difference between Christianity and Hinduism. The Hindu religion offers neither pity nor hope to fallen or down-trodden women, and makes no effort to transform or uplift them. Soon after, in September 1883, she and her little daughter, were baptized in the Episcopal church at Wantage. Of that time she writes: "My heart was drawn to the religion of Christ and I was intellectually convinced of its truth. I felt a great joy in finding a new religion which was better than any other religion I had known before. I knew full well that it would displease my friends and countrymen very much, but I have never regretted taking the step. I was hungry for something better than what the Hindu Shastras gave. I found it in the Christian's Bible and was satisfied."

However, Ramabai did not feel that she had really found Christ until a long time after she accepted the Christian religion. During the six years of her stay in England and America she studied the subject deeply, and for a time was much bewildered at the multiplicity of Christian sects and the confusion of their doctrines. In the differences of orthodox and unorthodox Christian sects, she met greater intellectual and spiritual difficulties, and for years her heart yearned for something that she did not find.

It was not until some time after her return
to India from America in 1889 that .she was
able to write: "I have come to know the
Lord Jesus Christ as my personal Saviour, and
to have the joy of sweet communion with him."
Since then there has been no doubt or dismay
in her spiritual life, and a zeal for evangelism,
to carry the gospel of salvation to others, has
been her consuming passion.

After nearly three years with the sisters at
Wantage and at the Cheltenham Female College, Ramabai came to America in February,
1886. The immediate occasion of the journey
was the graduation of her cousin, Anandibai
Joshee, from the Woman's Medical College in
Philadelphia. This cousin, who like Ramabai,
aimed to help the women of her native land,
was training herself for the work by securing
a medical education. Because the bond of the
common purpose between them was stronger
than the ties of blood, at home she had been one
of the few of the kin of Ramabai who had been
kind to her in the early days of her widowhood.
Her degree of Doctor of Medicine was the first
ever conferred on a Hindu woman. It was a
great loss to India when Anandibai Joshee died
in February, 1887, a few months after her return home, at the age of twenty-two.

When Ramabai arrived in Philadelphia, she
expected to return to England in a short time,
and thence to India. But Dean Rachel L. Bodley of the Woman's Medical College, who took
Ramabai to her heart and home, encouraged

her to remain and mature her plans in the United States. In England she had studied hard and had profited much intellectually and spiritually, but she was still with no well formulated method of procedure for her work in India. In America those plans soon began to take definite shape. It was in the public school system, especially the kindergarten and industrial branches, that she found the solution of her problem. With the help of her many new friends she began to consider the ways and means of realizing the great dream of her life.

While studying the working of the school system she wrote her book, *The High-Caste Hindu Woman*, which appeared in 1887 with an introduction by Dean Bodley. The introduction to the second edition in 1901 was by Mrs. Judith W. Andrews of Boston, long one of Ramabai's most loyal friends in America. From the first the book produced a deep impression, and aroused a widespread interest in the unhappy lot of the women of India and in the work that the author proposed to do in their behalf. Ramabai was the first writer to set forth from first hand knowledge the complete and intimate story of a Hindu woman's life—her hopeless and helpless position as defined by religion and custom, her few joys, her many sorrows and her great needs. She told of the practice of female infanticide, the child marriages, the contempt and cruelty that crush the sonless widow. Much that she wrote about was generally known in America through accounts of missionaries and travelers, but perhaps the general public had been inclined to regard their narratives as too highly colored. No reader could doubt what Ramabai wrote—it was all expressed so clearly, so earnestly, so authoritatively and yet so temperately. The masterly style of the book is as remarkable as the matter presented. Later, in 1907, she wrote another noteworthy book, *A Testimony,* which is an account of her own life, and especially of her religious experiences.

When her book had appeared in 1887, Ramabai began to make her appeal to America for funds to enable her to establish a school and refuge for the high-caste child widows of her native land. She asked, moreover, that her friends form themselves into an association to be the custodian of the money that might be raised and to which she should be responsible for its use.

In May, 1887, at a public meeting held in Boston, a provisional committee was appointed to consider Ramabai's plan, to act as far as possible, and to report at a later meeting. In December this committee presented a report that was accepted, officers were elected, a constitution was adopted, and the temporary American Ramabai Association became an organization. It sprang into existence, and Ramabai saw her long cherished plan take definite form. That night her joy was too great for sleep; when found sobbing in her room, she explained, "I am crying for joy that my dream of years has become a reality." Among the

officers of the association were Edward Everett
Hale, Phillips Brooks, Lyman Abbott, George A.
Gordon, Mrs. Mary Hemenway, Dean Rachel L.
Bodley, and Frances E. Willard—a rare body
of officers, Unitarian, Episcopalian, Congrega-
tionalist, Baptist and Methodist. The board of
trustees, consisting of business men and the
executive committee of philanthropic women,
were equally undenominational. The association pledged itself to the support of a secular
school for ten years—a school in which no religious instruction either Hindu or Christian
should be given. The Bible and the Vedas were
to stand side by side in the school library, free
to all. The caste rules were to be observed, but
there were to be no public religious observances
of any kind. This was Ramabai's pledge to her
own and the American people—a pledge she
kept inviolate.

After the formation of the association Ramabai considered herself its servant. From
May, 1887, to November, 1888, this dauntless
little woman of thirty, in the midst of a strange
people, strange customs and manners, eating
neither "fish, flesh or fowl," often hungry and
cold, showed a degree of mental and physical
endurance that was marvelous, even in the eyes
of Americans.

A lady who was present at one of her meetings described her appearance at that time:
"Ramabai is strikingly beautiful; her face is a
clear-cut oval; her eyes, large and dark, glow
with feeling. She is a brunette, but her cheeks

are full of color. Her white widow's saree is
drawn closely over her head and fastened under
her chin.''

The Boston association, however, was not
enough. Protected from insult by her pure
womanliness and strong personality, she traveled from Canada to the Pacific coast, lecturing, forming circles, studying educational, philanthropic and charitable institutions, omitting
nothing that might prove helpful to her people.
Reaching the Pacific coast, her appeals won the
sympathy of ministers of all creeds—Protestant, Catholic and Hebrew—of earnest women
and business men. As the result, an auxiliary
association was there formed that sent $5,000
to the treasury the first year. In November,
1888, with an assured annual income sufficient
for the support of a secular school of fifty pupils
for ten years, Ramabai bade good-by to a land
that had grown very dear to her, and turned
her face homeward, bright with hope, and with
a brave heart, though she knew not how her
countrymen would receive her.

She sailed from San Francisco for Bombay
by way of Japan and China, and in February,
1889, she stood again on the shores of her native
land, after an absence of six years. She found
many to welcome her and to encourage her in
her plans, and in less than six weeks the school
of which she had dreamed for many years was
opened in Bombay. There were two high-caste
child widows as its first day pupils—one of
them a girl who had thrice attempted suicide,

restrained only by the fear of being born again a woman. To her school Ramabai gave the name of Sharada Sadan—Home of Wisdom— for it was meant from the beginning to be a home as well as a school.

Such was the modest beginning in 1889 of the real work of Ramabai for the womanhood of India—a work that has now continued for almost a quarter of a century with constantly increasing scope and with greater and greater effectiveness. In the first year, the school gained in reputation and numbers far beyond the expectations of Ramabai or her friends in America. It was soon removed from Bombay to Poona, the former home of Ramabai and a stronghold of Brahmanism, where it has since remained. In 1893, when the number of pupils had grown to about fifty, the school was bitterly attacked by the Brahmans on the ground that its head was violating her pledge to keep the school a secular institution and not to lead its pupils away from their religion into Christianity. Over thirty of the pupils were withdrawn and the future seemed very dark. The investigation that followed vindicated Ramabai. It was shown that she had not broken her engagement to keep the school unsectarian, and that she was not to be blamed if some of her pupils, under the influence of her strong personality, contrasted her religion with that which they had known and sought Christian baptism. The clouds cleared away, the old pupils came back with new ones with them.

The agitation, however, resulted in a reconstruction of the Hindu advisory committee of the institution, and in the understanding that every pupil should henceforth receive religious instruction, while retaining perfect liberty of conscience. So, while the Sharada Sadan has remained nominally secular the Christian influence, resulting from the evangelical zeal of Ramabai, has radiated to every part of India.

When the school had been in operation a few years, Ramabai was able, through the generosity of American friends, to buy a large farm at Kedgaum, not far from Poona. Here she established an avowedly Christian home and industrial school which she named Mukti—Salvation. This estate has supplied Sharada Sadan with vegetables and milk, and its products have added materially to the funds available for her work. Moreover, on the farm itself, she has cared for and trained hundreds of girls and women.

The first great work at Mukti was in the famine year of 1897. She hastened to the famine-stricken district of Central India and rescued over five hundred child widows and deserted girl wives, of whom she sheltered and fed three hundred at her farm. These waifs of famine and ostracism are portrayed as "nothing but skeletons, and like the beasts of the jungle." Think what it meant for one woman to do this work of rescue under such conditions! At the same time she was superintending the erection of buildings, the digging of wells, the cultivation of fields and the establishment of various industries on the farm—not to mention the carrying on of the school at Poona.

The next year, 1898, saw the expiration of the ten year period for which the American Ramabai Association had pledged its support of her work, and, at the invitation of the Association, Ramabai made a journey to Boston to meet her loyal friends again, and to talk over the future. At the annual meeting of the Association in March the marvelous success of the first ten years' experience was reviewed. It was shown that the buildings and equipment of the Sharada Sadan at Poona were worth $50,000 and that they were wholly free from debt. This property was then, and has since continued to be, held by the Association, in accordance with the wish of Ramabai. The great farm and industrial school at Kedgaum are held by Ramabai herself. In those first ten years the American Ramabai Association sent $95,500 to the support of the work. The Poona school in that time had educated and sheltered three hundred and fifty child widows, of whom scores had gone forth to found schools of their own, to serve as missionaries or housekeepers or to become voluntary Christian workers in missionary fields.

As a result of this showing of definite results, the Association was incorporated and reorganized to carry on the work on a still larger scale. Ramabai went back to India happy in the realization that her fondest prayers were being an-

swered. In the following three years no less
than $50,000 was sent her—a sum which she
used wisely and prudently in meeting the great
needs of her undertaking. The financial support given by her American friends has continued to the present time. It cannot be
doubted that it will continue as long as she lives
to continue the work, or while her successors are
accomplishing results equally necessary and
valuable.

In 1900 Manorama, the daughter of Ramabai,
graduated from the Chesborough Seminary,
North Chili, New York, and unselfishly put
aside her hope for a college course to return
to India and become vice-principal of the Sharada Sadan. There she has taken on more and
more of the responsibilities and duties of her
mother, and the 1912 report to the American
Ramabai Association was wholly her own.
Then there were one hundred and fifteen girls
and women in the Sharada Sadan, and one
hundred and seventy-two on the farm and in the
Mukti school.

The name of Ramabai deserves a high place
on the roll of the heroic women of our time.
Overcoming almost smothering obstacles, she
has accomplished for her sex and her race a
work which only the Judge of all achievements
can properly estimate. The long, hard years
of preparation have been followed by almost
a quarter of a century of wonderful fruition
—a glorious harvest to crown all the service

and sacrifice. And in that vast empire where she has lived and labored million upon million of women yet unborn will learn to bless her name.

CHAPTER X

MAUD BALLINGTON BOOTH

BY R. V. TREVEL

A LIFE of action generally should be regarded as a panorama and Mrs. Ballington Booth is seen in a succession of all sorts of surroundings in various countries. For two decades and a half the Salvation Army with its drums and flags has furnished a shifting background to her career; later this background merges into another setting which throws into possibly clearer relief the works of this woman with her radiant influence in our civilization.

Nothing in the antecedents or environment of Maud Charlesworth—for such was the maiden name of the heroine of this chapter—pointed to a very exceptional life for the girl; but the good mind she inherited and the tinge of foreign blood in her veins no doubt had their effect. Her mother mingled in her veins the blood of French Huguenot and Scotch Calvinist. Her father, however, the Reverend Samuel Charlesworth was altogether English by race, as well as a clergyman of the English Church. Maud's girlhood, indeed, was typically English. Speaking of her birthplace, her father's rectory in the parish of Limpsfield, Surrey, she says, in

After 'Prison—What?: "The pretty tree-
shaded garden of Nutfield Cottage was bounded
on one side by the quiet village churchyard and
a little private gate opened on the path that
led through it to the garden of Nutfield Court,
where our special playmates lived. By day-
light one could run blithely enough between the
old quaint head-stones, moss-covered, and other
mounds bright with masses of blossom, when
the breeze was playing in the trees, the lark
singing praises from the blue sky, or the quaint
old ivy-covered tower of the church might send
forth its glad peal of chimes. There was so
much of life and beauty that children could run
or linger there with no thought of the death that
lay still and solemn beneath the smiling flowers
and whispering grasses. But it was a different
thing if one walked back after nightfall, with
senses alert to every sound, and heart beating
fast with unknown terrors. The rustle of a
bird in the ivy, the creaking of a dead branch,
the flitting of a bat-wing, or a play of moonbeam
and shadow—such things made the churchyard
a place to be avoided, for now memory was
vivid that it was a village of the dead."

The writer of this passage describes a natural
and normal little girl as well as an English
neighborhood. But what a comparison this remembered "village of the dead" was to give to
her in later years!

Ten years or more before this thoughtful
child was born in Nutfield Cottage, the Salvation Army—then called The Christian Mission

—was founded. The Salvation Army began
as a limb of English Methodism, just as that
church itself branched off from the Church of
England a hundred years before. The Salvation Army was organized as a result of the religious ardor and energy of two English New
Connection Methodists who married in 1855.
The man, indeed, who adopted the title of the
"general" of the movement, was a minister of
the New Connection, the Reverend William
Booth. His wife, Catherine Mumford, a spiritual woman of strong character, was strangely
well-mated with him and shared his determination to use effective measures, no matter how
unconventional, to extend the Kingdom of God
upon earth. Squads of their Army are a familiar sight in the streets to-day. No one mo-
lests them or jeers at their banner inscribed
with "Blood and Fire." That this motto of
theirs once expressed the open scorn and actual
violence which they had to meet is hard to realize now. Not so very many years ago, however, both General Booth and his eloquent wife
were arrested for commotions attending the
open-air meetings at which they won converts,
and their followers were often fined and imprisoned and sometimes beaten and maimed or
killed by the rabble. Why the Salvationists
were deemed unpardonable in the eighteen-
fifties and sixties is easy to understand. In
the first place, England is a quiet-loving country,
and the eyes of authority and the people could
see nothing but disturbance of the public peace

in the acts of these modern crusaders as, on country commons or city streets, they collected crowds which often became riotous. One sort of popular opposition came from saloon-keepers, drunkards, law-breakers and bitter women whom the fearless, if noisy, evangelists were trying to convert. The more the Salvation Army was persecuted and prosecuted, however, the more people did it convert, most of them from the less educated classes but not a few persons of rank, such as Lord and Lady Cairns, and Sir Arthur Blackwood. Towards the end of her life, Queen Victoria showed toward the Army a less distant consideration than at first; and her son had long been friendly, when as Edward VII he invited General Booth to take part in his coronation in 1902.

A number of factors have made for the success of the Salvationists in bringing thousands to Christianity and pure living. For one thing, the sect is absolutely sincere. Moreover—as was at first hard for the world to understand—the Booths did not from choice make use of tambourines, shouting, and red-scarfed parades, but adopted their noisy methods simply because they saw that in no other way could they catch the attention of a great mass of people. The Army's creed, as a matter of fact, differs from that of the Anglican Church simply in that the sacraments are not observed for fear of discussion that might prevent men and women from coming to Christ—the all-important matter. That their methods of campaign as well as its

object were fully approved from on high, both
General and Mrs. Booth firmly believed; this
clear conception, joined to executive force and
resourcefulness, in no small measure accounts
for their success.

It would be hard to point to any other quarter
where religion has shown such effectiveness
since the Salvationist era. After their first
hard conquest of British prejudice at home,
Booth sent his captains abroad and sometimes
went forth in person. George Scott Railton, as
a missionary, journeyed to Morocco in 1870; and
two years later James Jermey writes to the General from Erie Street in Cleveland, Ohio, that
"in the good Providence of our blessed Lord
I and family are all quite well, and at last I
am in the right field for mission work—glory,
hallelujah!" Detachments of the Army invaded the continent; Frederick St. George de
Latour Tucker in 1881 resigned his position as
a high government official in the Punjab to become the Salvation Army "Commissioner" in
India; and soon after a party sailed over seas
to far Australia, where the cause began to prosper from the first.

Although not formally incorporated and
named until 1865, this "religious organization
on military principles" more soundly dates, as
already noted, from the marriage of its high
priest and priestess ten years earlier. Definitely, the activities of the Salvation crusading
have been and still are these: the rescue of

unfortunate women who are housed and cared
for in Army "rescue homes"; the regular visitation, not to say invasion, of the worst haunts
of vice and sin, of drinking places and crowded
tenements; the furnishing of coal, clothing, food,
shelter, and lodging to all who need them; the
caring for children; the visiting of prisons and
hospitals; the providing of Christmas and
Thanksgiving dinners; and the finding of employment either inside of the Army or out of
it for those having none. At the same time, it
is the constant aim to bring all the men and
women who are thus helped into the Salvationist ranks and into a belief in the Saviour, who,
according to the doctrine which they preach and
practice, is to be served with utter self-abnega-
tion and with thought only of others.   The military structure under which this work is carried
on includes "corps," "regiments," and "out-
posts," and the ranks of "colonel," "lieutenant-
colonel," "major," "captain," and "lieutenant," while the rank and file are called
"cadets."   The General, whose "International
Headquarters" are in London seems always to
have a "Commander" as his right hand there,
a title which Mrs. Catherine Booth bore—for
titles are held by women as well as men—until
her death in 1890.

Since the death of General Booth in 1912, his
eldest son, Bramwell Booth, has succeeded him
as the General in London. The American
"Headquarters" are in New York. In coun-

tries where the Salvationist work is making its
beginnings its head is called the "Commissioner."

The General and Mrs. Booth had eight children, who, as fast as they grew up, were created
officers of the Army; most of them were like the
parents, pure spirits, stern yet happy in self-
requirement, their life objects seeming to be
just two—the service of their Redeemer and the
bringing of others to that Master for their saving.   The Booths must be characterized as the
hierarchy of their sect, for they are no less.
Clearness demands a chart of the family:

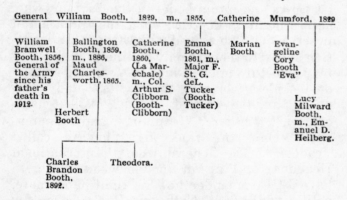

General William Booth, 1829, m., 1855, Catherine Mumford, 1829

| William Bramwell Booth, 1856, General of the Army since his father's death in 1912. | Ballington Booth, 1859, m., 1886, Maud Charlesworth, 1865. | Catherine Booth, 1860, (La Maréchale) m., Col. Arthur S. Clibborn (Booth-Clibborn) | Emma Booth, 1861, m., Major F. St. G. deL. Tucker (Booth-Tucker) | Marian Booth | Evangeline Cory Booth "Eva" |

Herbert Booth

Lucy Milward Booth, m., Emanuel D. Heilberg.

Charles Brandon Booth, 1892.   Theodora.

Of the whole body of the Salvation Army,
General Booth was the autocrat, exercising his
authority as fully over its members who were
also of his own family as over all the rest.   His
authority, too, seems to have been almost un-
limited in its extent; it suggests to the American mind the complete spiritual or moral con-

trol attributed to the heads of Mormonism;
though it must instantly be said that the Salvationists never have had marriage latitudes as
their dictator's rules of marriage are, on the
contrary, very restrictive. No minute details
of duty or the conduct of physical life seem to
have been excepted from the direction of General Booth, and no wedding could take place
without his permission. And the family appears to have been as faithful to his religious
dispensation as he was inflexible in enforcing
it. That outsiders who have married into the
family have taken its color almost completely
shows the coherence of the family. Major
Tucker, who married Emma Booth, not only
merged his life into the organization, but
legally changed his name to Booth-Tucker. So
did Colonel Clibborn, who similarly changed
his name when he married the eldest daughter,
Catherine, her whom the Parisians named "La
Maréchale" when her father and mother sent
her as a Salvationist Joan of Arc into France.
But there was one spirit, and that a woman's,
which became identified with the Booth family
and the Army without becoming absorbed in
them. That spirit belongs to her, born Maud
Charlesworth, who became Mrs. Ballington
Booth.

The education of Maud Charlesworth as child
and schoolgirl went forward through the dozen
years centered by 1875, partly in Belstead, England, and partly in Switzerland, with, however,
a good part of the time spent at home. The

family moved from the pleasant rectory in Surrey into a London neighborhood where Mr. Charlesworth assumed the large parish of Limehouse. Here she first met the Army in which she afterwards enlisted. In her *Beneath Two Flags* she records that first impression: "I remember as well as if it were yesterday my first sight of the Salvation Army. It was in my second home, a pleasant, shady, country-like place shut in by great high walls and gates, from the dust and bustle of East London, and on the gravel walk one bright Sunday afternoon knelt poorly-clad people while in their midst stood a man with hands uplifted in prayer. The crowd was augmented every moment from the crowded street without; poor women with sickly babes, lads of an unruly type, eying the lilacs and our windows in turn, while even drunken men leaned against the gate and stared in open-mouthed wonder. 'Strange people,' I thought, 'how loud they sing, and what funny words,' as their voices rose above the din and bustle in the thoroughfare without:

'O you must be a lover of the Lord
Or you can't get to heaven when you die.'

"Then I wondered why they knelt upon the hard gravel walk, and why they pleaded until their throats were hoarse with the crowd that sometimes laughed and jeered at them. The pathos of the speaker's voice and the tearful sobs of some of the witnesses could not be heard

through my window and the whole scene seemed
disjointed and grotesque compared with my
childish experience of Sunday and religion.
This was my first introduction to the Salvation
Army, then known as The Christian Mission.
'Very kind,' I had heard it said of my father,
to let them come into our garden when through
the influence of the saloon-keepers, the police
had stopped them from standing in the street
to preach to the passing multitudes.

"I saw them many times during the next few
years; marching the streets through rain and
snow, kneeling upon the hard ground, and sitting crowded together in a poor, broken-down
old theatre with the poorest and lowest of that
large East London parish. Yes, I sometimes
watched them, as their building stood just opposite our church; and strange the contrast used
to seem when we stepped in for a few moments
on Sunday night to listen to the merry joyful
songs. And then I heard them sometimes when
the singing sounded muffled through the stained-
glass windows of our church, and it could hardly
have been said to break the sacred stillness yet
I could catch the oft-repeated words, 'O you
must be a lover of the Lord,' and sometimes
they would come to my ears mixed in a strange
way with that familiar sentence, 'Lord, have
mercy upon us miserable sinners.' Ah, little
did I know that these people were sinners forgiven seeking sinners lost.

"Again as I lay at death's door with typhoid
fever I heard the same old song echoing down

the chimney sometimes varied with the refrain, 'Will you go, will you go to the Eden above?'

"And many a day after that I would run to the window as they marched past; by degrees I could hear fresh choruses and see larger crowds until finally there appeared a flag, with a bright star in its red centre and a blue border fluttering in the wind. I would move from one window to another to keep them in view, but, after all, to me they were only a crowd and some stirring scenes.

"Later on my childish thoughts were exchanged for other people's opinions and criticisms, until as the Army passed, with uniform and with colors flying, I learned to smile with derision, and to not only take credit, but repeat tales which had lost the little spark of truth with which they started."

But note the maturer attitude of the young girl:

"I turn from those days to a time when I saw them as rescuers of drunken fishermen in the streets of a seaport town famed for its wickedness and learned to know them as godly earnest people. Yes, it was then that my opinions changed and I saw them as they were and learned to love them; for they were pure in heart and filled with a love for others and disregard for self that gave them a strange fascination for me.

"But I pass to the days when I learned to look anxiously and lovingly through the rectory windows for the approaching of their blue-bordered flag, until I pause at *the* day when I myself, in the Army hall, saw Jesus my Saviour as I never had seen Him before, and gave up my life entirely to God—*my* God, the Army's God, and the drunkard's God. There I received into my heart the love and fire that sent me forth to do God's will and to follow the steps of Christ to Calvary. Indeed, I found that day that not only had I been looking at the Army, their methods and their work through a colored glass, but at my God—His will, His love, and His purposes, until they had become so dim, that I had never seen written across His life and sacrifice, '*Go thou and do likewise.*' I had a new purpose in life, and the present, ever-present consciousness of my Saviour's nearness. Of course everything looked different then—the Salvationists kneeling in the muddy London streets, associating with drunkards and sinners, the poor and despised, the singing at the risk of throat and lungs in frosty winter air. Ay, even the shouting for joy—all was understood, all was made clear. And then my thoughts traveled on through eight years of service—happy years in which I daily have learned to love the Army better, and have seen for myself what a blessed and wonderful power God has made it.''

Many a fine-hearted, fervent young creature might have thrown herself into the community of the enthusiasts, or at least have desired to do so. It is doubtful whether she would have been permitted to do so or whether she would have remained when once enlisted in the Army. This school miss was barely old enough to have been presented at Court, yet the Reverend Mr. Charlesworth let his earnest little daughter flock with these rag-tag and bobtail Christians. Moreover, the girl remained steadfastly with them from that time forward. What decision, courage, character and conviction in one not grown to a woman! The father on his part, although a formalist at least in profession, was a gentle Christian and a good man; he perceived the sincerity of these children of God, and had let the troop of them come out of the inhospitable street into the rectory garden. Then why might he not trust his child in the meetings and marches of these strangely holy folk if she really felt inspired from Heaven to go with them?

It was at this date, 1881, that the Booths sent their first crusade into France. Mrs. Booth traveled thither with the party, which she left there under the leadership of her daughter Catherine, who—think of it—had not much more than reached her majority. With "Captain" Catherine, went out little Miss Charlesworth as her "lieutenant." A dozen other maidens of similar ages made up Miss Booth's band, and it was now that she became the "Maréchale." Something of the campaign is recounted by Mrs. Ballington Booth:

"*God has left Paris,* is not only a statement printed in large letters as a newspaper heading, but is regarded as an accomplished fact by those who school themselves to believe in nothing supernatural or religious. Another paper rejoices in the fact that the Parisians have brought about *the abolition of God,* and having torn down His altars and banished His memory, they exalt the goddess of reason, the god of pleasure, and the mighty god of self, who only too readily asserts himself in every Christless heart.

"In a little hall, situated at the end of an alley, up a flight of stairs, the Army flag was first planted in a poor and communistic quarter. A strange little gathering it would have appeared to a stranger unacquainted with its meaning. A crowd of rough French laborers, dressed in their blue blouses, and women in their little snowy-white caps, knives and pistols not visible, but there nevertheless, hugged close to the citizen's breast. A rough hard crowd, as the words—'They have got in that hall half the cut-throats of Paris'—of the sergeant of the police prove. O, what a study of vicious faces, that look ready at any moment to do or dare anything, and on the platform only a few young girls! The one who is singing, with face uplifted, you might imagine to be some Catherine of Sienna or Madame Guyon; a sweet, holy, determined face, thin and worn with work, but full of courage and resolution. The crowds stare in wonder, spellbound and perplexed, as they listen to the simple heart-stirring song. Thus the Salvation Army began its work in France.

"Night after night the little band prayed,

sang, and spoke, until they were weary, but
to small effect. It seemed as though the first
convert would never come. The people remained immovable, though they came in crowds.
A French Christian who watched these strange
movements, turning to Miss Booth said: 'You
had better go home to your mother. The Salvation Army cannot possibly succeed here.'
Perhaps part of this comforting advice might
have found an outspoken echo in the heart of
one less consecrated. But the suggestion was
stifled by the brave answer, 'If I cannot save
France, I can die for it,' and mother and home
were not visited, until the visit could be taken
with news of victory.

"The people wept and were deeply impressed,
but as to definitely seeking salvation it seemed
far from them. But one night the Captain
made her way to the back of the hall and sat
down to a poor, dissolute working woman; she
put her arms around her and asked her if she
did not want Jesus as her friend and Saviour.
'I love you,' she said, looking into the woman's
face, while her tears fell on the hard-worked
hand. Those tears melted the heart which no
amount of preaching would have broken; and
this touch of divine love made the poor woman
long to find its source. So before the night
had passed the Army's first Parisian convert
had risen from the penitent form washed in the
precious blood of Jesus. The ice was broken
then, and although the fight was still hard, by
ones and twos their ranks were augmented, un-

til a nice little platform of French men and
women could be seen nightly in the new hall
on the Quai Valmy," to which the Maréchale
moved the camp when their position grew
stronger.

Needless to say that the French press found
high amusement in the enterprise of these pure-
faced little missionaries. Yet they did not always sneer, either; take, for example, the following picture by a reporter in the daily paper,
Paris. It does not require very hard guessing
to recognize the portrait drawn:

"In a café in the Quartier Latin, last month,
a numerous party was assembled by the usual
haphazard of public-houses. Drinking, smoking, card-playing, singing, speech-making, and
chatting were the order of the day.

"Suddenly the door opened, and after several seconds of astounded silence, a clamour
rose, tumultuous, extraordinary, formidable,
greeting the entrance of a woman cadet of the
Salvation Army.

"She was a young girl of some sixteen years,
of the Nell Horn type. With her delicate profile rendered still more delicate by being en-
cased in a great, black funereal bonnet, very
pale, her eyes bright and sad, erect in her
little old woman's dress, with a voice whose
English accent heightened its sweetness, she
offered the Salvation journal, *En Avant*.
They were free to buy it, or to let her return
as she came.

"But one woman knew no better than to insult her pure young sister. Some men had the weakness to laugh at the would-be joke.

"The Salvationist remained untroubled. She invited the girl who had insulted her to 'come to Jesus,' and explained to her the advantages of conversion, paraphrasing the dictum of her leader, 'You make pleasure your god, make God your pleasure.' The assembled café, delighted, received this little sermon with redoubled repartees, some few witty, many more idiotic. In spite of this brutal avalanche, aimed at that which was sacred to her, the face of the Salvationist kept its serenity.

"The conflict between one little devotee of sixteen years and a company of some sixty men and women, sceptical and shameless, was prolonged. At last a woman, moved by the spectacle of such strong faith, responding so bravely and generously to all kinds of insult, begged the assembly to leave off. *It was the woman who had begun it all!*

"This sudden change of tactics, provoked by an attitude more than human—heavenly—gave me the secret of the rapid religious growth of this organization. It possesses courage and resignation. These are the first virtues of apostleship, those which arouse in the masses admiration and pity."

In this other scene, intense is the interest because the simple Spirit of the Universe meets and awes the most artificialized civilization of mankind. That they might appeal to the well-to-do, pleasure-seeking Parisian, the Salvation-

ists rented a resplendent ballroom on the Boulevard Des Capucines. The heavy velvet hang-
ings, flashing mirrors, polished floor, gilded
furniture—what a contrast to the dingy Army
hall down in La Villette! But more striking
was the difference in audiences. Carriages
crowding the boulevard without brought ladies
clothed and bejeweled as for the opera, and
gentlemen in evening dress. The fashionables
of Paris filled every seat.

The Salvationists filed upon the platform.
Upon the little group of plainly dressed, sweet-
faced, stern lipped young women, hundreds of
opera-glasses were focused. Sneering comments arose from the audience. When Miss
Booth knelt in silent prayer, the audience arose
as one and stared at her in amazement.

"Is she sick?" asked one lady.

"No," answered another. "She is praying
to the good God." Exclamations of wonder
arose.

"Has God left Paris?" "What is the religion for France?" and "A lost soul," were
the topics of Miss Booth's address. As she
started to speak, her hearers took no pains to
conceal their amused wonder. "But after a
while," writes one who was there, "as the
power of God could be felt through the straight
yet tender words of the speaker, the listeners
for once forgot themselves and were lost in the
subject; fans would be folded, glasses forgotten,
and the mask of outward seeming would drop,
leaving on those faces a look of weary long-

ing, apprehension or pain, which showed clearly
that the heart beneath had not been quite dead-
ened by the false joy and empty etiquette of the
Paris world."

In one week the cadets of the Paris Training
Home which La Maréchale established visited
nine hundred and seventy-four cafés, speaking
and singing in most of them. "Wealthy merchants, ministers of the Gospel, would-be
suicides, drunkards, women of fashion, and
poor, lost girls—truly all manner of men and
women, were saved."

In 1883 Miss Charlesworth, now eighteen, re-
visited Switzerland, this time in company with
her superior officer, the Maréchale; Major
Booth-Tucker in his engaging *Life Of Mrs.
Catherine Booth* exclaims that, "In no country
has the Army encountered more bitter and
persistent opposition than in the freedom-boast-
ing republic." It does seem strange, as he
contends, that governments were so slow to
recognize and utilize the Salvation Army, "in
spite of its notorious success in purging and
purifying and transforming the outcasts of
society." In the midst of such brave endeavors, Miss Booth and her companions were
expelled from the country; but they returned,
and in September the Maréchale writes to her
mother from Neuchâtel Prison. "I have a
mattress, a blanket, and a shawl. The food is
very decent, and the bread not hard. . . . This
is all right. God is in it. If you could see our
soldiers, and how the town is awakened, you

would rejoice with me.   The rulers hate Christ
come in the flesh.   But He *is* come, and oh, if
you could have seen our meetings Sunday afternoon in the wood.   The tears, the prayers, the
shouts!''   General and Mrs. Booth in London
urged Earl Granville and Mr. Gladstone to take
measures for the release of the captive; La
Maréchale was soon free.   Miss Charlesworth,
though described as ''one of the most courageous and successful officers in the ranks,''
somehow escaped arrest; but a Miss Stirling
who was with them was imprisoned for one hundred days.   Thereafter, however, the Swiss authorities ceased to molest the Salvationists
among them; and the adversities already
suffered redounded to the advantage of the missions on the continent generally.

The scene as regards Miss Charlesworth
shifts from the Alps to Sweden.   In that country in 1886 at the head of a party, the young
girl is the heroine of an incident that includes a
touch of a lady's learning, very apt in the university city of Upsala.   ''As I went home,'' she
writes, ''late at night from my meeting I met
troops of young students, many of whom were
drunk and singing ribald songs.   Passing the
large saloons [this word reflects the later American life] I heard glasses clinking on the count-
ers, the rolling of billiard balls, and, looking
at the large lighted windows above, I was
told that those who were in before eleven were
allowed to remain all night.   Further, I heard
that these young men were the flower and hope

of Sweden, for in that city there were two thousand college students. Had any special effort been made by the churches to reach them? I was told that they were considered unreachable. We therefore determined to make an attempt in this direction. To have placarded the city with posters in the Swedish language, inviting these students to our meeting, would have been to have brought them, insulted and disgusted to break the windows, and probably even to attempt to wreck the building. We therefore published the following bill:

"CIVES ACADEMICI:—CRAS, DOMINICA—HORA III POST MERIDIANA—IN 'SALVATIONEM'—VOS OMNES VENITE! — 'MAUD CHARLESWORTH' — BRITANNICA ILLA, QUAE GLORIA BELLI HELVETICI FLORUIT, PUBLICE LOQUETUR. —NEMO, NISI CIVIS ACADEMICUS, IN 'ARCAM'—ADITUM HABEBIT.*

"What was the result? That evening the one topic in the saloons of the city was the Salvation Army's new departure. Swedes looked at the bill in open-mouthed wonder whereas the students were flattered with the idea of this meeting being exclusively for them,

---

* Citizens of the University, come all of you to-morrow, Sunday, at three in the afternoon, to the "Salvation" meeting place. Maud Charlesworth, the Englishwoman distinguished through the renown of the warfare in Switzerland, will address the audience. None but university students will be admitted to "The Ark" hall.

and of the Swedish populace being ignorant of
the purport of the invitation.

"At three o'clock on the Sunday afternoon,
with I must confess a little trembling and fear
as to results, I stepped upon the platform to
look down upon a sea of faces, for the newspapers estimated that out of the two thousand
students sixteen hundred were present." Nor
was this the only meeting, for later others as
successful and large were held, and the interest
and change manifested in many of those young
men was not only an intense joy to the Salvationists, but was also the comment of the whole
religious and secular press of the country.

She returned to England, and that autumn
married there Ballington Booth whose life was
consecrated to the cause that claimed her every
effort. He had just come home from the direction of affairs in Australia, but in 1887 the two
sailed to take charge of the organization in the
United States. Few English people have ever
understood America any better than Americans usually understand the United Kingdom,
and General Booth's Salvation Army in America has never reached its maximum effectiveness because its conduct has been too British.
For a number of years the General had tried
a succession of representatives, but it was hard
for them successfully to carry out the plans
mapped out for them by him at the far-away
London International Headquarters. Now,
Commander and Mrs. Ballington Booth had
hardly more than landed in New York before

the American separation began. They saw,
two very perceptive and practical people, that
American conditions were not met, and Ballington Booth, while faithfully preserving his subordination, endeavored to explain this state of
things in his reports to his father. The General, however, was imperiously conservative.
The Ballington Booths and serviceable friends
whom they had made begged General Booth to
come over and see the situation, and he finally
did come, but between the father and son there
was already a definite, if unspoken, disagreement; the old autocrat felt his junior to be pre-
suming in venturing to suggest to his authority,
while the capable young man, eager and chafing
to throw himself into the campaign before him,
felt that he was restrained from successful action only by the unadaptive policy of the distant chief. The breach was not lessened by the
tour that the three made of the country. The
intelligent Commander and his interesting wife
attracted even more attention than the gray-
haired founder himself—a situation unprece-
dented in his experience. It is impossible not
to sympathize with the mortified veteran; all
that he and his faithful partner, now dead, had
originated and accomplished had rendered the
career of Ballington possible; but it is always
hard for the vigorous father to realize that even
his son grows up, or to remember that the world
is a kaleidoscope in which things readjust into
new relations that are better seen by younger
eyes than by those that are growing dimmer.

The Commander resigned that title; he ceased to have anything to do with the Salvationists in the United States and indeed left the Salvation Army altogether. "Bring Maudie and come back," the General wrote from London—he had returned there—but Mrs. Ballington Booth was in accord with her husband and the step which she saw was necessary for their usefulness in the United States. The break grew definite and final—for some years they had been naturalized citizens when, in 1895, they set on foot the Volunteers of America with Ballington Booth named as its General and him and his wife as the joint presidents. Since that time, Mrs. Booth has in no way been associated with the Salvation Army.

The Volunteers of America is described as "a philanthropic, social and Christian movement," and this organization, although loosely modeled on the United States Army, seems less rigorous in its discipline than the parent Salvationist body; in fact the Volunteers use civilian titles along with their military ones, as for instance their General and his wife are also the Presidents, Colonel Walter Crafts is the Treasurer, Colonel James W. Merrill, the National Secretary, and so on. Their headquarters are in New York, and, although they have not branched outside of the United States, they are very active throughout the country in benevolent undertakings similar to those of the Salvation Army. Instead of a one-man régime, however, such as old General Booth held over his Army, the Volunteers' General or their two Presidents confer annually as to government with the Grand Field Council, which represents the minor officers throughout the country. If there is a material difference in the Volunteers' methods of preaching, singing, and conversion, it is that the Volunteer corps are perhaps a shade quieter than the Salvationists, although, as well as indoor services, the Volunteers hold meetings "in God's natural cathedral, our open-air stands." The portion of this work that is more familiar to the public the General of the Volunteers administers, while Mrs. Booth entirely devotes herself, as her share of the Volunteers' undertakings, to the class of people, cursed by society, whom she has regenerated for this world and the next.

So this is the second background to her life— her Volunteer Prison League. And what shall we say of this background? Is not the hard gray stone of prison walls a dreary surface against which to see a gentle form? But her visitation has, from Sing Sing to San Quentin, strangely thrown a warmth over cold prison walls, which no longer always seem to scowl in the sunlight, for they now wear a brightness that is new to them. Can the satisfied impulses of a woman's heart explain it all? This question, one must answer "No," and say that Christ has wrought the change with her as His means.

During Mrs. Ballington Booth's journeys with her husband before they left the Salva-

tion Army, she had become deeply interested
in prison work through her visit to San Quentin Penitentiary in California. In consequence, her Volunteer Prison League was
started at Sing Sing on May 24, 1896. The
atmosphere of the California institution seemed
to intimate a cessation of life; the stark cells
impressed themselves as little else than tombs;
they brought back to her mind the churchyard,
that "village of the dead," lying next her home
in childish days at English Limpsfield. "In
those days death held over me a great horror.
The thought connected with it that made me feel
most desolate, and the fact that when one was
dead, laid away in the earth and left alone in
some dark place beneath the tree shadows, to
be covered in by the snow or swept over by
howling winds or dismal rains, the world would
still go on the same as ever. For others, bright
home lights would gleam, laughter and fun,
companionship and love, life with all it means
would still exist, while the dead would lie forgotten and alone. I have thought of these
things and seen once more the vivid picture
and felt the thrill of those childish fears as I
have entered into sympathy with the 'boys' in
prison, for prison to many is a living death."

Mrs. Booth first went to Sing Sing at the
special request of Warden Omar V. Sage. The
invitation came from him without suggestion,
even, from the Booths. From that day the
work has grown, spreading from prison to
prison and state to state, "but I have always

visited each prison at the special invitation of
chaplain or warden, never pushing in my work
as something aside from theirs, but planning
to go as a helper to them in their field.   We
have the strong coöperation, sympathy and
backing of the officials all over the country.''
Major R. W. McClaughrey, formerly warden
of the United States Penitentiary at Leaven-
worth, Kansas, makes the same statement from
the officials' point of view: ''I am safe in
saying that Mrs. Ballington Booth's influence
in the prisons of which I have had charge, has
been more potent than the rules and regulations, formal discipline, or the 'terrors of the
law,' in producing a spirit of loyalty, cheerful-
ness and obedience that has greatly improved
conditions in every respect.   I cannot commend her work too highly, nor can I commend
her too strongly as an able, devoted, and consecrated Christian woman who deserves the confidence and help of all lovers of God and humanity.''   Very different language this from what
the warden might use in writing about many
ladies who have thought themselves called to
work among prisoners; Mrs. Ballington Booth
has no maudlin sympathy; from the first she
has known that though society, government and
law may be in fault the average prisoner is also
bad and needs reformation.   Their ''Little
Mother,'' as they call her, goes straight for
their hearts and souls—which she always assumes they possess—and so regenerates them

from the core outward to the improvement of
their lot from the beginning and to the end.

As in all effort, it was the hardest thing to
break ground. The men at her original meeting with them were at first ugly, and might
have tried to hoot her out of Sing Sing if it had
not been for the guards. Had they not known
men and women come to appeal to them before
who had done them no good? Yet slowly the
looks of the black-striped, shaven-headed assembly in the chapel altered. In the words of
Mr. Theiss: "A little woman, a queenly
woman, sat on the platform with her hands
folded. There were no harsh lines in her face,
there were no marks of sternness, no holier-
than-thou expression in it. Instead there were
understanding kindness, sympathy, love. It
was not the face of a reformer, but of a woman;
and the woman had rich, black hair, piled in
shining masses on her head; with warm full
lips, with cheeks that glowed, and with eyes so
dark, so full, so lustrous, that they began to
burn into the heart.

"With her hands folded, this unexampled
visitor sat studying their own upturned faces.
She saw scarred and scowling countenances that
expressed only hatred and passion. She saw
hardened visages in whose wistful look was a
lingering trace of goodness. She saw still innocent faces of young men who yet beheld life
fair before them. But on every face she saw
pain, suffering, and humiliation. And as she

surveyed them the look of love deepened on her face, and a mist came into her eyes.

"When the music ceased Mrs. Booth rose to speak. She told her hearers of the glad Springtime outside, of the birds and the buds and the blossoms, of the beautiful sun and the fragrant breezes, and of all the hope and joy of the new year. She paused a moment to let her words sink in. Then she said: 'Boys, there's a new life for you if you will have it. The sun of God's love is shining on you just as truly as the sun in the skies is shining on the earth. Let its beams into your heart and try the new life that will spring up. Give up the old life, so full of pain and suffering, and try the new with its peace and joy. Now, while we sing softly one stanza of 'Nearer, My God, to Thee' I want every one who will try to lead a better life to stand on his feet and remain standing.'"

Softly the music rose and filled the chapel, and died away again. Hardened faces began to work convulsively. Strong men bowed their heads and sobbed audibly. Yet no one rose. Coming close to the edge of the platform, the speaker stretched out her arms and said: "Oh, boys, boys, won't you come? Don't you know I want to help you? Don't you know I am your friend? If all the world turns against you, I will stand by you. Don't you know I love you?" Tears were rolling down her cheeks and she could control her voice no

longer. But she stood with her arms out-
stretched in silent appeal. Then an old convict arose, sobbing as a child. A second stood
up. Then another and another, until eighty-
three men were on their feet. That afternoon
a society of the inmates was started at their
own suggestion; and such was the beginning
of the Volunteer Prison League or the V. P. L.

Who can wonder that the genius of such a
scene now has her famous Hope Halls, and has
extended the membership of her League
throughout many penal institutions, until now
the V. P. L's number nearly ninety thousand
members, including both those in and out of
confinement?

If this is astounding, how much more so the
fact that she is successful with about three-
quarters of all those League members who come
to her care from the prison. Moreover, Mrs.
Booth splendidly asserts, and her showings
bear her out, that, even to begin with, "the
prisons are not filled with degenerate, vicious,
crime-loving men. There have been, and always will be as long as degenerating influences
are at work, some abnormal and brutal characters whose fiendish murders, assaults, and
schemes of robbery startle and shock the world.
It is unjust to judge all the prison population
by these few monsters," for of all who after
serving their terms have trusted her and their
higher nature she has made three-quarters decent, useful citizens.

In assuming Volunteer Prison League membership the entrant subscribes to these simple rules:

First.   To pray every morning and night.

Second.   To read the Day Book faithfully. [The Day Book is a manual of extracts from the Bible of a kind most helpful and cheerful to prisoners.]

Third.   To refrain from the use of bad language, and abstain from the use of intoxicants.

Fourth.   To be faithful in observance of prison rules and discipline, so as to become an example of good conduct.

Fifth.   To seek earnestly and to encourage others in well-doing and right living, trying where it is possible to make new members of the League.

Every man who joins receives a little white button with the League's blue star and its motto, "Look up and hope." A certificate of membership hangs in his cell as a daily reminder of his promises and his happier outlook. While the "Little Mother" does all that she can to win the "boys" into active Christianity, yet any man may enter the organization who will endeavor to lead a rightful life; likewise any member is received with welcome at the nearest Hope Hall for his fresh start at his discharge from prison, whether he be Catholic or Jew, or Protestant or infidel. They must all, by the way, come straight to the Hope Hall when they are free, for their own safety. No individual just out of prison is immediately fit for the now strange conditions of independent life; for a while he needs friendly care and preparation, both in mind and character, and commonly in health besides. Furthermore, one just out of prison is always a marked man, unfavorably so; and any observer can tell him; hardly any person will trust him to give him employment, and the police are likely to arrest him as suspicious. Sometimes Mrs. Ballington Booth meets with men who try to acquire the benefits of League membership without meaning to heed their obligations and amend; but they cannot deceive her. That her insight is as piercing in discovering evil as it is keen in reading good, must be a large factor in all she has accomplished. Moreover, she seems to have the happy faculty of turning intended evil into good.

A certain young man called one morning at the Volunteer headquarters and with the lively phrase and manners of the Bowery asked to see Mrs. Booth. When he was admitted to her Prison League office, "Well, 'Little Mother,'" he greeted her breezily, "I have come!" He explained that he had just come from "up the river,"—the vernacular for Sing Sing—that he was a thief and nothing else; he had spent as much time behind the bars as outside of them, and it was the strangest thing in the world for him to have come to see her. He was not even a member of the League, but when he was about to be discharged some of the V. P. L. boys got after him, telling him that the "Little Mother" would help him all the same, and they had induced him to pay this visit although at first indisposed to it. He was not religious; moreover, of all things, he detested work. Yet he was dissatisfied with what his life had been and he would like to try another; but under the peculiar circumstances, he supposed that he could not be entertained as a candidate for assistance. The lady answered that this was not at all the case, and she was very glad to see him. She talked with him and frightened him by persuading him to kneel down with her while she prayed for his future; then she sent him to the Hope Hall in the interior of the State. This man later made good in an honest position. But when Mrs. Booth told her Sing Sing friends of this reform, and then gave the man's name or nickname the corridors rumbled with the roaring laughter of the audience. The authorities were dumfounded; one officer said: "Mrs. Booth, we cannot believe you have got hold of that man and made him do honest work. He was born lazy and he was the most accomplished, notorious crook; he used to steal while he was here with us, and we had him in punishment most of the time because he just would not work. Why, we cannot think of his having turned over a new leaf. I wonder how long it will last." It has lasted now for sixteen years, and he is still a faithful Christian.

The first of the Hope Halls was the New York one, "Meadowbrook," but now their originator has three more, one each in Illinois, in Ohio, and in Iowa; but Mrs. Booth does not tell the public where they are, for that would be indelicate to the "boys." There is a nobility in the situation of those who go to these homes to complete the conquest of their old lower selves, and no sight-seers are admitted to the Halls. They are large houses in the country, with farm land around them, and in them the late prisoners live pleasantly and in comfort, working lightly but with ample time for reading and letter writing and companionship. Whether it takes only a few days or takes long months, a permanent position and opportunity is found at last for every comer, and he goes forth to it well prepared to do right. But the Hope Halls are not all, either. Many prisoners have families they leave in want, and the V. P. L. workers look after numbers of these where they live; but some of them, wives, mothers, children, and old fathers, have nowhere to live, and so Mrs. Booth has built another hall for them. She will not whisper where it is to ordinary sinners, but its name is "Rainbow House," and it must have the brightest rooms, for it has many windows.

In the volumes which Mrs. Booth somehow has found time to write, there is plenty of evidence that she shares her family's literary gift. Her sister, Mrs. Charles W. Barclay, is the author of *The Rosary* and an aunt, Miss Maria Louisa Charlesworth, wrote *Ministering Children,* well known to the last generation. In Mrs. Booth's books, the reader sometimes meets with little intellectual discussions and spiritual matters such as were heard from her father's pulpit; but most of her pages are devoted to things most easily understood. *Beneath Two Flags* is unlike "Ouida's" *Under Two Flags*. *Branded* and *After Prison—What?* relate obviously to their author's chosen field, and so do her *Wanted—Antiseptic Christians* and *Little Mother Stories*. It seems that Mrs. Booth's *Twilight Fairy Tales* and *Sleepy Time Stories* have been favorites with children, her own and others. Perhaps she has never written with more weight than in the following sentences:

"A learned writer some years ago published in one of our scientific papers a treatise concerning prisoners, in which he proved from his own mental conclusions that they could not be reformed. . . . To my surprise I was met at cell after cell with the question, 'Have you read, Little Mother, what Professor —— said about us?' and in some instances, by educated and sceptical men, it was used as an argument against the duty of trying to do better. If those who toll the bell of doom for the poor souls in bondage fully realized how the damning tones echo and re-echo in disheartening vibration from prison to prison, from cell to cell, they might understand that it is almost criminal to break the bruised reed and quench the smoking flax."

And probably nothing in Mrs. Booth's life is more gratifying to her than this,—that years after they are making a successful living and have happy homes of their own, many of the old residents come back on holidays to their Hope Halls to hold reunions there. What must they think of her?

BIBLIOGRAPHY

The writers of the foregoing chapters have drawn their material from diaries, letters, magazine articles, newspaper clippings and personal interviews too numerous to mention. They feel, however, that note should be made of the following works which were among those that they consulted:

Adams, Brooks,—*Emancipation of Massachusetts.*

Adams, Charles Francis, Jr.,—*Antinomianism in the Colony of Massachusetts Bay in 1636-1638.*

Adams, Charles Francis, Jr.,—*Three Episodes of Massachusetts History.*

Aikenhead, Mrs. Mary,—*Irish Sisters of Charity.*

Alldridge, Lizzie,—*Florence Nightingale, Frances Ridley Havergal, Catherine Marsh, Mrs. Ranyard.*

American Ramabai Association, Annual Reports of.

An anonymous comparison of Protestant and Roman Catholic ladies' good works in England.

Barberey, Hélène de,—*Elizabeth Seton et les Commencements de l'Eglise Catholique aux Etats-Unis.*

Baring-Gould, S.,—*Virgin Saints and Martyrs.*

Belloc, Bessie Rayner Parkes,—*Historic Nuns.*

Birrell, Augustine (Editor),—*The Heart of John Wesley's Journal.*

Booth, Ballington,—*From Ocean to Ocean.*

Booth, Mrs. Ballington,—*An Open Letter to Society, From Convict 1776.*

Booth, Mrs. Ballington,—*Branded.*

Booth-Clibborn,—*Ten Years in Salvation War.*

Booth-Tucker, Frederick St. G. de L.,—*Life of Catherine Booth.*

258

Butterworth, Hezekiah, & Brown, Theron,—*The Story of the Hymns. The Story of the Tunes.*

Chapman, Miss E. F.,—*Some Distinguished Indian Women.*

Clarke, Adam,—*Memoirs of the Wesley Family.*

Clarke, Eliza,—*Susannah Wesley.*

Coates, Thomas F. G.,—*The Prophet of the Poor. The Life Story of General Booth.*

Davies, Edward,—*Frances Ridley Havergal, a full sketch of her life.*

Dennis, James S.,—*Christian Missions and Social Progress.*

Duffield, Samuel Willoughby,—*English Hymns: Their Authors and History.*

Duncan, Canon,—*Popular Hymns, Their Authors and Teaching.*

Ellis, George Edward,—*Puritan Age in Massachusetts.*

Ellis, George Edward,—*Life of Anne Hutchinson.*

England, M.,—*The Salvation Army;* in, *London in the Nineteenth Century*—Sir Walter Besant, Editor.

Hallowell, Anna Davis,—*Life and Letters of James and Lucretia Mott.*

Hallowell, Anna Davis,—*Lucretia Mott;* in, *The Medford Historical Register*, October, 1911.

Harper, Ida H.,—*Life and Work of Susan B. Anthony.*

Havergal, Frances Ridley,—*Complete Poems.*

Havergal, Frances Ridley,—*Crimson and Gold Threads from [her] Life and Works.*

Havergal, Frances Ridley,—*Prose Works.*

Havergal, Frances Ridley,—*Specimen Glasses for the King's Minstrels.*

Havergal, Frances Ridley,—*Swiss Letters and Alpine Poems.*

Havergal, Maria V. G.,—*Memorials of Frances Ridley Havergal.*

Holmes, David,—*The Wesley Offering.*

Howe, Daniel Waite,—*The Puritan Republic of the Massachusetts Bay in New England.*

Hutchinson, Thomas,—*Anne Hutchinson in Massachusetts.*

Jameson, Mrs. Anna Brownell,—*Addresses on Sisters of Charity.*

Kirk, John,—*The Mother of the Wesleys.*

Lonsdale, Margaret,—*Sister Dora.*

Moore, Henry,—*Life of John Wesley.*

Nutter, Chas. S., & Tillett, Wilbur F.,—*The Hymns and Hymn-Writers of the Church.*

Ramabai,—*The High-caste Hindu Woman.*

Ramabai,—*A Testimony.*

Robinson, C. S.,—*Annotations of the Popular Hymns.*

Sadlier, Agnes,—*Elizabeth Seton, Foundress of American Sisters of Charity.*

Smith, Hannah Whitall,—*Frank; the Record of a Happy Life.*

Smith, Hannah Whitall,—*The Unselfishness of God, and How I found It.*

Sankey, Ira D.,—*The Story of the Gospel Hymns.*

Southey, Robert,—*Life of Wesley.*

Stanton, Anthony and Gage,—*The History of Woman's Suffrage.*

Stead, W. T.,—*Hymns that Have Helped.*

Stevens, Abel,—*Women of Methodism.*

Tyerman, L.,—*Life and Times of John Wesley.*

Tyerman, L.,—*Life and Times of Susannah Wesley.*

Van Alstyne, Frances Jane,—*Memories of Eighty Years.*

Van Alstyne, Frances Jane,—*The Blind Girl and Other Poems.*

White, Arnold,—*Truth About the Salvation Army.*

Whitehead, John,—*Life of Reverend John Wesley.*
Willard and Livermore,—*Women of the Century.*
Winthrop, John,—*A Short Story of the Rise, Reign
and Ruin of the Antinomians . . . of New
England.*
Wise, David,—*Ancestry of the Wesley Family.*

CHRONOLOGICAL OUTLINE

With the purpose of assisting readers in making for themselves a conspectus of each of the lives here studied and a broader conspectus of the relation of these lives to each other and to the events and movements with which they are bound up, this outline is offered. It is offered also by way of indicating the definite unity that binds together the book as a whole.

1590. Birth of Anne Marbury (Hutchinson).
1634. Anne Hutchinson comes to America.
1635. Anne Hutchinson becomes the leading exponent of antinomianism in Massachusetts.
1636. Sir Henry Vane, Governor of Massachusetts Bay Colony, becomes an adherent of Anne Hutchinson.
1637. Sir Henry Vane returns to England.
Anne Hutchinson is tried before the General Court of Massachusetts for sedition and heresy.
1638. Anne Hutchinson is banished from the colony, and goes to Rhode Island.
1643. Anne Hutchinson removes her home to Long Island, and is there killed by the Indians.
1662. Birth of Samuel Wesley, father of John and Charles Wesley.
Act of Uniformity passed in England.
1669. Birth of Susannah Annesley (Wesley).

1683. Samuel Wesley leaves the Dissenters and returns to the Established Church.

1688. Susannah Annesley marries Samuel Wesley.

1697. The Wesleys settle at Epworth.

1703. Birth of John Wesley.

1705. Samuel Wesley, Senior, imprisoned for debt.

1709. Rectory at Epworth burned; John Wesley, aged six, rescued with great difficulty. Birth of Charles Wesley.

1712. Susannah Wesley gathers in her home for religious instruction her servants and neighbors. This "conventicle" was the pattern for John Wesley's later congregations.

1729–42. Susannah Wesley constant adviser of John and Charles Wesley in their organization of the Methodist church.

1735. Death of Samuel Wesley, Senior.

1742. Death of Susannah Wesley.

1774. Birth of Elizabeth Ann Bayley (Seton) in New York.

1783. Evacuation of New York by British.

1793. Birth of Lucretia Coffin (Mott).

1794. Elizabeth Bayley marries William Seton.

1803. Death of William Seton in Italy.

1805. Elizabeth Seton is received in New York into the Roman Catholic church.

1807. Lucretia Coffin (Mott) attends Friends' School in Nine Partners, N. Y. Elizabeth Seton attempts to teach in New York; is prevented because of her religious faith.

1808. Elizabeth Seton opens girls' school in Baltimore. Sisterhood of St. Joseph organized by Elizabeth Seton who is placed at its head.

1809. Death of Harriet Seton, sister of Elizabeth. First death in the new sisterhood.

Lucretia Coffin (Mott) teacher in Nine Partners' school. James Mott teacher in same school.

1811. Lucretia Coffin marries James Mott.

1813. First American Sisters of Charity finally and formally established. Elizabeth Seton becomes Mother Superior.

1818. Lucretia Mott enters the ministry in the Society of Friends.

1820. Birth of Fanny Crosby.

1821. Death of Mother Seton.

1827. Secession of Hicksite Quakers from orthodox body. Lucretia Mott joins secession and is bitterly persecuted by the Friends because of her anti-slavery views.

1828. Fanny Crosby pronounced incurably blind. Writes her first poem.

1830. James Mott retires from cotton business because it depended on slave labor.

1832. Birth of Dorothy Pattison (Sister Dora). Birth of Hannah Whitall (Smith).

1833. Lucretia Mott participates in convention of American Anti-Slavery Society in Philadelphia.

1835. Fanny Crosby enters New York Institute for the Blind.

1836. Birth of Frances Ridley Havergal.

1838. Lucretia Mott participates in Anti-Slavery Convention of American Women in Philadelphia. Convention mobbed and hall burned.

1840. Lucretia Mott, with other women delegates to world's convention in London on abolition of slave trade, refused right of participation.

Lucretia Mott visits Quaker churches in England, Ireland and Scotland. Hostility of Orthodox Quakers follows her.

1847–58. Fanny Crosby teaches in New York Institution for the Blind.

1848. Hannah Whitall begins to study her religious life. Lucretia Mott, with Elizabeth Cady Stanton and others, plans first Woman's Rights Convention. Convention held in Seneca Falls, N. Y.

1851. Fanny Crosby does her first serious song writing, in collaboration with George F. Root.

Hannah Whitall marries Robert Pearsall Smith.

1854. Frances Ridley Havergal writes hymn *O Thine for ever*.

1855. The Christian Mission founded.

Fanny Crosby and George F. Root produce the first American cantata: *The Flower Queen.*

1857. James and Lucretia Mott retire to farm home on the Old York Road near Philadelphia.

1858. Birth of Ramabai, in Gungamal, India.

Hannah Whitall Smith "discovers the unselfishness of God."

Fanny Crosby marries Alexander Van Alstyne.

1861. Dora Pattison becomes teacher of a village school.

1864. Dora Pattison joins Sisterhood of Good Samaritans and is called Sister Dora.

1865. Sister Dora assigned to hospital in Walsall.

The Christian Mission incorporated under the name of The Salvation Army.

Birth of Maud Charlesworth (Booth).

1868. Death of James Mott.

Fanny Crosby writes: *Pass me not, O gentle Saviour, Safe in the arms of Jesus,* and *Rescue the perishing.*

1870–80. Maud Charlesworth (Booth) educated in England and Switzerland.

1872. Frances Ridley Havergal writes *Tell it out among the heathen that the Lord is King.*

1873. Frances Ridley Havergal writes *Take my life and let it be.*

Fanny Crosby writes *Blessed Assurance.*

1873. Hannah Whitall Smith "joins the woman's crusade."

1874. Sister Dora severs her connection with the Sisterhood of the Good Samaritans.

1878. The new hospital at Walsall opens "in the name of Sister Dora."

Death of Sister Dora.

Ramabai goes to Calcutta and studies and lectures there.

1879. Death of Frances Ridley Havergal.

1880. Death of Lucretia Mott.

Ramabai marries Bipin Bihari Medhavi, a Calcutta lawyer.

1881. Maud Charlesworth first works with the Salvation Army, in Paris.

1882. Death of husband of Ramabai. She de-

termines to devote her life to the welfare of the widows of India.

1883. Maud Charlesworth campaigns in Switzerland for the Salvation Army.
Ramabai studies in England.

1886. Ramabai comes to America.
Maud Charlesworth (Booth) in Sweden
for Salvation Army.
Maud Charlesworth marries Ballington
Booth.

1887. American Ramabai Association organized.
Ballington Booth and Maud Ballington
Booth sent to the United States to take
charge of Salvation Army there.

1889. Ramabai founds a free school in Bombay.

1895. Ballington Booth and Maud Ballington
Booth organize the Volunteers of America.

1896. Maud Ballington Booth organizes the Volunteer Prison League.

1898. Ramabai makes second trip to America.

1900. Manorama, daughter of Ramabai, gradu-
ates from American school and associ-
ates herself with her mother.

1911. Death of Hannah Whitall Smith.

INDEX

INDEX

Act of Uniformity of 1662, 25.

All the way my Saviour leads me, 126.

American Anti-Slavery Society, Lucretia Mott attends, 97.

American Ramabai Association, organized, 214; enlarged, 219.

American Sisters of Charity, founded, 84.

Annesley, Samuel, father of Susannah Wesley, 26; death, 38.

Antinomianism in Europe, 6; in Massachusetts Bay Colony, 8-10.

Anti-Slavery convention of American women, 99.

Anti-Slavery Society of New York, 99.

Blessed Assurance, 115, 126.

Booth, Ballington, marries Maud Charlesworth, 243; sent with his wife to the United States, 244.

Booth, Bramwell, succeeds William Booth as "General" of Salvation Army, 227.

Booth, Maud Ballington, 222-257; ancestry, 222; girlhood, 223; education, 230; first meets Salvation Army, 230; joins the Salvation Army, 234; goes to Paris in ranks of Salvation Army, 235; to Switzerland, 240; to Sweden, 242; marries Ballington Booth, 243; the two sent to the United States in interest of Salvation Army, 244; they organize Volunteers of America, 245; organizes Volunteer Prison League, 247; visits prisons, 248-251; methods of League, 252; organizes "Hope Halls," 253, 254; writings of, 256.

Booth, William, general of Salvation Army, 224.

Bradbury, William B., collaborates with Fanny Crosby, 124.

British and Foreign Anti-Slavery Society of London, 100; calls world's conference, 100; James and Lucretia Mott, Elizabeth Cady Stanton among delegates, 101; declines to seat women delegates, 101.

Consecration, 179.

Cotton, Reverend John, in Massachusetts Bay Colony, 2, 8, 12.

Crosby, Fanny, 115-133; birth, 116; ancestry, 117; girlhood, 118-120; pronounced incurably blind, 120; student at New York Institute for the Blind, 121; teaches there, 122;

271

first poems, 122; marries, 123; collaborates with George F. Root, 123, 124; with William B. Bradbury, 124, 125; with Philip Phillips, 125; with Robert Lowry, 126; with Mrs. Knapp, 126; with William H. Doane, 127; character of her work, 131, 132; friendship of Frances Ridley Havergal and Fanny Crosby, 133.

Doane, William H., collaborates with Fanny Crosby, 127.

Dora, Sister, see Sister Dora.

Dubois, Father Jean, friend of Mother Seton, 72, 75, 77.

du Bourg, Father William Louis, friend of Mother Seton, 71, 72; ecclesiastical superior of new Order of St. Joseph, 74.

Epworth parish, Wesleys move to, 40; parsonage burns, 45, 47; rescue of John Wesley, 45.

Filicchi, Antonio, friend of Mrs. Seton, 66, 67, 70.

Flower Queen, first American cantata, 124.

Foster, J. Ellen, and Hannah Whitall Smith, 165.

Friends, Society of, school at Nine Partners, N. Y., 91, 92; Lucretia Mott enters ministry of, 94; secession of Hicksite branch, 95; attitude on slavery, 98; persecution of Lucretia Mott, 98, 101, 102, 104, 106; John M. Whitall, 161-163; influence on Hannah Whitall Smith, 166, 170

Good Samaritans, Sisterhood of, 139; Sister Dora joins, 139; leaves order, 151.

Havergal, Frances Ridley, 179-195; birth, 180; education, 180; musical ability, 183, 184, 191; interest in temperance and Young Women's Christian Association, 185; hymns, 187-190; religious beliefs, 192, 193; friendship with Fanny Crosby, 133.

High Caste Hindu Woman, 213.

"Hope Halls," organized by Maud Ballington Booth, 253, 254.

Hutchinson, Anne, 1-22; birth, 2; girlhood, no record of, 1; marries, 2; comes to America, 2; as friend and neighbor, 4; social and religious life in Massachusetts Bay Colony, 5; antinomianism in Europe, 6; in Massachusetts Bay Colony, 8-10; excesses of, 9; trial of, 11-17; claims of Mrs. Hutchinson, 14-16; conviction, 16; sentenced to banishment, 17; excommunicated by church, 18; goes to Rhode Island, 19; goes to Long Island, 19; death of, 20; character of, 3-5, 21-22; Reverend John Wheelright, 2; tried for heresy by synod, 10; by court, 11; Reverend John Cotton, 2, 8, 12; Governor John Winthrop, 4, 12, 13; Thomas Welde, 4, 5, 17, 21; Sir Henry Vane, 11; Mary Dyer, 18.

I gave my life for thee, 187, 188.

Knapp, Mrs. E. L., collaborates with Fanny Crosby, 126.

Lowry, Robert, collaborates with Fanny Crosby, 126.

Lucas, Margaret Brice, and Hannah Whitall Smith, 165.

Manorama, daughter of Ramabai, 205, 220.

McClintock, Mary Ann, with Lucretia Mott and Elizabeth Cady Stanton plans first woman's rights convention in Seneca Falls, N. Y., 107.

Methodism, debt of, to Susannah Wesley, 53, 54, 55, 56.

Mother Seton, 57-87; birth, 57; ancestry, 58; childhood, 58-60; early religious emotions, 61; marries, 63; voyage to Italy, 65; death of her husband, 65; inclination toward Catholic faith, 67-69; return to New York, 68; embraces catholicism, 69; opens school at Baltimore, 71, 72; Sisterhood of St. Joseph founded, with Mother Seton as first Superioress, 74; home for order secured near Emmitsburg, Maryland, 75; hardship of the early years of the order, 79, 80, 82, 83; conversion of the order into first American Sisters of Charity, 84; growth of the organization, 85; death of

Mother Seton, 86; character of, 86, 87.

Mott, James, teacher at Nine Partners School, 92; leaves orthodox friends with Hicksite branch, 95; retires from cotton business because of its connection with slave labor, 97; death of, 113.

Mott, Lucretia, 88-114; birth, 88; ancestry, 88; girlhood, 89; attends Friends' school at Nine Partners, N. Y., 91; teaches there, 92; marries, 93; enters the ministry of Society of Friends, 94; leaves orthodox body with Hicksite branch, 96; Lucretia Mott and slavery, 97, 98, 99, 100, 106, 107, 112, 114; persecuted by Society of Friends, 98, 101, 102, 104, 106; delegate with Elizabeth Cady Stanton and others to world's convention called by British and Foreign Anti-Slavery Society, 100; refused a seat in convention, 101-104; home life of, 105, 108, 111; Lucretia Mott and woman's suffrage, 107, 108, 113; death of, 114.

Nine Partners, N. Y., James Mott teaches at, 92; Lucretia Mott attends, 91; teaches at, 92.

Old Jeffrey, ghostly visits of, at Epworth, 38, 39.

Pass me not, O gentle Saviour, 127.

Pattison, Dorothy Wyndlow, see Sister Dora.

Philadelphia Female Anti-Slavery Society formed, 98.

Phillips, Philip, "The Singing Pilgrim," collaborates with Fanny Crosby, 125.

Quakers, see Friends, Society of.

Ramabai, Dongre Medhavi, 196-221; birth, 196; ancestry, 197, 198; girlhood, 199-201; education, 201-202; religious convictions, 203, 204; marries, 205; Manorama, her daughter, 205, 220; becomes a widow, 205; widowhood in India, 205-209; Ramabai goes to England for study, 210; to the United States, 212; writes *High Caste Hindu Woman*, 213; American R a m a b a i Association, 214, 219; returns to India, 216; organizes school for widows in Bombay, 216, 217; Christian home school at Poona organized, 218.

Rescue the Perishing, 115, 127, 129, 130.

Root, George F., collaborates with Fanny Crosby, 123, 124.

Safe in the arms of Jesus, 127, 128, 155.

Salvation Army, organized, 223; character of, 224, 225; William Booth, 224; Bramwell Booth, 227; discipline of, 228.

St. Joseph, Order of, founded, 74.

Saved by Grace, 115, 128, 129.

Seton, Mother, see Mother Seton.

Sister Dora, 134, 159; birth, 134; girlhood, 135, 136; interest in the work of Florence Nightingale, 137; becomes teacher of village school, 138; becomes a sister of the Order of Good Samaritans, 39; is stationed at North Ormesbury, 140; at Walsall, 140-145; leaves Order of Good Samaritans, 151; hospital experience, 149-152; "missions" at Walsall, 152, 153; death of 158; character of, 143, 147, 154, 155, 157, 159.

Slavery, and Lucretia Mott, 97, *et seq.;* Society of Friends and, 98, *et seq.*

Smith, Hannah Whitall, 160-178; Quaker home and parents, 161; character of her father, 161-164; influence of her father on her theology, 165; girlhood, 166-170; Quaker teachings, 166; 170; marries, 171; religious experiences, 171, 172, 175; becomes student of Bible, 173, 174; goes to England, 175; influence on religious thought, 176, 177; connection with Women's Christian Temperance Union, and British Women's Temperance Association, 160, 176; death of, 178.

Somerset, Lady Henry, and Hannah Whitall Smith, 165.

Smith, Robert Pearsall, marries Hannah Whitall, 171; accompanies her to England, 175.

Stanton, Elizabeth Cady, co-delegate with Lucretia Mott to world's anti-slavery convention in London, 100; with Lucretia Mott plans first woman's rights convention in Seneca Falls, N. Y., 107.

Tell it out among the heathen, 189.
Thine forever, 182.

Underhill, Captain John, 9.

Van Alstyne, Frances Jane, see Fanny Crosby.
Vane, Sir Henry, 7, 11.
Volunteer Prison League, organized, 247; methods and character of, 252.
Volunteers of America, organized, 245; character of, 246.

Walsall, Sister Dora at, 140-152.
Welde, Thomas, bitter opponent of Anne Hutchinson, 4, 5, 17, 21.
Wesley, Reverend Charles, at deathbed of his father, 51; devotion to his mother, 52; help and advice from his mother, 53, 55, 56.
Wesley, Reverend John, letters from Susannah Wesley to, 36, 53; saved from burning rectory at Epworth, 45; preaches at grave of his father at Epworth, 51; cares for his mother, 52; advice from his mother, 54, 55.
Wesley, Reverend Samuel, Senior, born, 27; changes

religious faith, 28; student at Oxford, 29; made rector of Epworth parish, 40; political troubles of, 43; imprisoned for debt, 44; burning of Epworth rectory, 46; illness and death of, 50, 51.
Wesley, Susannah, 23-56; birth, 24; girlhood, 25; ancestry, 26-27; abandons dissenters' beliefs, 28; education, 29; marries, 29; early married life, 30-32; poverty, 33, 42; theories of education, 34, 35; devotion to her children, 36, 48, 53; character of, 30, 42; Old Jeffrey, 38, 39; at Epworth rectory, 40; burning of parsonage, 45, 47; rescue of John Wesley, 45; holds religious meetings for neighbors and servants, 49, 51; returns to London, 52; value to Methodism, 53, 54, 55, 56; death of, 56.
Westley, Reverend John, 26.
Wheelright, Reverend John, 2; tried for heresy by synod, 10; by court, 11.
Whitall, John M., 161-163.
Widows in India, condition of, 205-209; Ramabai organizes school for, 216.
Willard, Frances E., and Hannah Whitall Smith, 165.
Winthrop, Governor John, 5, 12, 13.
Woman's Rights, first convention planned by Lucretia Mott, Elizabeth Cady Stanton and Mary Ann McClintock, at Seneca Falls, 107.